CW01368629

PRINCE RUPERT OF THE RHINE

King Charles I's Cavalier Commander

Mark Turnbull

PEN & SWORD HISTORY

AN IMPRINT OF PEN & SWORD BOOKS LTD.
YORKSHIRE - PHILADELPHIA

First published in Great Britain in 2025 by
PEN AND SWORD HISTORY
An imprint of
Pen & Sword Books Ltd
Yorkshire – Philadelphia

Copyright © Mark Turnbull, 2025

ISBN 978 1 39903 321 3

The right of Mark Turnbull to be identified as Author of this work has been asserted by him in accordance with the Copyright, Designs and Patents Act 1988.

A CIP catalogue record for this book is available from the British Library.

All rights reserved. No part of this book may be reproduced, transmitted, downloaded, decompiled or reverse engineered in any form or by any means, electronic or mechanical including photocopying, recording or by any information storage and retrieval system, without permission from the Publisher in writing. NO AI TRAINING: Without in any way limiting the Author's and Publisher's exclusive rights under copyright, any use of this publication to "train" generative artificial intelligence (AI) technologies to generate text is expressly prohibited. The Author and Publisher reserve all rights to license uses of this work for generative AI training and development of machine learning language models.

Typeset in Times New Roman 10/12.5 by
SJmagic DESIGN SERVICES, India.
Printed and bound in the UK by CPI Group (UK) Ltd.

The Publisher's authorised representative in the EU for product safety is Authorised Rep Compliance Ltd., Ground Floor, 71 Lower Baggot Street, Dublin D02 P593, Ireland.
www.arccompliance.com

For a complete list of Pen & Sword titles please contact
PEN & SWORD BOOKS LIMITED
George House, Units 12 & 13, Beevor Street, Off Pontefract Road, Barnsley, South Yorkshire, S71 1HN, England
E-mail: enquiries@pen-and-sword.co.uk
Website: www.pen-and-sword.co.uk

or

PEN AND SWORD BOOKS
1950 Lawrence Rd, Havertown, PA 19083, USA
E-mail: uspen-and-sword@casematepublishers.com
Website: www.penandswordbooks.com

Contents

Preface vii
Acknowledgements ix
Introduction x

Chapter 1   Dear Little Creature 1
Chapter 2   Evill Newes 5
Chapter 3   Frayle as Glass 10
Chapter 4   Le Diable 13
Chapter 5   Fatherlesse 17
Chapter 6   Royall Unckle 21
Chapter 7   Untaynted 27
Chapter 8   Unsettled Spiritt 30
Chapter 9   Vlotho Re-examined 36
Chapter 10   Invincible Constancy 39
Chapter 11   Hart & Mind 46
Chapter 12   Flags and Formalities 50
Chapter 13   Brimful of Zeal 53
Chapter 14   Prince Robber 59
Chapter 15   White Hairs 64
Chapter 16   Scribbling Age 72
Chapter 17   Cheefe Actor 77

Chapter 18	Burning Love	85
Chapter 19	Successe in Armes	92
Chapter 20	Hannibal	100
Chapter 21	Den of Dragons	105
Chapter 22	Cry, Howl, and Yelp	116
Chapter 23	Vigorouse Remedyes	122
Chapter 24	Unjust Displeasure	129
Chapter 25	Great Error	139
Chapter 26	Prejudicial to Monarchie	147
Chapter 27	Heavie Tye	155
Chapter 28	Arch-Traytors	162
Chapter 29	Unhappily Cast Away	170
Chapter 30	Dark and Deep	175
Chapter 31	Brotherly Trick	183
Chapter 32	Surgery & Phisick	187
Chapter 33	Desdemona	197
Chapter 34	Albion's Patron	204
Chapter 35	God Zounds	208
Chapter 36	Popish Plot	212
Chapter 37	Great Rupert	217
Chapter 38	Ruperta and Dudley	220
Chapter 39	Lady Katherine Goring	223

Conclusion	230
Notes	231
Bibliography	250
Index	256

Preface

My passion for seventeenth-century history began at the age of 10. In 2023, my biography of King Charles I (*Charles I's Private Life*) was published and I seized the opportunity to write this book about his nephew, Prince Rupert, perhaps the most famous commander of the civil wars. There are so many facets to Rupert's life that make it so fascinating – army, navy, arts, science, trade, exploration, together with tragedies and triumphs aplenty.

In 1976, three biographies of the prince were published, the most well-known being by Patrick Morrah. General Frank Kitson came next, splitting Rupert's life into two books in 1994 and 1998, and then most recently Charles Spencer, in 2007. Since then, major research has been undertaken in two key battles of Rupert's life – Vlotho (1638) and Powick Bridge (1642) – and Professor Nadine Akkerman has remarkably transcribed and annotated the correspondence of Rupert's mother, spread across innumerable archives. These give much new insight that was not available to previous biographers.

Additionally, during research I built up several cipher keys and used them to unlock various coded letters to and from Rupert for the first time in centuries, which allowed me to get closer to the man himself during the Wars of the Three Kingdoms. There is fresh interpretation and evidence around Marston Moor and Rupert's mindset during the 1645 siege of Bristol. I consulted twenty-four archives and examined as many original sources as possible, rather than accept age-old narratives, which has identified historical inaccuracies and challenged myths.

The women who shaped Rupert's life have never had the focus they deserve and have been left as two-dimensional footnotes in his story, an omission that severely skews understanding of the prince. By addressing this, I can reveal more detail than ever before about Lady Katherine Goring, Frances Bard, and Peg Hughes.

In his day, Rupert was clouded by propaganda that either lauded him a hero or tarred him a villain. These are a selection of sobriquets given in his lifetime:

- Prince Robber
- Mars of the Malignants
- Diabolical Cavalier
- Duke of Plunderland

- Wizard Prince
- The Bloody Prince
- Rupert the Devil
- Plunder Master Generall
- Son of Blood
- Prince of Mischief
- Dutchland Devil

This book is no hagiography. Nor is it a military history of the civil wars. With ground-breaking detail, it reveals the remarkable story of the man that was Rupert of the Rhine.

Acknowledgements

I'm extremely grateful to all staff from the twenty-four different archives who assisted me with researching their collections, especially the Bodleian Library, Yale University's Beinecke Library, and The London Library.

Thanks to Professors Ronald Hutton and Nadine Akkerman, and Adrian Tinniswood, respected authorities of the period, for kindly reading my manuscript and providing endorsements. Professor Steve Murdoch and John Spiller for sharing their thoughts and respective research about the Battles of Vlotho and Powick Bridge. Eleanor Swift-Hook, Keith Crawford, and Claire Hobson, for reading over some particularly important chapters and giving honest opinions. Reverend Michelle Grace, of St John the Baptist, Aldbury, was good enough to take photographs of an interesting monument that mentions Frances Bard. Gregg Archer kindly created the excellent maps used in the book. The wonderful portrait of Rupert used on the cover is by Danelo Yarnold, after a painting by William Dobson.

Finally, none of my books would have been possible were it not for the loving support and encouragement of my wife, Kate.

Introduction

Azores. September 1651.

The *Constant Reformation* had been built at Deptford, London, in 1619 – the same year as Prince Rupert of the Rhine was born in Prague.

The fifty-two-gun vessel fought the Spanish and French, as well as Algerian pirates. But in 1642, along with the Royal Navy, it was turned upon King Charles I – Rupert's uncle. The Royalist cause was defeated in the brutal civil war, but the commander of the *Constant Reformation* and a few other ships defected to the king in 1648. After the shock of his uncle's execution the following year, Rupert took the war to sea, doggedly fighting on in his young cousin's name. The *Constant Reformation* became the prince's flagship. Over 100 foot long and weighing 700 tonnes, its wooden stern castle was a last bastion of royalism – a floating fortress – decoratively carved with royal coat of arms, images of ordnance, busts, and gargoyle-like figures. This nautical interlude is a lesser-known aspect of his military career, but it played a significant part in shaping both his character and future life.

Rupert did battle from the quarterdeck with the same feistiness he had displayed in the saddle as a cavalry commander. He hounded ships loyal to England's new republic, capturing, plundering, thwarting, and escaping them. The chase took him to the Azores, an archipelago of volcanic islands in the Atlantic, between Portugal and the New World. There, it was Mother Nature – and not his enemies – that proved the greatest threat.

On 27 September 1651, howling winds blew his ships out of Terceira and into the storm-tossed ocean. For three days this hurricane raged. At 3.00 am on 30 September, the *Constant Reformation* was in a bad way – within hours, a serious leak sprung beneath the foremast and the carpenter and crew stamped 120 pieces of raw beef between planking to arrest the flow. The ship's pinnace, towed astern, was washed away. By midday there was 6 foot of water in the hold and the crew began signalling to the rest of the fleet using flags and firing their guns. An hour later the beef gave way and 'flewe from the Decke' so fast that the ship lay at the mercy of the sea.[1] Of five pumps in the hold struggling to keep the ship alive, two were put out of action by casks of water that were scattered by the incoming torrent. Rupert's brother, Maurice, desperately tried to bring his own vessel alongside, but the storm was too strong. The 'hideous noise' drowned out the cries of each brother as Rupert attempted to communicate his final instructions.

At this crucial point, sixty seamen 'beseecht' Rupert to leave on a yawl – the last means of escape.[2] The prince declared that upon this 'last Pinch' he would not forsake them. Instead, he would 'Resolve to die' by their sides. The officers begged Rupert to put himself to the mercy of the sea in the small craft, arguing he was destined and appointed by God for 'greater matters'.[1] Resorting to force, they 'made the Prince goe in to it' and pleaded that if he did get to another ship, to use his authority and bring that vessel alongside.

Rupert, his page, and seven other men boarded the yawl. As it was lowered, another two leaped into it. At two o'clock, the crew cut down the *Constant Reformation*'s main and mizzen masts, abandoned the anchors, and cast overboard some guns from the upper deck. In the hold, bailing was stopped on account of casks that 'flew upe &: downe' in the water. The chaplain appealed to the crew – when they were 'past all hopes' they should come to him and receive the sacrament.

At four o'clock, all pumping was stopped and the men now 'expectid nothing butt dethe'. Yet it 'Plesd god' to protect Rupert, who miraculously made it to the *Honest Seaman*, before sending the yawl back to the foundering flagship.[3] Two men attempted to get inside via a ladder on the larboard quarter though the sea swept them away and they were drowned. Five others were successful. The four oars fought with the waves and carried them to the *Swallow*, but the yawl was then consumed by the tempest.

Flaming torches were set on the poop of the *Constant Reformation*. Night closed upon the tragic scene. By ten o'clock, the fires were enveloped as the vessel was sucked to its watery grave, along with 300 sailors and some of Rupert's dearest companions.

Their constancy and courage must have been heart-breaking to witness, and Rupert was tormented as he heard them 'sinke'.[4] Most items of value, which he had risked everything to amass, were also lost. Without the domineering presence of the *Constant Reformation*, his remaining ships were greatly diminished; the power behind the prince had gone. One year later, the sea would claim that which was most precious to Rupert: his loyal brother.

Chapter 1

Dear Little Creature

The sprawling palace of Whitehall was sandwiched between two of London's main thoroughfares – the River Thames and King Street, a road leading from Charing Cross to Westminster. It had gorged on Tudor finances and grown to cover 23 acres, reputedly able to house 600 courtiers. Imposing Yeoman Warders – like 'teriffic giants' – guarded it, dressed in red livery that sported an embroidered rose.[1]

Following the union of the crowns of Scotland and England in 1603, the monarch residing in this seat of government was King James VI of Scotland and I of England. By Christmas 1619, a replacement grand banqueting house was under construction; this was James leaving a mark of his dynasty. The rest of Whitehall Palace, however, remained largely unchanged with rusty fire irons still emblazoned with Henry VIII's coats-of-arms. Here, the 53-year-old James recuperated from a fever. The Venetian ambassador described him as having a red face and whiting hair, often walking with the support of his young favourite's arm, the handsome George Villiers, Marquess of Buckingham. Having lost his Danish wife earlier that year, and not being particularly fond of London, the despondent king was further weighed down by talk of war.

One year earlier, in 1618, the Bohemian Estates (Parliament) had deposed their king, who was also Holy Roman Emperor. Leading Protestant counsellors had rounded on the emperor's Catholic supporters and thrown some from a window of Prague Castle. The Secretary of State (who was of 'little stature') was fortunate enough to have landed in a dunghill, reputedly attributing his survival to 'a new miracle'. The Bohemians searched for a suitable leader to whom they could offer their vacant crown.

Ominous clouds swept across Europe when James's son-in-law, Frederick, Elector Palatine, accepted the Bohemian offer. James feared that Frederick's decision would spark a religious war – one observer noted that 'Germany is like to fall into combustion'.[2] Nicknamed '*Rex Pacificus*' due to his desire for peace, James had a will to live 'without vexation'.[3] Indeed, after prayers that Christmas of 1619, he rebuked one of his bishops for referring to Frederick as King of Bohemia. James shunned use of the contentious title and procrastinated over the stance his kingdoms should adopt in the conflict that was brewing. As the New Year of 1620 broke, a messenger from Bohemia arrived with altogether different news; James had become a grandfather for the fourth time. His daughter, Elizabeth – Frederick's wife – had given birth in Prague, between 9.00 pm and 10.00 pm on 17 December 1619, to a third son.

One correspondent in London remarked that the birth of the Bohemian prince did not prompt any public rejoicing. But behind closed doors James was jolly. Calling for a large beaker of wine, he drank to the health of the new addition. Handing a purse of money to the bearer of this news, he instructed the man to inform Charles, Prince of Wales – his son and heir – and to throw open the doors of his apartments if necessary. The birth of Prince Rupert offered distraction from looming hostilities.

Rupert's mother had been crowned Queen of Bohemia in November 1619, while she 'bore him in her wombe'. The glories of that hasty ceremony faded fast. At that time, Rupert's father was on campaign, recruiting both troops and allies in a bid to keep the new crown on his head. Frederick believed destiny had called him for a war between good and evil. Elizabeth was, understandably, very melancholy despite Frederick's letters encouraging her to do battle with her outlook. Before 1619 was out, the newborn prince, displayed in an ebony cradle, was presented as a means of bonding the royals with their new people. Because of his nationality, the Bohemian Estates proposed that Rupert should be designated heir to the throne, thereby circumventing his two older brothers. The motion was defeated by a single vote. Despite the 'infirmities' of infancy, it was recorded that there appeared appropriate 'rayes' of majesty in the child.[4]

On Sunday, 31 March 1620, the little prince was christened in St Vitus Cathedral, carried to the font by the wife of Bohemia's chief burgrave. He was named after a fifteenth-century ancestor, King Ruprecht III, and the godfather was also a political choice. Bethlen Gabor, rumoured to be half-Turkish, had been elected King of Hungary after that kingdom, like Bohemia, deposed the emperor. This made him a key ally. Bethlen, like Frederick, was on campaign and not present at the ceremony, therefore he sent Count Turzo, attired in Hungarian costume and replete with armour, as his representative. Following the service, the party, presided over by Elizabeth, moved to an array of silk tents on the riverside for a seven-hour feast. Gifts galore were also served up in Rupert's honour; a silver alms dish in the form of a ship, and a bejewelled black horse, given on behalf of Bethlen. They were prophetic gifts; Rupert would go on to be an exceptional cavalry and naval commander.

While Elizabeth kept up appearances, the most important battle of Frederick's life fast approached. The black horse that Bethlen had gifted was most likely the one that Frederick was riding at Rokycany in October, weighed down by continual hardships of war. Though he received kindly messages of paternal affection from his father-in-law in England, practical assistance amounted to little more than two roving ambassadors and a nationwide collection, which made Frederick's cause appear more of a charity case. When edicts were issued for a second donation, many only proffered letters of excuses. Meanwhile, the Spanish donated something infinitely more practical in support of the emperor – an army – and marched it into the Lower Palatinate, part of Frederick's ancestral homeland. Things looked bleak, indeed.

Frederick and Elizabeth had four children in the autumn of 1620, with a fifth on the way. Charles Louis and Elisabeth had been left with paternal family in Germany. On 15 September, their eldest son, Frederick Henry, left Prague Castle and was spirited away to Holland. Rupert remained with his mother in Prague.

Elizabeth understandably fretted. Turning in desperation to her pen, she wrote to her brother, the Prince of Wales, criticising their father's 'slakness'. On the same day another missive to Buckingham, the royal favourite, asserted that her enemies would regard her father's 'blowes' more than his words.[5] Frenetic exchanges of letters with her husband were, as always, full of expressions of love as they sought to shore each other up. While Frederick shared her trust in God, he also advised that 'one must be prepared' for the worst, preferring that she left Prague sooner and in a 'good order' rather than having to beat a hasty escape.[6] Remaining in the capital, however, prevented disorder and though her bags were packed, Elizabeth attempted to maintain an air of confidence. This meant that Rupert (their 'dear little creature') remained in situ to reinforce his – and the family's – fledgling Bohemian bonds.[7]

The roar of cannon shot could be heard in Prague night and day. Frederick, Elizabeth, and Rupert were in the eye of the storm. Frederick's men grew restless as the days passed; one general, Count Ernst von Mansfeld, prepared to defect while another, Count Hohenlohe, had a leg blown off and died. Cold nights froze soldiers to death on both sides and winter threatened to put an end to the campaigning season. The Catholic League had to strike – and soon.

On 8 November 1620, while Frederick and Elizabeth lunched in Prague Castle, his army remained on sandy high ground, which sloped down to the city. On the face of it, the position was a strong one, being interposed between the enemy forces and Prague, but before the royal couple had finished their meal, the Catholic army struck. Within an hour, Frederick's defeated troops were streaming into Prague. The city was overrun with confusion and panic. Although the casualty rate had been almost equal on the field of battle, Frederick's force had lost almost twice the number in their retreat. Closeted away in the old town, Frederick, his wife, commanders, and council met to decide their next steps. The two English ambassadors advocated opening communication with the enemy, and letters were duly despatched. The defeat had practically eroded all hope and plans were made next day to evacuate Elizabeth. Her departure was the final nail in the coffin and soon enough Frederick realised his best option was to leave with her. A cavalcade of carriages and baggage duly wound its way out of the capital, and soon afterwards Catholic forces took possession of the city.

Amidst the chaos, Frederick left the crown itself, but it's said that something even more precious was almost forgotten. While the coaches streamed out of the courtyard, baby Rupert was supposedly discovered during a final check of the royal apartments, whisked up, and thrown into one of the carriages. It's an unlikely story. A second tale also found its way back to England; that the victors had discovered a square clock in the library, half a foot tall, standing on four globes. Described as a 'Hieroglyphicall' clock, with the words 'you will not hear me, but you will see me' inscribed in Latin around the dial, it was reputedly found to contain some parchment sheets. On one, where Roman numerals equalled the year 1620, a lion (representing Bohemia) was trodden down by a double-headed eagle with the arms of Austria on its breast. A sable lion (denoting Burgundy and Flanders – or the Spanish Netherlands) was also 'thrusting [the Bohemian lion] through' with a spear.[8] Whatever the origin of these stories, both are indicative of the family's utter defeat.

Two Englishmen (both friends) accompanied Frederick and Elizabeth in their flight; Ralph Hopton and William Waller were army volunteers. Twenty years later, they would find themselves on opposing sides in the civil war that tore through England, Scotland, and Ireland, and their enduring friendship still personifies that war without an enemy. Just prior to the flight of 1620, Waller's horse had been killed under him and he had escaped the fire of a group of 'Cossacks' with only a graze to his head. Now, as snowy weather took its toll and impeded the retreat, the pregnant Elizabeth had to alight from her carriage, whereupon Hopton led her horse for 40 miles.

All through this ignominious escape, Frederick attempted to maintain a stiff upper lip, but all eyes were on his 'incomparable Lady'. Elizabeth refused to let her 'dignitye' fall below that of a queen and her countenance and discourse were of an 'unchangeable temper'.[9] Her plight attracted immense sympathy and respect, fostering a groundswell of chivalric outrage. In England, one official supping with thirty of his household drank a health to her. With sword held aloft in the other hand, he kissed it and swore an oath to live or die in her service, before passing wine and blade around. The cult of the Queen of Hearts had begun. It would be forty years before Rupert, a fugitive almost from birth, would find somewhere he could call home.

Chapter 2

Evill Newes

One person that Elizabeth's situation didn't seem to move was her cautious and canny father, who had feared this outcome from the very start. Powerless (and penniless) to send any significant assistance, James must have read letters from his fugitive daughter, now in Breslau, with much concern. She called on him to 'have a care' and send help, otherwise they would be 'entirely ruined'. To be perfectly clear, she emphasised the need for 'proper' help. She vowed never to leave her husband, warning that if he perished, then she would also.[1] They were stirring words.

King James's reticence to enter a major religious conflict was understandable – after all, it would have been costly in terms of money and lives, as well as a gamble on the outcome. Having become King of Scots at the age of one, following his mother, Mary, Queen of Scots's forced abdication, he was well experienced in how uncomfortable a seat the throne could be, and once wrote that crowns could be composed of thorns as well as jewels.

The deaths of James's parents offered no comfort either. When he was 8 months old, his father, Henry Stewart (Stuart being the Anglicised version), was staying at a house in Edinburgh when it was blown up. His dead body was found outside in just a nightshirt, a case of murder in which his wife was thought by many to be complicit. James's mother would eventually flee Scotland after a revolt by leading nobles and seek sanctuary from Elizabeth I of England, only to suffer an eighteen-year imprisonment. This ended with her execution. With such family history, James sought peace over war, hoping to avoid the family trend for unnatural endings. To do this, he plumped for a one-size-fits-all approach to politics, attempting to please both Catholic and Protestant alike, but ending up alienating both. His neutrality projected an image of weakness to the world.

Elizabeth and Frederick found more tangible support from the latter's family. Frederick's hard-drinking father had been the driving force behind their union, despite accusations that his son was punching above his weight in the marriage market. The last act of Frederick senior was his somewhat convenient, if untimely, death aged 36, which did more than anything to bring his son's marriage to fruition. It saw Frederick become Elector Palatine at the age of 14, one of seven electors entitled to appoint emperors of the Holy Roman Empire, and head of a Protestant

League – a band of princely brothers. The serious-minded young man (a committed Calvinist) had accepted the throne of Bohemia with the backing of his maternal family – the Dutch House of Orange. Frederick's mother, Louise Juliana, was the sister of Maurice of Nassau and daughter of William the Silent – the man who had secured Dutch independence from Spain.

The Dutch were therefore natural allies welded by bonds of blood and religion. In Frederick's time of need, ousted from Bohemia, and with Spanish troops overrunning his lands in the Lower Palatinate, Uncle Maurice offered a safe haven.

Elizabeth was heavily pregnant when she arrived at Küstrin Castle, a seat of Frederick's brother-in-law, the Elector of Brandenburg, in December 1620. She saw the gloomy fortress as a place of exile; it was as cold as the welcome, for Brandenburg had been warned against harbouring her. Lonely as she was, Elizabeth remained hopeful that although the Battle for Prague had been lost, the war could still be won.

When Frederick eventually reached Küstrin, his stay was brief, for he left again to attend to military affairs. Elizabeth gave birth to her fifth child on 16 January 1621, naming him Maurice after the Dutch Stadtholder. Despite scandalous propaganda that both mother and child had perished, the baby was healthy, which was more than could be said for the cause of the Winter King and Queen. In Prague, some twenty-seven of Frederick's supporters were tortured and executed, their remains deposited in key positions along the Charles Bridge as a stark warning for all to see. An Imperial ban, issued that January, officially outlawed Frederick from the empire and decreed his lands forfeit to the emperor.

Despite the extreme cold, Elizabeth, Rupert, and the newborn left Küstrin on 29 February, stopping off at Berlin, another seat of the Brandenburgs, where Maurice was left in their care. From there, Elizabeth and Rupert travelled to Stolzenau, in Westphalia, where Frederick joined them in March. Uncle Maurice's cavalry arrived to escort the trio to Holland the following month, where the tired fugitives took stock of their situation. Frederick V, King of Bohemia and Elector Palatine, was reduced to merely 'ye name and meritt' of a monarch.[2] Elizabeth confided that she expected little aid from her father, who her enemies did mock and jest, but she was at least reunited at The Hague with her eldest son. The 7-year-old Frederick Henry penned an update to his maternal grandfather, in which he reported the whereabouts of his siblings; Rupert (who had fallen sick) was with him at The Hague, Charles Louis and Elisabeth with their paternal grandmother, and Maurice at Berlin.

The powerless royal couple became ever more entrenched as months passed. Their continued exile was embarrassing, with English MPs declaring their children 'jewels of this crowne' and Holland the nation's 'outworks'.[3] These rumbles of nationalistic outrage led King James to lodge an official protest at the Spanish invasion of the Lower Palatinate, calling for the territory to be restored to his son-in-law. He remained silent over Bohemia. The Upper Palatinate, together with the dignity and title of Elector Palatine, would be granted by the emperor to Maximilian of Bavaria. The infuriated Elizabeth heard that despite her father's lacklustre demand, there was no let-up in his plans to match her brother, Charles, with the Spanish Infanta – the enemy. She bitterly wished for the death of the entire Spanish race, most especially the females. When King James sent her a jewelled ring containing his portrait, she could not contain her frustration – he might have sent 1,000 soldiers in place of each diamond, she had retorted, which would have been infinitely more valuable.

Fortunes ebbed with each passing day. Uncle Maurice provided a home stocked with wine and beer, followed by a modest income of 10,000 guilders. Somewhat like Queen Victoria and Prince Albert, Frederick was serious-minded and of a delicate constitution, whereas Elizabeth was made of sterner stuff. The couple's devotion to one another filled their letters and was demonstrated by the birth of eight more children between 1622 and 1632. Louise Hollandine came along soon after their arrival in Holland in 1622; Louis, in 1623, only to die the same year from teething; Edward, in 1624; Henrietta, in 1626; Philip, in 1627; Charlotte, in 1628; Sophia, in 1630; and Gustavus, in 1632.

Despite her continuous pregnancies, Elizabeth went out hunting and cut a dazzling and charming figure, which increased her following immensely. As the nursery filled, Uncle Maurice provided a former convent in Leiden for the children, around 13 miles by water from The Hague. Named the 'Prinsenhof', it comprised large dining rooms and bedrooms on the ground floor that looked out onto a courtyard; there was also a well-kept garden. The décor was plain, but seven rooms on the first floor afforded views of the Rapenburg canal, across which lay the 'great Accademy' that was Leiden University.[4] A steady stream of tutors and professors made the Prinsenhof a true seat of learning, described as one of the most 'composed & regular' courts.[5] Tutors included Elizabeth's secretary, John Dinley; artist Gerrit van Honthorst; and soldier Sir Jacob Astley.

Frederick and Elizabeth were very careful over their children's carers, shunning one candidate for Rupert's governess because she was 'a great misery'.[6] Their choice eventually fell on the more trusted and familiar shoulders of Count Volrad von Plessen and his wife, Sybille. The count had once been an extraordinary ambassador to England and was one of Frederick's senior advisors, having 'long managed' his affairs, while the countess had been Frederick's own childhood governess.[7] The aged von Plessens kept a tight ship, assisted by their daughters, who looked even older and were described as 'frightful'.[8] Girls were educated separately to the boys.

The utterance of Rupert's first words, reported by his oldest brother, were 'Praise the Lord' in Bohemian. It was the start of what would become an excellent grasp of languages and his father would pen praise over how the 3-year-old Rupert understood so many. They were surrounded by Dutch, French, German, and English. Rupert would go on to speak all of these, including some Italian and Spanish. Such skills would stand the boy in good stead, whether his future lay in the most cultured courts or on the bloodiest battlefields. Indeed, at the age of 4, he was proposed for command of 100 Scotsmen that were traditionally kept in the service of the King of France, which had, until the union of the English and Scottish crowns, been entrusted to the King of Scotland's heir. This is the first stirrings of a martial destiny.

In later life, Princess Sophia would drily recall the 'weariness' of learning at the Prinsenhof.[9] At the heart of studies – and the children's existence – was the premise to love God and fear the devil. They were taught the catechism in German, rose at 7.00 am each day to study the bible, and were transferred from teacher to teacher in brisk fashion. Divines visited every Sunday and Wednesday. A despairing Sophia would recall the odd grimaces of one tutor who brushed her teeth rather fervently during lessons. Days ended as they had started, with bible study, followed by bed at 8.30 pm. It was a decidedly Calvinist upbringing in line with their parents' instructions, designed to ward off even the slightest whiff of Catholicism.

Religion was seen as the 'foundacon' (foundation) of everything and the want of it in princes was considered 'fatall'. It was said of Rupert, in contemporary biographical notes, that his early education led him to abhor the 'debaucheryes' of the age.[10] The same source (couched with grandiose praise) accounts that his judgement was so well advanced that he decided what topics of study a prince might do without – or 'honourably bee ignorant of'. He excelled in art, as did his sister, Louise. But above anything else, war soon became Rupert's 'great inclinacon [inclination]', framing his body and mind entirely to that exercise.[11]

Consequently, he excelled at handling a horse, weapons, and armour, as well as the art of fortification. This was augmented by natural courage and determination, meaning that as he grew up, he became ever more impatient to partake in war and 'nothing could allay or calme' this desire. Listening to veterans stirred feelings of inadequacy that lay upon him like 'blemishes' for not having proved himself. Instead, all he could do was take heart from their example and wait.[12]

A decidedly English influence ran through the Prinsenhof's curriculum. Upon being appointed tutor, John Dinley sought direction from King James and was told to 'breed' Frederick Henry, the eldest Palatine, in a love of English whilst protecting him from Puritanism – considered as equally dangerous as Catholicism.[13] The young Princess Elisabeth, Rupert's sister, was also described as a very good 'Englishe woman'.[14] There was method and reason behind all of this. Charles, Prince of Wales, was single and childless, meaning that Elizabeth of Bohemia remained second in line to her father's three kingdoms.

After being bedridden with eight fits of a tertian ague, or fever, King James died on 27 March 1625. Though the 'evill newes' of her father's loss was a blow to Elizabeth, it meant that her loving brother was now king, and her hopes flourished as a result.[15] Charles had long worked hard to instil fighting spirit into his father, and now he was in the driving seat, Elizabeth had good right to think that next to God, her saviour was her brother.

Just one month after James's death, Stadtholder Maurice, Prince of Orange died. The Protestant cause took a further blow in May, when Spanish forces led by Ambrogio Spinola captured the Dutch town of Breda after a nine-month siege.

As her brother's heir, Elizabeth and her family's standing naturally increased. Should anything happen to King Charles, she would inherit her brother's three kingdoms. All of this was not lost on the late King James's favourite, who had been promoted to Duke of Buckingham. He retained a destructive influence over King Charles I and was bold enough to advance his daughter as a match for Frederick and Elizabeth's eldest son. To pave the way, he used his influence to negotiate a financial grant for Elizabeth, which was very welcome to her.

Buckingham even de-camped to The Hague and met young Frederick Henry and his siblings. As the most important non-royal representative of King Charles's three kingdoms, the handsome Buckingham must have impressed. Frederick Henry understood his duty perfectly. Writing to Buckingham in February 1627, he thanked him for honouring them with a visit and professed an assured friendship. The matchmaking, however, would come to naught. Just one year later, on 28 August 1628, Buckingham was stabbed by a minor officer in Portsmouth, as he readied the fleet for war with France.

Buckingham had planted his people in every corner of government, raking in a fortune and accumulating a vast array of posts and positions for himself. He also garnered much hatred as a result. As blood gushed from his mouth, the state went into meltdown, because he occupied practically all senior positions. King Charles heard the news whilst at prayers and suffered 'great mental distress'.[16] Ports were closed. Rumours abounded, notably that it was a Catholic plot, which stoked memories of the 1605 Gunpowder Treason.

At both The Hague and the Prinsenhof, news filtered in slowly, which prolonged the shock over this 'suddaine and unspeakeable a losse'.[17] For three weeks rumours remained unconfirmed. Once it became clear that the assassin had harboured grievances over his salary and the execution of a relative for mutiny, panic began to subside. King Charles, officially at war with France and Spain, decided to push on with plans to support Protestants besieged by the French king at Ile de Re. Although Elizabeth wished that her brother's ships and soldiers might have been directed against Spain, any active support of the Protestant cause in Europe was infinitely welcome.

Along with the eldest Palatine, Frederick Henry, the other brothers' futures seemed inextricably linked to King Charles. On 14 December 1628, just four months after Buckingham's demise, Charles Louis assured his uncle that he was bound to his service and the prosperity and greatness of his crown. Despite the 11-year-old's grand words, that crown was in a poor state. The king had been reduced to plucking out its jewels and giving them as gifts to parting ambassadors, such was his parlous position.

Chapter 3

Frayle as Glass

Elizabeth gave birth to thirteen children in rapid succession over eighteen years. New arrivals streamed through the doors of the Prinsenhof, but there was also the occasional exit. When Louis died in 1624, aged just 4 months, his mournful mother lamented her prettiest child. Charlotte followed him to the grave in 1631, aged 3.

The year 1629 got off to an encouraging start for the family's sixth year in the United Provinces. The Dutch West India Company had achieved spectacular success at the end of the previous year by capturing the Spanish treasure fleet and these prizes had now arrived in Holland. A jubilant Frederick and Elizabeth directly benefitted because they had shares in the company, therefore would be entitled to a portion of the 15 million guilders' worth of spoils.

While Frederick celebrated at The Hague, his eldest son fell ill. Frederick Henry, deciding that maternal affection might help him feel better, took a three-hour trip from the Prinsenhof to his mother's bedchamber. When his father arrived home, talk of the treasure fleet at Amsterdam left the boy eager for the opportunity to go and view it. The public ferry on which father and son travelled had to navigate a challenging waterway full of sandbanks, but dense fog doubled the hazards. A collision occurred and the vessel capsized, throwing its royal occupants into the icy waters. Frederick was unable to save his son, whose calls for help soon gave way to a deathly silence.

The poor boy's frozen body was recovered the next day entangled in the rigging. Though Frederick was hauled to safety, a part of him was lost with his child, and the trauma of it haunted him for the rest of his days. Grief-stricken, Elizabeth was consoled by loyal Sir Thomas Roe, a roving ambassador devoted to her family, who said the boy had been 'ripe for God' and had now gone home. Roe implored her to look up to her son in heaven, but then down to her surviving children, who were all pledges from the Almighty. Young Frederick Henry had been intelligent, serious-minded, and virtuous.

> A [fruit] too ripe: a star too shining bright
> A Comett, that did braue Heauens greatest light
> Now he is not; we wonder what he was,
> Rich as a Diamon[d], yet as frayle as glass.[1]

The loss of his nephew greatly upset King Charles I, who sent one of his closest friends, Sir Robert Kerr, to represent him at the funeral. Despite the failure of military initiatives in support of the Palatines, Charles remained a loving uncle. Kerr carried not just written assurances of this, but more tangible evidence. Charles Louis – the new heir – would receive his dead brother's pension and Rupert was granted £300 per annum. Both boys wrote replies, sealed with black wax, giving thanks for this benevolence. It was a key moment in the relationship between Rupert and his uncle, sowing the seeds of a strong bond of loyalty to this distant figure of authority, who was now a father-figure.

For the anguished Elizabeth, on the back of her personal loss, there was much speculation that her brother would imminently make overtures of peace to Spain. Amidst death and calamity, she might have mused over the loss of her elder brother seventeen years past and wondered if he would not turn in his grave over the very prospect. Prince Henry had been a fierce opponent of Catholicism and a staunch adherent for an alliance with the Protestant League. Upon his death, swathes of people had hoped Elizabeth's younger brother, Charles, might be a like-for-like replacement.

From the moment of his accession in 1625, Charles had prepared for war, even though Parliament was unwilling to grant him Tonnage and Poundage revenues, previously given to monarchs for life. His honour was tainted by his sister's sad situation. Thus, by mortgaging his lands, blowing his personal reserves and the dowry from his marriage, he had attempted to bypass Parliament's intransigence. This was nowhere near enough to offset the costs of equipping and supplying ships and soldiers for war. Though the personal intent was admirable and noble, he got what he could pay for, and it was woefully inadequate. Coupled with his favourite, the Duke of Buckingham, being given command, the result was abject failure. Parliament kept a stranglehold on the purse strings and with financial crises taking Charles to the brink of a nervous breakdown, by 1629 he was left with little alternative but to broker a peace and tend to his own country's political divisions.

To Elizabeth, this was a blow that bordered on betrayal. Attempting to reassure her, Charles sent his Secretary of State, Sir Henry Vane, to whom, like many of Charles's ministers, she had mischievously assigned a nickname. While Vane was a 'great fat knave', the Earl of Carlisle was 'ugly camel's face'; Sir Thomas Roe 'honest fat boobie'; and Jacob Astley 'my little monkey'. She didn't particularly like Sir Henry, deeming him Vane by name and monstrously vain by nature. Yet, through him, King Charles assured Elizabeth that he retained a chief ambition to do her service and that talks with Spain were like mere 'Physickes' to attempt to cure his situation.[2] Elizabeth responded with gratitude for her brother's plain dealing. She was reassured that no peace would be agreed unless it came with Frederick's restitution to the Palatinate. Considering how unlikely this was, she saw negotiations as dead in the water. A treaty with France, on the other hand, was acceptable, as the latter could become a useful ally against Spain.

When a heavily pregnant Henrietta Maria attended a Te Deum in celebration of a subsequent peace with her native France, she returned to Greenwich Palace for her confinement. There are two different versions of what occurred next. Either she fell to the decking of her boat as it ran the rapids at London Bridge, or a fight between two great dogs scared her; what's certain is that she went into labour ten weeks early. Her husband was by her side throughout, showing 'great love'. Sadly, the baby boy was 'cut down' the moment he saw light.[3]

As Spanish diplomats continued negotiations, Charles and Henrietta Maria's appetite for war was on the wane. Had the royal baby lived, he would have supplanted Elizabeth in the line of succession – on account of which whispers were heard that she would 'not be sorry' for the child's demise.[4] Undoubtedly, she sympathised with her brother and sister-in-law, but gifting them a painting of her own children (the 'munkeyes' as Elizabeth nicknamed them) was particularly ill-timed.[5] Showcasing her healthy, growing brood, the possibility of them inheriting the British throne caused monarchs and princes to hedge their bets and strive for her favour.

The year 1629 also brought a pause in the regularity of childbirth. Frederick, frustrated by what he called the feeble arm of England, occupied himself with a building project. Purchasing an old monastery from the Province of Utrecht, it was as if he sensed he would not be restored to his lands anytime soon. The new palace he built at Rhenen proved a good distraction and, thirty years later, would be inherited by Rupert. Located just 40 km from the Spanish fortress of s-Hertogenbosch (also called Bois le Duc) which they had been strengthening since 1598, Rhenen was right on the front line. A scale model was shipped to King Charles, who approved it 'exceeding well', though he expressed concern that the multitude of windows would expose it to extremities of heat and cold.[6]

Bois le Duc was duly besieged on 15 June 1629 by Dutch and English forces, joined by Frederick. For nearly three months Elizabeth, in Rhenen, could hear musket and cannon shot, almost as regular as the letters from her husband. Then, in September, a large explosion blew a hole in the ramparts and the town surrendered. Exhilaration over such a hard-fought victory soon soured on the back of the increasing likelihood of an Anglo-Spanish peace deal without the all-important restoration of the Palatinate. This prompted Frederick to look for more reliable allies. It was a different accord, one that involved Sweden and Poland, which seemed to answer his prayers.

Chapter 4

Le Diable

In 1630, aged 10, Rupert entered Leiden University. 'Rupert le Diable', as his siblings would call him, was headstrong and determined, itching to take his martial studies to the next level. Of a practical and outdoor mind, never one for being idle, he got out and about at Leiden and The Hague, escaping the confines of royalty and ambassadors. He met sailors, with compelling stories of adventure, danger, and exploration, as well as soldiers from flashpoints across Europe. These 'inflamed' in him an 'extreame affeccon' (affection) for conflict, and it grieved him that such glories were passing him by.[1]

When King Gustavus II Adolphus of Sweden made peace with Poland, this was but a precursor to something bigger. The Lutheran monarch made ready to enter the Thirty Years' War against the Catholic Holy Roman Empire, fearing their success might see Baltic ports occupied and thus threaten Sweden. Rupert must have followed events closely. Gustavus was a formidable figure with the means to champion the Protestant cause.

Against this backdrop, Queen Henrietta Maria, in London, went into labour at 2.00 am on 29 May 1630. King Charles 'stayd al the while' in the room, which was separated into two parts; the queen and her ladies on one side, Charles and the lords on the other, while her 'cryes' rang out.[2] A Scotsman was duly sent to Frederick and Elizabeth with news that a healthy boy had been born. By the end of June, Gustavus was preparing to deliver 10,000 troops to the Baltic coast. This news provided more hope than that from England, where focus centred on the new arrival's christening, and thus the Palatine demotion. A star would be seen in the sky over London, leaving onlookers undecided whether it was Venus or Mercury. Elizabeth was certainly conflicted by love and war.

On 30 May, Charles Louis obediently wrote to his uncle and aunt congratulating them on this 'happie' occasion, adding rather sweetly, 'I maie hope to know my Cosen, the Prince of Wales, one daie.'[3] Elizabeth also despatched letters, but about a very different topic. Concerned over how her brother's terms with Spain might tackle Frederick's restoration to the Palatinate, she made her displeasure perfectly clear. Two 'perplexed' letters to King Charles entreated him to continue demonstrations of love and favour and avoid Spanish temptations.[4]

During his summer progress at Beaulieu, on 16 August 1630, Charles tackled the rift head-on. Making sure to demonstrate understanding of his sister's position, he tactfully assured her that peace would not see him 'lay my armes a sleepe'. Instead, he promised to 'doe what lyes in mee' to engage the likes of France and Holland in an offensive and defensive treaty for both the restoration of the Palatinate and the liberation of Germany from the Catholic emperor and his Imperial troops. Parliament's intransigence over finances had crippled Charles's military offensives, so he resolved to bring soft power to bear, coupled with volunteer forces. These, he hoped, would 'helpe and harten' Gustavus of Sweden.[5]

It became apparent that the Swede had little need of assistance. Having spent time galvanising his authority, Gustavus had forged a strong central government that united Sweden. It was this that allowed him to make such a striking entrance upon the European stage. He attended divine service numerous times every day and led firmly from the front, writing articles of war in his own hand, which became the code by which his soldiers operated. Frederick followed every move of the 36-year-old King of Sweden, as did his older children – Princess Elisabeth would remark on Gustavus's 'habitual wisdom and experience in war'.[6]

Within four weeks, Pomerania was under Swedish occupation, and soon a base was set up at Stettin. This posed a serious threat to Imperial forces. In May 1631, Gustavus was marching towards Magdeburg, intent on its relief. By contrast, Johann t'Serclaes, later Graf von Tilly, the emperor's 70-year-old commander, hoped Magdeburg's capture might prove a firebreak that would stop the Swede's blazing advance. When the town duly fell to the Catholics, their actions were so horrific that they would never be forgotten. Burning Magdeburg to the ground, its civilian populace was massacred and reports circulated that children were thrown into the flames or skewered on the ends of pikestaffs. It became synonymous for brutality and the death toll of 42,000 caused a wave of revulsion throughout Europe. This was no time for waverers.

Finally, Tilly and Gustavus came face to face 4 miles north of Leipzig. At the Battle of Breitenfeld, on 17 September 1631, the Catholics suffered a crushing defeat. It seemed as if there was no stopping Gustavus. He continued his incursion, advancing to the Rhine, and by mid-November had occupied much of the Palatinate. Frederick's curtain-call, it seemed, was approaching. In December, Gustavus finally halted at Mainz, and there he took stock and enjoyed a well-earned rest. Now joined by his queen, Protestant leaders gravitated towards this radiant royal.

Frederick was in 'high spirits'.[7] Though forced to rely on handouts, such as an allowance from his brother-in-law, it amounted to a modest income. He had been saving for a rainy day, and with the sun set to break through, he took 100,000 crowns and visited his children at Leiden. Charles Louis and Rupert were taking part in a public exam, which their father proudly observed. The newest addition to the family was christened Gustavus in honour of the victorious Swede.

The year prior, Frederick's nephew had arrived at the Prinsenhof where he found his cousins living 'very happily and affectionately together' and engaged in a frenzy of activities.[8] Every day, he had noted, was crammed with activity, both to educate as well as keep them from being devilishly idle, which was sure to corrupt. Elizabeth would issue strict rules against gambling with cards, excessive eating and drinking, and fraternisation between male and female servants. She ensured the children were taught together under one roof and not separated. The boys rode, pole-vaulted, fenced, danced, played musical instruments and exercised with pikes and old Sir Thomas Roe even shed a tear at the sight.

As their father made ready to join the King of Sweden, the Palatine children must have shared his excitement. Unfortunately, Gustavus did not reciprocate the same enthusiasm for the exiled King of Bohemia when he arrived. The purpose of Frederick's attendance was to strengthen his position and anticipated restoration to the Palatinate, but Gustavus was wary of self-interest.

Frederick's brother-in-law, King Charles, seemed incapable of mastering his own subjects. To make matters worse, an English ambassador extraordinary was sent to the King of Sweden at the end of 1631, and the choice could not have been more disastrous. Sir Henry Vane failed to impress Gustavus. As if this wasn't bad enough, the thousands of volunteers levied in Britain and sent to the Swede were, as usual, cobbled together. King Charles had dissolved his mutinous Parliament on 2 March 1629; therefore, these volunteers were assembled on a shoestring budget. Speed was of the essence, and a royal order scraped the bottom of the barrel by calling for vagrants to fill the ranks. Of the 12,000 that joined Gustavus in the middle of 1631, barely 700 were left at the end of that year due to famine and plague.

Gustavus treated Frederick with respect but set expectations. Firstly, Lutherans living in the Palatinate must be given the same rights as Calvinists (Frederick being the latter). There was also speculation that Frederick might be required to become a vassal of Sweden. Ironically, it had been Frederick's acceptance of the Bohemian throne that had started this religious conflict, but now it looked increasingly apparent that he would not be central to its conclusion. He was yesterday's monarch.

Further action delayed talk over divisive conditions. On 6 April 1632, Gustavus's second victory against Tilly was made even more decisive when the latter was killed. Tilly's end might be thought to preclude that of the empire. Augsburg and Munich were added to Gustavus's cache of towns. The desperate emperor was forced to go cap-in-hand to Albrecht Wenzel Eusebius von Wallenstein, a turncoat commander who had abandoned him, but was now his best hope of reversing matters.

Frederick had lost Prague after his forces had been defeated by Tilly at the Battle of White Mountain twelve years earlier. Of his beloved Palatinate, the upper part had been doled out as a reward to the Catholic Maximilian, Duke of Bavaria, while the Spanish still occupied the lower. Swedish victories had now killed Tilly and ejected Maximilian from his Bavarian homeland, and Frederick might have savoured the sweet taste of revenge. But once again fate proved fickle, and Gustavus's forces were soon held in check around Nuremburg, in Bavaria. In September 1632, the titans clashed, and Wallenstein defeated Gustavus.

Frederick, in his own words, had lost nearly all hope. He continually questioned Gustavus's intentions and wrote that the Swede was keeping him as 'low' as he could.[9] Frederick's requests to raise his own army had been blocked, and Gustavus made no promises about the Palatinate. Entirely eclipsed, Frederick slipped away from his ally's side, resolving to send messengers to King Charles I and the Prince of Orange for advice on how he should proceed. In such bleak vulnerability, it was said he desired only Elizabeth's loving company and dogs to go hunting. He proceeded via Frankfurt and Oppenheim (which had been half-burned) to Mainz, which he grew weary of after a few weeks. Though putting out feelers for a return to The Hague, Frederick was set for a very different destination.

Chapter 5

Fatherlesse

Like many allies throughout history, the relationship between Frederick and Gustavus fractured as ultimate victory drew ever closer. On 6 November 1632, Gustavus approached the German town of Lützen. With a heavy mist made bleaker by gun smoke, the Swedes did battle once more with the formidable Wallenstein. What emerged was a stunning Protestant victory, but Gustavus – the 'Lion of the North' – gave his last roar. The King of Sweden was shot dead.

King Charles I, grappling with conflicting reports of Gustavus's fate, laid a bet of 70 pieces at 100-1 on his survival. When the truth became clear, Elizabeth reacted with equal detachment, claiming that the king's death troubled her 'not a little'.[1] He had, after all, disregarded her husband and their self-consuming desire for restoration. But two weeks later, the feverish Frederick gained a heavenly crown when he died at 7.00 am on 19 November 1632. On that very same day (King Charles I's 32nd birthday), Elizabeth was gripped by fever, therefore news of her widowhood was withheld. There was genuine concern that she might prove unable to bear the grief, and though she went through 'fire & water, sighes & teares' the Winter Queen was made of stern stuff.[2] In a touching letter, King Charles accepted that he could not 'by a few lines, efface the just grief' of her loss, and implored her to settle in England.[3]

No sooner had Elizabeth recovered than King Charles next fell ill after a bout of tennis. When 'redd spottes' appeared on his face and chest, smallpox was diagnosed. Keeping to a warm room in a 'furr'd gowne' he was remarkably unaffected, remaining merry whilst eating and drinking heartily. Queen Henrietta Maria, as devoted as ever, refused to 'be out of his company' and lay with him at night at great risk to herself.[4]

At the Prinsenhof, amidst such instability, the loss of the great Gustavus reduced the 13-year-old Rupert to floods of tears as much as the death of his father. This unusually emotional outburst shocked his young brother, Philip, who assumed the entire Protestant cause was lost. Rupert's reaction shows a degree of hero-worship for the renowned King of Sweden – they certainly shared many characteristics. In Gustavus, Rupert had seen a man infinitely more successful and dynamic than his own father, and who he might one day emulate. Charles Louis termed his father's death as the loss of 'the bringer up of my youth, and Provider for my estate'. He committed himself to the 'perpetuall honoring of his memorie'.[5]

Rupert, together with brothers Charles Louis, Maurice, and Edward, addressed themselves in a pitiful letter to King Charles. Committing themselves to their uncle's protection, they lamented having no friends, fortune, nor great honour except this blood tie. Should the king not maintain them, then God knows, they asserted, what might become of them. Rupert took up his pen again in January 1633, thanking his uncle for the favour shown to them all and boldly asserting he desired nothing more than to 'grow up for your Majesteis servise' and to live by the king's bounty.[6] Rupert sought a new idol.

King Charles had despatched the Earl of Arundel to The Hague. The peer had escorted Elizabeth out of England after her marriage to Frederick, and now he came to take her back. The king invited his sister to return to England and settle there, but Elizabeth, determined to fight for her son's restoration, refused. On 5 February 1633, as Arundel waited on board the *Victory* for a good wind, he noticed a small craft. Charles Louis and Rupert were being rowed to the *Victory*, and once in sight of it, Rupert rejoiced and 'would needes helpe to rowe', so impatient was he to board it. Once standing on the deck – created from England's great oaks – Charles Louis 'sweetely' exclaimed that he was happy to finally set foot upon his uncle's dominions.[7]

Fortunately for the Protestants, their cause still had a worthy commander in the Prince of Orange. Rupert's great-uncle had captured a trio of Spanish fortresses – Venlo, Roermond and Maastricht – while Gustavus had been storming through Imperial territory. Now besieging Rheinburg, the Prince of Orange sent for Charles Louis, the eldest Palatine. The young elector needed to take on his late father's mantle and this opportunity would teach him how to both lead and fight, but determined not to be left out, Rupert petitioned to accompany his brother. Surprisingly, his mother agreed that he could not be soon enough a soldier in these active times. Rupert's first taste of warfare awaited him.

Frank Kitson, in his 1994 biography of Rupert, suggests the prince was an aide-de-camp or messenger. Speaking with his own military experience, Kitson ventures the opinion that Rupert's first campaign gave him a particular flair for capturing or relieving fortified towns. The prince showed such a natural affinity with the world of war and the life of a soldier that his mother quickly got cold feet. Concerned that his morals were under assault, she recalled him home, much to Rupert's irritation. Frederick Henry interceded, and Rupert no doubt bombarded his mother with teenage outrage, which made Elizabeth relent. At one point during the siege representatives of King Charles arrived at Charles Louis's tent to formally invest him with the Order of the Garter, something which must have appealed to the chivalrous Rupert. Though it only took a short time to bring about Rheinburg's surrender, both princes proved their 'ingenious and manly carriage'.[8] It was the world's 'first proof of [Rupert's] Valour and Conduct'.[9]

Apart from fighting it out on the field of battle, or battering towns, there was a less deadly way in which the Palatines might turn their situation around – marriage. Elizabeth, together with King Charles, became matchmakers-in-chief.

On 8 September 1631, following negotiations for a union between Princess Elisabeth and Prince Vladislaus of Poland, King Charles had hosted a Polish ambassador in Whitehall Palace. Escorted by the earls of Arundel and Carlisle, the man was welcomed at the gate with two volleys of shot from the trained bands. Negotiations turned sour when Poland demanded the princess's conversion to Catholicism. To make matters worse, another Polish envoy deliberately attempted to hand over persuasive letters about religion to the princess herself, without her mother's knowledge. This all so enraged King Charles that he shunned the match. A union between Rupert and Marguerite, daughter of the French Duc de Rohan, also fell through, most likely to Rupert's relief. At that time, he was married to the idea of being a soldier.

Though the family's fortunes were at their lowest ebb, Rupert's towering presence – standing 6 foot 4 inches – coupled with his good looks, gritty determination, and brave demeanour, attracted many ladies. There was a romanticism about his plight. There are similarities with the early life of Prince Philip, husband of Queen Elizabeth II, whose family were twentieth-century royal exiles. As a boy, the independent, determined, and rather abrasive Philip was shuffled from relative to relative, without a place he could truly call home. The same was true of Rupert. Both princes made the best of their nomadic upbringings, thrived in the military, and ended up settling in Britain.

After Rheinburg, the winter of 1633 passed peacefully, much to Rupert's chagrin, and he spent most of this 'respose' wishing for an end to it. There were some distractions, one of which was a medieval-style tournament arranged by the Prince of Orange to mark the military successes, which included running at the ring. Eagerly taking the opportunity to show off his prowess, and break the tedium, Rupert entered the fray. During one course, running for the honour of the 'Ladyes', the 14-year-old stole the show with his 'gracefull aire' and drew the 'ye eyes & hartes' of the audience. He emerged victorious and lifted the prize. This performance was applauded as much as if he had just 'gained a battail or conquered a Kingdome' and the ladies ended up competing amongst themselves over who would crown him with the glory.[10] One, described as more eminent than the rest in quality and beauty, ensured that Rupert knew the sense she had of his worth, though tantalisingly she is not named.

Notwithstanding Rupert's eminent admirer, the spring of 1634 could not have come soon enough. But his hopes for 'warr & glorie' were dashed by a lack of suitable military operations.[11] Matters improved the following year when France declared war on Spain, sending an army of 25,000 to assist the Dutch in attacking the Spanish Netherlands. Rupert, along with Charles Louis, eagerly joined the Prince of Orange as volunteers in his lifeguard and subsequently took part in the capture of Tirlemont (Dutch: Tienen) and the siege of Louvain (Leuven) amongst other actions. Tirlemont was a particularly brutal affair that included civilian massacre. Blame was laid squarely on the French, who were alleged to have been so 'inhuman and barbarous' that their allies now found them entirely 'distasteful'.[12]

The plague in Leiden, where 1,500 were dying every week, was seen as divine punishment, and as the architect of the alliance with France, the Prince of Orange's popularity took a beating.

Thus, Rupert experienced the horrific side of war. It was noted that his bravery astonished veterans, and that he would have done more had the commanders 'suffer'd him' to do so. Instead, concerned by Rupert's reckless disregard for his own safety, particular 'care' was taken of him. While Frederick Henry pounded the walls of Leuven, he was most likely bombarded by letters from Rupert's mother.[13]

What's clear is that the prince was certainly not averse to giving his great-uncle the benefit of his opinion, which was in favour of 'charging ye enemy' – valour was better than virtue. Rupert, aspiring to be a great soldier rather than a politician it was said, learned a great deal about the former at both sieges. Accounts of his experiences extol his principle that 'before wee overcome others wee should learne to overcome our selves'.[14] This motto was the same one his uncle, King Charles I, had adopted at that age – it shows a clear connection between the two, though the prince didn't always manage to abide by it. As the approach of winter brought the curtain down on the campaign of 1635, it was, aptly, England that beckoned.

Chapter 6

Royall Unckle

The landing of Charles Louis at Dover, in November 1635, was the precursor to another royal arrival. Queen Henrietta Maria was pregnant with her fifth child and her due date was fast approaching. Christmas passed in a blur of preparations. The baby girl, born on 28 December 1635, was christened Elizabeth in honour of her aunt in Holland. Like any parent, King Charles's heart filled with joy over his new daughter, while simultaneously his purse emptied. A new bed, cradle, chairs, and stools for the birth alone had cost £2,481. A pension of £300 was also granted to Charles Louis's eldest sister (another Elisabeth) along with a gift of horses, as she turned 17.

Charles Louis had not come to meet his newest cousin; his trip was politically motivated and covered by his uncle's exchequer to alleviate his mother. After setting aside £1,000 for Charles Louis's expenses, the king must have heard with dismay that the actual costs incurred for just two months were double that. Then Rupert joined his brother in February 1636.

On the surface, the royal court in England was lavish. Adorned by the finest art collection in Europe and operating with a formality that made it divine-like, it was as though the boys had been elevated to somewhere between heaven and earth. Certainly, the grand court masques and their allegorical acting furthered a fairy-tale image with the king and queen as central characters. The horror of European warfare must have seemed a million miles away. Beneath the surface, however, bubbled a melting pot of discontent.

The sole purpose of this visit was summed up well by roving ambassador, Sir Thomas Roe; in the heart of King Charles lay the counsel, maintenance, protection, supplies, armies, victories, and restitution that Charles Louis required – if the boy played his cards right. The pressure was on. Politics and manipulation were arts Charles Louis would, by necessity and character, become quite adept at. His mother tried to ease his passage by asking none other than Sir Henry Vane to look out for him. She was certain her son would commit many errors, being so young, but she most feared how 'damnably' he would perform with the ladies, being a 'verie ill courtier'.[1] Vane was entreated to intercede and desire them not to laugh too much at the young man.

Elizabeth had made more practical preparations in advance. King Charles's two greatest ministers were Thomas Wentworth, Lord Deputy of Ireland, and William Laud, Archbishop of Canterbury. Together they coined the phrase 'Rule of Thorough' in reference to their united efforts to reform government and church at all costs – nobody was to be spared, and even King Charles was blocked from enclosing Oatlands Palace on account of the cost. Laud's leadership of foreign affairs made his support crucial to the Palatine cause, and as such, Elizabeth cultivated a relationship. Of Wentworth, more distant in Ireland, she felt a negative vibe. Having never corresponded with him, and sensing a mutual lethargy, she decided she could not find it in her humour to begin.

Having written to Laud in July 1635, Elizabeth had plainly expressed hope that her brother might give her son the means to take the Palatinate, as opposed to forcing him to 'sitt still'.[2] In her eyes, the time for treaties had passed.

For Charles Louis, a rather cold and awkward 18-year-old, burdened with immense expectations, he rapidly lost patience. Clinging to a hollow title, the crushing powerlessness of his situation, coupled with teenage self-righteousness, infuriated him. Every exiled Palatine had to deal with inferiority, being reduced to handouts and goodwill, but after just three months in England, Charles Louis was having to be persuaded to stay. He was annoyed that his uncle did not show him letters relating to Palatinate affairs, and even having his height measured, to ascertain if he was taller than his brothers, stirred emotional insecurity. The pace of diplomatic progress was slow, making him 'mad' that despite encouragement, nothing ever came to fruition.[3] In Charles Louis's defence, he was perceptive, shrewd, and able to weave a web of influence so quickly that he soon understood the underlying tension in England (to which his uncle seemed oblivious) and knew which opposition leaders to befriend.

There were fewer difficulties for Rupert. By comparison, he seemed to settle into his sabbatical with surprising enthusiasm and was awestruck by England. He was (so Elizabeth warned) 'giddie' and, uncharacteristically, Rupert soon put aside his obsession with war to plunge into the pleasures of court life.[4] Calling on Sir Henry Vane once more, Elizabeth charged 'vanely' with the dubious task of telling Rupert when he did 'ill' and reassured the man that the prince was 'good natured' enough to take it.[5]

The truth of the matter facing the Palatine cause was that King Charles was rendered powerless by a fissure at the heart of his government. The royal court was but an image, cast by the king at the projector, with Wentworth and Laud directors of the show. Behind the scenes, the duo worked hard to unify the three kingdoms politically and religiously, and it would have been folly to jeopardise this on account of the Palatinate. The rule of 'Thorough' was delivering, and by June 1636, Wentworth reported that Ireland was £96,450 better off due to his management, while its church had been brought further in line with England's.

King Charles was playing the long game by necessity. He was entirely sympathetic to his nephew's cause and desired nothing more than to be a Protestant champion like Gustavus, but he was aware of current limitations. First and foremost was Parliament, who used money as a bargaining tool for reform. After he and MPs had clashed in 1629, Charles had dissolved Parliament and ruled alone, which wasn't unusual – his father had done so for nearly ten years on one occasion. By attempting to get his house in order, King Charles was following the late Gustavus, who had created a strong, central government in Sweden, reinforced by an effective army, before entering the Thirty Years' War.

King Charles's plans to strengthen his kingdoms and his own authority were symbolised, in a manner, by the building of a great ship, the largest and finest ever made in England. At 1,637 tonnes, the hulk that became the *Sovereign of the Seas* was taking shape in Woolwich dockyard, and the king made frequent visits. On 28 March 1636, he proudly took Charles Louis and Rupert to see the launch of two small pinnaces, built from the waste material. As the *Roebuck* and *Greyhound* joined the Royal Navy, so discussion centred on plans for Rupert.

Having experienced the Gunpowder Plot in 1605, Elizabeth of Bohemia held a healthy fear and detestation of Catholics. She did her utmost to imbue this in her children. As soon as whispers reached her that Rupert was often in the circle of Queen Henrietta Maria, Elizabeth began to fret. Letters from Charles Louis seemed to confirm her worst fears, when he wrote of Rupert's 'great friendship' with Endymion Porter, whose wife was a zealous Catholic and the queen's lady-in-waiting.[6] True, Mrs Porter would be involved in the conversion of the Countess of Newport and came close to winning over the Puritan Marchioness of Hamilton. But the fact that Endymion was also a worldly-wise diplomat, poet and art connoisseur was not mentioned, nor that he entertained a variety of artistic figures that must have greatly appealed to the impressionable Rupert. However, at Porter's *soirées* might be found William Davenant, whose nose had been eaten away by venereal disease, or his friend Sir John Suckling, a soldier-poet and hardened gambler who could not be trusted to repay a debt of sixpence. So, it's understandable to see why Rupert's family fretted. Charles Louis simply did not know how to steal his brother away from this group, short of going there in person and pulling him out.

The cold truth was that the headstrong Rupert didn't entirely trust Charles Louis, and would not heed warnings over the Porters. Charles Louis complained his sibling was 'very shy to tell me his opinion'.[7] At one point the topic of Rupert's marriage to Marguerite de Rohan was resurrected, only to fade again through the prince's lack of interest – he was discovering the world and was not ready to be pinned down by a dynastical marriage, no matter how beneficial it might have been for the family. Another idea he rejected out of hand was becoming a bishop in the Church of England.

A scheme for conquering Madagascar and founding a colony there under Rupert's sovereign rule did attract the prince's interest. Sir William Davenant even penned 446 lines of poetry in praise of Rupert and this venture, with Endymion Porter writing the front piece. Calling the whole idea a romance inspired by Porter, who desired to go along with the prince like a squire, Elizabeth likened it to a

Don Quixote tale and asked friends to put such 'windmills' out of her son's head.[8] Patrick Morrah, in his 1976 biography of Rupert, states that Henrietta Maria's objective had been to ensnare Rupert and convert him. On returning to his mother, Rupert supposedly admitted as much, saying that had he remained just a few days longer he would have succumbed. This seems uncharacteristic and Rupert never swerved from Calvinism at any other time.

News that King Charles was sending an envoy to the Holy Roman Emperor also attracted Elizabeth's displeasure, as did her brother's idea of marrying Charles Louis to the emperor's daughter. She complained that the woman was 'oulde and unhandsome' and argued that the emperor had previously duped her father.[9] In the end, she had no alternative but to accept a last-ditch attempt at a peaceful resolution to the issue of the Palatinate.

As diplomacy dragged on, the two princes engaged in rounds of hunting, plays, country progresses, and naval inspections. Rupert was prone to over-exercise, whereas Charles Louis did not do enough, and the latter admitted that 'my body kan not indure soe much as his'.[10] After one shopping trip, the king and queen visited Bedlam to see the 'mad folkes' – a well-known attraction for the curious and wealthy – and found there more than they bargained for. Two women frightened the royals out of the place by 'forole [feral] talk' but not before they flashed at them too. One 'puld upp her cloathes before' while the other 'puld upp all behind' and 'shewd all'.[11] It's unclear whether the princes accompanied them, but they would surely have heard all about it. Another escapade did certainly include the boys. They visited the Temple to see William Davenant's masque called *The Prince d'Amour*, played in honour of the elder. Queen Henrietta Maria and three of her ladies disguised themselves as citizens and sneaked in to watch, along with her circle of favourites, the Earl of Holland, Lord Goring, Henry Jermyn, and Henry Percy. It's easy to see why the vivacious and fun-loving side of his aunt appealed.

Rupert was observed to have an active spirit, full of observation and judgement. Moreover, he was likely to be a good 'sword' if his edge 'be sett right'.[12]

> whatsoever he wills, he wills vehemently; so that to what he bends, he wilbe in it excellent ... [his Majesty] takes great pleasure in his unrestfullness; for he is never idle, and in his sports serious, in his conversation retyred, but sharp and wittye, when occasion provokes him.[13]

Elizabeth was counselled to recall Rupert from England by gentle means, but her brother stepped in and insisted that the boy should stay. King Charles thoroughly enjoyed his down-to-earth nephew's company; the pair shared a love of outdoor pursuits and a seemingly limitless energy. In April 1636, when the Earl of Carlisle died, the resulting lucrative vacancy as First Gentleman of the Bedchamber – a trusted official always at the king's side – was for a time rumoured to be earmarked for Rupert to keep him in England.

Bonds were forged that would later see Rupert give his all for his uncle. Though the king never had that same level of affinity with Charles Louis, he showed all signs of love to him too. If Rupert was King Charles's favourite, at this time Elizabeth admitted to Sir Thomas Roe that Charles Louis had always been her golden child.

The two brothers were immortalised during this visit by the artist Anthony van Dyck. William Cavendish, Earl of Newcastle, captured the essence of van Dyck's skill by saying that when he looked upon the man's portraits, they appeared more 'Nature, & nott Arte' – meaning extremely lifelike. Van Dyck, he went on, held a power over the 'Eyes of Man-kinde' to epidemical proportions.[14]

The full-length portrait of Charles Louis and Rupert was destined to hang in Whitehall Palace, its gilded frame carved with martial weapons. The elder sports a golden Garter chain and baton, looking out of the canvas with a knowing expression, but the younger stands much taller and gazes pensively into the distance, cutting a very noble figure. Charles Louis's armour gleams, reminding viewers that he is the elector, but Rupert needs no such adornments to shine, with sharper and more handsome features. The great artist also produced individual portraits of the pair, each wearing a leather buff coat. The differences between those are immediately apparent. Rupert's stance is confident and at ease with himself, crimson breeches and gold lace embroidery giving a colourful contrast. One hand grips a cane, while the other arm rests on his sword's hilt. His brother seems as washed-out as the watery-blue ribbon of the Garter around his neck. The weight of responsibility and frustration could not be disguised in his features, even by van Dyck, though he did capture Charles Louis's perceptive eyes, which assess the viewer from a distance.

A change of scenery marked the halfway point of the visit in the summer of 1636. With plague raging in London, the court went to Oxford for the end of their summer progress, where Archbishop Laud entertained them. A former student of St John's College, he was Chancellor of Oxford University from 1630, and is described today by the Bodleian Library as almost its 'second founder'.[15] He had beautified the college chapels of St John's, Merton, and Lincoln, as well as numerous churches and cathedrals across the country. To sober Puritans, however, this smacked of Catholicism, and worse still, railing off altar tables distanced the congregation from the Almighty.

When the king, queen, and their nephews arrived at the university, they were greeted with gifts. For the king, a velvet-covered bible embroidered with the royal arms and a pair of gloves. Henrietta, Charles Louis, and Rupert all received their own pairs too. Laud selected *Caesar's Commentaries* (in English) for Rupert.

Students were instructed not to wear their hair long, with boots and loose stockings also prohibited. Chosen from the king's retinue were fifty-seven people to be awarded honorary degrees. After being proposed by Sir Nathaniel Brent, Warden of Merton College, Prince Rupert, in a scarlet gown, became an honorary Master of Arts on 30 August 1636. A dinner followed, in which the king, queen, and Charles Louis dined on one table, and Rupert with the lords and ladies on another. Though his martial manner was not entirely at ease with such a grandiose court, it's testament to Rupert's personality that he won applause from all quarters, especially many women. At some point during the visit, he would have met the enchanting Mary, Lady Herbert, daughter of the king's late favourite, the Duke of Buckingham. After the latter's murder in 1628, Mary had been brought up in the royal court and treated by the king and queen as one of their own children. Rupert and Mary's friendship would blossom during the civil war, though by then she had gone on to marry the king's cousin, the Duke of Richmond and Lennox.

As months passed, the social calendar could not distract any further from the ultimate question: what King Charles was prepared to do for his nephew's restoration. At Newmarket, on 23 October 1636, Charles Louis and his uncle engaged in debate over the preference for treaty or troops. The elector was firm for the latter, but the king well knew that once taken up, the sword was not easily sheathed again, and any army would need financing for at least three years. In the face of continued discussion, the king declared that he would not hazard so much on uncertainties, requesting his nephew commit his rationale to paper. Charles Louis delegated the task to the faithful Sir Thomas Roe. By November, King Charles was offering up to £12,000 to his nephew, a sum that would equate to a whopping £1,400,000 today. But the offer disappointed Charles Louis and his mother, the latter declaring that it would be better her son was in his grave than to remain with his uncle. All the world, she countered with maternal outrage, was in action for him.

Chapter 7

Untaynted

While Europe tore itself apart, King Charles's three kingdoms looked on at the horrors from which they had been spared. It seemed as if the Stuart dream of uniting their countries, in both religion and government, was drawing tantalisingly close. It was a logical strategy. With a singular focus, the resources, loyalty, and priorities of all three might be better harnessed. After that, the king could become a major player on the world stage, intervening militarily to secure the right outcome, or playing the peacemaker to his own advantage. Religious uniformity – their churches united on a middle road – would surely see God crown these islands with his favour.

Scotland was the last part of the jigsaw. An unusually savvy Charles had made minor alterations to the liturgy in 1634, which were then enhanced by a further change in 1636. The Archbishop of St Andrews and 'his Brethren' had, however, been given royal authority to stick to the first if they saw 'apparent reason'.[1] The king was treading carefully.

Throughout spring of 1637, perhaps encouraged by progress, King Charles started to discuss military support for his nephew. It was an unusually hot season. In Holland, Rupert's mother remained fearful that he was about to be swallowed by the flames of apostasy. Extracting him was a priority and this time she wrote pushing the excuse that the Prince of Orange was about to take the field 'very suddenly'. Events of 1637 were moving so fast that she termed it an active world – one which Rupert should fully partake of. This time she would not back down and resolved to 'hinder' any who thought to hold her son back.[2]

Sir Thomas Roe reassured that Rupert's religious beliefs were 'untaynted'. The enemy, he wrote, was a serpent as well as a wolf, but Rupert had remained 'impregnable' against conversion attempts. Furthermore, the boy showed infinite potential, because 'whatsoever he undertakes, he doth it vigorously, & seriously' – he was compared to steel, a metal that needed the right tempering and disposing.[3] At one point during the visit, Rupert was bled due to 'heatting himselfe' too much with exercise during the hot weather.[4] In April 1637, another burning issue (according to Walter Yonge, an MP from Devon) was that Papist books had been printed with the supposed blessing of Archbishop Laud, and upon discovery of this the Earl of Pembroke (a Puritan peer) threatened to resign from the Privy Council if the king did not act. Adamant that this had been done without his knowledge, the king was said to have ordered the burning of 300 offending books.

Offering military assistance to his nephew would at least dispel ridiculous rumours that the king was a closet Catholic. A plan was hatched between King Charles, France, and Holland that each would provide 3,000 soldiers to Charles Louis. In terms of vessels, fourteen ships of the Royal Navy were to be loaned, while the French and Dutch agreed to stump up another thirty between them. When deciding who could command the forces – both by land and sea – Rupert's name was proposed, such was the confidence in his qualities. King Charles was positive that his nephew would 'acquit himself very well' when the moment presented.[5] Unfortunately, matters came no closer to fruition than the madcap Madagascar scheme, for the Chancellor of the Exchequer made it clear that the three kingdoms were unfit for war.

How should we assess Rupert's English interlude? Frank Kitson thought it allowed the prince to become an established member of the royal family, and meet the leading nobility and gentry, not to mention see England's towns, roads, and rivers. The royal progress of 1636, for example, had taken the prince through eleven different English counties, from Lincolnshire down to Hampshire. Charles Spencer ventured that Rupert had found his 'spiritual home'.[6] There's no doubt that Rupert had been enraptured by his uncle and aunt's magical court. For sixteen months he was treated with more respect than ever before – for the eternal exile who had been bred to fight, England was a rock of stability involved in all aspects of his life. He ignored the faults, factions, and fissures. The contemporary and anonymous *biographical notes* record that Rupert went to England to seek employment, only to be absorbed by 'ye divertissements of ye court' that made his warlike heart delight in the 'softnesse' of peace. The kindnesses of his uncle and aunt were 'powerfull charmes'. Indeed, he only left because he felt duty bound to his brother's cause. When the boys sailed away, the author records that they did so full of resolution and hope.[7]

The brothers' opposing emotions highlight their differing characters and motivations. Charles Louis stayed a little longer than intended just to obtain a donation of £10,000 from the king. A subscription also came from William, Earl of Craven, a rich noble who dedicated his life and fortune to the Queen of Bohemia and her family. Admitting candidly to Sir Thomas Roe, Charles Louis later declared that he had been loath to part from the man, but not from England. At one point during the visit, he had complained about the 'perpetual hunting and changing of lodgings'.[8] Rupert, on the other hand, had gone hunting with the king on the very morning of departure. Unable to contain his regret, he expressed a desire to 'break his Neck, that so he might leave his Bones in England'.[9] His image would remain, at least, hanging in the hallowed Privy Gallery at Whitehall, along with over seventy Tudor and Jacobean portraits. Busts of the princes were also commissioned by the Earl of Arundel.

Just days after their departure in the *St George*, an apt choice for the knightly Rupert, three Puritans were pilloried at Westminster in June 1637 after being condemned by Archbishop Laud in the Star Chamber. William Prynne, Henry Burton, and John Bastwick had their ears cut. Spectators wept. Blood poured from each man and the crowd 'strewed' herbs and flowers before the trio.[10] The letters 'S.L.' for 'seditious libeller' were branded on Prynne's cheeks for having published writings condemning both Laud and his religious policies. Prynne, a barrister of Lincoln's Inn, was a longstanding voice of opposition. Some years earlier, he had incurred the king's personal animosity by publishing a book that condemned female actors as 'notorious whores' on the eve of the queen's masque, in which she had a central part.[11] Such ear-cropping was not confined to Puritans – a Catholic called Pickering suffered the same fate after claiming the king was a Papist at heart and all Protestants were devils.

As Rupert headed back to Holland, the ships were engulfed by a tempest. Archbishop Laud noted that the topsails of the princes' ship were affected, and that water came in through the lower ports of their pinnace. Luckily, they arrived safely, though both brothers were stricken by seasickness. Within five years, a very different storm would draw Rupert back to his uncle's side.

Chapter 8

Unsettled Spiritt

With the distractions of courtly life behind him, Rupert was once more unable to 'live wthout accon [action]' in the summer of 1637.[1] His brother, Maurice, was already at Breda with the Prince of Orange's besieging force. The town had fallen to the Spanish in 1625 and now the Dutch were determined to take it back.

Having joined the siege, Rupert 'let noe day passe' without taking part in exploits that surprised or inspired his comrades.[2] Many Englishmen also arrived, their names a roll call that would go on to serve in the Wars of the Three Kingdoms; the Earl of Northampton, Viscount Grandison, Sir Jacob Astley, Charles Gerard, Charles Lucas, George Goring, George Monck, and Henry Wilmot. By August, Charles Louis turned up, hoping to secure the Prince of Orange's cooperation in furthering a treaty between England and France that was favourable to the Palatinate. He also expressed concern to his mother about Rupert, venturing that his brother needed a better man to look after his business – and, in effect, to keep him from trouble.

Another volunteer who arrived was Jeffrey Hudson, Queen Henrietta Maria's favoured servant, who was just 18 inches tall. One traveller at the time noted tongue in cheek that Hudson's 'Gygantisme body made the bulwarks of Breda tremble'.[3] But Elizabeth recounted testimony that Hudson did 'as much as anie bodie yet against the ennemie [from] within the trenches'.[4] Indeed, the Dutch were so strongly entrenched with 'extraordinary' siegeworks that the Spanish barely managed to disturb them.[5] With every passing day, the trenches were dug closer to Breda, like arteries ready to carry soldiers to the fortress's very walls. Charles Louis wrote that the English and French who were part of the Dutch force had managed to get past the 'ditche' of the enemy's horn-work – an earthen defence.[6]

One evening, the high-spirited Rupert and Maurice sneaked into the trenches and crept along them. As they neared Breda, they overheard the defenders' voices. Now, more than ever, Rupert's bilingual skills proved valuable, and the brothers ascertained that the Spanish were planning to sally out from the town and attack the Prince of Orange's army that very night. Even the gate involved was obtained. They hurried back to their great-uncle and made him aware, resulting in the Spanish being beaten off.

Jacob Astley, a former tutor, had been assigned to Rupert and Maurice to keep them from high jinks as well as danger. Luckily, this escapade did not reflect negatively on him, as Elizabeth praised his being 'so diligent in waiting on my sonns'.[7] Such risky behaviour was probably not unexpected of Rupert. Throughout his life, he never seemed cowed by danger – instead, it spurred him on, as if the possibility of being killed did not even enter his mind. Like Churchill, who during the Blitz took to the roof to watch air raids during World War II, Rupert and Maurice seemed anxious to be at the forefront of action; to feel the adrenaline and to prove themselves. The Palatines, due to their situation, had an inferiority complex that drove them on.

Rupert, a stubborn and determined character, wanted to be the best at whatever he turned his hand to. This headstrong manner and bloody-mindedness often took precedence over the greater good, which didn't bode well for someone who would one day hold senior command. When a force of English volunteers was tasked with capturing a horn-work, Frederick Henry felt sufficiently concerned to specifically ban Rupert from joining the fray due to the danger involved. By way of consolation, the prince was permitted to deliver the order to attack. Unsurprisingly, when the instruction had been duly passed to Captain Monck, Rupert got into the front line and charged with them. This could have been one of his first direct dealings with George Monck, who would one day become not just a kingmaker, but a monarchy-maker.

Rupert emerged unscathed (luck that would stick with him for the next ten years) but a number of other men did not fare so well. George Goring was shot in the 'Ancle-bone' and invalided out of Holland on crutches.[8] Amputation was a stark possibility. Though often legless through alcohol, the man kept his lower limb, but would forever walk with a limp. A bullet tore through Henry Wilmot's cheek and ear, leaving him deaf on one side. For Peter Apsley, brother of Lucy Hutchinson, it was a shot to his mouth. This took away part of his tongue, causing light-hearted mirth to King Charles I on account of the man's outspokenness.

Breda surrendered on 10 October. Rupert's stint in the siege had lasted just over two months. Charles Louis did not stay to see the victory – instead, itching to have an army of his own, he had left to visit his mother. Elizabeth was at Rhennen hunting and haring while in England, King Charles and Queen Henrietta Maria watched the launch of the *Sovereign of the Seas*, which would carry 144 guns and 11 anchors.

One notable death at Breda was the Landgrave of Hesse, which left his army leaderless. Charles Louis saw his chance and sent representatives to sound out the Landgrave's widow as to the possibility of his assuming command. King Charles's envoys were still working to seal a treaty with France, hoping to draw European powers into supporting Charles Louis.

An anecdote from this period is symbolic of the political manoeuvring over the Palatinate, and the many interlinked factors required to attempt Charles Louis's restoration. While out hunting, one of Rupert's favourite dogs followed a fox into a hole. When it stuck fast, the prince squeezed down and grabbed the dog's hind legs but became trapped himself. A man called Thomas Billingsley then took Rupert's legs and pulled the prince out, still clinging to the dog, who still had the fox in its teeth.

If Charles Louis could get himself at the head of an army it might give impetus to his cause and encourage French and British investment – certainly, it would be more likely they would support an army rather than provide one. A pearl of wisdom from trusted family friend, Sir Thomas Roe, was if the elector laid the cornerstone, then others might add to it. By December, word was reaching England that Charles Louis was of a will and resolution to sell his remaining jewels and die fighting at the head of his few loyal supporters. In the end, he decided against attempting to use the Hessian army, concerned that he would never have full control over its operations and staffing.

The first campaign was one of recruitment. Rupert naturally answered his brother's call, but Maurice and Edward were sent to France to complete their studies. Donations rolled in; £20,000 from his mother, and the same figure from King Charles, along with a whopping £30,000 from the ever-faithful Lord Craven. On receiving a further £5,000 from Craven and £4,500 from his mother, Charles Louis (on the Prince of Orange's advice) bought the small town of Meppen, in Westphalia, from the widow of a Swedish officer, to whom it had been granted. Meppen came with a garrison and was intended as a rendezvous for his troops, while the annual income generated from the town was 25 per cent more than the cost. No sooner had the transaction been completed than Catholic troops seized the place. It was not a good start. The unfazed elector instead resolved to march his army into the eye of the storm and to the Palatinate itself.

Command of three regiments of cavalry were given to Sir Thomas Ferentz, a German officer and close supporter; a man called Loe, of whom little is known; and Prince Rupert. To bolster the force with experience, the elector had been counselled to persuade James King to join him – a Scotsman who had long served in the Swedish army. Elizabeth called King a 'verie worthie man'.[9] As such, envoys, Sir Thomas Roe and Richard Cave, successfully worked their magic on King, who had achieved the rank of General Major with the Swedes. He had been operating around Minden for one year. As well as bringing a Swedish contingent to Charles Louis's small army, the man was familiar with the area and its topography. King took the mantle of Lieutenant General, the most senior officer under the elector. Lord Craven led a regiment of guards.

In October 1638, the force set off 'full of hopes and courage' towards Minden, a Swedish-held town that offered them a safe haven should they need it.[10] Until now, the Palatine element of this force has always been painted as being the largest, but Steve Murdoch and Kathrin Zickermann disagree. During research for 'The Battle of Lemgo, 17 October 1638: An Empirical Re-evaluation', within *Miltärhistorisk Tidskrift*, they concluded that the Palatine element could not have been above 2,000 (including men from across Britain as well as the German dutchies) whilst the Swedes numbered 3,000.

On passing the Imperial (Catholic-held) town of Rheine, a detachment broke away and drew close to it. The custom was for both sides to offer 'an affront'.[11] This saw three troops of Rheine's garrison form up outside their walls and usual practice was that shots would be exchanged in a short, controlled standoff. After that, the elector's army could get on its way. Prince Rupert, Lord Craven, and Richard Crane (who would later command Rupert's civil war lifeguard) were the leaders of the reconnaissance detachment, but custom was far from Rupert's mind.

Seeing the enemy draw up was too tempting, and the prince decided to give battle, leading three troops of horsemen to the attack. This was no medieval show. Instead of halting, firing, and wheeling about, Rupert and his band charged right into the enemy. The clash was devastating. The Imperial horsemen were forced back towards to the town, and in the melee, Rupert was almost swept inside too. Once again, his luck held when 'a soldier, with a screwed gun, snapped at the Prince within ten yards of his body' but happily it misfired.[12]

The prince's example encouraged his men, and such shock-and-awe would become his trademark. According to Thomas Roe, far from eliciting the praise of Lieutenant General King, Rupert's action instead earned 'a gentle reprehension', which was the first rumble of concern in the two men's relationship.[13] Roe was inclined to agree with the admonishment, terming Rupert an 'unsettled spiritt'.[14] The gung-ho action of a young novice certainly posed a significant risk and this reaction from King is crucial to understanding what followed.

After this clash, instead of continuing to Minden, the elector's force turned to besiege Lemgo, in Münster. Just 20 miles south of Minden, this Imperial town proved a fatal distraction. Nadine Akkerman, biographer of Elizabeth of Bohemia, states that James King's encouragement to attack Lemgo was because it fitted with Swedish interests. Additionally, King had been Governor of Lemgo before it had been captured by Imperial forces, so had a vested interest in retaking it.

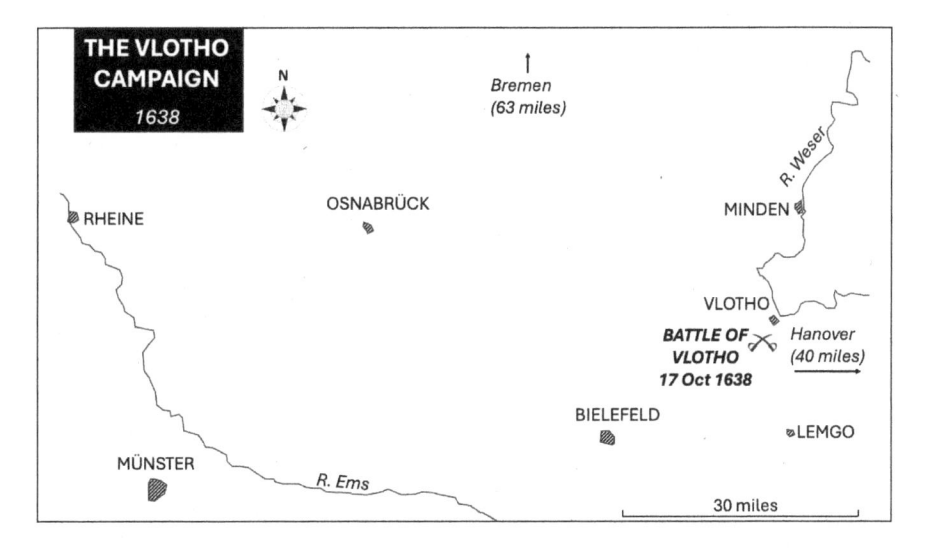

THE VLOTHO CAMPAIGN 1638

BATTLE OF VLOTHO 17 Oct 1638

The delay allowed a large Imperial army commanded by Melchior von Hatzfeldt to close up. As the elector's officers met to discuss the situation, Rupert was 'of a disposicon rather to charge an enemy, then to make retreates' but was persuaded that falling back was essential on this occasion. The army needed putting into a better condition, and there would be 'noe losse' of reputation over such reasoning.[15]

Accordingly, Charles Louis lifted the siege and attempted to escape his pursuers, but each of the two routes to Minden had their own difficulties; one would involve crossing the River Weser, which would slow them down, while the other would take them perilously close to Hatzfeldt's force. The opinion of James King, as the most senior military officer, took precedence; avoiding the Weser, they went via Vlotho. Hatzfeldt discovered Charles Louis's plan from prisoners and subsequently had his army of 8,000 traverse a mountainous route to cut off the elector. When both sides met, King suggested drawing the army up on a hill called Eiburg. While the cavalry did just that, he withdrew to bring up the foot and guns.

With King's departure, historians have placed German professional, Count Hans Christoff von Königsmarck, who had served with King in the Swedish army, as next in seniority. He is blamed for promptly ordering the army to march down the hill and into a valley; a fateful decision. The landscape of the valley protected the flanks of the elector's troops and meant that the larger Imperial force could only attack on a limited front. The risk was that the elector's army would have little manoeuvrability, and if those front ranks broke and fell back upon the rear, it could become chaotic. There would be hot work for those in the van, who would bear the brunt of the Imperial assault. The four cavalry regiments were drawn up in lines, and here Königsmarck is again blamed for refusing to have his own men at the front; Charles Louis and Loe took that perilous position, followed by Ferentz in the second line, Rupert third, and Königsmarck at the rear. The Battle of Vlotho Bridge (also known as Lemgo) was about to begin.

When the Imperials unleashed their might, they punched straight through the first two lines. Unperturbed, Rupert spurred his troops forward to counter them. Once again, the prince's unorthodox approach met with success; the sheer force of his onslaught stopped the enemy in their tracks and then went on to buckle and break them. Calling on Königsmarck to reinforce him, Rupert had no intention of reining in his men, but nor did he consider the wider implications of his continued charge. Königsmarck did not budge. As a result, the prince reached the end of the protective valley only to be attacked by fresh forces, which he beat off with the support of Lord Craven, who had fought his way through. Though Rupert 'sustain'd ye courage of his [small] party', he and Craven could not hold back the waves of Imperial troops. Valour had to 'yeild to multitudes', especially when those multitudes seized the opportunity to attack the prince's exposed flanks. Others penetrated the valley, turned about, and then struck in his rear. The battle 'continued along tyme in suspence'.[16]

While Rupert's body of men inevitably crumbled, the enemy missed the prince, who found himself alone but unhindered. Wearing a white cockade on his helmet, he was unaware that the enemy had chosen the same field sign – a means of identifying colleagues in the heat of battle. In those brief moments Rupert had a thousand thoughts 'revolving in his mind' but flight was not one of them. Spotting a cornet, who bore one of the elector's standards, being assailed on all sides Rupert charged in to help the man. By doing so, he blew his cover.

During the encounter, one Imperialist bolder than any others 'laid hould on [Rupert's] bridle'. The prince escaped by swiftly 'cutting [off] at one blow, ye fingers of ye hand' that had been laid upon him.[17] Well and truly singled out, Rupert attempted to escape by jumping a stone wall, but his exhausted horse could not manage it. Now on foot, the prince fought like a bated bear until he was overpowered and pinned to the ground. Colonel Lippe, an Imperial commander, on hearing about the exploits of this armour-clad officer, arrived to question him. Lifting the vizor, Lippe demanded to the man's identity. 'A colonel,' came the reply. It prompted an exclamation that he was a young one at that.

Chapter 9

Vlotho Re-examined

Charles Louis and James King escaped the battlefield in a coach, only to face other perils when it became stuck in flood water from the Weser. The elector saved himself from drowning by clinging to an overhanging branch and swam to safety. He was said to have despondently made his way back to Holland remarking that 'Fortune was not yet weary of afflicting his Family', though this is nothing but later propaganda.[1]

Vlotho has been extolled ever since as a disaster for Charles Louis, though as Murdoch and Zickermann point out, the 'orthodox understanding' of the battle narrative stems from Hatzfeldt's grossly exaggerated narrative. They have scrutinised contemporary Swedish, German, and English accounts to uncover a very different perspective; Hatzfeldt only took 1,000 prisoners, meaning that 'nearly all the cavalry and most of the infantry' had successfully retired to Minden. Within just over two weeks, the Palatine forces were 'greater in number' than before Vlotho after receiving thousands of new recruits, some of whom came from Britain. Murdoch and Zickermann concluded that Vlotho was 'far from being the "last flicker of an independent Palatine cause" as often claimed'. From October 1638 to June 1639, while Rupert was incarcerated, the Palatine-Swedish army 'inflicted so much damage' on Imperial forces and took so many prisoners that most of the high-ranking officers captured at Vlotho were successfully exchanged or ransomed.[2]

In the aftermath, the Queen of Bohemia wailed that she would rather Rupert was dead than in the hands of the emperor – and therefore subject to dreaded attempts to convert him. She had also lost a sizeable amount of money, leaving her entirely at the mercy of her brother and the pension he afforded her. In one letter, she put the failure of the siege of Lemgo down to bad weather. Blame was a tangled web of recriminations that was nothing to do with the elements – fresh study sheds light on the actions of those who directed the elector's army.

James King

The last three biographies of Rupert do not mention a rivalry that lay at the heart of the elector's army preceding its formation; King was extremely jealous of Sir Thomas Ferentz, to the degree that the Queen of Bohemia feared it would entirely prevent King from joining her son's force. Matters were somewhat patched up when King was confirmed as the most senior commander.

King forever blamed Rupert for racing up the valley and exposing his cavalrymen to the full might of the enemy before the rest of the army had been brought up. The day had been lost, the Scot asserted with much justification, by the prince's forwardness. It should be recalled that he had already chided Rupert for such behaviour at Rheine, prior to Vlotho. James King's advice to use the hill as a defensive position had been overridden, probably without his awareness, and he was not present when battle commenced. Out of all the leaders, King was the one whose reputation was unfairly slandered over Vlotho – the fact he sent his baggage to safety before battle commenced is hardly evidence of treason.

Prince Rupert

Though Rupert's headlong charge opened the defensive confines of the valley and allowed Imperial troops to penetrate its confines, his initial success did halt the enemy onslaught. He believed that he could have further exploited this if Count Königsmarck had backed him up. There was much praise for Rupert's courage, and though that cannot be taken away from him, it has very much taken precedence over his failing. Additionally, his battle exploits and capture have overshadowed his brother's achievements in the campaign post-Vlotho.

Count Königsmarck

The *biographical notes* relating to Rupert's life, written at the end of the seventeenth century, apportion clear blame on Königsmarck for drawing the army down from the advantageous hill. The anonymous author doubly condemns Königsmarck's failure to back Rupert's charge. But Königsmarck's placing himself in the rear, and his failure to move, is more an indicator of a Palatine-Swedish conflict of interests than personal cowardice. The Swedes simply wanted to preserve as many of their men as possible and it seems Charles Louis had no option but to accept that.

According to Patrick Morrah, who followed from Eliot Warburton, who in turn followed the *biographical notes*, James King's departure from the hill just prior to battle is said to have left Count Königsmarck as the most senior and experienced officer – 'eldest Colonel'. He reportedly expressed a dislike of the position on the hill (supported by Rupert) and commanded the army to descend and draw up in the long valley.[3] Warburton was categorical in accusing Königsmarck of misconduct and cowardice and the *biographical notes* clearly lay the decision on him.

I'm indebted to Steve Murdoch, who kindly checked further contemporary sources (such as Swedish muster rolls and Imperial records) to validate

Königsmarck's army rank and standing. The man fails to be mentioned, indicating that his rank and influence may have been significantly exaggerated over the centuries. His name crops up much more from 1639, when he replaced the subsequently disgraced James King in the Swedish army. With primary archives failing to mention Königsmarck in any senior rank prior to Vlotho, the decision to descend the hill should not be attributed so certainly to him alone. Who was responsible remains unclear, but because it was the elector's army, Charles Louis must have sanctioned it.

The *biographical notes* admit that Rupert was active in support of the decision to descend the hill, and that he (rather uncharacteristically) left the decision to Königsmarck. In my view, there is a strong possibility that Rupert was the prime advocate for the move, and this was subsequently played down and covered up. The headstrong act would fit with Rupert's behaviour and character. It would also account for James King's lifelong criticism of Rupert, and the accusation that the prince lost them the day – not Königsmarck.

But what of the decision to attack Lemgo, which helped bring about the battle at Vlotho? King and Königsmarck were inextricably linked, having been released from their positions under Johan Banér to serve the elector. Banér was a field-marshal in Swedish service. His instruction that King should ensure the elector's force attacked Lemgo delayed the elector's army, and allowed Hatzfeldt to trap them. Capturing Lemgo would have provided a foothold and means of supply, but it was certainly not essential. Elizabeth of Bohemia noted that it was to have served as winter quarters. The twenty-four-hour delay before reaching the town made all the difference in preventing the elector's army from getting safely to Minden.

Furthermore, in 2014, Alexia Grosjean and Steve Murdoch's *Alexander Leslie and the Scottish Generals of the Thirty Years' War* details that Banér was the one who slandered James King's reputation with unfounded allegations of treason post-Vlotho. Banér's refusal of a promotion to King was the final straw that saw the latter proffer his resignation from the Swedish army.

The stain of dishonour naturally made James King extremely bitter. Vlotho also planted a seed of vulnerability in Rupert's mind. From this would spring the roots of disaster, when the duo were brought back together six years later, at the Battle of Marston Moor.

Chapter 10

Invincible Constancy

During the confusion when Rupert was taken prisoner, it was thought he might have been the Elector Palatine. When the dust settled, it became apparent the Imperial army had captured Prince Rupert, Lord Craven, Sir Thomas Ferentz, and Richard Crane. Rupert was initially held by a regiment of dragoons under the command of Irishman, Colonel Walter Devereux, renowned for having killed Albrecht von Wallenstein. After offering some gold pieces to Devereux, Rupert would most likely have escaped with his connivance, had an Imperial detachment not arrived to take the prince.

The captives were escorted south by a guard of forty horsemen. Ironically, as a prisoner, Rupert further experienced his ancestral lands while being taken through the Upper Palatinate. The emperor had officially handed the title of Elector Palatine to Maximilian of Bavaria. Such was Rupert's renown that Maximilian feared the young man's presence and forbade anyone to even look at him – 'no notice' should be taken and there should not be 'anie kinde of usage'.[1] Two poor men broke the rule and were arrested. In fact, Maximilian tried desperately to get the rising star into his clutches, desiring to be his captor, but the emperor would not sanction it. Fearing Maximilian might even seize Rupert, Emperor Ferdinand III ensured the prince's route avoided Bavaria. At Bad Salzuffren, a sympathetic woman tried and failed to help the prince escape and then at Warrendorf, near Münster, they paused. Lord Craven, who had been shot in the thigh and hand, needed time to recover.

The party eventually continued south to Würtzburg, turned east to Bamberg, and then headed towards Austria. Craven was allowed to go free after paying £20,000, though attempts to double the sum to include Rupert were declined. Richard Crane was also released, and through him Rupert sent word to his mother to reassure her that 'neither good usage nor ill shoulde ever make him change his religion or partie'.[2]

On receiving this message, Elizabeth's relief was evident in a letter she wrote to Sir Thomas Roe, but wrestling with her Catholic demons, she possessed a gnawing doubt. Trying to convince herself that her plucky son would stand firm, she reasoned that he had never before betrayed her, even though he was 'stubburne and willfull' to others.[3] She would rather 'strangle' her children with her 'own hands' than see any of them convert.[4] The prince also tasked Crane with delivering a second message. According to one contemporary document, having been refused pen and ink, he resorted to (etching?) some brief words upon a piece of 'table' that was duly sent to King Charles I, urging him to continue his friendship.

Rupert was then isolated by order of Ferdinand III, who had been elected emperor only two years earlier. From Bamberg, his journey proceeded to Linz in February 1639, where he was committed to the castle overlooking the River Danube with Alpine foothills as a backdrop. Situated 100 miles from Vienna and described as a 'very fine' building, it had been enjoyed by a succession of Holy Roman Emperors, before being almost rebuilt and then fortified.[5] Often alluded to as a foreboding place, its appearance and location were not as bleak as might be imagined. The gardens were described as pleasurable. It was the restricted existence that would prove bleak for Rupert's inexhaustible mind and spirit – his wings would be clipped for the next two and a half years.

At first the prince was confined to his rooms, with only brief periods of exercise. Requests by his mother and uncle to have a gentleman attendant were turned down; instead, he was allowed only a page and two servants, who were described by the Venetian ambassador as being an Englishman, Irishman, and Scotsman. The envoy also noted that Rupert was well treated, and his captors observed him to be of superior manners, charm, and ideas.

Count von Kuffstein, a military veteran, was Governor of Linz Castle. He developed such a respect for Rupert that he served the prince 'as farr as his fidellity and ye trust resposed on him would permit'.[6] The prince was allowed to dine with Kuffstein and no doubt conversation touched on the late Battle of Vlotho.

In the aftermath of that battle, it was thought Rupert had been killed. Edward Nicholas, an official close to King Charles, had written as much in November 1638. When Richard Crane reached England, he found the king preoccupied. A rebellion had occurred in Scotland over attempts to impose a new Prayer Book, leaving the monarch visibly distressed; when Crane recounted Rupert's survival, the relieved king took his hand several times and explained his own desperate situation with a 'passionate affection'.[7] King Charles would later write to his sister with a warning that he would have to look upon his own family's safety first.

As Rupert's survival seeped through to the outside world, the prince and his courageous exploits were discussed across Europe. His hot-headedness was easily overlooked. Coupled with bravery before the sieges of Tirlemont and Louvain in 1634, his having emerged unscathed from Breda in 1637, and the lucky misfire of the screwed rifle before Lemgo, the legend of his invincibility started in earnest. Rupert's reputation held many in awe. Royalty coveted his services, men wanted him as their commander, and many women desired to be acquainted with him.

Count Kuffstein's daughter, Susanne Marie, was only a few years younger than Rupert and through circumstances the pair would become very close. It is Frank Kitson's opinion that Susanne seemed in love with Rupert, while Charles Spencer states they were in love with one another. Patrick Morrah is not so certain, writing that there was no evidence of any lasting effect. That the prince thought her 'one of the brightest beauties of her age, no less excelling in the charms of her mind than of her fair body' is evidence of some mutual affinity.[8] The author of the *biographical notes* claims that Rupert's bravery and misfortune combined to make 'sencible imprescons' on Susanne and rendered him 'altogether Illustrious' in her eyes.[9] For the warrior who rarely let anyone or anything distract him, I think Susanne was Rupert's first attraction – a crush – and captivity allowed the prince to appreciate such feelings like never before.

Susanne must have observed the prince as he occupied his inquisitive mind with science and art, topics which he always gravitated to during opportune moments, including times of personal difficulty. He sketched, developing an instrument that assisted with drawing in perspective, which in later life he would go on to demonstrate to the Royal Society in London. Albrecht Dürer, a German artist of the Renaissance, had 'revolutionized printmaking, elevating it to the level of an independent art form' and Rupert admired his work.[10] Perhaps this was a precursor to the prince's interest in mezzotint engraving, which he would later revolutionise.

Solitary confinement was mitigated by Rupert's 'invincible constancy' and eased by the presence of various pets.[11] He demonstrated a loving patience towards them that was not always replicated to humans – animals could never betray him and were loyal companions that never answered back. By training them to carry out various tricks, they behaved more like little friends. A hare would often sleep on his bed and when the bolt of his door was pulled back, she would reputedly jump down and open it with her teeth. The Earl of Arundel gave him a bitch called 'Puddle' of a breed so renowned that the Great Turk instructed his ambassador to secure one of the litter.[12] The prince's way with animals was so great that it would bewilder his future enemies.

Puddle was also recorded as sleeping on her master's bed so must have coexisted happily with the hare, until Rupert, deciding that it was unfair on the latter to be cooped up with him, released it. The author of the *biographical notes* specifically stated that the 'bitch' was 'called' Puddle. Contemporary spelling of 'poodle' was sometimes written as 'puddle', but unless the author got it completely wrong, this is the name and not the breed. Morrah speculated that Puddle might have been the mother of Boye, a hunting poodle who was with Rupert in England during the civil war.

Though Rupert filled his days, he was by no means a content captive, and from the moment he arrived, escape was contemplated. A Scotsman was at the forefront of such plans throughout most of 1639, but it seemed as though fate would take a more direct hand. Swedish forces had been drawing ever closer to Linz, causing 'alarme' in Vienna.[13] But when Imperial troops defeated the Swedes on the frontiers of Bohemia in October 1639, it ended hopes of Rupert's liberation.

The victorious commander was Archduke Leopold, brother of Emperor Ferdinand, and instead of immediately returning to Vienna, he paid a visit to Rupert. Leopold, nicknamed the 'Angel', was a sweet-tempered and pious man, five years older than the prince. The pair quickly struck up a good friendship. When Leopold returned to Vienna, he put Rupert's case to the emperor and pushed for extended liberties. Once again, Maximilian of Bavaria tried to exert control and opposed the move, sending his young second wife (the emperor's sister) to plead his case. Leopold, however, enjoyed Empress Maria-Anna's full support and together they carried the day. Maria-Anna, a sister of the King of Spain, had at one time been spectacularly courted by Rupert's uncle, King Charles I, who had gone to Madrid incognito in a failed bid to secure her hand. That had been in 1623, but perhaps it had some bearing, or maybe she just sympathised with the famed prisoner at Linz. Additionally, diplomatic pressure from both King Charles and France for Rupert's release was regular.

The results of 'soe powerfull a mediation weere quickly seene' and Rupert was allowed to leave the castle for up to three days at a time.[14] He gave his word not to escape, and this ended his plotting. Outdoor pursuits that the prince loved, such as hunting, tennis, and horse riding, were indulged. As soon as the gentry and common people encountered Rupert, his charisma rubbed off on them, and it was said that they treated him with such respect, 'as if they were his subjects'.[15] Such stories showed just how much Maximilian, the usurper of the Upper Palatinate, had to fear. Rupert even made frequent excursions to Upper Bavaria, being the guest of a Count Kevenhuller, whose home was a 'pleasant' place.[16]

Such an improvement in fortunes was not without expectations. The emperor's ambition was to secure Rupert's conversion and then employ him as a commander. A proposal that two Jesuit priests attend him was rejected by Rupert unless he could also have the benefit of two Protestant ones. Count Kuffstein attempted in vain to influence the prince, being himself a convert from Lutheranism. After around two years of imprisonment, the emperor proposed to free Rupert if he agreed to become a Roman Catholic. 'They thought a young prince [which] shewed noe passion but for warr would willingly redeeme himselfe at soe easy a rate and readily sacrifise all ye reaisons of religion to those of fortune.'[17]

Rupert refused to sacrifice his religion and leave captivity via the 'gates of Apostacy'. Still the emperor persevered. If Rupert would not convert, then he should ask to be pardoned for having supported Charles Louis's rebellion. The prince's answer was no less blunt; he would not seek forgiveness for doing his duty. To do so would be to 'make himself [a] criminall'. By his answer, Rupert let them know 'hee was as little disposed to betray [the] cause of his family as hee had bene [the] cause of God'.

With his patience running thin, the emperor's next suggestion was that Rupert accept a military post in the Imperial army. This received another refusal. It would lead to him fighting against 'antient allies & friends of his Country' who had championed his father's cause – the very suggestion was offensive.[18] With Maximilian of Bavaria whispering in his ear, the emperor withdrew Rupert's privileges, and the prince was kept under close guard by a file of twelve musketeers.

Matters in the outside world offered no encouragement. In October 1639, Charles Louis had been seized and imprisoned by the French. The other brothers, Maurice, Edward (and perhaps Philip) were studying in France. The situation must have left their anguished mother in a state of despair. The reason behind the incarceration was an attempt on Charles Louis's part to take over the army of the late Duke of Saxe-Weimar, the commanders of which were ready to accept him. France, however, objected to the move. Travelling incognito to Alsace, Charles Louis was arrested in Paris and confined to the highest apartment of a tower at Bois de Vincennes.

By the middle of 1640, Charles Louis had been released on condition he stay with the English ambassador in Paris, while Edward and Philip were also required to remain in France. Maurice had returned to his mother, serving a short stint in the Swedish army. The summer of 1641 saw events move rapidly and Rupert's release was openly discussed with the emperor's envoys. In May, King Charles made it known that he wished for Rupert to serve in the Venetian army upon his release, but the Doge's ambassador felt bold enough to insist that first Charles Louis should correct a slight that he had given him. King Charles met the ambassador and gave much polite reassurance, whereupon he resumed his advocacy of Rupert with a veiled warning that only a favourable outcome would prove Venice's friendship.

As a young boy, King Charles himself had entertained ambitions of fighting for Venice, and this had been heartily encouraged by them. Times had changed. The Venetian ambassador was sent clear instructions to 'dexterously' remain noncommittal and let the matter of Rupert drop amidst 'profuse assurances of affection and esteem'.[19]

In August 1641, King Charles entrusted Sir Thomas Roe with responsibility for negotiating Rupert's release, leaving it all to his 'wisdom' to manage accordingly.[20] The 60-year-old envoy had worked as far afield as the Mughal court in India, as well as Turkey and Poland. He was infinitely bound to Elizabeth and her family and held their implicit confidence. Rupert was in a 'great deale of hopes' over the matter of his liberty.[21] He, too, was willing to empower Roe and on 17 August 1641 wrote to assure the veteran diplomat that he trusted him as a friend, leaving all conditions to his judgement. During the Imperial Diet (a forum for political negotiation and policy making) held at Ratisbone, Roe accordingly mediated on Rupert's behalf. The prince, scenting freedom, despatched further letters of encouragement. King Charles wrote kindly to the emperor calling for his nephew's release as the start of a more durable, public peace in Germany. Proposals were laid out to restore Charles Louis to the Lower Palatinate, though the upper was retained by Maximilian for the remainder of his life.

Such care was taken to ensure that Roe's work at Ratisbone was not undermined. A parliamentary declaration referencing Rupert's mother as 'Queen of Bohemia' was amended and that title 'scraped' out, much to her anger.[22] Rupert's eldest sister, Elisabeth, closely followed events, but was not hopeful. She felt the Diet was but a 'comedy' with delegates acting as great men, whereas they were merely servants of the emperor.[23] Roe himself amusingly compared Ratisbone to rat's poison, which at the time was termed 'ratsbane'. Rupert, she thought, would continue to be held hostage in order to safeguard Imperial interest.

The Palatines were so used to disappointment that they feared becoming too hopeful. By October 1641, Roe's efforts seemed close to achieving the impossible. In high spirits, Elizabeth's daughters acted out a play at her home in Rhenen – Louise, playing the part of a man, was said to greatly resemble Rupert.

Frank Kitson wrote that Rupert's incarceration had 'accentuated a natural bloody-mindedness' that was never far below the surface.[24] But as Roe nudged matters towards a positive conclusion, the prisoner prince was eager to please and displayed uncharacteristic meekness. He wrote to Roe on 19 September 1641 to thank the diplomat for reminding him of his faults, which he would endeavour to amend, but ventured that the matter of concern had been exaggerated. It seems that Rupert may have offended someone.

In another letter, the prince offered Roe all that was in his power to give at that moment, which was his sincerest thanks. When Ferdinand proposed to release Rupert if he promised never to bear arms against him, the prince baulked. He despatched a letter to King Charles I for advice and on being told to accept, duly did so. Next, the emperor wanted this agreement documented, signed, and sealed. To Rupert, this suggested a slight upon his honour, so he warned that if the matter was put to such formalities, the wording must be well considered. The request was dropped, and it was agreed that Rupert's kissing of the emperor's hand would be enough to seal the deal.

The orchestrated moment arrived, ironically, while Rupert was out hunting near Linz. As the Holy Roman Emperor approached, Rupert, on foot, had just killed a boar with a spear and was receiving adulatory congratulations from the assembled crowd. Ferdinand rode close, extended his hand, and Rupert paid his homage.

Upon the breaking news, Sir Thomas Roe was feted from every angle. Rupert's mother acknowledged the 'double obligation' she had to the ambassador, who had not only 'wrestled' to overcome all difficulties, but had secured such honourable terms.[25] Indeed, she recognised the emperor's magnanimity, and was even prepared to compliment him for it. A more practical gift of thanks was in store for Roe, when Rupert's artistic sister, Louise, agreed to provide 'recompence' for the ambassador's achievements that was within her power; a painting of his adoptive daughter, Rupa.[26]

Charles Louis, in Scotland with his uncle, praised Roe's care and industry over the 'master-piece' of diplomacy, praying that it augured well for continuing negotiations over the restoration of the Palatinate.[27] English politician, Richard Cave, was certain that Rupert's freedom would 'redound' to Roe's present and future honour.[28] Many shared the hope that after twenty-three years, the war in Europe – which had started when Rupert's father had accepted the crown of Bohemia – might draw to an end after his son's release.

When Rupert left Linz, the final step in the road to freedom was Vienna, where he travelled to take formal leave of the emperor. The prince was accompanied by

Roe, having promised to follow the man's 'consel [counsel] in alle'.[29] Within letters to Roe, there is a certain rawness to Rupert's English writing, likely reflective of the fact that the language had not been his prime method of communication these past few years. In England, £3,000 was earmarked for Roe and Rupert's expenses and King Charles wrote of his desire for a speedy conclusion.

In Vienna, the Venetian resident met Rupert (accompanied by Roe at all times) and remarked on his courtesy. When inevitably asked about the Palatinate, the prince tactfully replied that the matter was left in God's hands – or more precisely, Roe's, who was more direct. Roe replied that for 'good or ill' the finishing strokes would be put to negotiations to have back that which belonged to them.[30] Rupert's mother, however, felt sure that by defying Maximilian of Bavaria and freeing her son, the emperor would not 'dare' intercede over the Palatinate.[31]

Having the chance to become more acquainted with Rupert, the emperor tried one last attempt to persuade him to enter Imperial service. Though the prince again refused, he left a very positive impression on everyone at court, and was shown the 'honnours [that] weere due to his birth & merrit'. 'The ladies alsoe vied [with] their civillities and labour'd to detaine him ... by their charmes when ye Emperours caresses failed But ye Prince wanted not prudence to break through such soft obstruccons.'[32]

Finally, after a few weeks spent at tennis or hunting, Rupert made ready to depart with four followers, leaving Roe to continue his work. His mind had long been made up to go straight to his uncle and give thanks for the efforts made to bring this moment about. But first, not forgetting his manners, he paid a brief visit to Archduke Leopold to express his specific gratitude to the 'Angel'.

Heeding the emperor's parting warning, to avoid the lands of Maximilian of Bavaria, Rupert took his post horses and journeyed via Prague, the city of his birth. At Dresden, he refused to indulge in alcohol-fuelled celebrations, choosing instead a spell of hunting, before getting on his way. Apart from a burning desire to go to his uncle, the competitive prince was adamant he would reach his mother before despatches announcing his departure from Vienna, and thus surprise them all. Like a greyhound released from its trap, Rupert made it to Holland on 10 December 1641, with the letters arriving hot on his heels that same day.

Chapter 11

Hart & Mind

Rupert's mother had genuinely fretted for him. The journey would be an 'ill' one, she had feared, due to the 'extreme cold and a great snow'.[1] When he turned up in The Hague she was just sitting down to supper. Elizabeth was shocked and overjoyed, considering her son 'leaner and growen' but not otherwise altered, while everyone from the highest to the lowest made great show of his return.[2] Rupert relayed how the emperor had treated him with 'soe much honour & kindnesse' and the question naturally arose about what to do with the prince now.[3] If he stayed in Holland, Elizabeth pondered, then he would live idly, but in England, his aunt might finally 'gain' him and notch up another conversion.[4] The prince's great respect for King Charles would make him extra vulnerable. For Rupert 'nothing was able to wthhould him' from hasting to his uncle for his 'hart & mind' was there, and barely three days after arriving in Holland, he was attempting to secure passage.[5]

The prince's sister, Elisabeth, thanked Sir Thomas Roe for his exertions, admitting she was ashamed at offering 'bare words' in exchange for his deeds.[6] Her mother was also acutely aware of the need to reward Roe and urged King Charles to make him Lord Treasurer of England. Unfortunately, the king was fast becoming a fugitive in his own capital, with Parliament attempting to take control of all appointments to government positions.

Charles Louis had been by his uncle's side for months, hoping that he might wheedle out more men or money for his cause. He had arrived in London without securing advanced permission, and what's more, did so to protest at the marriage of his cousin – King Charles's 9-year-old daughter, Mary – to the 14-year-old Prince William of Orange. Rather embarrassingly, Charles Louis attempted to intercede for the girl's hand, even at this eleventh hour. To add insult to injury, turning up at a time of serious civil unrest in London, when the king's opponents might look to him as an alternative monarch, fostered much gossip. Yet King Charles remained polite and courteous and made his nephew welcome.

While Rupert and Roe had been in Vienna, a bloody rebellion had broken out in Ireland on 23 October 1641. Recognising that this would 'hinder' her brother's support, Elizabeth of Bohemia 'verielie' (verily) believed that the rebellion was orchestrated by either the emperor or the King of Spain.[7] Despite the former's generosity over Rupert's release, she had in mind an Italian proverb, 'those who are kinder than usual either have betrayed or will betray us'.[8]

The situation in Ireland came on the back of King Charles's failed attempts to impose a new Prayer Book on Scotland. Two subsequent wars with the Scots over the matter – in 1639 and 1640 – had exhausted his treasury and earned him much enmity. In England, during 1641, he had been forced to grant a raft of concessions to his enemies in Parliament that significantly weakened the royal prerogative. There would be no taxation unless sanctioned by MPs, Parliament would be summoned every three years, the Star Chamber (a court used to uphold crown government) was abolished, and most spectacularly of all, he had been forced to sanction the execution of his most loyal and able minister.

Thomas Wentworth, created Earl of Strafford, had almost brought the Stuart dream of politically and religiously unifying the three kingdoms to a reality. As such, Parliament knew it had to remove this able and gifted politician to achieve its own counter-reforms. When a Treason trial invariably collapsed, MPs introduced a Bill of Attainder, meaning Strafford would be executed if the Bill was approved by the Houses of Commons and Lords, and then the king. It was judicial murder. With London in uproar and menacing crowds ready to pull anyone apart who dared support Strafford, both Houses sanctioned it and Charles signed with tears in his eyes. He did so for his wife and children's safety, a mob standing ready to storm the palace, but also from genuine hope that this might assuage his enemies. Parliament's leaders smelled blood. There was no let-up in ever more revolutionary demands and Charles made fatal errors of judgement that mismanaged the critical situation. The increasing power of such hard-line Puritans was of particular concern to Irish Catholics and fear they might be targeted was one of the reasons that sparked their rebellion.

Christmas 1641 was a subdued affair in Whitehall Palace. The king received support from a group of moderates who felt his concessions offered a workable balance between Crown and Parliament. Troops were needed to restore order in Ireland, and this caused a rupture over the fact that the king would lawfully control such a force. Secretary of State, Edward Nicholas, hoped for a 'hearty and perfect union' between the king and his MPs, otherwise they would all be confounded. The Venetian ambassador was sceptical that a solution could be found 'without bloodshed'.[9] Pinning hopes on the support of moderates, Charles ordered over 200 MPs to return to Parliament in the New Year.

It was into this constitutional flashpoint that Rupert was headed. On 29 December 1641, the Lord High Admiral ordered a pinnace to transport the prince, but Mother Nature took a hand and storms dashed his hopes. In England, a political tempest broke.

Three days into January 1642, Sir Edward Herbert, the king's Attorney General, addressed peers in the House of Lords. Acting on royal orders, he accused six men of 'divers great and treasonable Designs and Practice'. A mutter of discontent spread as Lord Mandeville, the long-faced heir of the Earl of Manchester, was named.

A sergeant-at-arms made his way to the House of Commons to arrest five MPs: John Pym, Sir Arthur Haselrig, John Hampden, William Strode, and Denzil Holles. As the men's trunks were sealed, the house rang to cries of 'breach of privilege'. At the palace, the king was dismayed to hear that those accused had resisted arrest.

Things rapidly went from bad to worse. Reports that six pieces of ordnance had been brought into the city, and that people of mean quality had begun to hoard arms and ammunition, led the king to order searches of houses. The loyal Lord Mayor doubled the watch, had chains seal off the streets, and firefighting equipment was prepared. The palace was 'thronged' with supportive gentlemen and army officers. In the afternoon, Charles appeared in their midst and declared, 'My most loyal subjects and soldiers, follow me.' Entering a coach, a military escort followed him into the street where passage was hindered by vast crowds. A stray officer also slipped out of the palace, reaching Westminster ahead of the king to tip off the six targets. The Countess of Carlisle, one of the queen's ladies, had also sent warning.

When the king's cavalcade finally arrived, he had his soldiers wait in Westminster Hall and then entered the House of Commons, accompanied only by Charles Louis. The monarch respectfully removed his hat. The seats of the five MPs were still warm. He asked the Speaker's leave to borrow his chair, glanced around the hundreds of faces, and apologised for entering the chamber. It was clear to the king that his 'Birds are flown' but all the same, he asked the Speaker of their whereabouts.[10] William Lenthall was a quiet man who had tried to give up the job one month earlier, claiming that it 'exhausted the labours'.[11] He now fell to his knees. 'I Have neither Eyes to see, nor Tongue to speak in this Place, but as the House is pleased to direct me, whose Servant I am here.'[12]

After leaving the chamber empty-handed, the monarch's opponents successfully portrayed his actions as the behaviour of a tyrant. Next day, the king set off in his coach again, this time to the Guildhall. Symbolic of the worsening situation, an ironmonger managed to throw a paper through the window of the carriage, bearing the words 'to your Tents, O'Israel', biblically referencing Israel's rebellion against its king. Before the Common Council, the beleaguered monarch declared his missing traitors were 'Shrowded' within London. He also addressed malicious rumours that he was a Catholic sympathiser or convert – despite having long persecuted them – by assuring that he would prosecute all who opposed laws and statutes, whether 'Papists or Separatists'. With his life, he would maintain and defend that 'true Protestant Religion which [his] Father did profess'.[13]

After concluding, he began private discourse with some aldermen, but was interrupted by repeated cries for 'Privileges of Parliament'. Silence was called for and Charles asked if anyone wanted to speak. One man peremptorily told him to take his Parliament's advice. The king countered that he already did, and would continue to do so, though there was a distinction between that body and a few traitors within it. As voices of discontent started up again, Charles calmly asserted that 'no privileges' could protect a traitor from legal trial. It's remarkable that the king was willing to engage with protestors and no arrests were recorded.

Parliament's leaders blamed the attempted arrests on his wife, an easy target, who they alleged was conspiring against the 'public liberty'. The image of a Catholic she-wolf in the royal bed was designed to discredit the monarch and provoke fear. For the king, it stoked concern that the queen would be targeted. On 8 January, he sent orders that his ship, *Bonaventure*, should upon the 'first opportunity of winde' head for Portsmouth and await further orders.[14] The intention was that the vessel might spirit his endangered queen out of the kingdom. On the evening of 10 January 1642, with violence threatening to erupt, Charles took his wife and three eldest children and left the capital. The youngest two were left with their household, as the king expected to return as soon as he had seen off his wife.

Hampton Court had not been prepared for the royal family's arrival, and they all huddled together in one bed for warmth, before moving on to Windsor. As dawn broke over London, the six Parliamentarians came out of hiding and processed to Westminster, feted by jubilant crowds.

During this gravest crisis so far, Charles found solace in his family. Rupert's friend, Endymion Porter, a Groom of the Bedchamber, observed the royals and remarked, 'I envy their happiness.'[15] The king did not know what to do for the best, but surprisingly, was not shaken by events. He fully expected tempers to calm in a short time. Dismissing offers of mediation from the ambassadors of France and Holland, he also turned a deaf ear to Charles Louis. Whereas his nephew urged a reconciliation with Parliament (which would suit Palatinate politics), Henrietta Maria 'would not heere of it' for fear of dishonourable conditions. Back in The Hague, Elizabeth of Bohemia rued that her sister-in-law 'doth gouerne [govern] of all the kings affayres'.[16]

The king thought it advisable for his wife to leave the country for her own safety, therefore reason was given that she had to escort Princess Mary to Holland. The family travelled by way of Greenwich and Canterbury to Dover. Parting from the queen, who Charles loved 'beyond expression', as well as his eldest daughter, was a cause of suffering to him.[17] But this sad moment would also see a reunion.

Chapter 12

Flags and Formalities

With a break in the weather, Prince Rupert had boarded the *Expedition*, and a fair wind carried him to Dover. There, on 17 February 1642, he finally thanked his uncle for aiding his release from captivity, though there was more to the meeting than such polite formalities. The king knew the plots against him were deep-rooted and 'ye abettors mighty & numerable' therefore Rupert, as might be expected, offered some advice. 'His Councill therfore to ye King was, to put him selfe wth all ye Speed hee could into a Posture off defence [then] when ye sword was in his hand, ye rebells would better understand his reasons & hee might use it as little as hee pleased.'[1]

Matters had not yet degenerated to such a point. Even if they had, his uncle was unable to put himself into any posture of defence, nor did he wish to; appeasement was once more his preference. Free pardons had been granted to the six men he had tried to arrest, conceding that he was 'wholly to desert any further Prosecution'.[2] At such a sensitive juncture, the continued presence of a military figure such as Rupert was inadvisable. There was even a rumble of discontent about it within the royal entourage. The Marquess of Hamilton felt the need to sound out the prince's intentions and ambitions, and though Rupert explained he was to leave very soon, the meeting ended with a dispute between the pair. It was enough of an issue to reach the king's ears. This new snippet of detail shows what a divisive figure Rupert could be, even with those who shared his loyalty to the king, and especially at such an early stage in his uncle's troubles.

It was decided that Rupert should leave with Henrietta Maria and Princess Mary. Beneath the shadow of Dover Castle, King Charles did not know how to 'tear himself away' from his wife. After tears, 'sweet discourse' and affectionate embraces, he watched her ship until it vanished over the horizon.[3] The queen took a train of 380 men, four priests and four ladies, one of whom was Mary Villiers, Duchess of Richmond and Lennox. When Rupert had visited his uncle's court in 1636–37, Mary was aged about 15, but now, five years later, she was married to the king's cousin. Cooped up aboard ship, the seasick Rupert who did 'very ill brook ye sea' was likely in no mood for exchanging pleasantries. There would be ample opportunity over the next five months as he helped his aunt raise men, money, and munitions – termed 'considerable Succours'.[4]

On the surface at least, Rupert's aunt and mother got on exceedingly well when they met one another in Holland. But, on King Charles's dire situation, they were entirely divided. Henrietta Maria believed Scotland would assist the king against the English Parliament, but Elizabeth was not so sure. The former believed that force was necessary to restore order, whereas the latter did not wish to see her homeland riven apart, not least because it provided financial subsistence. Henrietta Maria expected she would only be in Holland for a few weeks or months at most, but her stay would last over a year. Rupert, having fully intended to return to England with her, was in no mood to wait so long.

Unlike Rupert, Charles Louis never lost sight of the family's priority – restoration to the Palatinate. The first half of 1642 offered numerous avenues to advance his siblings' military experience and bolster alliances that might assist. The elector's first preference for Rupert and Maurice was Swedish service but he admitted the chances looked slim. Yet again, Venice politely turned Rupert down. There was still the option of joining the emperor and battling the Turks, though Ferdinand III felt somewhat let down that his former prisoner had not kept up correspondence with him. The monotony of letter writing would never be one of Rupert's strong points.

The last option of a bad bunch was the 'Irish warres', but Charles Louis knew that his uncle's opponents would not brook Rupert in a military role and would instead prefer their own men. Nevertheless, he assured his mother, he would 'speak with some of them' about it. King Charles himself was 'enough inclined' to Rupert taking up a post in Ireland, going so far as to suggest General of the Horse, and pressing Charles Louis to intercede for it with leading Parliamentarians.[5] In April 1642, the king even entertained the idea of joining Rupert in such a venture.

Declaring himself 'grieved at the very Soul' for his good Irish subjects, the king let it be known that he intended to raise a personal guard of 2,000 to accompany him there and offered to sell or pawn any of his parks, lands, or houses to do so. Playing to patriotic hearts, he asserted that to 'adventure his life to preserve his Kingdom' was necessary and worthy. Parliament warned that any who accompanied the king would be deemed enemies of the state, fearing the monarch's true aim was to 'win the affection' of Irish rebels and enlist their support.[6] But at Westminster, only one-third of MPs and a quarter of peers were attending sessions and the assembly no longer had any claim to be representative of the nation.

In March 1642, Parliament pushed to have control of England's militia. 'By God, not for an hour,' the monarch had declared, insisting that they had asked of him that which 'was never asked of a King'. This transformed the crisis into a full-blown revolution. Parliament justified their unprecedented power grab by citing apprehension for their safety. 'Lay your hands on your hearts,' the king retorted, and asked them to consider whether he now had cause to fear for his own. The dreaded breach came when Parliament published a Militia Ordinance on 5 March, taking control of the armed forces on their own authority. Officials up and down the country were forced to decide whether king or Parliament held the greater authority.

Now facing an abyss, the monarch was 'much disconsolate and troubled' especially so by his wife's continued absence. Prince Charles said so in 'sad Lines' to his sister Mary, including his own desire for peace. 'Dear sister, we are, as much as we may, merry; and, more than we would, sad, in respect we cannot alter the present distempers of these turbulent times.'[7]

Heartened by the arrival of the 9-year-old Duke of York, brought safely to York despite Parliament's attempts to intervene, the king called for a Chapter of the Order of the Garter. He hoped to counter his opponents by prevailing upon men's honour. It was a noble thought, but many were driven more by their own religious and ideological desires, or simply personal ambition. Nevertheless, he made Prince Rupert a knight in absentia – an award that must have appealed greatly to the prince, and which strengthened the bonds between uncle and nephew. From Holland, Queen Elizabeth kept a close eye and, removing rose-tinted spectacles, commented dryly that 'all goeth ill enough' at York.[8] Like Charles Louis, she was wary of being entangled with the stricken monarch and foundering with him.

On 22 April 1642, the king sent the reticent Elector Palatine and 9-year-old Duke of York to Hull to 'sound the intentions' of the Parliamentarian Governor, Sir John Hotham. When the royal party was admitted and treated with respect, the king's hopes were kindled. On St George's Day, Sir John's loyalty was put to the ultimate test in an epic showdown. Accompanied by 150 men of his household, the monarch gave a few hours' notice of his own arrival, but found the drawbridges raised and gates closed. Following demands for admittance, Hotham appeared on the walls and called out his apologies. Declaring himself a faithful subject, he nevertheless refused to compromise his orders from Parliament. The rasps of a royal trumpeter pronounced Hotham a traitor, but still nobody moved, and though in a 'great wrath', the checkmated king withdrew with his dignity in tatters.[9] Inside the town, the Duke of York and his entourage were sent to their lodgings and calls for their release momentarily fell upon deaf ears.

Hotham had been forced to decide between king or Parliament, and the incident prompted Charles Louis to make up his mind, too. Six weeks earlier, he had admitted to his mother, 'I protest to God, I would not staye a minute in this Kingdome' if affairs could be better served elsewhere. As the king's position became ever weaker, so Charles Louis grew ever more fickle and then absconded. Leaving England, he claimed to have been 'inticed' to go to Hull and was 'totally ignorant of what was else intended'.[10] His mother also distanced herself, agreeing that her son had been 'surelie catched in'.[11] Though she didn't approve of his leaving England, she accepted he was 'of age to governe himself' and resolved not to meddle.[12] Continuing to believe that the king did nothing without his wife's approbation, Elizabeth felt Henrietta Maria was showing herself to be 'agaynst anie agreement with the Parliament but by warre'.[13] As Charles Louis shrunk away, Rupert took his cue, assured by his aunt that the post of General of the Horse was earmarked for him.

Chapter 13

Brimful of Zeal

When Rupert and Maurice first attempted to get to their uncle's side, they did so via the Royal Navy's *Lion*. Not long after the princes boarded, a footman arrived with a letter for the captain. It didn't take Rupert long to ascertain that something wasn't right, and soon enough he wheedled the truth out of the messenger. The prince's mother had sent instructions to stay their journey, but an army of footmen could not stop Rupert. The captain was persuaded to set sail regardless.

The *Lion* left Hellevoetsluis in the first week of July 1642 but after a couple of hours ran into storms. For three days and nights the ship was battered. Considering Rupert was prone to seasickness, reports that the brothers were left in a weakened state can't be underappreciated. Debate about it even reached the House of Lords, where it was said the elder had 'cast much Blood'.[1] Captain Fox took the sensible course of action and turned the *Lion* about, putting his passengers off and promising to pick them up later. Caught between a rock and a hard place – the opposing wishes of the Queen of Bohemia and her son – Fox took the opportunity to escape both. He sailed for home. The Royal Navy had by this time come under the control of Parliament, therefore the *Lion* was seized, and the captain questioned about his recent activity. Rumours abounded that Rupert's landing in England was 'dayly expected'.[2]

As weeks passed, Rupert struggled to contain his impatience. Being so helpless must have inflamed similar frustrations to those he had felt during his imprisonment at Linz. With his mother unwilling to bless his departure, publicly at least, Rupert went to the Prince of Orange to get what he wanted: a new vessel. Frederick Henry duly provided a forty-six-gun ship, together with a smaller one 'laden wth Armes', and the two princes boarded as soon as could be. For Rupert, the zeal he had to serve his uncle made him so gung-ho that 'dilligence it selfe was [deemed] lazy' – caution was thrown to the wind.[3] Joining him were Bernard de Gomme, a military engineer; Bartholomew de la Roche, an explosives expert; along with, Daniel O'Neale and faithful Richard Crane. Not forgetting the prince's pets: Boye, his white hunting poodle, and a monkey.

Meanwhile, the Parliamentarian fleet was lying in wait. King Charles had done his best, 'taking precautions for securing Newcastle', but with his own navy turned against him, he could do precious little.[4] When Rupert's ships neared the Yorkshire coast, they were unsure where to land and the Parliamentarian *London* intercepted them off Flamborough Head. Exhilarated, Rupert stood on deck wearing a mariner's cap alongside the captain. When the *London* enquired of their purpose, the reply that they were cruising, and that the smaller ship was a Dunkirk prize, was met with scepticism. The Parliamentarians intended to search Rupert's vessels, but the prince had the guns run out in response. The *London* fired a salvo, signalling for assistance.

The prince's ships raced north, and off the coast of Northumberland, they encountered more enemy warships. Another wrangle ensued, which supposedly necessitated landing munitions on Holy Island (once a religious haven off the coast) but Rupert and his followers managed to escape. Finding the way to Tynemouth clear, the princes were rowed into the harbour beneath the looming castle and priory that dominated the headland.

News of Rupert's presence off the coast spread like wildfire. Word was that one of his vessels had been sunk, leaving historian Simonds D'Ewes to write 'what is become of [the prince] is not yet known certainly'.[5] While waiting 'impatiently' for authenticated updates, the Venetian ambassador feared the princes had drowned.[6] Upon being advised that the king was at Nottingham, 'ye moment [the prince] landed hee tooke post' and rode south. As confirmation of the prince's survival spread, they were credited with cheating death. Such was Rupert's talisman-like effect that his uncle was said to be 'more encouraged by his presence' than by the array of arms and munitions in tow.[7] MPs, however, heard the news with dismay and were 'incensed'.[8]

At some point on the frenetic journey to Nottingham, Rupert's horse slipped and 'pitching him upon his shoulder put it out of joint'.[9] After a brief stop to set the bone, the prince was back on his way. He rode through the gates of Nottingham that night, dismayed to find that the king had left, and so took some much-needed rest. At Coventry – whose 3 miles of walls were as imposing as London's – the king faced the nightmare of a second insult when it mimicked Hull and closed its gates on him. Worse still, on this occasion the garrison took pot-shots at his party and killed some of his servants.

Determined to get into Coventry one way or the other, orders were sent to Nottingham for two petards – explosives adept at blowing holes through gates. In the arsenal, the bewildered George Digby had no idea what they were and woke Rupert for assistance. Together with Captain William Legge, an Irishman, the trio were unable to find a petard, but Legge used two great mortars and mocked one up. Legge would go on to form a lifelong bond of friendship with Rupert, while Digby became his mortal enemy.

Digby, son of the Earl of Bristol and a friend of Henrietta Maria's, had a chequered past. He had urged the king to arrest the six Parliamentarian leaders back in January 1642, and after the failure, had fled to Holland. When attempting to return some months later, he was captured and taken to Hull, whereupon the hapless soul tried to pretend that he was a Frenchman. After revealing his identity to the governor, Digby became convinced that the man would defect and turn over the town and its huge magazine. Therefore, he had persuaded the king to march troops to the town and go through the motions of a siege in July 1642, which would sate the governor's honour and provoke his surrender. It was the first of many schemes to backfire. The golden-haired and blue-eyed courtier also had a silver tongue, which managed to cultivate the king's confidence regardless of these mishaps.

The affair of the petard has been described as Rupert's first negative impression of Digby, but it was much more. On the eve of war, it sparked a conflict between the pair that would go on to erode the Royalist cause from within. A letter Digby wrote to Rupert at Nottingham is only briefly mentioned by Kitson, but it evidences the seriousness of the situation and warrants fuller examination. 'I am tolde by [Mr O'Neale] that your highnesse hath not soe right an understandinge of mee, as my affection to yr person and service made mee hope.'

Ulster-born Daniel O'Neale had been employed as an agent for Elizabeth of Bohemia, and she thought him a faithful and worthy man. With this closeness to the Palatines, he had come to England with Rupert and is the go-between mentioned. In this frank letter, Digby references whispers that the prince had taken ill an 'expression of mine Concerninge you' but protests with 'Confidence and truth' that he had always honoured the prince. The issue related to a 'friendshipp of honour' between an anonymous party and Rupert ('soe gallant' a prince), and had prompted Digby's remark that little people should be kept at a greater distance. We can only speculate as to the circumstances, but it sounds like Digby was caught indulging in gossip over Rupert engaging with those of a lower social standing.

Closing the letter with an assertion that he would serve Rupert with 'affection and industrye' in all things, the courtly language cannot hide Digby's patronising manner.[10] It was a particular skill of his to wriggle out of trouble by masking private machinations with public protestations of loyalty. This must have infuriated the prince, who wore his opinions firmly on his martial sleeves. Coming so very early into Rupert's arrival, the episode suggests that tensions stemmed back to their time in Holland with Henrietta Maria.

On 21 August 1642, the day after the prince's arrival at Nottingham, he sought out the king, who was now at Leicester. Rupert was quick to take stock of the stark reality. 'Till now the King was not able to resolve on [a] violent remedy … how great Soever their provocacon [provocations] weere nor forget his Enemies & subjects weere ye same.' The prince found his uncle melancholic and surrounded by a sense of defeatism. That was a mood alien to Rupert. The Earl of Southampton insisted that peace envoys should be sent to Westminster. Sir Jacob Astley, once Rupert's tutor and now Sergeant-Major-General, warned if the enemy approached, the king had so few troops that he might easily be captured. The ignominy of his uncle having been shut out of Hull and Coventry rankled with Rupert and was a sign of how the king's 'gentelnesse served nothing' and that the more indulgent he was, 'the more insolent they weere'.[11] As Rupert's mother had written back in 1636, no monarch of England had ever 'got any good' by treaties, and most commonly had lost by them. Wars, she was certain, always made a 'good' peace.[12]

In Rupert's self-righteous young mind, he was the instrument of war – his uncle's sword – which would not be sheathed until the king was restored to his rightful glory. All the tragedies of Rupert's life were as if mere preparations for this crusade, and it gave him a clear purpose. Without doubt, his dominating presence changed everything. Anyone who clung to peace was left out in the cold, but those who advocated war gathered around their greatest ally. The biographical notes claim it was Rupert who urged his uncle to formalise the conflict as soon as possible. '[T]here weer two motives wch encouraged [the king] – first ye Justice of his cause ye second the presence of his Nephew, in whom was found all ye Quallities yt make men victorious & renown'd.'[13]

Nottingham Castle was rooted in England's history, having been built on top of a high rock just after the Battle of Hastings. The town was ideally located within the road system of the Midlands. On 22 August 1642, a giant pennant was unfurled that portrayed the royal coat of arms and embroidered onto its length was a hand pointing to a crown along with the words 'Give Caesar his Due'. King Charles called upon loyal subjects to defend him against Parliament's army of 15,000, led north by the Earl of Essex. Royalist recruitment had been far less successful given the king's propensity for concessions, and many avoided pledging support in case he backed down. With scarcely 1,000 troops, the monarch prayed this ancient ceremony would bring in recruits, but only a meagre 30 responded.

The standard was hoisted to the heavens two times; the first had been in a field nearby, where twenty men had used knives and daggers to dig a hole for it. Trumpets had rasped and drums rattled in the presence of the king and his two eldest sons, along with Rupert and Maurice. When it was blown down the same night, the flag was unfurled again at the top of the castle's tallest tower. It was a symbolic act that in most history books is given as the formal start of the English Civil War and often incorrectly termed as the king levying war on his people and/or Parliament. The act declared the army raised against the king to be rebels, engaged in unlawful armed rebellion.

King Charles was 'forc'd to declare warr, but in a tyme when his forces and provicons [provisions] weer soe unequall to those of his enemies'. The king knew as well as anyone else that it would be foolish to make matters formal before he was able to secure victory. Nor did he wish to do so, until he had left 'nothing undone wth God and man'.[14] Matters, as often was the case, moved too swiftly for him. In Portsmouth, the unreliable George Goring, son of the queen's friend, had turned coat and declared for the king – but he did so on 2 August, way earlier than anticipated. As a result, Parliamentarian forces were sent against the town, but the king was in no position to assist Goring. Portsmouth, he had hoped, could have been a means of receiving foreign aid or supplies the queen was gathering. Now it was doomed to fall.

The fact is that both sides had been mobilising and skirmishing long before they each cared to admit it, and certainly since MPs seized control of the militia that spring. Though Parliament had no standard it could hoist, its Members issued a remarkable (and extremely rarely referenced) declaration on 4 August 1642 – three weeks before the royal standard went up. The wording of this crucial public statement had been painstakingly debated in both Houses and signed off days earlier; MPs and peers announced that they were engaged in a 'necessity' to take up arms. Every key moment was listed to justify hostilities against a 'malignant' party that surrounded the monarch.[15] Just as the king summoned troops when he raised his banner three weeks later, Parliament's declaration called men to the Earl of Essex's colours. Sir Simonds D'Ewes considered it 'full of virulent expressions against the king'.[16] The Venetian ambassador was in no doubt that the English Parliament had just declared war on King Charles. On 9 August 1642, a second statement went even further and condoned the killing and slaying of Parliament's enemies. These offer a completely different slant on the start of the war. Esteemed historian, Conrad Russell, one of the few historians to make reference to the declarations, judged that they 'called for war.'[17]

When considering the facts in this fresh context, it's clear that King Charles was on the back foot when he raised his standard. During much of the lurch towards hostilities, he had been embarrassingly reactive, and this frustrated Rupert. The standard was an attempt to take back the initiative, and it was an absolutely essential reaction to the two provocative parliamentary declarations.

On 6 September 1642, Parliament announced that anyone who did not support it was a delinquent and their property liable to be sequestered (or seized). Ironically, this forced the issue of partisanship and recruits swelled Royalist ranks to 2,000 cavalry and 1,200 foot-soldiers. Apart from men, the Royalists also lacked money. On the very same day as Parliament's edict, Rupert took matters into his own hands and sent a threatening demand to the Mayor of Leicester. The official had ignored a summons to present himself before the prince, and anxious to marshal his uncle's subjects into line, Rupert demanded a loan of £2,000, which would be repaid in 'convenient time'. To ensure the mayor was under no illusions, Rupert warned that he would enforce the request with an army the following day, declaring that it was 'more safe to obey than to resist his Majesty's command'.[18] Unsurprisingly, the incident was condemned by the Parliamentarians. Royalist lawyer, Edward Hyde, also criticised it in his multi-volume work on the war, deeming it a 'full inexperience of the customs and manners of England'.[19] Even the king felt it was a step too far. Horrified, he wrote to the mayor assuring that he did 'abhor the thoughts of it' and claimed it had been done without his knowledge.[20]

Rupert's behaviour was used to tar him as a violent foreign interloper. Given numerous derogatory sobriquets in his lifetime, this was added to in 2023, just after his 400th birthday, when Dr Jonathan Healey labelled him a 'Thuggish toff' in *The Blazing World*.[21] In the prince's defence, he merely played bad cop to his uncle's good cop. Visits made to the estates of prominent

Parliamentarians, where Rupert extracted money for his uncle's war chest, were akin to Parliament's sequestration of Royalist assets. 'Brimful of zeal', the prince's energy knew no bounds, even on the Sabbath, when he rode up to Caldecote House, in Warwickshire.[22] The home of Parliamentarian Colonel Purefoy resisted Rupert, and shots were duly exchanged, killing two of the prince's officers. This led him to set the barns, stables, and outhouses alight. When Caldecote finally flung open its doors, Rupert was shocked to find the lady of the house emerge and fall to her knees. She had mounted the defence, assisted by her daughters, servants, and son-in-law. Impressed by their valour and resolution, Rupert offered the latter a commission (which was refused) and promised that not a penny worth of goods should be taken from the house.

The trained bands of Leicestershire were next on the receiving end of Rupert's wrath. Henry Hastings, the Sherriff, gave troops the option of serving the king or surrendering their arms. When it became clear they had no intention of doing either, Rupert and Maurice arrived and the former 'clap'd his pistol' to the head of the spokesman.[23] Unsurprisingly, the men laid down their weapons and, it's asserted, this example secured those of Nottinghamshire and Derbyshire.

In light of such leadership, 'ye most timorous weere ashamed to show feare under such a Generall'. Those Royalists who opposed Rupert went underground but did not disappear. For now, the military held dominance with the king, and the prince became the backbone of the war effort with his 'new miracles'. Commanders held him in such 'great esteeme' that his reputation was transformed to a whole new level.[24] In the Royalist camp he was feted publicly and disliked privately, while to the Parliamentarians, he became the ultimate bogeyman. These opposing opinions have cast long shadows and clouded judgement of the real man and his actions.

When news of Rupert's behaviour reached Westminster, his enemies responded with 'indignation' and spoke of drafting a proclamation to exile him. After rational thought from those 'less rabid' the measure was dropped, most likely because it would be impossible to enforce, but also in view of the prince's royal status.[25]

With the Earl of Essex and his large army closing in, the king took his small band to Shrewsbury, from where he hoped to draw recruits from Wales. En route, he was joined at Stafford by Rupert. While the royal party stood in a garden just 60 yards from St Mary's Church, the prince took a shot at the weathercock with a cavalry pistol and sent a bullet through the tail. King Charles quipped that it was a fluke. In answer, Rupert successfully put another hole in it, a feat that would be remembered forty years later. The prince was itching to take aim at the Parliamentarians and would soon get the chance to put his skills to better test.

Chapter 14

Prince Robber

The 'diabolical Cavaleere' was closely watched by Parliamentarian troops in the Midlands. From Northampton, on 13 September 1642, Nehemiah Wharton reported that soldiers were 'madde' (mad) to be at Rupert after hearing about the latter's threat to Leicester. They drilled at 6.00 am every day in preparation. In the meantime, Wharton's men occupied themselves by plundering and feasting upon venison belonging to 'malignants' – or Royalists.[1] Frustration was taken out upon altar rails, prayer books, and 'glased picturs' inside churches. The sermons of Puritan divines fanned the fires that burned in their bellies.[2] Upon an alarm that Rupert was plundering Market Harborough, they hastily mustered, only to hear that their enemy had flown away as fast as he had landed.

Rupert's hit-and-run tactics struck terror into the hearts of his opponents. Nobody knew just where he might show up. There was a chance, albeit slim, that a long-awaited battle might be enough to shock both sides to the treaty table, because sustaining troops could not be maintained indefinitely. In Abingdon, for example, Royalist Lewis Dyve petitioned on 21 September for the 'inlarging' of his quarters'.[3] The country was so heavily charged to maintain his troops, yet the proceeds fell short of requirements. On the day that Dyve wrote this entreaty, the king, in Shrewsbury, took up his pen and confirmed Rupert's 'desire' for a battle 'if hee sees fitt'.[4] Given the royal green light, the prince made ready to seek out and destroy the enemy. Dyve would accompany him.

Oxford University had long been doing its utmost to plug gaps in the king's army and finances. Scholars enlisted and university plate was donated. Despite Parliament declaring such donations illegal and imploring neighbouring counties to keep strict watch to hinder the passage of future convoys, Sir John Byron ran the gauntlet. After rounding up recruits, horses, and arms, as well as money and university plate, he left Oxford on 10 September 1642. Heading west to Worcester, Byron was chased by horsemen and dragoons from the Earl of Essex's nearby field army, but the city was not fortified enough to safeguard him. With royal blessing for a battle, Rupert hammered south to Worcester with as many as 2,000 cavalrymen to safeguard Byron's booty.

Nemiah Wharton, meanwhile, harboured hopes of confronting the elusive 'Prince Robber'. He and his comrades marched via Rugby and joined the main field army of the Earl of Essex at Dunsmore Heath on 20 September 1642. There, they heard that the prince was on his way, and Wharton hoped his path might finally cross with his foe.

He dressed in his best, purchasing a new soldier's 'suit' for winter that was edged with silver and gold lace, and wore a scarf that his mistress had sent him. Suitably apparelled, Wharton was resolved not to stain them unless it was in 'the blood of a Cavaleere'.[5]

Other soldiers were not so affluent and grumblings over lack of wages had to be addressed. Wharton recorded one novel method. While en route to Worcester they met a horseman who pelted along with news that both sides were 'in fight' near the city. The men were spurred on by it, crying, 'To Worcester, to Worcester,' and 'ran shouting for two miles' in foul weather.[6] Wharton called this fake news, spread to encourage a speedy march, but with both sides closing in no chances could be taken. A detachment of horse and dragoons under the command of Colonels Edwin Sandys and John Browne, sent to prevent Byron leaving Worcester, now crossed to the west bank of the River Severn and took up position near Powick Village on 22 September.

When Rupert reached Worcester, he was met by welcoming cheers, especially from the mayor who was eager to treat him to civic entertainment. Unused to dealing with a royal like Rupert, in circumstances such as these, the mayor was rebuffed in no uncertain terms. If the story is true, Rupert swore an oath and exclaimed, 'God damn him, he would not stay, but would go wash his hands in the blood of the Roundheads.'[7] The prince certainly didn't dally and almost immediately proposed to scout out the enemy. His second-in-command, Henry Wilmot, opposed the plan but Rupert 'prevailed'.[8]

The 23 September 1642 was a fine day. The prince and his force headed to Powick Bridge, just one mile southwest of Worcester. The countryside was described as pleasant, fruitful, and rich, abounding in corn, woods, pastures, hills, and valleys. The locals were also benevolent, assisting the prince's men with information and guides.

Wilmot was sent forward with a small party to check for signs of the enemy. When he returned asserting that there were none, he suggested they might leave. The account of Edward Hyde, later Earl of Clarendon, a Royalist lawyer who later penned a history of the conflict, has formed the basis for the hitherto accepted version of events. This has since been shown to be inaccurate. He described how the prince and his leading officers took a break in a 'green meadow', subsequently removing armour and weapons.[9] Beneath that field was another that led down to a lane, beyond which was Powick's stone bridge, barely 8 foot wide. The crackle of gunshot supposedly stirred the Royalists, whereupon a shocked Rupert, along with his senior officers, mounted up without donning armour. The prince was said to have charged to battle not looking to see if his men had followed.

In 2022, John Spiller published a research article that reassessed Powick Bridge using eyewitness testimonies. These differed from Clarendon's version, which Spiller stated had caused misinterpretations, omissions, and errors in the accepted narrative of the skirmish. Concluding that Powick Bridge was far from a chance encounter, Spiller puts forward convincing evidence that Rupert sent a false message to lure the Parliamentarians into a trap. Nor was he resting in a meadow – far from it. An account printed six weeks afterwards, most likely by Parliamentarian Captain Nathaniel Fiennes, as well as those of Puritan minister Richard Baxter, and Royalist officer Richard Bulstrode, paint a very different picture.

Powick Bridge - 23 Sept 1642

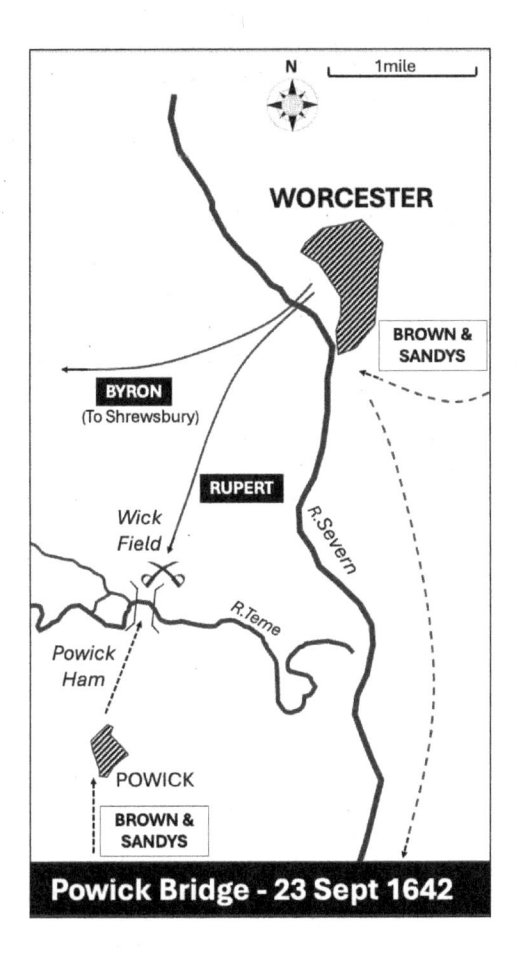

Rupert was aware of enemy horse and dragoons under Colonels Sandys and Browne at Powick. A letter written from Shrewsbury explained that the prince was made aware of the force on his arrival in Worcester, which would account for his shunning civic hospitality. Nemiah Wharton asserted that the common people assisted the prince with scouts and intelligence, while the Parliamentarians at Powick made no secret of their presence. Additionally, a turncoat gave away vital intelligence about the Parliamentarians.

Both sides were of almost equal strength, at around 1,000–1,500 men, with the Royalists possessing slightly more dragoons. East of Worcester, the Earl of Essex's main field army was planning an attack on the city. The aim of the Sandys-Browne detachment had been to cut off one possible escape route for Byron and his treasure. Numerous Parliamentarian accounts attest to a 'false message' that arrived at 4.00 pm on 23 September and was written as if from the Lieutenant General of Horse in Essex's army. This message – initiated by Rupert – was 'implying' that Sandys and Browne should cross Powick Bridge and head back towards the city.[10]

Nemiah Wharton, with Essex's field army, later recounted his understanding that the message told Sandys and Browne that the 'Cavalleeres were all fled'.[11] Far from taking his leisure in a meadow on the other side of the bridge, the prince had in fact stationed dragoons in an approach lane and drawn his force up in Wick Field. There he waited for the fake message to take effect.

Perhaps Rupert's men deliberately let off shots to back up their ruse and make it seem like Essex had engaged the Royalists. Spiller explains that musket fire, coupled with the message, led Colonel Sandys to believe that there was an attack in progress. Accordingly, despite cautions from three captains, who warned that they may be being drawn into a 'snare', Sandys had his units cross the bridge without sending scouts ahead of him. Nor did he wait for his fellow officer, Browne. This sealed the Parliamentarians' fates. The account of Richard Bulstrode, an officer in Rupert's force, bears out the premise that this was a trick by describing how the Parliamentarians crossed the bridge expecting to meet a vanguard of troops from their own main field army. Instead, they ran into the Royalists, who had 'stood very quietly for some time'.

The prince, as per his plan, allowed only a portion of Sandys's force to muster opposite him. It was essential that battle should commence before all the Parliamentarians were deployed, meaning that they would be outnumbered. Rupert was then in full control. The account of Captain Nathaniel Fiennes confirms that they found the Royalists formed up and that the prince's dragoons had been tactically placed to fire on them in an 'ambuscardo' – or ambush. Another describes the Royalists as being 'in battalia'. This 'well-planned trap', as Spiller calls it, saw Rupert choose the place to attack and the numbers of enemy to engage, and as a result, he was able to outnumber them two-to-one.[12]

Nemiah Wharton (though not present) later heard that the prince and Sandys had gone head-to-head. Rupert had supposedly demanded to know Sandys's allegiance, who replied, 'King and Parliament.' 'Not the king alone?' Rupert questioned before going on to cry, 'For the King have at you,' and discharging his pistol.[13] Whether the verbal exchange is factual or not, such close-quarter action between the two is plausible.

When battle commenced, the prince unleashed his unorthodox cavalry tactics. Rather than halt at a distance to discharge pistols, and only engaging the enemy when firepower had been spent, the prince and his troopers charged headlong into his opponents. If the clash didn't finish them, the discharging of his men's' pistols at close quarters would. The Parliamentarians were quickly pushed back towards the bridge, and despite Captain Nathaniel Fiennes putting up a stout resistance, they broke soon enough. To cap it all, the Royalists were served well by the wind, which blew the smoke of gunshot, dust, and dirt into the enemies' faces. Fighting is thought to have lasted just fifteen minutes. It resulted in the deaths of thirty to forty Parliamentarians and fifty to eighty captured. Nevertheless, it was an impactful clash.

In Royalist minds, Rupert could *achieve* anything, whereas to the Parliamentarians, he was *capable* of anything. Edward Hyde thought the skirmish proved of 'unspeakable advantage and benefit' to the king, and being the cavalry's first action, imbued them with confidence. Powick rendered the name of Prince Rupert 'very terrible' and 'exceedingly appalled' the enemy.[14] The Venetian ambassador reported home that those Parliamentarians who survived the encounter owed their lives to the 'suppleness' of their legs and 'swiftness' of their horses, and he saw their defeat as testimony of the Almighty's support for the king.[15] Outraged, Nemiah Wharton predicted that a pitched battle was now inevitable. Such an encounter would, he thought, prove hot work because his enraged colleagues would show no mercy.

Clarendon was not a particular admirer of Rupert, and whether deliberately or not, his work furthered an enduring image of a reckless, hot-headed Rupert being caught off guard. Spiller, however, concludes that Powick Bridge was a 'short but fierce culmination of a plan' that was both well-conceived and well-executed by the prince – who deserves 'far more credit for his actions than historians have hitherto given'. I very much agree that it challenges perceptions of Rupert; we see a more level-headed and calculating commander. But why would the prince's own account make no reference to his spectacular plan? Spiller is of the opinion that the fake message might have been branded 'ungentlemanly' and detracted from the glory. Of course, Rupert may have just wanted to keep his tactics secret.[16]

The Parliamentarians added their own confusing smokescreen, declaring that Powick had been a marvellous victory for them. But when their broken units returned to the Earl of Essex's army at Pershore the earl – whose own lifeguard had been trounced – must have wondered how effective they might be if his life was ever on the line. He insisted that his men be trained to use their arms readily and expertly with focus given to the necessary rudiments of war over ceremonial discipline. By comparison, the Royalists received few losses. Prince Maurice took a wound to the head, Wilmot (having redeemed himself) was slashed on the back, and Dyve shot in the shoulder. Rumours reached Nemiah Wharton that Rupert had been wounded, but once again the prince had emerged unscathed.

Chapter 15

White Hairs

Kentish iconoclast Colonel Edwin Sandys had desecrated the cathedrals of Canterbury and Rochester before moving on to Worcester's. Sandys might have survived the clash at Powick, but he had been mortally wounded in three places and captured. Henry Wilmot, Rupert's second-in-command, was credited with this. All the injured Parliamentarian prisoners were deposited at Worcester where Sandys then died, ironically laid to rest in the cathedral alongside the likes of Prince Arthur Tudor and King John. Rupert's enemies alleged that he and his men stripped, stabbed, and slashed the dead bodies of the Parliamentarians in a most 'barbarous manner' and imbrued their hands in the blood.[1] But, more truthfully, no less a person than Nemiah Wharton conceded that the prince had in fact passed order that the wounded should be carefully tended to. By midnight, the prince had successfully extracted Byron's booty, left Worcester, and was heading back to the king at Shrewsbury.

Richard Crane, commander of the prince's lifeguard, was sent ahead with news of the victory, reporting only three Royalist casualties. Rupert extolled Crane's gallantry with a call for his knighthood, which was readily granted. The king wrote back commending his nephew's 'courage and conduct' but equally urged him to take care of Worcester and preserve his horsemen for a full battle.[2]

From the north, praise for Powick was fulsome; the Earl of Newcastle, a wealthy peer, poet, and master equestrian, wrote in appropriately grandiose terms. Just as Rupert came to be frustrated by the mixed messages of Lord Digby's private and public opinions, Newcastle's gushing prose might have masked the fact that this proud peer was not willing to be anyone's subordinate. 'I as hartely Congratulate your saftie, as your victorie, for your person Sr is to bee valewed above a kingdoume.'[3]

The earl credited Rupert with not simply bringing good fortune to the king's cause, but by making that good fortune himself. Of 'taking the bull by the horns' we might say today. Attention such as Newcastle's must have flattered Rupert and reinforced self-confidence in his ability to win the war for his uncle. Three days after Powick, King Charles was recruiting levies with Rupert's support. The king took the opportunity to warn the Earl of Newcastle that the rebellion 'is growen to that height, that I must not looke what opinion Men ar'. The monarch instructed him to employ all loving subjects without 'examining' their consciences – to embrace Catholics.[4]

Meanwhile, the 51-year-old Essex mustered his hymn-singing army, up to their ankles in mud, and occupied Worcester, where they took pot-shots at a bronze statue of the king in the cathedral. Pulled along behind Essex's force was his winding sheet and coffin, signifying a readiness to live and die with his men. As both sides prepared for a pitched battle, the king – attempting to gain the legal upper hand – considered whether Essex should be indicted for his act of rebellion. Learning from his failed attempt to arrest the six members in January 1642, the monarch called for evidence and tasked Rupert with providing it. The prince was ordered to send soldiers from his force who could bear witness against a list of ten principal Parliamentarians, topped by Essex, Lord Brooke, and the Earl of Stamford. From the outset of the war, the king had ensured evidence was meticulously stored for a day of reckoning; enemy pamphlets and proclamations were deposited in Oxford University and Edward Hyde would later receive a royal commission to write a history of the conflict.

Rupert, though, had his own ideas about how to deal with rebellious leaders. On 10 October, the day when the Royalist army marched out of Shrewsbury in search of Essex, the prince issued an open letter to the peer.

> I hear you are General of an army, sent by the agreement of both Houses of Parliament ... we greatly fear you aim at some higher power, namely, your own sovereignty. If your intents are such, give but the least notice thereof, and I shall be ready, on his [majesty's] behalf, to give you an encounter in a pitched field, at Dunsmore Heath, 10th October next. Or, if you think it too much labour and expense to draw your forces thither, I shall as willingly, on my own part, expect private satisfaction as willingly at your hands for the same, and that performed by a single duel ...[5]

Rupert, the king's champion, was ready to settle the war by a pitched battle or personal duel. The king had consistently forbidden duelling at his court and what he thought of this is unrecorded. However, it's doubtful that anyone, even Rupert, felt it would be taken seriously, but it contributed to the growing cult surrounding the prince. Charles Spencer attributes part of this growth to the popularity of gentlemen outlaws at the time, and suggests Rupert was, like Robin Hood, being woven into folklore. Several tales did indeed circulate. One had Rupert bribing a farmer, switching clothes, then riding an apple-laden cart through the Earl of Essex's army and selling them to the troops. He was later said to have paid the farmer to go amongst the Parliamentarians and ask them how they enjoyed the fruit sold personally by Prince Rupert.

Another claimed that Rupert, scouting the size of Essex's army, sought refreshment at the house of an old widow near Worcester. As the woman rustled up food, she grumbled about the Royalists and called them rude knaves, reserving special vitriol for Prince Rupert (who should have stayed where he was born) and calling down a plague to choke him. Her undercover visitor agreed, tipped her handsomely, and then reported her to the authorities for having entertained Prince Rupert in her house.

Kitson judged these stories to be by 'no means unlikely' given Rupert's admiration for Gustavus Adolphus, who had been the star of similar ones.[6] Undercover assignations of this sort were not confined to Rupert. Nemiah Wharton, in September 1642, reported that the Royalist Earl of Northampton 'by stealth' entered the town of Northampton to assess enemy strength, staying overnight and escaping next morning after being discovered.[7]

Within days of Rupert's challenge to Essex, it seemed that fate – or more specifically the prince's mother – might prevent any encounter. A pamphlet appeared on 11 October 1642 reporting a speech that Rupert was supposed to have made to the king. Having received letters from his mother in Holland who was 'discontented and troubled in mind' over his actions in England, Rupert reportedly agreed to return to her.[8] This is almost certainly fake news, but there was truth in that Elizabeth did publicly distance herself from his activities. The fact is that Rupert remained by the king's side and his enemies would soon be under no illusions as to his constancy.

On the evening of 22 October 1642, King Charles quartered around Edgecote, south-east of Warwick, while Prince Rupert was set to billet his troop at Wormleighton, around 7 miles away. George Digby had taken 400 horsemen to 'find out' if the area was clear of enemy troops and reported back with an affirmative.[9] The prince's horsemen were astounded to discover enemy quartermasters scouting Wormleighton for the same purpose, and following a brisk action, took eleven prisoners. After questioning them, and sending out a second patrol, it was discovered that the Earl of Essex's army was at Kineton, barely a day's march away. Campfires could be observed. Though Rupert was ready to attack Kineton first and ask questions later, he was reminded that the king should be the judge in a matter of such magnitude. After receiving a note from Rupert, the monarch – at 4.00 am – readily agreed to get the infantry to Edgehill for the morning. 'I have given order as you have desyred; so I doubt not but all the foot and canon will bee at Eggehill betymes this morning.'[10]

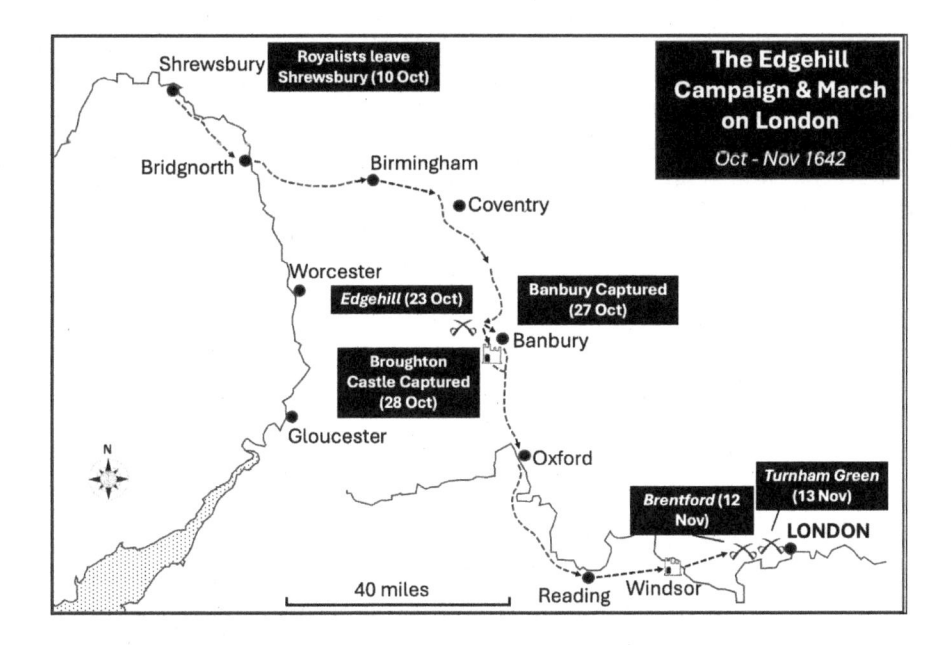

The Edgehill Campaign & March on London
Oct - Nov 1642

As a cold dawn broke above the 650-foot escarpment, Rupert eyed Kineton in the distance. Frustratingly, he was in for a long wait. He had instructed the cavalry to arrive by 8.00 am but the last units didn't get there until three hours after this, by which time the foot were beginning to arrive. The Earl of Essex had received warning of Royalist concentration as he went to church that morning and then set about marshalling his army in the vale, one and a half miles from the foot of Edgehill. It was open ground – 'a faire meadowe land' – with some rows of hedges and thick brushwood.[11] Though the king arrived at midday, it would take another hour for the remainder of the Royalist foot. Essex, too, was waiting for his force to come together, some units having been quartered 20 miles distant.

Latest estimates put both sides at an equal strength of 14,000, though the Parliamentarians had nearly double the artillery. Since the royal standard was raised in Nottingham two months earlier, the Royalists had transformed their position, with Rupert's energies and example undoubtedly playing a huge part. Sir Philip Warwick later reminisced that the prince had 'put that spirit into the king's army, that all men seemed resolved'.[12] On the summit of Edgehill, however, the king's commanders first did battle with one another. At the heart of the dispute was Rupert. When given his commission as General of the Horse, he had insisted on being directly subordinate to the king, and not the Earl of Lindsey, who was Lord General. This suited Rupert, but was also normal practice for European royalty, and Charles Spencer puts forward the premise that 'Princes of the Blood outranked marshals in the Field'.[13] But taking matters further, the prince arrogantly took umbrage at receiving royal orders via the hands of a Secretary of State, fostering much enmity.

When the 59-year-old Lindsey proposed drawing up the army in the traditional Dutch style – line formation – Rupert opposed the plan, likely with characteristic bluntness. He advocated Gustavus Adolphus's diamond-shaped formations, which allowed flexibility and better defence against cavalry. Lindsey, a veteran admiral and general, who in his teens had fought for the Dutch Prince of Orange, stood firm. When King Charles came down on his nephew's side, Lindsey threw his marshal's baton and declared if he was 'not fit to perform the office of Commander in Chief, he would serve [the king] as a Collonell'.[14] With that, he took up position at the head of his own regiment.

The Royalist army was hastily put into the hands of Patrick Ruthven, Earl of Forth. At 70 years of age, the Scotsman had been a major general in Swedish service, but in 1639–40 had indomitably held Edinburgh Castle for the king during the Bishops Wars, fought against Scottish Covenanters. At one point, the audacious commander had carcasses of beef thrown over the walls to give the impression he had more than enough food to hold out. A hard drinker and martyr to gout, he was, nevertheless, completely loyal and in sympathy with Rupert. Judgement was that Forth's 'white hairs' (or experience) would temper Rupert's 'ardour'.[15] The decision to support Rupert and Forth shows how much stock the king, who was militarily inexperienced, put in his nephew. Yet the fact Rupert didn't get the top job is a reminder that despite his successes, he was an extremely divisive figure.

Coming to realise that Essex had no intention of attacking uphill, the Royalists descended. Adorned with blackened armour and a velvet coat lined with ermine, King Charles rode through the army calling for his men to show courage and resolution. He took the opportunity to reinforce his devotion to the Protestant religion, privileges of Parliament, and rights of the subject. This he had also publicly stated on coins minted at Shrewsbury with the inscription 'Pro religione et parlamento'.[16] The king's speeches caused 'Huzza's thro' the whole army. He reminded senior officers that as their king, he was 'both your cause, your quarrel and your captain'.[17] The glittering sight of the royal standard and accompanying cheers goaded Essex, who responded with a salvo of roundshot, supposedly aimed at the Royalist 'cavalrie'.[18] According to Sir Philip Warwick, the king had given order that his army should not engage until the enemy had first 'shot their cannon at our body of men'.[19] Battle had commenced – it was 2.00 pm.

Five Royalist infantry brigades had been arranged with three forming a front line and two behind. The cavalry was split in two and placed at each end, with Rupert commanding the right wing and Wilmot the left. The prince urged his horsemen to ride in close formation and avoid discharging carbine or pistol until they were amongst the enemy. Considering his men suitably prepared, he led his wing forward, three lines deep, with the battle cry 'The King and the Cause'.[20] There had been no time to warn his officers that an enemy troop had, at the eleventh hour, declared their intention to defect. The aptly named Sir Faithful Fortescue had his men tear off their tawny scarfs (signs of Parliamentarian allegiance) and fired his pistol into the ground.

Essex's left wing of cavalry, with defection in their midst, watched as Rupert's men increased to a canter at perhaps 200 yards. It became clear the Royalists were not going to draw up to fire, and instead charged like an equine juggernaut. With Rupert's reputation preceding him, cavalier blades had barely started cutting and thrusting before the Parliamentarian left wing collapsed. Though Rupert and his men had 'curagiouslie' got the battle off to a good start, the prince was unable to rein in his jubilant troopers.[21] Pursuing the broken Parliamentarians for 2 miles, the Royalists fell to pillage. Henry Wilmot, the prince's second-in-command, delivered a like success on the opposite wing before pounding off. Thus, the Royalist infantry was left alone. Sir Jacob Astley, Sergeant-Major-General, kneeled and uttered his famous prayer. 'O Lord! thou knowest, how busy I must be this day: if I forget thee, do not thou forget me.'[22]

Upon rising to his feet, the silver-haired Astley led his 'boys' forward with resolve. As the infantry slogged it out, a small reserve of two cavalry regiments, retained by the Earl of Essex, revealed themselves to devastating effect. The first, led by Sir William Balfour, broke through one of the five Royalist brigades (Richard Fielding's) and made it to the king's artillery. Unluckily for Balfour, he could find no nails to spike the guns and put them out of action, but one of his men nearly captured the 12-year-old Prince of Wales and 9-year-old Duke of York. The former, cocking his pistol and declaring that he was not afraid, was only saved when the assailant was finished off with a poleaxe.

With the battle hanging in the balance, King Charles rode amongst his struggling infantry to reinforce morale, whereupon a footman was shot in the face. He was vulnerable to all the 'greattest hazertis' (hazards).[23] The Earl of Lindsey, having resigned that morning, fought like a lion in the hope of personal combat with the Earl of Essex. When Lindsey was shot in the leg and mortally wounded, his son stood over him and fought off the enemy until the Royalist lines were pushed back and the pair captured. News that a 'blue riban' (Knight of the Garter) had fallen spread fast. A more significant loss was to come. Sir Edmund Verney, bearer of the royal standard, resorted to using the point of the flagstaff to defend himself but was eventually felled and the prized flag snatched from his death grip. It seemed like all was lost. Luckily for the king, a few hundred of Henry Wilmot's cavalrymen, led by Sir Charles Lucas, returned and rescued the standard. As evening fell and more Royalist horsemen returned, Wilmot was urged to give one last charge that might break the enemy but he refused, declaring that they had already won the day and should live to taste the fruits of it. With both sides exhausted, 'as if by mutuall consent' the infantry disengaged.[24]

The prince's last three biographers are all in agreement that he did not join the chase with his men for long, nor did he put plunder above tactics. Instead, he is credited with doing his utmost to rally as many horsemen as he could, an almost impossible job in view of their racing adrenaline and the fleeing enemy. Crucially, it's also unclear when Rupert realised that the second line of his wing had charged with him, instead of remaining in position. Had they stayed put, which was the order, the infantry would have had key support – perhaps enough to tip the outcome to a Royalist victory. An enemy pamphlet went so far as to ascribe Rupert's pursuit of the Parliamentarians as being motivated by cowardice – to escape from both action and responsibility.

Darkness shrouded the scene of carnage as night fell. A bitter frost froze the survivors in situ, though neither side was willing to leave. For some of the wounded, the falling temperatures tended to them better than any physician. Sir Gervase Scrope, with sixteen wounds to his head and body, was stripped and left for dead for nearly two days until his son discovered him. Despite this ordeal, the cold stemmed blood loss and facilitated a miraculous recovery. Sir John Culpepper warned that if the king withdrew from Edgehill that evening, he would be ruined – the monarch agreed and 'incamptit [encamped] the nyt wth in halff myle' of the enemy.[25]

The following day, unwilling to resume the battle, Essex withdrew and headed to Warwick Castle. By doing so, he left the road to London open, and the Royalists masters of the field with a tactical victory. If the vulnerable capital fell to the king, the war would be over. Rupert was ready to gallop to the city and overawe it, but the Earl of Bristol (father of George Digby) cautioned against the feisty prince who might burn it to the ground. Bristol was playing on Parliamentarian propaganda and Rupert's hot-headed manner. King Charles refused to sanction an attack, more from a desire for an ideological victory than any worry over his nephew's unbridled spirit. London took no chances and many streets were given barricades of heavy chains, while trenches were dug in the approaches to the city, and small earthwork forts erected. Young Princess Elisabeth and Prince Henry, in Parliament's custody, were considered useful hostages and moved further into the city.

The capital braced itself. King Charles, however, relieved Banbury and then secured Oxford. Anxious not to be branded a bloody warmonger, he refused to conquer the city; far better to let Londoners' hearts move them into shaking off the traitorous yoke within Parliament. This blinkered idealism sprung from a deep belief in kingly responsibility and that God would never let traitors prosper. The first chance at winning the war was squandered. Rupert the realist must have seen how this risked invalidating everything so far achieved. He could never appreciate his uncle's complex role, being Captain General of the Royalists, but king of all combatants. It's said that King Charles was both affected and conflicted by the horrors of Edgehill, where losses included his cousin, and perhaps this exacerbated his reticence. In the weeks after Edgehill, he was certainly worried about Rupert, adding a postscript to an official letter in which he conjured his nephew, 'as ye love me', not to needlessly hazard himself.[26]

Believing the majority of enemy troops had merely been led astray, the king offered a free pardon after Edgehill to all except his leading opponents. It was an attempt to encourage an ideological peace. Rupert, by comparison, sated his frustration by skirmishing with Essex's retreating army, on one occasion seizing thirty waggons of arms and ammunition. What he could not take with him was spectacularly blown up. One interesting find when Essex's plate and cabinet of letters were taken showed that a Royalist called Blake (Rupert's own secretary) had been betraying secrets. As a result, the prince had the man hanged.

Post-Edgehill reports and rumours make fascinating reading. Continuing for weeks afterwards, they demonstrate the deep significance of the action, even to those who had been nowhere near it. In Suffolk, rector John Rous recorded what he heard in a diary that offers brand new insight. Nearly four weeks after Edgehill, it 'remained as a doubt whether Prince Rupert were not slaine'. Rous was told that the prince had returned to the field after plundering and was then 'cut [off] by the middle' or, as others said, 'beate [off] his horse'. To evidence this, Rupert's helmet and plume had supposedly been retrieved, and a 'George' (Knight of the Garter) had been found amongst the slaine – the prince having been raised to that Order months earlier. It was all wishful thinking on the part of the Parliamentarians – the 'George' was the Earl of Lindsey, who had perished. Extraordinarily, it was even alleged that Rupert's death was being concealed and that an imposter had taken his place – 'still a Prince Rupert is feined in the campe'.[27]

Mary, Princess of Orange (King Charles's daughter), recounted stories that reached Holland. Rupert was credited with killing 1,500 men by his own hands and called a 'divell' with 'cloven fett' – a cloven-footed devil.[28] Ironically, Rupert's mother was still referencing him by his childhood nickname, Rupert le Diable. Henrietta Maria wrote of men that attested to having seen and touched the prince's corpse. There was also Rupert's magical 'devil dog' called Boye, who it was claimed had called down vengeance upon Royalist Lord Taafe. Having previously shouted at the animal, tales spread that Taafe's death wound at Edgehill – a shot to the mouth – was no coincidence.

These spectacular rumours offer insight into the post-Edgehill climate. Their origins are evidence of just how high-profile and effective a role the prince was playing within the Royalist cause; his exploits terrorised the enemy both physically and psychologically. Edgehill saw propaganda about the prince skyrocket, but his actions at Brentford would add a deep-seated loathing.

Chapter 16

Scribbling Age

Only in November, when the Earl of Essex started to march his army back to the capital, did the king finally stir. The Royalist army set off in pursuit, but the Parliamentarians evaded them and reached London on 7 November. This despite the best efforts of Rupert and his cavalry. The Royalist initiative after Edgehill was well and truly lost, so the prince set his sights on Windsor Castle as a base. Unleashing his guns on the fortress had little effect and the king intervened to call it off. At this juncture, Parliament proposed peace talks. Though more a means of buying time, commissioners duly travelled to meet the monarch, while the Parliamentarian army began a slow and threatening advance.

Peace negotiations opened at Colnbrook on 11 November, just 20 miles from the capital. This was not Royalist territory, whereas the Earl of Essex's troops were abundantly supplied by London. Both sides outwardly committed to the negotiations while keeping a tight grip on their swords. The king made his own attempt on Windsor Castle, proposing that it be handed to him as a sign of Parliament's genuine intentions, to serve as a royal base from where peace could be thrashed out. This was rejected out of hand.

Parliament's army seemed poised to cut off royal supply lines by encircling them in a deathly embrace. If this occurred, the king could be held hostage to any terms. According to the Venetian ambassador, Prince Rupert was keeping a close eye on matters, and learned of artillery and 'warlike stores' that were being shipped in to 'hurt' the Royalists.[1] These were stored in Brentford. As a result, he proposed an immediate attack on the town to counter the threat – the place could be used as a foothold. The king had little choice. If he didn't agree to the operation, then he would have to do battle with Essex, or retreat with humiliation.

Taking just under four thousand infantrymen and four cavalry regiments Rupert traversed Hounslow Heath at night and advanced along the London Road. When darkness lifted its veil, a loyal mist replaced it, and Rupert's undetected men arrived at a crossroads, at which stood the house of Sir Richard Wynn. The regiment of Denzil Holles garrisoned it. To the east was Brentford End, a small outcrop that led to Brentford's main street, courtesy of a bridge over the Thames. The crossing was held by Lord Brooke's purple-coated regiment.

The Parliamentarians were caught off guard. In the resolute fighting that ensued, Holles's men retreated from the house and attempted to get to Brentford, but were relentlessly pursued and cut down, many drowning in attempts to cross the water. Every house in Brentford was fought over. The single street was a killing ground and inevitably some buildings were fired in the process. The Parliamentarians fired from windows, across gardens and orchards, until they could no longer hold off the Royalists.

In the House of Lords, the noise of war interrupted debate about the cessation. Distant smoke rose from the houses set alight. The attack blazed through the Parliamentarian news sheets as well as the imaginations of Londoners; there was no smoke without fire. The blackened king was accused of breaking his word and attacking during a period of truce. *Speciall Passages and Certain Informations* whipped up anger when it tarred king and Catholics as one: 'The world may see the counsells and plots of Jesuits are prevalent with the king in causing him to violate his words, and the knowne law of Armes.'[2]

True, Rupert's men did plunder Brentford, but few, if any, civilian deaths are certain. In Holland, Henrietta Maria optimistically considered that she might be able to sail home directly to London, so high were her hopes of the king being back in Whitehall. Parliamentarian propaganda grossly exaggerated Brentford and compared it to the sack of Magdeburg where over 20,000 civilians had been slaughtered. They expressed 'most violent sentiments of indignation'.[3] Nothing could erase the stain, whatever the mistruths, and Rupert's name was synonymous with it. As such, when the king and his army did appear at Turnham Green, on the outskirts of London, they were met by the Earl of Essex, whose troops were powerfully augmented by the city's trained bands and apprentices. Just two days after Brentford, their resolve in the face of the Royalist army was strong. Both sides watched each other warily and, in the end, the outnumbered king had no alternative but to withdraw his troops.

The forlorn monarch let it be known that he would fall back to Oxford like a 'pitiful prince' where he would wait either for negotiators or the Earl of Essex's army.[4] A newssheet of 16 November claims that before departing, Rupert (at 6 foot 4) dressed as a woman and viewed London's defences. If true, he must have regretted not putting them to the test immediately after Edgehill.

The year 1642 was heading for a disappointing close and the king pined for his wife. Henrietta Maria had intended to sail home with her stash of munitions, money, and men, but was forced to stay her departure due to enemy activity in the north of England. The Royalist war machine would be hard pressed to enter 1643 without her supplies. The queen bitterly complained of Parliamentarian raiding parties commanded by Captain John Hotham and the king subsequently implored the Earl of Newcastle to vanquish this threat. A stream of royal instructions was despatched urging the earl to send 'continuall advertisements' of the state of the north and every 'materiall accident' that happened there, so that the queen could make informed decisions about her voyage.[5] Paperwork was only a minor part of the weighty expectations heaped on poor Newcastle. He was to lose no time in securing Yorkshire, though Derbyshire, Cheshire, and Lancashire were all described as standing in need of him. Taking Nottingham and Newark would also put Lincolnshire in a better place. In short, the peer was deemed the 'principall instrument in keeping the Crowen upon [the king's] heade'.[6]

Though hostilities lessened as winter loomed, Rupert found himself engulfed in a war of words. The Parliamentarians were already blaming him for lapses in Royalist military discipline, even when he was not present, such as when Baron Strange (later Earl of Derby) attacked Manchester in September 1642. Strange demanded a contribution of £2,000 towards his army's upkeep, and Rupert's bad example was judged to be the cause of this 'injurious innovation' to England.[7] Lord Wharton had made a speech in London just days after Edgehill, in which he falsely accused Rupert of charging off the field and killing civilians – 'poore women' and their children. The prince, and the Royalists in general he said, aimed at nothing but 'pillage, and baggage, and plundering' and were nothing short of murderers.[8] With Wharton's words fresh in many minds, Brentford ignited an inferno of hatred towards Rupert – later in the war twenty Bedfordshire men would band together and vow to 'pistoll' the prince, after first pretending to offer themselves to his service and then assassinating him.[9]

The late Queen Elizabeth, the Queen Mother, reputedly stood by the mantra 'never complain, never explain'. In this way, today's royal family avoid engaging in debate over scurrilous stories. Outraged at such lies about him, Prince Rupert, 300 years earlier, could not contain himself and sallied forth in print. The results are extremely revealing. They tell us a lot about the man and his thoughts and are worthy of being explored in detail.

No sooner had Wharton's speech been printed than the prince issued a reply, in which he acknowledged his 'knowne disposition' was so contrary to this 'scribling age' – not being an avid writer. He railed that every morning there was a new malicious pamphlet that attempted to render him more odious by pedalling bold and impossible untruths. His anger doubled when the king was also targeted, for his uncle was only guilty of being 'too good' a person and too clement a monarch.

Lord Wharton's accusation of 'barbarousnesse and inhumanity' was as fabricated as anything that had been spoken or printed in two years, Rupert countered, and full of 'grosse falsities'. He could produce a thousand witnesses to counter the 'fowl untruths' printed in such 'hackney railing' pamphlets, which were used to deceive the poor and abused citizens of London. Detailing his martial principles, the prince made it clear that he deemed any man who struck, much less killed, a woman or child to be no soldier or gentleman, though with remarkable honesty, adds the caveat 'if it be in his power to doe the contrary'. He knew as much as any that civilians are almost always inextricably caught up in warfare. Rupert therefore demanded evidence – the times, persons, or houses – where any woman or child lost so much as a hair from their heads by him or his soldiers. Counteraccusations of Parliamentarian abuses were put forward, along with a further reminder that looseness and incivility in soldiers was common to any great army.

Final paragraphs offer defence against Royalist *and* Parliamentarian accusations that he would destroy London. Reminding readers that he had refused to change his religion despite 'wretched close imprisonment' in Linz, he ventured the greatest victory would be for the king to enter London without shedding one drop of blood, nor any citizen plundered of 'one penny or farthing'. Moreover, any man who had a design to enrich himself through pillaging the capital should be cursed. Rupert's resentment over the Earl of Bristol's bold assertion that the prince might burn the capital is palpable.[10]

Having unburdened himself, Rupert now faced the king and his council at Oxford, in December 1642. When they had been delayed at Reading a month earlier, on account of the Prince of Wales having measles, Rupert had inspected the defences. The results concerned him greatly. He now presented these findings, pragmatically judging that if war continued into 1643, it was essential to strengthen cities, towns, and places of advantage by erecting sconces and forts. This betrays his hopes that the war might have been brought to a successful close in 1642, but now a more drawn-out conflict was inevitable. To emphasise the point, he drew upon experience and explained how the Prince of Orange had 'tired out' the might of Spain through fortifications. The siege of Breda was quoted as a prime example, as was Ostend, having held out for three years – which Rupert bluntly calls an 'arrant dog-hole' in comparison to English towns! He even uses his family's failure to regain the Palatinate, attributing it to the fact that the Spanish and Bavarians had repaired old fortresses and built new ones. With key English locations fortified in this way, any rebel armies that posed a threat to them could be picked off by the 'brave and gallant' Royalist cavalry, operating as a flying relief column. Of course, this was all dependent on whether war did continue, and he headed off accusations of being a warmonger by assuring the council that he prayed with all his 'soule' for a peaceful resolution.[11]

The Cavalier Commander did not confine himself to the horse. He warned that 1643 would require more infantry, otherwise there would be 'no hope' of opposing the enemy, who were numerically superior in foot. Crécy, Poitiers, and Agincourt were cited, proving his grasp of history. As a solution, he advocated calling back the four English regiments serving under the Prince of Orange, whose experience would be invaluable. If the States General of Holland objected, then he suggested the Prince of Orange, as Generalissimo, could overrule them. The comparison to King Charles, whose authority was under complete attack, could not have been starker.

These rallying words are honest, blunt, and very matter of fact, much like Rupert's character. One quote he employs is 'though I cannot talke I can fight' – a phrase originally made by Duke of Brunswick to the prince's grandfather, King James VI/I. Rupert's use of it betrays an appreciation that he isn't one for courtly ways or polite exchanges, which he writes off as unnecessary, because fighting is the 'businesse'. 'I cannot like an Oratour in excellent English expresse my intentions.'

Enemy attacks had criticised his accent, to remind people that he was no Englishman and in turn marshall xenophobia against him. They questioned the declaration, suggesting it was too elegant to be written by him – instead painting him as a foreign mercenary lacking in both morals and intelligence. Rupert, however, hit back, asserting that he could speak sense – and being a 'downe right honest martiall man' could clearly deliver his meaning. The world and his 'maligners' he felt should at least give him credit for his substance.[12]

Searching for likeminded allies to surround himself with, he appointed William Legge sergeant-major and captain of cuirassiers on 1 November. Theirs was a bond of trust that would remain until Legge's death, thirty years later. The prince also made use of the honorary doctorates, which the king was granting thick and fast as a means of recognition. Rupert intervened with his uncle and made a 'motion' to obtain the 'title and dignitye' of a doctorate for Mr Peachye, chaplain to the new Earl of Lindsey, whose father had so spectacularly resigned as Lord General at Edgehill and was subsequently killed.[13] Lindsey had been in Parliamentarian captivity ever since, and would not be released until 1643, so perhaps Rupert was making amends for his part in the pre-battle quarrel. At any rate, he would need all the personal support he could muster, for the pamphleteers were far from finished with him. On top of that, he could attract enemies as fast as he could attract fans.

Chapter 17

Cheefe Actor

The devil prince seemed impervious to human frailties. Despite winter quarters beckoning, he could not bear to be contained by the season, inspecting, recruiting, attacking, and dealing with administration. This constant activity made him appear phantom-like, manifesting anywhere from Abingdon, Reading, Oxford, Thame, Deddington, and Aylesbury. Rumours even reached the Royalist Charles Cavendish in Lincolnshire that Rupert was about to enter that county. The man was 'overjoyed' but the news proved untrue.[1] Tellingly, Cavendish requests permission to leave his post and recruit, which was, he accepts, going against a specific order from the king. Like many Royalists, Rupert's authority was often held in higher regard, as if his influence might lever what they required. Indeed, the prince had already secured command of the Duke of York's troop for Cavendish.

On 24 November 1642, after the Parliamentarians had reinforced Marlborough, alarm bells rang in Oxford. Lord George Digby wrote to Henry Wilmot of intelligence that 500 enemy dragoons had arrived in the town, which was just 30 miles from the Royalist capital. With a further 1,000 on their way, it threatened to interrupt the king's communication with his forces in the West Country. As Digby warned, if they were not 'nimble' in their response, the town would become a 'terrible thorne' in their side.[2] Digby's attempt to take the town next day was too pre-emptive and, lacking men and artillery, was beaten off. Joining forces with Wilmot, the pair returned and took the place on 5 December. Victory at Piercebridge, 20 miles south of Durham, also came on 1 December 1642. The Earl of Newcastle drove the Hotham's out of County Durham and back to their Yorkshire stomping ground, securing key bridges that linked the counties. With Newcastle in control of Northumberland and Durham, and soon after occupying York, the queen would be able to land in the north. These two victories demonstrate that Royalist commanders other than Rupert furthered the cause as the year closed.

In 2004, the Home Office discovered a thousand seventeenth-century pamphlets, including one that detailed the prince's alleged attack on the Parliamentarian army at Worcester, on 10 October 1642. Attempting to surprise the city, he was supposedly repulsed after two hours' fighting. Two days later, he was reportedly pillaging his way through Wiltshire with 5,000 men, only to be rebuffed at Marlborough.

One newssheet asserts that the prince was next intercepted by 4,000 enemy troops led by Philip Skippon, who had them arrayed in Swedish fashion. Skippon, a noted orator, is said to have made a speech to his men prior to the engagement in which he acknowledged that they were not engaged against any 'foreign enemy' but were nevertheless opposing 'domestic and intestine foes'. Battle was said to have lasted seven hours, with Royalist casualties numbering three hundred infantry and five hundred cavalrymen, compared to sixty on the opposing side.[3] Almost certainly fake news, these do not fit with Rupert's known movements. Ronald Hutton has noted similar parliamentarian pamphlets from this period, which he described as 'totally fraudulent'.[4] The paradox here is that parliamentarian propagandists were simultaneously crediting the ethereal prince and his dog with malignant magic as a means of excusing Rupert's victories, whilst at the same trying to make people believe that he had also suffered numerous defeats; the latter by default challenged the powers mentioned in the former. What's certain, however, is that parliamentarian propaganda played a huge part in furthering Rupert's legendary reputation.

Before the year was out, the indomitable prince managed to seize one last success. When several thousand Parliamentarians from Northamptonshire struck at Royalist Banbury Castle, a huge concentric fortress near Oxford, Rupert only had to approach with a similar strength of dragoons before the enemy abandoned it. Christmas offered little festivity. The prince was beset by pleas for assistance, and numerous officers such as those in Deddington, near Banbury, were begging him to make 'all ye hast you can to us'.[5]

For all the mountain of letters Rupert received, there was a conspicuous absence of word from his family. Immediately after the Battle of Edgehill, Rupert had penned a hasty message to his mother, but that was the last known interaction between them. The hiatus in communication is understandable on Rupert's part, considering that at the time of Edgehill, Charles Louis had issued a statement distancing himself and his mother from Rupert's actions. Elizabeth was petrified that Parliament might find in her correspondence anything 'to theire prejudice' which might affect her pension being paid, though she discreetly supported Rupert's actions.[6] Parliament had indeed debated punishing the entire family and considered withdrawing support for their restitution to the Palatinate. Baulking at such prejudicial talk, Charles Louis complained bitterly that he and others had failed to stifle Rupert's 'youth and fieryness' nor persuade him to leave England.[7] Then, in January 1643, a letter from Elizabeth to Rupert was intercepted in Yorkshire.

After a three-month spell, Elizabeth wrote to encourage Rupert in his services to King Charles. She also revealed that her sister-in-law, Queen Henrietta Maria, had left The Hague bound for England with a mountain of warlike supplies. Charles Louis had refused to accompany her because she was not going as an 'angel of peace'.[8] The remainder of Elizabeth's letter contains a warning that the world is very wicked, and that some of the closest to us do the most harm, which is always a danger to those with a good nature. More details were to be verbally imparted by the messenger. Elizabeth seems to have been attempting to indirectly excuse

Charles Louis. She asks Rupert to put in a good word about his brother with the king and queen, who didn't hold Charles Louis so well in their minds, lamenting that the young man had simply had some bad advice – but not from her, she hastily adds. Rupert was unhappy over Charles Louis's attempts to control him. Never one to mix his loyalties, he likely dismissed any notion of intervening on his brother's behalf. Old Sir Thomas Roe, the ambassadorial architect of Rupert's release from Linz, wanted Elizabeth to return to England and act as a mediator. He even went so far as to suggest she might rein in Rupert, who needed 'a bridle to moderate him'.[9]

The year 1643 would see Rupert's star rise to its zenith. The Twelfth Night festivities were in full swing when he rode out of Oxford at the head of an army. He had his eyes on Cirencester, one of a trio of towns that studded the route to the southwest and impeded Royalist expansion. The Marquess of Hertford had requested support to capture the town and put increasing pressure on the enemy at Gloucester. Rupert, having been despatched, aimed to catch Cirencester while its garrison was full of festive spirit. His nocturnal march saw 'fire falling from heaven like a bolt, which with several cracks, break into balls and went out about steeple height from the ground'.[10] The prince exhibited a fiery display of his own when after three days he was obliged to withdraw empty-handed and with some loss. Sir Arthur Aston, a Catholic, and Governor of Reading, wrote on 11 January 1643 to express relief that the prince had returned from a mission planned by irresponsible civilian advisors. Aston was one of Rupert's close allies and naturally excused the prince from all failure, but the letter highlights the ever-present civilian-military rivalry.

Never one to back down, the capture of Cirencester became intensely personal. Rupert would not fail a second time. Between the end of January and early February, orders were sent to the south-west for waggons, spades, and bullets of all sizes, together with mortars, cannons, and hand grenades. Horses, scaling ladders, and 3,900 pike heads were also commandeered, it being noted that Rupert intended to march with twenty pieces of ordnance. The prince's shopping list shows his determination. While this equipment was gathered, he issued a challenge to Sir William Belford, a Parliamentarian who had captured Rupert's close comrade, Viscount Grandison. Belford, having agreed to release Grandison on the proviso that the man returned to present himself every six days – akin to conditional bail – nevertheless reneged upon the deal. Grandison consulted Rupert on the matter of honour, and they resolved that a duel or pitched fight 'to try the valour' of each other could decide the matter.[11] The message was sent under the prince's own warrant, but Belford reported it to his superiors and there the matter dropped. Rupert did get a fight though. On 2 February 1643, after making a feint towards Sudeley Castle, he turned his 4,000-strong force about and arrived before Cirencester.

Noticing that the enemy had not destroyed the suburbs, Rupert used them as cover and had a mortar brought up. A barn was set ablaze and plumes of smoke used to Royalist advantage as they broke into the town. Henry Wilmot made a diversionary attack from the north, while Rupert led the cavalry and Colonel Lewis Kirke brought up the infantry. When the turnpike to the west of town was taken, the Royalists found waggons and casks strung across the streets to block their path. For an hour and a half both sides fought courageously house to house. Doggedly clinging on, the Parliamentarians refused to give up this lucrative town, worth £4,000 per month, without a good fight. When eventually they surrendered 300 of their number lay dead, but the spirit of resistance lived on in others who stubbornly continued to fire on the Royalists and pot-shots were taken at Rupert. This flouting of the 'rules' of warfare ignited Royalist resentment and they turned to firepikes to burn the persistent Parliamentarians out of their holes.

The victors rounded up 1,200 prisoners, some of whom were kept in the church. Parliamentarian news sheets described how 'the [Royalists] entered the town and being much enraged with their losses put all to the sword they met with; men, women and children, and in a barbarous manner murdered three ministers, very godly and religious men'.[12] The tremors of Rupert's success rocked the West Country. Parliament withdrew garrisons from Tewkesbury, Malmesbury, Devizes, and both Sudeley and Berkeley Castles. Strongholds fell like ninepins, and with Gloucester wobbling, Rupert appeared before the town hoping that his presence might give him a full strike. Despite the citizens being 'at their wits end ... like men amazed', the town held firm and the unabashed prince moved on.[13]

Horses, harnesses, wool, hemp, linen, flax, brimstone, iron – not forgetting cheese – all rumbled off to Oxford. Prisoners, bound two by two, were also led to Royalist HQ, where peace talks were under way. The next day, Sir Edward Nicholas, the King's Secretary of State, heard the 'welcome News' and wrote congratulating Rupert's 'admirable dexterity & courage'.[14] It had 'strooke a great terror' into the enemy.[15] King Charles also 'snached' time away from business to congratulate his nephew and deemed this victory to be all the more welcome because Rupert was the 'cheefe Actor'.[16]

Cirencester and its alleged atrocities furthered the pamphlet wars. 'A looking-glasse, wherein His Majesty may see his nephews love' was written just afterwards, as if directed to the king. A stark warning was given that Rupert was a danger 'lying hid under an open shew of friendship' and that given half the chance, the prince would 'bid as fair for [his uncle's crown] by the sword'. The prince was, it accused, accumulating so much power under the colour of serving the monarch that he had become more of a direct threat than the Parliamentarians. Coupled with his 'Germaine' manner of plundering, which earned Rupert a bedrock of support from soldiers of fortune, it was judged that these men already acknowledged him as their 'Chieftain and Prince' and were 'like enough' to make him king. Internal Royalist discontent was the aim. Claims that the king had lost his peoples' hearts and the law its force, and that whoever held the sword would hold power, were very prophetic – in six years Fairfax and Cromwell would use their sword (the New Model Army) to cut through Parliament and the law.[17]

It wasn't just Rupert that was targeted by the printing presses – they stamped out vitriol about his hunting poodle, Boye, branded a 'very downright Divell' with Popish tendencies. Parliamentarian spies supposedly even trailed the animal, warily watching its every move. Deemed to have once been a handsome 'Lapland Lady' now morphed into a dog, Boye's magical abilities were suitably employed to excuse numerous disasters; he was a good get-out clause for their failure.

Boye could find concealed goods, the reason why Royalists discovered so much hidden plate in Oxford, which Parliamentarians, Lord Saye and Sir John Seton had missed. By speaking many languages – Boye's own being something between Hebrew and High-Dutch – the dog could eavesdrop and thus 'all our spies are discovered'. Being 'weapon-proofe' and catching bullets in his teeth, he was able to make his master similarly invincible, neatly accounting for all Rupert's death-defying antics. Importantly, this replaced supposition that the Almighty was protecting the prince and the Royalist cause, and instead ascribed it to black arts.

One Parliamentarian had given Boye a 'very hearty stroke' with a dagger only for it to slide off the dog's skin as if it was anointed with quicksilver. Should readers not be convinced by this, the canine was also credited with the ability to make people invisible, which was the reason Lord Digby managed to sneak in and out of Hull, and how both Daniel O'Neale and Will Legge escaped imprisonment. Adopting disguises, such as Tom the barber or Philip the shoemaker, the animal would convey misinformation to the Parliamentarians in frequent trips to London. Lastly, 'mysticall meanes' had allowed Rupert to disguise himself as an apple seller, a woman, and a cabbage net seller, to successfully carry out undercover reconnaissance. On a more intimate slant, Rupert and Boye were alleged to lie in the same bed – the prince sometimes upon the dog and vice-versa – prompting the question of what this might produce. A clause, the author urgently suggested, should be added by the Common Council of London to have the dangerous dog entirely removed from the king's presence. One bizarre allegation was the dog's weekly bath in two tubs of 'Custard-stuffe'.[18]

When Rupert got back to Oxford, the king capitalised upon his nephew's presence on account of peace negotiations. Parliament's envoy earls – Northumberland, Pembroke, Holland, and Salisbury – must have been suitably in awe of the prince and his dog, but their diplomatic efforts were being undermined by colleagues. The Venetian ambassador reported that MPs were using stories of Rupert's behaviour at Cirencester to 'stir up feeling' and divert desire away from peace.[19] There was also discord in the Royalist camp, with Rupert unhappy that the Marquess of Hertford (in his mid-50s and brother-in-law to Parliament's Lord General) had been promoted to General of the West.

Success heightened demand for Rupert's presence and there was no time to bask in glory. From his home at Ashby de la Zouch, Colonel Henry Hastings sent congratulations, but warned that the enemy were attempting to take Stafford and Newark. Hastings requested 400 muskets, match, powder, and cannon to help correct the situation. Nearby Warwick Castle was on the king's hitlist – it was 'His Majesties pleasure' that 'something' should be attempted upon it.[20] Rupert passed on the monarch's desire to the Earl of Northampton and suggested (rather instructed) the peer to march the following evening for Warwick, to be there at break of day for maximum effect. He also sent his 'fireworker' – Bartholomew de la Roche – to assist. Northampton and his commanders were ready to 'ventur our lives' but were not convinced, counselling that failure at Warwick would bring them dishonour and recriminations to the Royalist prisoners held in the castle.[21] Moreover, Roche brought only two petards, yet there were five doors that would need forcing. Another hitch arose when word came by an 'expresse Messenger' from the wife of Henry Hastings, that her husband had been besieged in Lichfield.[22]

After consulting the king about the hindrance over Warwick, Rupert wrote back at midnight and urged Northampton on – if a man called Ingram was in command of Warwick, then he would make little resistance. As if the matter was already solved and the castle taken, Rupert added the relief of Lichfield to their charge. This was a less-than-ideal response from the preoccupied prince. Next, no doubt frustrated by what he assumed was Northampton's reticence, Rupert decided his personal intervention was required to galvanise them, and he started to gather troops. Luckily for Northampton, who had no desire for the prince to meddle in his sphere of command, the situation improved without Rupert. Lord Brooke, a leading Parliamentarian and commander of their Midland Association, was picked off by a sniper and killed at Lichfield. The killer shot was to his eye, which was ironic as he had supposedly declared a hope that he might one day see the king and church 'pull'd downe'.[23]

On 19 March 1643, the Earl of Northampton defeated a Parliamentarian army at Hopton Heath, near Stafford. Though this stabilised his region, Northampton had been cut off in the action and unhorsed. In a death resembling that of King Richard III, he was hacked across the head with a halberd and then disfigured with a slash to the face. Refusing to hand back the peer's corpse, the Parliamentarians bartered over it, calling first for the return of their captured artillery. Northampton had been a close friend and servant of King Charles. The earl's son now interceded with Rupert for the inheritance of his father's military command, in view of the 'unwisht for honor fallen uppon mee'.[24] He also made it abundantly clear that there was no longer any need for Rupert's presence in the Midlands, it being not 'fitt for yor Army to bee in [this] parte' due to the county being so poor and provision for men and horse so spent.[25]

Free to focus elsewhere, Rupert had his eyes on Gloucester, hoping to complete the subjugation of the west. In the king's mind, capturing Bristol should take precedence, as there was a plot to betray it, and then after that, the relief of Sherborne Castle. But these preferences were, the king explained, only to help Rupert make the most informed military judgement and he did not want his nephew to put Gloucester entirely 'out of [his] mynde'.[26] On 7 March, Rupert accordingly set off for Bristol, but on Durdham Down outside the city, he heard that Royalist plotters had been foiled and so returned to Oxford. The situation at Gloucester was little better. Lord Herbert of Raglan, son of the wealthy Marquess of Worcester, was investing the west side of the town. By the end of March, Sir William Waller, a

Parliamentarian commander nicknamed 'William the Conqueror' defeated Herbert at the Battle of Highnam and pursued him into South Wales. Prince Maurice was therefore despatched to deal with Waller, as Rupert could not be spared.

Militarily, the king's eye had been focused on the west, but his heart was firmly in the north. The Earl of Newcastle was master of most of it, with the key exception of Hull, but until his wife was safely landed in Yorkshire, the king remained anxious and agitated. On 13 February 1643, King Charles had written to Newcastle 'never Woeman with Chylde more longed for anything, then we for newes from you'.[27] Imploring the peer to write once, if not twice per week with news, the king placed his wife and her safety above everything. He had cause for alarm. Lack of updates about the queen gave rise to rumours that 'some mishap' at sea had overtaken her.[28] Particularly 'skurvy' rumours from London reported that she had failed to leave Holland due to illness, which 'vext' the king even though he refused to believe it.[29]

Appointing the Earl of Newport and Lord Saville to welcome his wife, the king was shocked to discover that they had in fact laid treacherous plans to detain her. Choice of the duo was poor judgement on the monarch's part. Lord Saville did not wish to see the king 'trample' over Parliament, nor brought so low that common people might 'rule us all'. By using the queen as a hostage, Newport and Saville's idea was to force the matter and secure a balanced peace. Their letter to Parliament had been intercepted by the Earl of Newcastle, who subsequently arrested them.

Evading Dutch officials, who attempted to stop her leaving Holland, the queen had written to her husband: 'Adieu, my dear heart … if it happen that I could not come to you, it would be [due to] my death, since I can live no longer without seeing you. Believe this, for it is very true.'

She finally landed at the little harbour of Bridlington, on 23 February 1643. Parliamentarian warships had shadowed her and in the early hours, while she slept in a small cottage on the harbour front, they opened fire. With no time to dress, 'bair feet and bair leg', she hurried outside to get out of range.[30] Forgetting her dog, Mitte, the indomitable queen, at four and a half feet tall, returned in the face of this barrage to recover her. Afterwards, with dog in her arms and shot whistling overhead, the queen leapt into a ditch and kept up morale until the rebel ships departed. She had been more concerned about her munitions than her own person and recounted as much to her husband.

It was not until 1 March 1643 that Henrietta Maria's landing was reported to the king. 'I never till now knew the good of ignorance; for I did not know the danger that thou wert in,' he admitted.[31] His next objective was to be reunited with his wife and obtain her much-needed military supplies. To that end the town of Lichfield, which had eventually fallen to the Parliamentarians, was now a key obstacle on the road south to Oxford. At the end of March, Prince Rupert was sent to recapture the town and thus clear a route for the queen – the king had promised that she was his 'first and chiefest care' and expressed his impatience to 'hasten Our meeting'.[32] Rupert, with 12,000 horse and dragoons and 600–700 foot, could not avoid having

George Digby accompany him. The man was just as eager to be reunited with the queen, his greatest friend and ally.

On the day that Rupert reached Stratford-on-Avon, 30 March 1643, Royalists enjoyed a timely victory at Seacroft Moor, in Yorkshire. Lord George Goring, who had returned with the queen, scattered Sir Thomas Fairfax, and captured 800 prisoners. The latter described Seacroft as the greatest loss he ever received. Rupert kept his focus on the Midlands. Tipped off that 500 Parliamentarians had gone to Birmingham, just 14 miles from Lichfield, and that they might 'speedily attempt somethinge' it was essential he tackle the growing threat.[33] Birmingham was exceptional; 'it manifested a virulent and spontaneous Parliamentarianism', having supplied the Earl of Essex with 15,000 swords.[34] On Easter Monday, 3 April 1643, the prince arrived before the town and by 3.00 pm, his six artillery pieces thundered against it.

Chapter 18

Burning Love

Taking Birmingham should have been a straightforward task as it was only defended by one troop of horse and a company of foot – in the region of 140 men. In practice, Rupert's Royalists were beaten off twice over the space of an hour and the town ended up being severely burned and plundered when eventually they prevailed. Two versions of events survive. Parliamentarian accounts (one entitled *Prince Rupert's Burning Love to England Discovered in Birmingham's Flames*) claim that the Royalists fired eighty houses and prevented anyone from saving their goods or fighting the flames. All bar two of these were set alight, it alleges, in cold blood a day or two later. Rupert, it continues, spared neither friend, nor foe, in his quest to take the town and his men behaved like 'so many Furyes or Bedlams'. That night saw many Royalists 'drinking Healths' to Rupert's dog.[1]

A more sympathetic letter, from a Walsall man to his friend in Oxford, suggests that the prince fired two houses to get around some street barricades, but quickly ordered their dowsing. It does, however, confirm that buildings were set alight later, when the Royalists marched out of the town – though the excuse, that the prince's men were incensed after being called 'Cursed doggs, devilish Cavaliers, Popish Traytors', is a lame one. Rupert, it is said, exited Birmingham before his troops, and was not present when (quite mutinously) they supposedly ignored his orders to preserve the place. On being informed, the prince 'immediately sent to the inhabitants of the towne, to let them know that it was not done by his command'.[2] Sensitive to bad press, it seems the prince did try to control his men during the action, but to leave the town ahead of them was pure folly.

Few Royalist casualties had occurred, but the Earl of Denbigh, a middle-aged peer, was mortally wounded. It was also rumoured for a time that Digby had been killed, but unluckily for Rupert, that was not true. Unsavoury news about Birmingham soon reached royal ears. Two weeks later, the king wrote an official letter to Rupert in which he extolled the prince's military knowledge but ordered him to 'mingle Severity with Mercy' and to 'take their Affections rather than their Towns'. Those opposing the king's armies must be converted and not destroyed.

> teach our People to be undeceived in us their merciful King; let your fair Actions make it appear that you are no Malignants, no evil

Counsellors, but that you stand in Defence of us as much as they pretend to do, and that you seek not the Ruin and Destruction of our Kingdoms, which Aspersions are cast upon you.[3]

By April, Queen Henrietta Maria was at York, waiting for Rupert to take Lichfield. With the latest admonishment fresh in his mind, Rupert wondered how he might speedily coax the enemy into surrendering their town, and resolved upon a mine. On the prince's behalf, Colonel Henry Hastings rounded up a small army of skilled miners, as well as faggots and provisions. Colonel Arthur Trevor hastened ammunition. The king and his ministers, for their parts, supplied a steady stream of letters. Secretary of State, Sir Edward Nicholas (one of Rupert's key supporters) congratulated him on the taking Birmingham. Using a cipher, Nicholas also reported the king's view that there was 'little or noe hope' of any good from ongoing peace talks, but some Royalists, he also warned, were for an accommodation at any rate.[4] Another communication went further, advising Rupert that in his absence many principal army officers were advocating a cessation. It suggests the prince was of the opposite view and saw conquest as the best means of ending the war. Division became stark as the Royalists edged towards a military upper hand.

On 9 April 1643, the king urged his nephew to deal with Cheshire after Lichfield, yet gave him final say on his ultimate 'Desynes' as long as they conduced to 'my wyfes comming hither' to Oxford.[5] Nevertheless, Arthur Capel expressed hopeful expectations that the prince would soon be in Cheshire, which 'wilbe a very greate comfort' to all there.[6] Each dawning day had the potential of heralding events that would scupper the best-laid plans – the siege of Lichfield lasted thirteen days from 8 to 21 April.

Dealing with correspondence from his own side was one thing, but the enemy was not silent. A pamphlet entitled 'Joyfull Newes From Lichfield' opened on 16 April with a taunt that Rupert had from his arrival in England been very active in 'promoting, countenancing, and personally executing those destructive, dishonourable, and so much detested designes of pillaging and plundering'. An accusation that he only attacked places where he expected least opposition reeked of cowardice. It lamented (rather bitterly) that the kingdom would have been better off had he been killed at Edgehill defending the royal standard with Edmund Verney.

The pamphlet goes on to describe operations at Lichfield, claiming that Rupert's men attempted to undermine the walls of the fortified 'close' with pickaxes. After a five-day bombardment that had little effect, the rock and water put an end to such designs. Next, scaling ladders were called in, but the assaults were fended off. The garrison hanged one Royalist prisoner from the walls, likening his swinging corpse to the type of 'signe' suspended above taverns and other businesses – the act certainly advertised their defiance.[7] Worse still, Rupert was called upon to shoot the man down if he wished to save him. The enraged prince sent a messenger with terms, only to be told the garrison would rather die – they even offered an extra barrel of powder so he could step up his bombardment. Between bouts of cursing,

Rupert vowed to continue operations until Michaelmas if needs be, but time was not on his side.

The Royalist town of Reading, barely 40 miles from London, was a strategic outpost that would prove beneficial to any future march on the capital. It was also key to the protection of Oxford, which was increasingly vulnerable. At the end of 1642, Rupert had warned that Reading's outer defences were not strong, being without palisades, and the ditches dry. Despite the Governor, Sir Arthur Aston's unquestionable experience and loyalty, the prince felt that a resolute enemy might prove fatal to Reading. Nevertheless, it was thought that an intercepted letter from Aston to the king, complaining of the town's poor defences, was a ruse designed to draw the enemy to attack it. When the Earl of Essex rose to the bait, he found Reading in a better state than expected. Aston was in regular touch with Rupert and from 28 February, he labelled the enemy as cowards, advising, 'I am shuer they are fearfull.' All the same, he told the prince it would be better if 'yr selfe in person bee heer' and then matters would work out better.[8] Aston would be in for a long wait.

Cracks soon appeared in Aston's confident assertions. He implored Rupert to put in a good word with the king for money to pay Reading's garrison. There also came an admission that his officers had been inflating the numbers of men in their musters, which led to a request for 1,000 soldiers, otherwise the result would be disastrous. Also, Monsieur de la Roche, Rupert's acclaimed fireworker, lacked enough grasp of English to effectively command the town's artillery. By 12 April, Aston was regretting ever soliciting command of Reading, wishing that Rupert had never granted his request and had instead 'Ajudged mee to have lost my hed'.[9]

Reading's inconvenient truths only increased the pressure upon Rupert at Lichfield. The prince sent for 200 more foot and horse, as well as ten barrels of powder. On 13 April, Prince Maurice stabilised the West Country and South Wales by winning a victory against William Waller at Ripple Field. Reading's plight led to Maurice's recall. Then, on 15 April 1643, Rupert received word from the king that the rebels had 'ataqued' Reading. Though he 'could be content' with Rupert's presence, the king avoided summoning him – but urged him to lose no more time at Lichfield than he 'must needs'. Moreover, nothing should 'retard my Wyfs' coming south.[10]

The following day a 'somewhat differing' missive ordered Rupert to leave Lichfield with what force he may.[11] It was deemed preferable that Staffordshire be lost, than Reading. These contradictions have been labelled as dithering, but as a military novice King Charles was beholden on the advice of his commanders. Whenever Rupert was not present, that advice was often inconsistent, because the councils of war lacked his strong presence, which often controlled members and drove a coherent plan. For all Rupert's brusque manner, he was focused entirely on victory; he had no estate to consider, no family or friends to protect, nor business interests to contend with that might provide undue influence.

Stepping up his progress at Lichfield, Rupert had his men drain ditches and build walkways across the mud. Lord Digby mucked in, waist deep, while Will

Legge was, for a time, captured. From Yorkshire, George Goring, who had accompanied the queen back to England, wrote on behalf of his 'sacred mistris'. Whilst understanding and esteeming Rupert, her needs were reiterated; to be conducted safely to the king 'where by all right and merit shee ought to be'.[12] Jocularly styling herself 'Her She Majesty Generalissimo', the queen was titular leader of 16,000 foot and 3,000 horsemen, which would transform the situation in the south and perhaps make possible another bid for London. Rupert was therefore responsible for the queen's safety, as well as that of Reading, and Cheshire.

Governor Aston soon made another stark admission to Rupert that the calibre of Reading's garrison was so poor he (rather prophetically) feared he would lose his head and 'Reputation both at worste'.[13] On 20 April, news broke that a chimney brick or roof tile had been dislodged during bombardments and struck Aston's head, leaving him delirious. One day later, Rupert was warned that should he not come speedily to Reading, the place would be past hope of relief. The king was preparing to go in person.

On the same day Aston was incapacitated, Rupert finally detonated his mine (the first of its kind in England) and blew a 20-foot breach in Lichfield Close. It broke the prince's chains. The following day he accepted the surrender, granted generous terms, and personally congratulated the enemy commander. By 25 April, he was at the king's side and en route to Reading. With Aston out of action, his deputy, Richard Fielding, had opened negotiations under a flag of truce. When king and prince arrived with a relief force, they attempted to fight their way through the enemy army at Caversham Bridge, expecting Fielding to sally out of the town in support. The new governor didn't budge. Rupert managed to speak to Fielding and when the latter explained that he was honour-bound to the cessation, the prince told him categorically that 'there was no treating to be admitted'.[14] Despite Rupert's promises to supply gunpowder, Fielding concluded a surrender and left the humiliated king with no option but to withdraw.

Unsurprisingly, Richard Fielding was put on trial in Oxford at the start of May. One of the terms of Reading's surrender struck at the heart of royal honour. Fielding had agreed to hand over all Parliamentarian defectors in Reading – this flew in the face of King Charles's April proclamation offering protection to such people. During the court martial, the king made a public statement that he was never privy to the clause, which saw all those who had reverted to his side handed back to the enemy to face massacre and murder. Fielding was found guilty and sentenced to death, though Rupert stepped in, understanding the difficult circumstances the man had been subjected to. Sending the 12-year-old Prince of Wales with a plea for clemency proved successful and Fielding was spared, though he would never again hold a senior command in the king's army.

At the same time, Rupert took an active part in another more personal court martial, sitting as a judge alongside the Earl of Forth and Henry Percy. At the end of April 1643, good friend Sir Richard Cave had been condemned for surrendering Hereford to William Waller. After several days of witness testimony, Cave was exonerated, and it was declared his reputation had unjustly suffered. Rupert was fiercely loyal to his friends and again appreciated the complications faced by those in command of besieged garrisons.

Throughout May and June 1643, Rupert focused on doing all he could to protect Oxford. He put a garrison in the key town of Abingdon, spending much time there, and rode to various locations to inspect and oversee. Perhaps getting out of Oxford was also good for Rupert's soul. Secretary Nicholas wrote on 11 May 1643, admitting that the king was 'much troubled' by Rupert's discontent and wished that some 'busy bodies' would desist from meddling.[15] Keeping active was a good means of distraction from intrigue.

The selling out of Parliamentarian defectors in Reading did not put off a new turncoat, this time one of high profile. Sir John Urry (or Hurry) arrived at Oxford with news that the Earl of Essex was at Thame, lacking horses, and with troops that had empty bellies and purses. A pay convoy of £21,000 in coin was heading towards them – if captured, it might prove the final nail in the coffin for his army. Unable to resist such an opportunity, Rupert left Oxford at 4.00 pm on 17 June 1643, with around 2,000 troops, accompanied by Urry, Bernard de Gomme, and Will Legge. After a few hours rest, the force reached Tetworth at 1.00 am on 18 June. At Postcombe, two hours later, they briskly took nine prisoners. By 5.00 am, they arrived at Chinnor and in an engagement that lasted over an hour, killed 50 enemy troops and took 120 prisoners.

At Chalgrove, Rupert lured the pursuing Parliamentarians into a trap. After studying the reassessment of Powick Bridge, it's clear that tactics employed there were mimicked at Chalgrove. He secured the bridge at Chiselhampton, which would be the route of his retreat. According to de Gomme, the prince then made a show of withdrawing, which lured the enemy into pursuit, at which point he turned to face their advanced units. With the Parliamentarians firing from hedgerows, and their main force drawing up in a cornfield beyond, Rupert shunned advice to fall back, fearing this would prove more dangerous. Instead, seeing that the enemy were not coherently formed, he seized his chance and attacked. In this way Rupert maintained control, lured the enemy on, and managed to negate their superior strength by a brisk attack before they had fully deployed. These were becoming his trademark tactics, consistent with Spiller's revised interpretation of Powick.

Lieutenant Colonel Dan O'Neale took the prince's regiment around the hedges. Yelling 'this insolence is not to be endured', Rupert then jumped a smaller hedge and scattered the enemy dragoons lining them.[16] After sufficient horsemen had leaped across after him, the prince led them forward to support O'Neale, who had engaged the enemy. Attacked front and flank, the Parliamentarians resisted one charge and then broke.

Reports of the devil prince's nocturnal raid, and his soaring over the hedgerow like a phantom, must have seemed to validate the fantastical stories about him. Commandeering carts for Royalist dead and wounded, and the spoils they had accumulated, he rounded up all loose horses and sent Urry ahead with news of the victories. At Oxford, the turncoat was knighted by a jubilant monarch. Rupert then arrived with his haul of 200 prisoners and eleven standards. The fact that the valuable pay convoy had escaped did not matter as Essex's army had been proved ineffective; their morale took a beating, and the earl even proffered his resignation, though it was not accepted. In London, talk of the raid was confined to 'whispers'.[17] It also transpired that John Hampden, a leading Parliamentarian, had received a 'deathly wound' at Chalgrove, having been shot in the shoulder.[18] He died on 24 June. From Bletchingdon, just 7 miles from Oxford, Rupert's troublesome deputy, Henry Wilmot, sent congratulations. 'I hope the fright of it will persuade many that tis safer and beter being at their homes then soe neere you.'[19]

The twenty-four hours of lightning strikes at which Rupert excelled were, Frank Kitson suggests, based on tactical reflection from his imprisonment at Linz. The Battle of Vlotho had come about because of Hatzfeldt's ability to move his force so rapidly, and thus surprise his opponents. Operating at speed came naturally to Rupert, who was unwilling and unable to take his ease.

Three days after Chalgrove, the Earl of Berkshire (childhood friend of King Charles and tutor to the Prince of Wales) attempted to extract a favour from Rupert and would have done so in person 'had I have beene sure to have found you at Oxford'. Instead, hearing that the prince was 'soe often abroad' (moving around locations) he submitted it in writing.[20] During the raids, Rupert had captured Lord Sheffield, grandson of the Earl of Mulgrave. Berkshire's son, Harry Howard, had been taken by the Parliamentarians and was being held at Thame and it was proposed that Sheffield might be exchanged for Howard. This was not to be. Having taken the wounded Sheffield's parole, and left a surgeon with him, Rupert was angered to find that the man had broken his word and absconded. But Harry Howard survived the war to become a playwright, and according to much later gossip, may have even been the father of Nell Gwyn – one of King Charles II's mistresses.

Queen Henrietta Maria, now in Newark, was notified that she should be confident in the safety of her supplies and could send them on to Oxford. They would nourish the Royalist cause. Whilst King Charles had been urging his wife to hasten south, he also wanted the Earl of Newcastle and his army to do so. The queen had her own thoughts, suggesting the earl might go to the assistance of Lancashire, while rebuking him over other minor matters. In fact, her presence caused such a distraction in the northern army that she pushed for a war council to debate the matter at Pontefract. It wasn't so much that she intended to be disruptive, but a mini court and alternative centre of authority had formed around her, which exacerbated internal Royalist strife.

Newcastle must have been relieved to hear that she was ready to go to the king. Defeating the Fairfaxes at Adwalton Moor on 30 June 1643, the peer next wished to deal with Hull before following her. The baton passed to Rupert. As the queen and her troops fought their way south, defeating the enemy at Burton-on-Trent, Rupert was consulted as to their best route. He became a go-between for the royal couple. The king favoured his wife travelling via Worcester, rather than Stratford-upon-Avon, explaining that 'certainly our game is so faire that it is not fit to hazard a Battayle [until] our forces wer joyned'.[21] The monarch's view did not prevail, and on 11 July, Rupert met his aunt at Stratford.

At Stratford, the queen set out expectations for her friends – men like Henry Jermyn who had loyally served her – and pushed for their preferment. So determined was she that she supposedly refused to 'Ly wth ye king' until this was agreed.[22] On 13 July, king and queen were reunited on the site of the Battle of Edgehill and a silver medal was struck to commemorate the event. By and large, her nominees were shoe-horned into roles and husband and wife could delight in one another's company once more. Marriage was a topic that had been presented to Rupert at the beginning of the year. The king had corresponded with the prince's mother and the pair put forward Marguerite de Rohan, who had been suggested eleven years earlier. The lady had duly opened communication with King Charles that January. The French, it was said, were ready to allow the marriage as being conducive to their political interests and the king knew that Marguerite was a wealthy woman. Rupert, however, was having none of it and was 'resolved to give negatively'.[23]

As the summer of 1643 blazed on, the Royalists won a spectacular victory against William Waller at Lansdown Hill on 5 July. The Royalist Western Army had courageously fought their way up the hill and savaged the Parliamentarians perched on top. Waller's forces were dislodged, but the price had been high for the Royalists; one of their most prominent leaders, Sir Bevil Grenville, was killed, and they lost many cavalrymen. Sir Ralph Hopton, a driving force behind securing Cornwall for the king was temporarily blinded and paralysed when a powder waggon exploded. The tables soon turned on the battered Royalists, now pursued to Devizes by Waller, who had been reinforced. There they holed up in the town. Prince Maurice broke out, gathered reinforcements from Oxford including Henry Wilmot, and Sir John Byron, and led them back to confront Waller at Roundway Down on 13 July. The Royalists swept the enemy from the top of this imposing Iron Age hill fort, with many Parliamentarians fleeing to their deaths over a steep chalk escarpment.

In the middle of this military service, Maurice was tasked with duty of a very different kind. Always in Rupert's shadow, he was required to take his brother 'hansomly off' and marry Marguerite. Though 'Mars be now most in voag', King Charles coaxed, Hymer may still be remembered.[24] The king declared that he had no time to argue the matter and pushed for a quick reply, warning that delay was as ill as denial. The match came to nothing. Rather, both Rupert and Maurice's eyes were set upon the fair city of Bristol.

Chapter 19

Successe in Armes

At Roundway Down, Sir Arthur Haselrig had been relentlessly chased by a Royalist trooper. Clad head to toe in cuirassier armour, the impervious Haselrig survived a multitude of close-quarter attacks with pistol and sword. The king reportedly quipped that had Haselrig been victualled within his steel shell, he might have withstood a long siege. The man eventually escaped his pursuer, but that day the Parliamentarians lost 1,200 men that had been drawn from Bristol's garrison. England's second city was wounded, and the Palatine brothers moved in for the kill.

On 18 July 1643, Rupert left Oxford and met Maurice. They observed Bristol from Clifton Church, within musket shot of one of the forts that studded the 4-mile perimeter. Rupert had brought 5,500 men from Oxford. The Marquess of Hertford, commander of the Western Army (and Maurice's superior) was content to delegate. Rupert wanted a quick victory and dismissed suggestions for a formal siege. On 24 July, a summons was sent calling for the city's surrender, but Nathaniel Fiennes, with a weakened garrison of 1,800, refused. Rupert's plan was to harass the enemy throughout the night of 25 July to keep them on edge. Maurice's force would be stationed to the south and his own to the north, then at dawn, upon an agreed signal, they would mount a joint assault that would split the defenders.

In the early hours of 26 July, the Cornish attacked. Said to be somewhat earlier than expected, Rupert hastily committed his troops in the north, but the Royalists were thrown back time after time. Over the next few hours, Bristol's outer defences were littered with dead and dying Royalists, including numerous officers. Maurice passed 'from regiment to regiment encouraging the soldiers [and] desiring officers to keep their companies by their colours'.[1] Rupert drove his men back to the attack after each repulse. While riding between detachments, his horse was shot dead and it was said that the prince continued on foot 'without even so much as mending his pace'.[2] Not many commanders could have sustained such a relentless offensive as the two brothers, who worked in tandem with complete trust and support.

Eventually, dead ground between the forts of Windmill Hill and Priors Hill on Rupert's side allowed a crucial breach to be made in the perimeter. Waving firepikes, the wild Royalists soon had defenders retreating into Bristol's inner sanctum. Fiennes then withdrew all his men from the forts and outer walls, fearing that they would be cut off. This meant that the Royalists could turn the guns of the forts on the city, which lay in a hollow and was therefore extremely vulnerable. One brigade requested permission to begin fires to compel a surrender. Having learned from Birmingham, Rupert refused outright – he wanted Bristol taken intact and kept his men on a short leash. The following day, when the garrison marched out according to the terms of surrender, some Royalists set upon them, but Fiennes reported, the princes 'did ride among the plunderers with their swords, hacking and slashing them' to restore order. Moreover, Rupert 'did excuse it to me in a very fair way, and with expressions as if he were much troubled by it'.[3]

There's no doubt that the assault of Bristol would have faltered were it not for Rupert's towering presence, but Maurice played an equally strong part and is often overlooked. The Royalists gained the city but lost 500 men, including Colonel Henry Lunsford. The price lay heavy on the king's conscience and his subsequent aversion to taking towns by storm would kill off the advantages so newly won. Bristol's capitulation made many in Westminster tremble, while the booty amounted to 6,000 firearms, eighty artillery pieces, and a welcome trove of gunpowder. There were also vessels taken in the harbour, which would form the nucleus of a Royalist fleet.

In the aftermath of 1642's stalemate, Rupert had been a prime player in dragging the Royalist cause up by the boot strings and putting it into a position to win. Victory was now closer than ever. The Earl of Newcastle once again put pen to paper on hearing of Rupert's fresh success.

> Noe Creature Is more over joyed to heer of your victories then my selfe nor doth more harteley congratulat them to you but I must tell you trewly as theye are [too] bigg for any bodye else so they Apeer to Little for you ... Longe maye you live a Terror to your Uncles Enemies & a preserver [of] his servants.[4]

Despite being at the height of his power and prestige, and exhausting himself in his uncle's cause, Rupert was increasingly subjected to friendly fire. Whilst his blunt manner amassed opponents on his own side, so too did jealousy. As successes rolled in, complacency and apathy grew, and there were those who simply didn't want an all-out military victory. Two spheres of influence – each around the king and queen – accelerated factionalism. Rupert did not enjoy court life, nor did he thrive in the cut-throat world of politics, therefore he was immediately vulnerable. Military victories bring short term personal success if they are continued. By failing to simultaneously achieve success in relationship building and politics, Rupert was unwittingly giving himself a shelf-life. The latter elements did not come easily to the introverted prince.

From the point that Rupert rode to Bristol on 18 July, throughout his activity there, and in the aftermath of success, he was sent a string of terse letters by one of the queen's inner circle. Henry Percy, newly appointed General of the Ordnance, and created Baron Percy of Alnwick, berated Rupert as if he had also been made the prince's schoolmaster. He sarcastically thanked Rupert for choosing not to acknowledge his letters, and when Rupert sent Percy a cipher to code their correspondence, the latter took it as a 'just reproach' – as he also did the two days it took for the prince to respond. Another missive hints of a falling out between Rupert and Henry Wilmot (his second-in-command) and John Culpeper (Chancellor), the king having tasked the queen with making them all friends again. On the day Rupert took Bristol, Percy acidly reminded him 'your successe in armes I hope will not make you forgett your civility to Ladyes' – in other words, to use precious time writing polite letters to the queen. Henrietta Maria had complained that she had not received anything from her nephew in the space of nine days. Despite the military preoccupations, this was a fault Percy charged the prince with repairing.[5]

A line in Percy's letter of 26 July 1643 alludes to Rupert soon having absolute power put into his hands, most likely the top job of Lord General of the king's armies, which would have meant replacing the aged Earl of Forth and Brentford. Percy actually gives good and poignant counsel; when that day should come, Rupert should comply with the king's affairs and do what might content many and displease fewest. He correctly anticipated the prince's weakness in handling the political aspects that would be vital to such a position. Edward Hyde also noted the same when, with hindsight, he concluded that the prince had an 'unpolish'd roughness of his Nature; whch render'd him less patient to hear, and consequently less skilful to judge'.[6] A 'sharpness of temper' and 'uncommunicableness in society or council (by seeming with a pish to neglect all another said, and he approved not)' was apparent also to Sir Philip Warwick.[7] But local commanders, more temperamentally aligned to the prince, flocked to serve under him and vied for his approval, and their support was Rupert's bedrock.

King Charles's message of congratulations over Bristol was delayed due to more pressing concerns. Though he acknowledged, 'I know you doe not expect complements from me,' the king recognised that 'cheefe thanks' for the victory lay with his nephew.[8] The previous evening, he had been consumed by a very delicate decision that Rupert would be in full agreement over – the recall of the Marquess of Hertford. Command of the Western Army was to be transferred to Prince Maurice. Rupert's political shortcomings, however, resulted in one last tactless wrangle with the departing marquess. Having conquered Bristol, the prince assumed governorship of it without first seeking royal permission. The king seems to have offered it to Will Legge, while the Marquess of Hertford (considering the city within his sphere of command) appointed Ralph Hopton. As the saying goes, 'too many cooks spoil the broth' and the trio served up a first-class faux pas.

The king finally settled the post on his nephew, despite mutterings of discontent over a foreigner governing England's second city, which didn't bode well for Rupert's chances of becoming Lord General. Acting swiftly, King Charles made a personal visit to Bristol and with great tact confirmed Rupert in the post, but had him appoint Hopton as deputy – Legge, the loyal character that he was, did not object. This was one of many gaffes over governorships that would embarrass Rupert.

No sooner had harmony been restored than a council of war met in Bristol on 3 August. Some of the queen's circle were, like her, all for an immediate offensive against London, whereas others proposed taking Gloucester first. Agreement landed on the latter, but the king did not wish to incur similar losses to Bristol, and therefore refused to countenance storming the town. Instead, a formal siege was ordered. Knowing this would take critical time and resources, and risked gambling away the initiative he had just secured, Rupert refused to take command. Instead, it devolved upon the Earl of Forth. Victories increased the prince's reputation, which was the biggest safeguard against internal opponents, while defeat would have made them bolder. His reticence would protect him from any fall-out should the siege fail, but he would join the besiegers in a voluntary capacity to prove his unflinching devotion to the cause.

From the very outset, Rupert ensured his supporters channelled their energies towards Gloucester. Sir Arthur Aston was to deliver the summons. Will Legge was sent to the governor, Edward Massie, a man he had served with before the war, and who had given indications that he might turn the place over to the king. On 7 August, Aston informed Rupert that Legge's negotiations had proved fruitless. He also warned the town was just as strong as Bristol, and compared to Nathaniel Fiennes, Massie was 'a mutch better souldier'. As the Royalists pushed ahead with preparations, damming streams that drove the town's mills, Aston assumed that Rupert would not play a part in the siege, predicting 'wee shall Proseede but very sleepely without you'.[9]

On 10 August, the siege commenced. The king appeared before Gloucester in person, hoping his presence would induce capitulation, but there was no let-up in the town's resolve. It was another personal embarrassment to add to Hull and Coventry.

Reports, requests for help, warnings, and intelligence from the many Royalist garrisons in various parts of the country continued to flow to Rupert at Gloucester. Lancashire was in a dire situation. In Lichfield, due to lack of weapons, the garrison resorted to cudgels. Even in Bristol, where Hopton was repairing the defences, powder was 'an irreparable want att present'. The prince's own regiment, though strong at 300 men, had arms for only ninety-three. Money was no better. Lord Herbert, heir to the wealthy Marquess of Worcester, had promised a whopping £20,000 but supplied only £400 because 'monyes fayle him'.[10] Though the Royalists currently held the upper hand in the war, it was clear to Rupert just how fragile that lead was.

Time was rapidly running out before Gloucester's walls. Its fate galvanised the Parliamentarians into action; if it fell, the loss of revenue, territory, and prestige would be crushing. News that the Earl of Essex was preparing a relief force stirred Rupert. As soon as he heard this, the prince must have rued the town not being stormed, and counselled the king about the risks posed by Essex's relieving force. Defeat of Essex would, like Edgehill, open the road to London – the main prize. A letter from Henrietta Maria, in Oxford, shows that Rupert also lobbied his aunt on the matter. She attempted to reassure him (incorrectly) that Essex was only holding a muster at Hounslow Heath and was not on the march but promised to keep Rupert up to date with developments, adding that the Royalists should have time to take Gloucester.

Meanwhile, at an Elizabethan manor called Matson House, princes Charles and James whiled away the boring days in an attic room, carving notches into a stone window ledge. From the siegeworks, progress was equally laborious. Bad weather hampered mining, and to keep up morale Rupert and other commanders engaged in what would be described nowadays as 'back to the floor' – mucking in with the troops. Spending time working in the trenches, he was hit on the head by a stone and narrowly missed by a grenade. He drafted miners from Lichfield to help make all speed with the siegeworks. As Essex drew closer, Rupert and Henry Wilmot attempted, unsuccessfully, to skirmish with his army on 2 and 4 September, in a bid to delay them. The following day, Essex fired four artillery pieces as a signal to beleaguered Gloucester. From the town smoke spiralled skywards, though this was the retreating Royalists destroying their camp and lifting the siege.

The pipe-loving, plodding Essex had displayed a renewed sense of purpose that saw him save Gloucester. After resting his men for two days, on 10 September he set out for the perilous return journey to London. Making a feint northeast towards Royalist Worcester, Essex then turned about and escaped the king's army. With a head start, the Parliamentarians made all haste for the capital, with Rupert hot on their heels. At one point, the king is reputed to have alighted from his coach and sat down on a milestone, whereupon his 9-year-old son, James, asked when they might go home. 'We have no home' was the despondent reply.[11]

If Rupert was downhearted, he didn't show it – there was no time to be forlorn. By 16 September, he had the cavalry assembled on Broadway Down, having caught up with Essex. An attack might just bring him to battle. Waiting for royal permission to engage, evening soon drew in, and the infuriated prince charged off with a page and a gentleman to seek out the king. Voices drew them to one farmhouse and upon looking through the window into the candlelit room, Rupert saw a card game taking place. King Charles was versing Lord Percy at pickett with Lord Forth watching. The prince stormed inside, declaring his desire to attack the enemy and calling for the army to be marshalled and sent after him. Forth and Percy objected. This opposition was brushed aside, with Rupert 'insisting' upon his plan and duly securing 1,000 musketeers to support it.[12] The Royalists marched that same night, and all through the following day, until at 1.00 am on 18 September, word arrived from the Duke of Richmond. The king was 'loath to wearie' his infantry any further, but the prince's relentless drive had clawed back a second chance.[13]

With approximately 5,000 horsemen, he swept down upon Essex's 13,000-strong army at Aldbourne Chase and inflicted considerable casualties. Most importantly, delaying Essex meant that the Royalist army reached Newbury first, and therefore blocked the road to London. While tired Parliamentarians spent a night in the open elements, the Royalists quartered in and around the town. Mother Nature's necklace of natural defences were draped around Newbury – hills, lanes, hedges, and a river – but as dawn broke on 20 September, they lay unclaimed by the Royalists. That the king's army failed to occupy the high ground was a criminal act of negligence that would cost dearly. Seizing the opportunity, Essex's army quickly deployed upon Round Hill, giving their artillery a bird's-eye view of the town and the flat expanse of Wash Common. Immediately, the tables were turned, and the Royalists found themselves in a battle for ground that should have been theirs.

Fighting through terrain criss-crossed by hedgerows, from whence Parliamentarian musketeers loosed a deadly hail of lead shot, the Royalists aimed for Round Hill. Their infantry onslaughts faltered until the most they could do was pitifully cry out for cavalry support. Sir John Byron's horse was killed under him, while some soldiers scrabbled at the base of one hedge, attempting to hack a gap in it so that their desperate offensive might continue. Viscount Falkland was a peace-loving intellectual and one of the king's two secretaries of state. A volunteer in the army, engaged in a war he was weary of, he suddenly spurred his horse towards the small chink in the hedge and attempted to jump it. This lone rider was peppered with shot and brought down.

While Falkland's blood soaked the field, from Oxford the other Secretary, Edward Nicholas, dried the ink on a letter he had just written. Nicholas noted that Sir William Waller had lamented 'God doth not fight' for Parliament's cause.[14] On the battlefield of Newbury, it looked like the Almighty had since turned coat. Falkland's courageous end spurred the Royalists on, but the Parliamentarians and their defences were too formidable an obstacle, and on the Royalist left wing, Prince Rupert was also struggling. He 'commonly bore the first and most dangerous brunts' and led his cavalry across Wash Common three times before dispersing Sir Philip Stapleton's horsemen.[15] This time the prince's men did not lose themselves to pursuit, and instead turned to attack the flank of Essex's infantry, but it was not enough. At one point Rupert was on foot and in discussion with officers when Stapleton rode up to the group and shot his pistol at the prince. Miraculously, Rupert was unharmed.

With neither side able to break the other, and the death toll at around 1,000 each, both sides settled down for an uneasy night. Tactically, the Royalists had continued to obstruct the way to the capital. When Thomas Fuller catalogued the features and history of England's counties in 1662, he said of the Battle of Newbury that both sides had no 'stomack' to breakfast on another round of fighting the following day.[16] The Royalists certainly had precious little gunpowder left to feed their weapons. Though Rupert was all for engagement, the council prevailed, and order was passed that the army should steal away.

When the Royalists had abandoned Gloucester's siege, the young Earl of Sunderland had remarked that the failure had 'hindered us from making an end of the war this year'.[17] The king's decision not to storm Gloucester, for fear of high casualties, meant yet again his lack of ruthlessness eroded the hard-won military initiative. The window of opportunity, created by one year of fierce fighting, had slipped away within the one-month siege. At Newbury, Sunderland was killed by a cannon shot. Another peer, the Earl of Carnarvon, was run through the gut with a blade. After Viscount Falkland's stripped body was recovered, the vacant post of Secretary of State was later conferred upon none other than George Digby. The effect of this was a mortal wound to Rupert and the Royalist cause.

Days after Newbury, Queen Henrietta Maria attempted to keep up appearances by lauding the battle as a victory, proudly asserting to the Earl of Newcastle that the army she had led out of the north had contributed. Many Parliamentarian women, she wrote, had come to the battlefield to find their lost husbands. This communication did nothing to encourage the northern commander to bring his army south to join the king, which was still desired. Instead, the Earl of Newcastle penned his own letter; another congratulatory message to Rupert. 'God give you Joye of your late great victory, which I am confident the Rebells will never recover so that uppon the platter one may Salute the Kinge Agen, & only by your Hande Sr.'

As much as the queen tried to deflect the truth about Newbury, Newcastle was staring cold facts in the face. He warned Rupert that his army was 'dayley Threatned' by news and rumours about the 'Scotts their Coumeing In' – entry into the war as Parliament's allies. The fact was Newcastle had never wanted his army amalgamated with the king's, but most especially with the Scots at his back door. He continued 'not In dispayre' before Hull, but lost valuable time there in what looked increasingly like a futile re-run of Gloucester.[18] He kept his force in the north, and as a result preserved his own position and standing, as well as his lands and houses – for now.

During the siege of Gloucester in late August, the Scottish Earl of Montrose had turned up to consult the king. He had brought word that his countrymen were, indeed, in talks with Parliament. For all the man's eloquence, the king and queen had shunned him, preferring to believe the Duke of Hamilton's vow that he would keep Scotland neutral – the question was, for how long? Hamilton, the king's cousin, had earned a dukedom for that promise, which was made on his life. Around the same time as Montrose arrived, so too did a posse of peers, who had fled Westminster. The earls of Northumberland, Holland, Bedford, Portland, and Clare had wished to transfer their allegiance to the king. The queen had led hard-line hostility to show that siding against the monarch brought consequences, but the practical Rupert had chosen to welcome them in the hope their example might encourage others to follow suit. For marching the men into the royal presence, the prince had earned a rebuke, but he was undoubtedly correct to have done so. The cold-shouldered peers had little choice but to return cap-in-hand to Westminster within six months. Montrose and Rupert were kindred spirits. While trying to shake the king and queen from their delusions, the pair struck up a respectful friendship.

Throughout the strains and stresses of fighting for his uncle, of stomaching the personal propaganda, and enduring great sacrifices, Rupert's biggest supporter was his brother. Without Maurice's unswerving loyalty and trust, it would have been so much harder to shoulder the burden. Maurice had taken Exeter and Dartmouth, and by October 1643 was besieging the key town of Plymouth, where he was taken ill. The weather was foul. Dr William Harvey, the king's physician, was sent to Maurice's sickbed and kept Rupert closely informed. On 17 October 1643, Harvey diagnosed Maurice's illness as the 'ordinary raging disease' of the army – a 'slowe feaver with great dejection of strength'. His sleep had been very unquiet, but that morning the prince had at least recognised Harvey, who recounted the king's great concern over his health. Maurice showed a 'humble thankefull face' and acknowledged that he was weak but was very glad to hear of Rupert. 'Cordyall Antidotes' were prescribed, and he was moved to Dartmouth.[19]

Royal physician Sir Theodore Turquet de Mayerne had once expressed concern that Rupert's father had not believed in his doctor. Mistrusting professionals, Mayerne accepted, was what 'most princes do'.[20] Rupert was no exception, and he sent Richard Crane to ensure Maurice received every care and that the doctors did not embellish the truth in their reports. As Maurice's incapacity continued into November 1643, Harvey became comfortable enough to leave the patient, though he was 'not strong'. In London, reports circulated of his death, while in Holland, Maurice's mother was so concerned that she did not attend the Princess of Orange's birthday celebrations. On 4 November, Crane reported Maurice's desire to get back to the siegeworks at Plymouth, though 'uppon tryall he finds himself too weake for the journey'.[21]

Two days after Crane's letter, Rupert led an attack on Newport Pagnell. Duty prevailed, despite his personal worries. The necessity behind this action came after the Royalist garrison had been withdrawn from the town on the night of 26 October 1643, though the order to do so had been a mistake. The king's opinion had been misunderstood by an official and miscommunicated as a result. Rupert's wrath at such incompetence led the king to promise that he would in future be more careful about those employed to convey his commands. When Rupert attempted to rectify the situation and regain the place on 6 November, his men fought their way into the town but were beaten back out again. Newport Pagnell would have interfered with the supply of food to London, therefore its loss was a major setback.

As Maurice fought off his disease, it was the Royalist cause that faced a sickly decline. With the Scots massing near the border, the king finally accepted that an urgent remedy was required. To administer it, there was no better choice than Rupert.

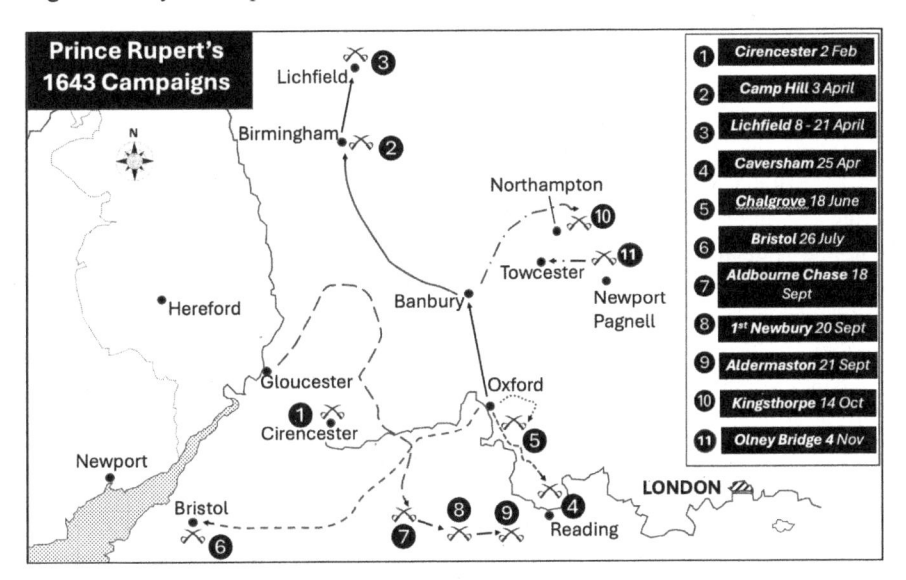

Prince Rupert's 1643 Campaigns

1. Cirencester 2 Feb
2. Camp Hill 3 April
3. Lichfield 8 - 21 April
4. Caversham 25 Apr
5. Chalgrove 18 June
6. Bristol 26 July
7. Aldbourne Chase 18 Sept
8. 1st Newbury 20 Sept
9. Aldermaston 21 Sept
10. Kingsthorpe 14 Oct
11. Olney Bridge 4 Nov

Chapter 20

Hannibal

Fire had torn through Oxford in October 1643. Many brewhouses, bakehouses, and malthouses had gone up in the inferno, leaving skeletal frames of charred timber across the town. Gossip and intrigue heated up the headquarters the month after.

In Rupert's absence, his friends rallied to his defence. On 9 November, the Duke of Richmond stepped in over scurrilous rumours, the source of which was Lord Digby, who had made some 'wrong judgements' about the prince. Rupert suffered much 'vexation' by it all – an understatement if ever there was one.[1] But Richmond cleared matters with the king and queen, assuring Rupert there was 'no scruple' about his business.[2] Whatever the precise details, Digby protested that he had merely passed on intelligence reports. Arthur Trevor also revealed that the army was much divided and the prince 'at true distance with many of the officers of horse'.[3] By 13 November, the king was soothing Rupert's frustrations and reassuring him that when his work at Newport Pagnell was done, 'you shall be welcome hither'.[4] He certainly had need of his nephew.

Having fled Scotland, the untrustworthy Duke of Hamilton had raced to the king and confirmed the Scots were mobilising, despite his promise to keep them out of the war. King Charles called on Rupert to step in. Reassuring him that rumours 'my Wyfe and I ar treating for a Peace' were nothing but a 'damnable' lie, he consulted his nephew over how best to protect the north.[5] But first, Rupert set about protecting himself.

Tired of the backbiting, the prince marshalled his allies. To Sir Arthur Aston, he wrote a warning that the man's enemies were circling at court. It speaks volumes that Aston, a staunch supporter of Rupert, became Governor of Oxford before the year was out – the prince was securing key posts for his friends. When another, Sir John Byron, desired 'first to be made' governor to the Prince of Wales, it met with less success, but he did receive a barony.[6] Rupert received his own titles in the New Year of 1644, created Duke of Cumberland and Earl of Holderness. Increased levels of intrigue accentuated the prince's suspicion and bloody-mindedness. George Porter, son of Endymion Porter of the king's bedchamber, fell foul of Rupert's blackening mood. That December of 1643, George bitterly complained about the prince's frown, which was 'cast upon mee at my comming away'. This frosty parting left George with a great affliction and a will to regain the favour he 'soe undeservedly lost'.[7] His journey north was to take up a post in the Marquess of Newcastle's army (the peer having recently been raised to that dignity) a move that would see him eventually reunited with the prince to fight the biggest battle of the civil war.

George Porter had barely arrived in the north when an extraordinary snowfall blanketed the kingdom for eight days in January 1644. A Scottish army had just crossed into England. The borders of Scotland and England had been subject to lawlessness for as long as anyone could remember – livestock was regularly stolen, and houses burned by feuding families. Some of them now fired their own homes so the Scots should 'not find any comfort'.[8] Similar destruction across the north was ordered by the Marquess of Newcastle for the same reason. Having kept up regular correspondence with Rupert since Powick Bridge, he wrote again on 10 December 1643. 'Noe man breathing Ever had more obligations to any then I have to your Highnes, & shall Ever acknowledge Itt whilst I have breath with my faythfull service to you … This Armey Is asaylde [assailed] on all sides.'

Newcastle candidly warned that he could not 'drawe a Considerable Bodye Into the fielde to hinder the Scotch their Couminge' and urged Rupert to make the king aware of these 'great truthes' before it became 'to Late to helpe Itt'. First and foremost, he called for Rupert to divert the enemy by taking Lancashire 'off my hands' – to neutralise the threat of Parliamentarians from that county.[9] The prince's trusted subordinate, John Byron, now Baron Byron of Rochdale, commanded in Cheshire and Lancashire.

Rupert became the man of the hour once again. On 31 December 1643, hearing rumours that the prince was to be made Captain General of North Wales, Cheshire, Lancashire, Worcestershire, and Salop, Byron declared of his troops 'the world hath not braver foot … nor fitter for such a Generall as yr Self'. Within two weeks, Bryon celebrated 'happy newes' that Rupert's commission had been confirmed – verbally at least.[10] Rupert was also promised the Presidency of Wales, which would help bolster his authority, but until matters were signed and sealed the prince could not rest assured.

While Bryon rejoiced, the Marquess of Ormonde, the king's Lord-Lieutenant in Ireland, was informed that his proposed commission for commanding the very same counties had been countermanded at the eleventh hour. Rupert, he was told, 'must have it', though it was merely to accommodate the prince and no slight upon Ormonde.[11] Unsurprisingly, Digby was involved in this duplicity. He sent to Ormonde, claiming (falsely) that he knew nothing of Rupert's appointment until after it was confirmed, adding very tellingly, 'I beinge not then soe happye as to have any part in his highnesses counsels [or confidence].'[12]

Rupert was keeping Digby at arm's length. But four weeks later, on 14 February 1644, the Presidency remained at a standstill, due to doubts that Digby was making over formalities. The Rupert–Digby split deepened considerably, evidenced by a letter in which the latter attempts to assure the prince of his 'faithfullnesse' and claiming no man living would execute Rupert's commands with more affection.[13] As the two squabbled, the Scots reached the town of Newcastle on 3 February, and laid siege to it.

The Marquess of Newcastle made a (rather obvious) forecast to Rupert that the north would be the 'Seate off the warr'.[14] His own army was 'nott halfe' that of the Scots and could not be expected to survive long against such odds.[15] Rupert was in no place to assist – indeed, he barely had time to write – and the most he could do was despatch Sir Charles Lucas and some cavalry to the marquess. On 18 February 1644, the prince stated his intention of moving to Shrewsbury, reassuring the northern commander that it was 'a step neerer'.[16]

Without the Presidency of Wales confirmed, Rupert's attempts to gather supplies for his northern venture was a battle in itself. Though one correspondent assured the prince that his uncle was his biggest advocate, there were 'such uncertaintyes' at court that even this was not always enough to help.[17] A quarrel between the meddlesome Lord Percy and Monsieur de la Roche, Rupert's 'fireworker', meant that explosives the prince requested did not materialise. As General of the Ordnance, Percy also controlled gunpowder, but Rupert's governorship of Bristol and its city stores offered him some independence. In early 1644, however, Percy dipped into that stash and Rupert perceived this to be to the prejudice of his northern preparations. A dispute arose. Percy exclaimed that he did not realise he had lost so much of the prince's favour. Recalling how the Royalists had been forced to disengage from Newbury due to lack of powder, Rupert directed his complaints to Percy's patron, the queen, warning that he only had twelve barrels and would be ruined without more.

Struggling to cope with these stresses and strains, Rupert became petty and vindictive. He clung on to newly pressed soldiers in a bartering manner, preventing them from joining the king, which prompted a forthright royal letter. The way Rupert 'retarded their cuming' caused serious problems his uncle stated – after all, the king's infantry were 'much wasted' and garrisons 'very weake'. Worse still, Rupert was not setting a good example, and this might 'much discuradge my service in the lyke kynde from the Western parts'. That said, the monarch recognised the crux of the issue and ended with a resolution to assist the prince with gunpowder, promising to punish the 'ill faylors [failers]'.[18]

An unlikely ally in the queen's household was Henry Jermyn, who also interceded on Rupert's behalf. Jermyn went on to become a key intermediary between the prince on the one hand, and the king, queen, Digby, and Percy on the other. Rupert sent Jermyn a list of his grievances and eventually, on 15 March 1644, the king gave a full answer to each one. He emphasised that he would take as much care of Rupert as 'anie of my children' and that he would not trust him 'by halfes'.[19] Accordingly, Rupert received the munitions, along with a promise he would be repaid £400 lent to the queen, and that he could replace the Governor of Shrewsbury (which would be his headquarters) with a man of his choosing.

The first quarter of 1644 had hit Rupert's morale hard. Internal politics had temporarily stalled the Royalist machinery and brought the prince to a crisis point. That he had to face so much just to marshal his own side must have at times made him wonder why he was putting himself through the immense toil and strain. Piecing these personal details together in such a way very much gives a fuller understanding of how Rupert started the year and the seeds of disaster that were planted at this time. Their harvest was yet to come.

Impetus for addressing the bad blood was helped by another crisis: the siege of Newark, a key link in communication with the north. A force of 8,000 Parliamentarians had arrived before the town and Newark was 'not wele provided of necessares' so could not hold out above fifteen days. Rupert was nominated to save the town and the king was crystal clear; he could not do the monarch a greater pleasure than relieving a place of 'soe neere consequence'.[20]

Galvanised into action, Rupert sent Will Legge 'speeding away' to beg, steal, and borrow troops from various garrisons.[21] He also gathered up English soldiers sent back from Ireland, who, despite being Royalist reinforcements, were often passed around like an inconvenience. Lord Byron had sent 1,700 to Shrewsbury (commanded by Colonels Tillier and Broughton) because he could not make provision for them. From there, the issue was summed up as a lack of money, clothes, shoes, weapons, food, and wages. But they found a ready home in Rupert's crack force.

Moving swiftly from Chester, via Wolverhampton, Lichfield, and Ashby de la Zouch, within seven days Rupert was just 8 miles from Newark. The unwitting Parliamentarians had only heard rumours – the prince had moved cross-country and having started with only a small band of men, this had not raised alarm bells. According to 'His Highnesse Prince Ruperts Raising of the Siege at Newarke', the prince's force marched the last leg by moonlight to maintain cover. As they made ready to move against Newark, the prince told Legge about a dream that he had beaten the enemy. He'd even commanded none other than Lord Percy to pray for his success. These two facts suggest that Rupert had a degree of concern and vulnerability about the task before him, which cannot have been helped by the cloak-and-dagger politics of past months.

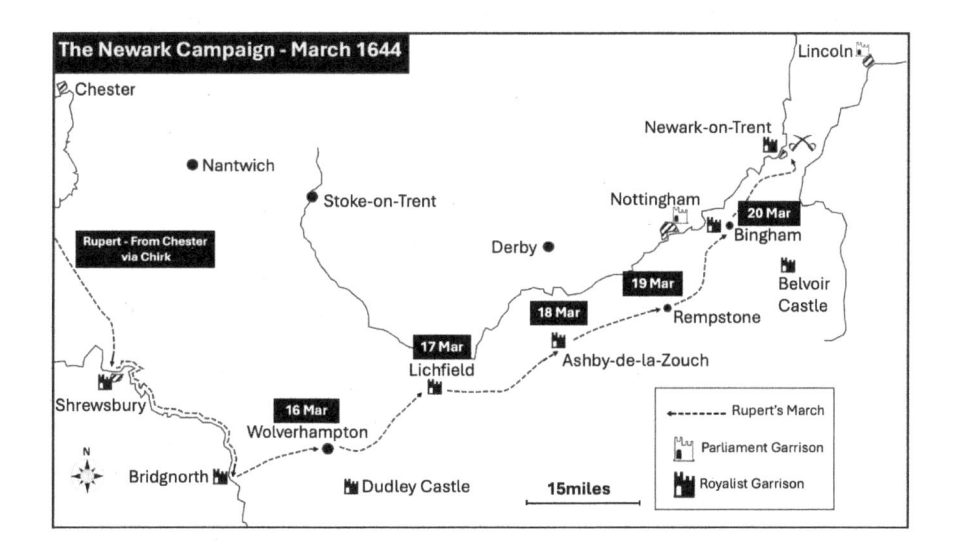

Just before dawn, the 6,000 Royalists arrived to see 5,000 besiegers, commanded by Sir John Meldrum, appearing to withdraw. At 9.00 am, Rupert, as was his wont, decided upon immediate attack while the enemy remained unorganised. Leading his cavalrymen downhill with the battle cry 'king and queen' he smashed most enemy horsemen, but those who fought on became a threat to the prince's safety. While the Royalist main body hurried up in support, Rupert remained in the thick of it. Three 'sturdy Souldiers' came at him; he killed one with his blade, another was 'pistolled' by his French gentleman, Mortaigne, while the third had his hand almost dismembered after attempting to grab Rupert's collar.[22] Meldrum retreated onto an island, but when 500 Royalists managed to get onto the western side of it, and those from Newark sallied out of the town, Meldrum's position became untenable. Although the Parliamentarians were allowed to march away, 4,000 muskets, fifty barrels of powder, and thirteen pieces of ordinance came to Rupert's hands – defeating the enemy proved a much easier way of gaining supplies than fighting with Royalist officials!

Success was Rupert's lifeblood. It sustained him, enhanced his power and prestige, and made him an inseparable part of victory. For this reason, despite his curt manner, bloody-mindedness, and the resulting personality clashes, most of his detractors grudgingly acknowledged his skills and driving force. Newark gloriously reaffirmed this. Often cited as his most spectacular success, the prince's enemies lined up in praise. Lord Percy extolled Rupert's 'great glorie' while Digby declared that fortune was now his servant to a degree beyond imagination.[23] In Bridgnorth, Lewis Kirke described rejoicing that continued all night, while Arthur Trevor added that courtiers, scholars and 'people of all Ages, all Sexes, all Facultyes Bells and Bonefyres' were grateful.[24] To Sir Philip Warwick, Rupert was the life of the Royalist armies. Although King Charles was a little too enthusiastic in judging Newark the 'saving of all the North', its relief gave a transfusion of hope. Likening his nephew to Hannibal, the king asserted that Rupert did 'imitat him in getting of Victories'.[25]

Chapter 21

Den of Dragons

The force that Rupert welded together at Newark was only a brief apparition. It coalesced, haunted the Parliamentarians, but then had to disappear. Time was of the essence. The troops were returned to their various garrisons and Rupert made for Shrewsbury to plan his next move.

The Marquess of Newcastle's latest letter balanced praise over Newark with stark truths. The Scots were 'as bigg agen' as he was in foot.[1] If Rupert did not come soon, then the king's 'great game' was over.[2] The marquess had already laid out his situation in detail to King Charles; with Northumberland lost and a sudden thaw melting snow, his withdrawing troops had struggled through floodwater. Though the Scots laid siege to Newcastle, their main force simply bypassed the town and continued south. Scottish numbers were estimated at 14,000 foot and 2,000 horse. Sir Thomas Fairfax, after a victory at Nantwich, in Cheshire, was now able to threaten West Yorkshire, while his father, Lord Ferdinando Fairfax, could strike from Hull. Newcastle sought orders – should he remain on the defensive in the hope of relief, or attack and risk all?

Another peer pressured Rupert to move. The Earl of Derby had a personal motive for urging a route north by way of Lancashire, claiming that it would strike 'a terror to that wicked partie' and give life to the half-dead Royalists there. It would also alleviate pressure on Derby's wife, defending his besieged family seat of Lathom House. Derby's earnestness stemmed from concern 'for her that is soe deere to me'.[3]

The fate of Lathom became an incendiary issue in the Rupert–Digby war. Henry Jermyn had been interceding between them and had kept a particular 'watche' on Digby. Giving Rupert full assurances that Digby had not 'fayled' in supporting the prince of late, Jermyn encouraged Rupert to use Digby's services for the greater good of the king's affairs. This was the prince's duty, he argued. Yet, despite Digby writing often, Rupert had not sent back 'one answer'.[4] Unfortunately, the prince could not bring himself to entertain his rival, and this made him appear unjust and arrogant. On 13 April 1644, Arthur Trevor commented on a letter Digby had sent Rupert regarding the relief of Lathom. It was so 'ill received' by the prince, that Trevor, one of the many people attempting to maintain good relations between the pair, considered his work to be at an end. The prince, Trevor asserted, has 'no present kindness' towards Digby.[5]

Amidst all this, Rupert was also forced to deal with other people's vendettas as well as his own. Quarrelling between Lord Loughborough, Richard Bagot (Governor of Lichfield), and Thomas Leveson (Governor of Dudley Castle) was out of control. Rupert was charged by his uncle to bring together and reconcile the men. No doubt the king felt this appropriately timed task might enhance the prince's tact and make him reflect on his own issues with Digby.

Throughout early 1644, Parliamentarian victories ratcheted up the pressure. Sir Thomas Fairfax defeated Royalists at Selby, thus threatening York, while from the south, Sir William Waller inflicted a crushing defeat on Ralph Hopton at the Battle of Cheriton on 30 March 1644.

The Marquess of Newcastle was in despair. The queen had expressed herself glad that he had not been driven to eating rats, though this was hardly designed to help reassure him. The king, too, could offer little more. Forced to place the north second to his own worsening situation around Oxford, the monarch pointed out 'consider that wee, lyke you, cannot doe alwais what we would'.[6] If his own royal army was defeated, and the headquarters fell, then the cause was finished. Royalist high command was in meltdown.

Fearing his forces in the south were at risk, the king backtracked on the northern venture and ordered Rupert to return to HQ. Lord Digby had been avoiding passing commands on to Rupert, instead leaving the job to his 'brother secretary' Sir Edward Nicholas. At this moment Nicholas was ill. On 3 April 1644, making it clear that having to convey such an order was 'very unwelcome' to him, the reticent Digby admitted he was 'afeard' it would not be pleasing to Rupert – this exchange demonstrates the chasm between the two men. Defeat at Cheriton had caused such 'disorder' that even the 'reputation' of it risked the total ruin of the south-west, which, in turn, caused the king's fears for Oxford.[7] Thankfully, next day there was a U-turn. Digby wrote again with relief that Rupert should 'stay in those parts [Shrewsbury] till further directions'. This, he guessed, would 'bee more pleasinge unto you'.[8] Indeed it was – for two days after that, Digby thanked Rupert for 'soe civill a returne'.[9]

The Parliamentarians were as confused about where Rupert might be sent as the prince himself. Contradictory intelligence had him heading north to Yorkshire, east to the Eastern Association, and southwards. The Earl of Denbigh even aided his recruitment drive by spreading a rumour that Rupert was drawing close. But on 21 April, the prince received instructions direct from the king. Should the Earl of Manchester move to Yorkshire, then Rupert was directed to 'keepe your Boddy intyre' (entire – not to split it) and place the saving of Yorkshire above Lancashire.[10] With the military situation on a knife-edge, the king attempted to convey instructions for all possible scenarios, but only succeeded in confusing matters. His letter, he added, was to conclude and not to command. Such lack of cohesion stemmed primarily from the king's desire above all things to protect his wife. Now seven months pregnant and suffering extremely, Henrietta Maria searched for a safe haven to give birth.

One day after the above letter, 22 April, the king wrote again, but this time abandoned his prescriptive instructions. Knowing that the Marquess of Newcastle would 'not be able to withstand the Scots' without Rupert's support, the king now stated, 'I will not give you any positive Order.' Instead, he would leave decisions to his nephew, assured that he would 'doe what shall be best for my service, trusting still to your judgement'.[11] This is not a letter that I have seen quoted before in the chronology of events leading up to the battle for the north. Its existence shows just how confusing and contradictory the situation was for Rupert.

Unable to stand it any longer, Rupert went to Oxford to seek clarification and restore some semblance of order. As the Parliamentarian Committee of Both Kingdoms put it, he wanted more defined orders, to free himself from blame in the event of any ill success that might occur – there was probably much truth in that. Rupert lobbied the king and council, imploring them to go on the defensive at Oxford, and thus allow him to do battle in the north while Maurice subdued the west. Sir Edward Walker, secretary to the council of war, noted that the prince had sent many messages to this effect before coming in person to advance the proposition. The king should reinforce Oxford, Wallingford, Abingdon, Reading and Banbury, then send the remainder of his cavalry to Prince Maurice. With Oxford protected by this ring of garrisons, and the two princes inflicting pressure in the north and west, Parliament would have to split their forces, which by default lessened the threat upon Oxford. The policy was duly adopted.

After about a week in Oxford, Rupert left on 5 May 1644. Barely had he ridden out than his advice was overturned; Reading was abandoned. So too was Abingdon, and according to the king's Secretary-at-War, Sir Edward Walker, it was done on the orders of Henry Wilmot without the monarch's knowledge. As Rupert moved north his efforts had once again been undone, and the reversal of policy triggered an explosive letter to the king from Whitchurch on 19 May. Well might Sir Lewis Dyve rue the way of things since 'the light and comfort of [Rupert's] presence was removed'.[12] The king was just as candid in his reply: 'I confess the best had been to have followed your advice.'[13]

Two further letters on 26 May confirm how deep the issue was. Digby assured Rupert that withdrawal from Abingdon was done after mature deliberation – clearly supporting it – and warns against listening to 'rumors and reports' that 'flye'.[14] The king, like a double act on the same day, expressed hope that matters did not 'disharten' Rupert too much or turn him from his northern expedition. He appreciated the 'freedom' (or outrage!) expressed in the prince's letter from Whitchurch and resolved that Rupert would never have cause to 'repent' any expressions of 'kyndeness' shown towards his uncle. This is evidence of a very intimate breach. The relationship between uncle and nephew had never been more strained. Rupert felt a lack of faith on the king's part. The letter ended with a 'fancy of my owen' when the king suggested making Maurice General of the Horse in Rupert's absence.[15] This was a means of repairing trust; that Maurice might fight Rupert's corner and keep the commanders in check. The fact that the king seemed powerless to control his courtiers understandably made Rupert extremely vulnerable. This eroded his confidence and burned him out just at the point when he needed all his strength to save the north.

June saw the Scots besiege York, the jewel in the king's crown. From before the city, the Earl of Eglinton described the plan to 'hounger [hunger] them out'. The forces of Lord Fairfax and his son Sir Thomas joined the Scots, and the Earl of Manchester was ordered to prevent any relief force from approaching.[16] Nothing, however, could stop Rupert. On 27 May 1644, he relieved Lathom House, where Charlotte, Countess of Derby – a cousin of Rupert's through his father – had been holding out with a small garrison. The brave countess had conducted so determined a defence that when the Parliamentarians brought up a mortar, her small band sallied out, captured it, and dragged it inside Lathom. Now the besiegers fled at Rupert's approach. Lady Derby showered her guests with gifts; Rupert received a ring worth £20 and was presented with the prized mortar, which he would take to York. Will Legge got four candlesticks. In return, Rupert presented her with twenty-two enemy standards, which the countess promptly displayed as trophies.

The following day, 28 May, Rupert stormed Bolton. It was defended by 2,000 Parliamentarians and 1,500 Clubmen, civilians who grouped together to protect their locality. With time of the essence, Rupert crushed opposition, especially after one of his captured men was labelled an Irish Catholic and hanged. Bolton would become a byword for brutality. With claims of indiscriminate massacre, it's difficult to say how many civilian deaths occurred, and whether they were in cold blood, or simply caught up in the encounter. Parliament's commander, Colonel Rigby, claimed that he lost less than 200 men and that most had fled, though he was almost certainly playing down his failure.

The truth is further marred by exaggerated compensation claims, which still rolled in nine years afterwards, and which played on Rupert's blackened reputation to strengthen their case. Most list plundering of goods, or the death of soldiers in defence of the town, which left their families destitute, a sadly inevitable outcome that manifested across the kingdom, rather than civilian massacre. One petitioner in 1653 complains that others from outlying villages had suffered less but received greater relief. 'An exact relation of the bloody and barbarous massacre at Bolton', supposedly written by an eyewitness, gives a combined death toll of 1,200–1,500 for both sides. Despite such numbers, it only specifically names three women and two men as being either robbed or badly treated, and a further three killed in cold blood. The assertion that only a few surviving women and children were left in Bolton is absurd. Parish registers list approximately seventy-five dead, while the active engagement of civilian Clubmen in the military defence is a big problem that blurs lines. The most we can be sure of is that Royalists trounced the garrison, and many were killed in action, while others were slaughtered in the pillage that followed – civilian deaths (those not playing any part in the defence) have been grossly over-inflated and most likely numbered between seventy-five and one hundred and fifty.

Next on Rupert's list was Liverpool. A tough nut to crack, it fended off multiple assaults. In the end, being vastly outnumbered, the garrison evacuated by boat on 11 June. It was said the capture of the town had cost 100 barrels of powder and the lives of many Royalists, but it did give the king a key port through which to receive reinforcements from Ireland. Seven captured ships were also pressed into royal service. Though he prevented his soldiers from plundering the town, Rupert was powerless to stop a 'great number of Ratts' from doing so. An extraordinary sight, they left vessels at low tide, marched in troops to the town and took provisions, before returning.[17]

The prince requested the Bishop of Chester to arrange collections in his diocese for the benefit of Royalist wounded. The Parliamentarians would eventually grant £28 to over fifty 'poore widdowes' of Liverpool – their husbands and/or sons having been killed in the fighting. Ellen Banke claimed she was shot and wounded, while Elizabeth Robinson was 'sore wounded and brusd', but neither received any payout.[18]

These successes were spectacular, but they took much time – something both the king, and York, were preciously short of. According to Arthur Trevor, while Rupert gave his all, his enemies in Oxford whispered that it was 'indifferent whether the Parliament or Prince Rupert doth prevaile', one being as bad as the other. Digby, Culpepper, Wilmot, and Percy were reputedly behind this. When Rupert found out, his outrage contributed to a week's delay in which he offered up his commission to the king and resolved to leave for France. It's remarkable that at this critical time he faced such opposition, but equally concerning was the fact that that it affected him enough to proffer his resignation. It is a vitally important indicator of his state of mind just prior to the biggest civil war battle.

In the end, time and a 'Lady' cooled his blood, according to Trevor.[19] In the last years of the war, the Duchess of Richmond often intervened to soothe the prince's anger, so she is most likely the glue that kept him bonded to his uncle's cause at this moment. Re-examination of sources for this book identified a poignant mismatch. Morrah, in quoting Trevor's letter, substituted 'Lady' for 'frend' and this has been followed since. The one-word change gives quite a different slant. Though the lady helped pacify him, Rupert still wrote to the king and demanded the four men's removal – a naive act that pitted the prince against his foes and made his fall essential to their survival. Sir George Radcliffe certainly thought fear of Rupert's greatness 'may do harm' to the prince.[20]

While Rupert paused in Lancashire, the king was playing a game of cat and mouse in a bid to spin out time. The aim, he had explained to Rupert on 7 June, was to defend himself 'until you may have time to beat the Scots, but if you be too long in doing it, I apprehend some great inconvenience'.[21] Oxford's vulnerability was a direct result of the U-turn over Rupert's advice to garrison a ring of towns as protection from enemy field armies. With the Earl of Essex and William Waller having joined forces, the king had left Oxford and marched west, drawing them away from the headquarters. Soon enough, Essex irresponsibly gave up the chase and marched off to the south-west, deciding instead to relieve the town of Lyme. His bemused subordinate, Waller, had been left to shadow the royal troops.

The Road to Marston Moor - 1644

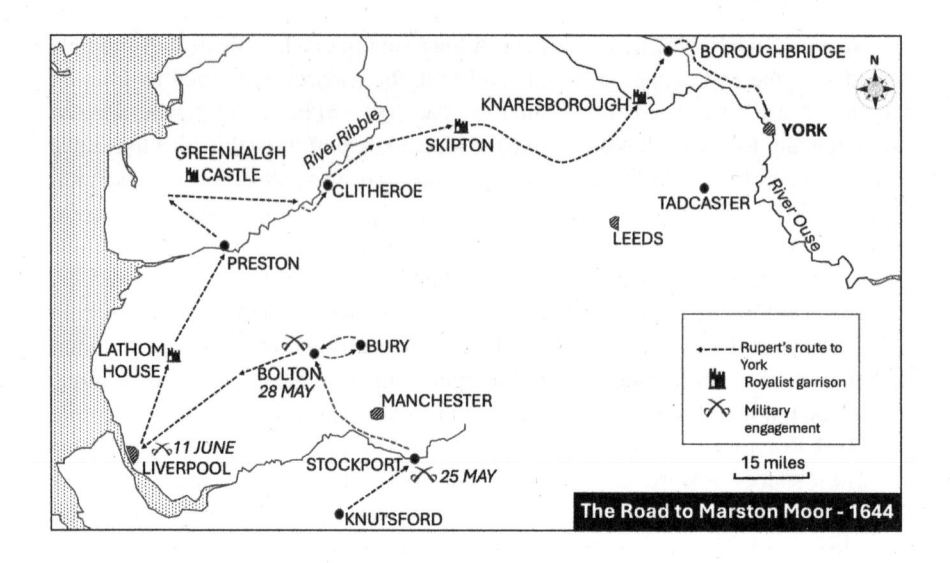

The king was in a desperate quandary. Essex marching into the southwest alleviated his own situation but threatened the pregnant queen in Exeter. Greatly concerned, he wrote to Rupert on 14 June, declaring that his nephew's successes were 'no more welcome to me, that you ar the meanes'.

> If Yorke be lost, I shall esteeme my Crowne litle lesse, unlesse supported by your suddaine Marche to me, & a Miraculous Conquest in the South ... but if Yorke be relived, & you beate the Rebelles Armies of bothe Kingdomes wch ar before it, then [inserted handwriting: 'but otherwais not'] I may possiblie make a shift (upon the defensive) to spinn out tyme, untill you can come to assist mee.

The order was fairly clear so far; relieve York by defeating the armies before it. The next part told Rupert that if he discovered the city was already freed from its besiegers he should 'imediatly March with [his] whole strength, directly to Woster to assist me & my Army, without wch, or your having relived Yorke by beating the Scots, all the successes you can afterwards have most infallibly, will be uselesse unto mee'.[22] Once again, trying to provide instruction for all scenarios made this a dubious tangle of words – but the premise at its heart was to fight the rebels and relieve York, or if the city should *free itself* (presumably without Rupert's intervention) then return south and join the king.

In 2005, Malcolm Wanklyn and Frank Jones quoted an undated note from the king, which they think was written on 15 June 1644, the day after the aforementioned letter, but despatched with it. The note is described as having previously been 'totally ignored' by historians. In it, the king reaffirms that York's relief is 'most absolutely best for my affairs' and asks his nephew to speedily prosecute it. If this was no longer possible to achieve, he should march south to the king immediately. Whichever goal was adopted, it must be carried out without 'engaging yourself in any other action' – in other words, put an immediate end to the conquest of Lancashire and relieve York, or come south.[23]

On receipt of these writings, Rupert made for York with an intention to battle the enemy – that is perfectly understandable based on what was written. He had a definite order to fight and relieve York as long as it was besieged. To the outside world, however, matters seemed on a knife-edge. On account of the king's plight and Rupert's delay in Lancashire, Sir William Davenant warned that such uncertainty would doubtless hit York's morale hard.

Outside the northern capital, the besiegers proudly got their best battering piece ready; a 64-pound cannon. The noose tightened daily. While Rupert marched by 'crooked and lengthy routes' to evade and confuse his opponents, Parliamentarian sappers tunnelled closer to York.[24] Mines were sprung, making a breach in the walls near St Mary's Tower, but the garrison repelled the incursion. A celebratory bonfire burned on top of York Minster. The Marquess of Newcastle had played every card during the siege; he bought time with hollow negotiations and arranged for letters to fall into enemy hands that suggested he was in dire straits – or at least worse than he was.

On 30 June 1644, King Charles's army marched along one side of the River Cherwell, in Oxfordshire, watched from the opposite bank by William Waller's troops. As the king's ranks became strung out, Waller seized his chance, very nearly securing a great victory. However, the Royalists quickly rallied, and a brisk action ensued around Cropredy Bridge that lasted until sunset. Waller came off worst, losing eleven guns. The king's position was now infinitely better.

One day later, on 1 July 1644, Rupert was at last nearing York. The triple armies subsequently withdrew from their siege lines to Marston Moor, where they expected the Royalists to engage them in battle. Rupert sent a cavalry screen along the Knaresborough road to give the impression he was heading to the moor, but sent his main force north via Boroughbridge, and thus put the River Ure between him and his enemies. Turning east, he approached the north side of York unopposed and relieved the city. A ruse might have assisted this outmanoeuvring. Newcastle had long been sending false messages, which served to hoodwink the allies, and a Scottish account from 5 July 1644 noted that they broke up the siege of York because of an intercepted letter from the king to his nephew. It warned that nothing but 'impossibilities' should prevent Rupert from defeating the Scots in battle. The wording of this much clearer instruction, to do battle at all costs, suggests it was a different letter to those of 14 and 15 June quoted earlier.[25]

The letter referred to by the Scottish source has never been mentioned in histories as a reason for the allies withdrawing to battle positions on the moor. Coupled with Rupert's cavalry feint, it certainly helped convince the prince's enemies that he did intend to do battle on 1 July, resulting in them leaving York's siegeworks – much to his benefit and their embarrassment. The letter, in my opinion, was almost certainly a clever trick akin to his ruse at Powick Bridge.

The Relief of York
1 July 1644

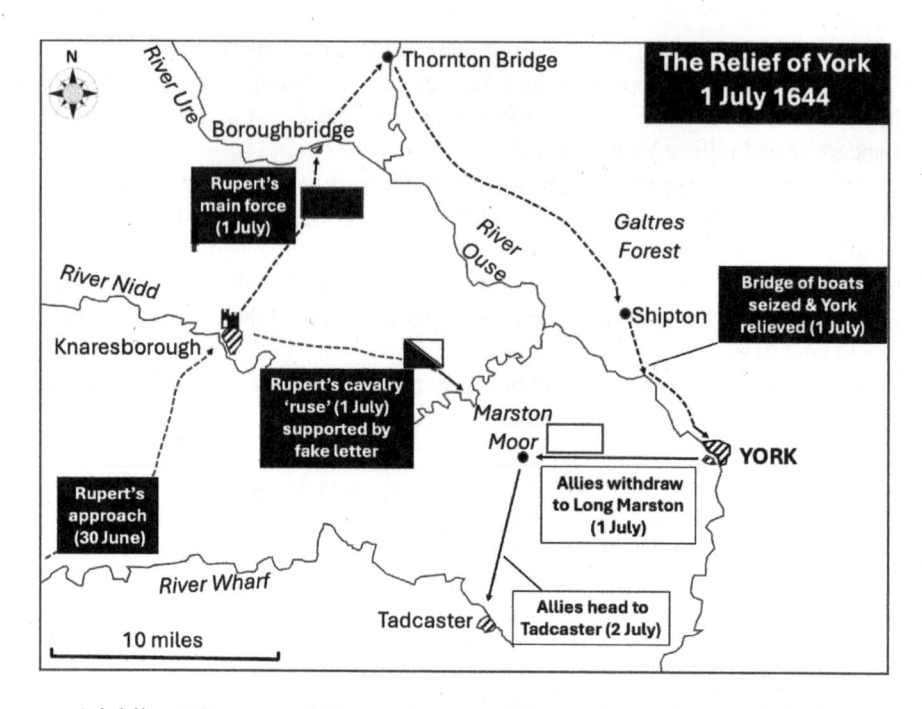

Map features:
- Thornton Bridge
- Boroughbridge
- River Ure
- Rupert's main force (1 July)
- River Ouse
- Galtres Forest
- River Nidd
- Knaresborough
- Shipton
- Bridge of boats seized & York relieved (1 July)
- Rupert's cavalry 'ruse' (1 July) supported by fake letter
- Marston Moor
- YORK
- Rupert's approach (30 June)
- Allies withdraw to Long Marston (1 July)
- River Wharf
- Tadcaster
- Allies head to Tadcaster (2 July)
- 10 miles

A jubilant Marquess of Newcastle termed Rupert the 'redemer off the North', welcome in so many ways that it was beyond his 'Arethmetick' to number.[26] Rupert did not go into York to meet the peer, instead sending George Goring on his behalf. While the allies slept that night at Marston Moor, Rupert laid his plans. The prince's last three biographers are all agreed on his intention to launch a dawn attack upon the triple army at Marston Moor, and as such, he sent instructions for the Marquess of Newcastle to get the garrison there for 4.00 am.

Much has been written about the absence of a conference between Rupert and Newcastle. It has been presented as a major failing on the prince's part, evidenced as his arrogance, and cited as key to Newcastle's subsequent opposition at Marston Moor – in short, a significant reason for the loss of the coming battle. But the proud peer was not a petty child. Newcastle had much respect for Rupert, a prince of the blood and a duke. Since Powick Bridge, he had followed the prince's every success, lauding him with congratulatory letters. Rupert, with the enemy just a few miles away, would have been foolish to leave his post and go to Newcastle, especially as he was planning an almost immediate clash. *Subsequent* disagreement between the two men stemmed from Newcastle's firm belief that a battle was unnecessary.

The Venetian ambassador later noted that the prince caused his own will for a battle to prevail on account of confidence that the enemy would flee. A 1656 book (which infuriated Rupert on publication) claimed that the prince joined his forces 'though not his opinion' with Newcastle, who disagreed over venturing all so soon.[27] The unfortunate truth is that the York garrison would have struggled to get to the rendezvous anywhere near 4.00 am. They had been under siege for nine weeks and duly made merry when it came to an end – even the best commander would have struggled to move them. In their absence, Rupert called off his dawn attack.

Following a difficult night, the triple army withdrew in dismay on 2 July and began a headlong retreat to Tadcaster. The intention was to receive significant reinforcements, whilst also blocking Rupert from joining the king or striking Lincolnshire. When Newcastle, in his coach, joined Rupert at around 9.00 am, he made clear his opposition to any attack until his men were present. With the triple armies totalling 27,000, Rupert hoped to even the odds by adding the garrison to his own 15,000. Matters were still hopeful. The enemy were vulnerably strung out on the road to Tadcaster when the prince took his men to Marston Moor. The massing of Royalists soon caused alarm. Captain William Stewart, serving with the Scots, confirms their vanguard was within a mile of Tadcaster when orders came to turn back to York.

Rupert could have assaulted his opponents there and then, but with their lines so strung out, this would not have delivered the knockout blow he wanted. They were not concentrated enough to inflict severe casualties. In line with his tried and tested tactics, Rupert let his opponents return to the location he'd chosen and watched carefully as they started to deploy. This way he could choose the appropriate time to attack, and as a result, the numbers he would face. Not only would this negate their numerical superiority, but they would still be in a state of unreadiness. However, as the allies returned in ever greater numbers, Rupert didn't budge. That was his mistake. Additionally, the king's two written instructions did not cater for a scenario where Rupert had relieved York *without* fighting the allies. As such, his stance to do battle, rather than return south, would be open to question.

Though the prince had spectacularly employed his proven tactics to get the battle he wanted, Newcastle was in firm control of the timing, opposing any offensive until his troops were present. Far from Rupert going against the peer, he reluctantly accepted the man's opinion, though against his better judgement. Six months of internal opposition and Rupert's near resignation, combined with his cancelled dawn raid, had sapped his confidence just when everything was at stake. Were he to sideline Newcastle, attack before the York men arrived, and then lose the encounter, he would be entirely blamed for the loss of the north. Agreeing to wait for the garrison was an attempt to safeguard himself. By suppressing his proven instincts and respecting Newcastle's advice (the very thing he's often accused of not doing), the prince set himself and his men up for a brutal clash. What he couldn't have known at this juncture was just how long it would take Newcastle's men to arrive. The morning soon vanished.

The triple army secured an advantageous corn hill, which meant that the sun would shine into Royalist faces and wind blow against them. The fact they managed this was another failing on Rupert's part considering he had the pick of the ground. Though he tried to dislodge them with a regiment of redcoats, this was unsuccessful, as also were attempts to change Newcastle's mind over the merits of an all-out attack. As the afternoon went on, the upper hand Rupert had seized the day before ebbed away. Newcastle must have been equally uneasy over the whereabouts of his York garrison. Accounts vary as to when they eventually put in a show, but it was somewhere between 2.00 pm and 4.00 pm. Their numbers were much lower than expected at only 2,500 and 'those all drunk'.[28] They were led by James King, now Baron Eythin, who had been in charge at Vlotho – no love was lost between him and Rupert. On being shown the prince's battle plan, Eythin replied, 'By God, sir, it is very fyne [on] the paper, but there is no such thinge in the ffeilds.'[29] Rupert offered to move his lines back, and increase the distance between the opposing armies, but it was too late. Eythin reminded the prince that his forwardness had lost the day at Vlotho, nearly six years ago.

By this point in the day, Eythin's blunt words had little bearing and there is no sign they caused Rupert undue anger or frustration – in fact, he is recorded as being tactful and accommodating. Newcastle's cautionary advice and King's late arrival had already destroyed his plans. Now the prince fell back on the last option – a dawn attack on 3 July. Newcastle demurred, concerned that the enemy might strike first, but Rupert dismissed the notion; the Royalists had utilised every ditch, hedge, and lane to secure their defensive position. He gave orders for his army to have supper and fill their bellies in readiness for the morn.

Why did Rupert not place Eythin in command of one of his cavalry wings? Eythin was indeed a fine cavalry commander, but it appears he was assigned command of Newcastle's Whitecoats – infantry so called because of a vow to dye their coats in the blood of their enemies. Keeping Eythin with the York garrison has logic, for he had commanded them during the siege and, considering the effort to get them to the moor, was best placed to handle them. Eythin's late arrival was reason enough to pass him over for a prominent role, rather than a result of any longstanding vendetta on Rupert's part. The army had already been deployed and command of the cavalry wings most likely assigned during Eythin's absence.

The Royalist army was spread across a two-mile front, positioned defensively behind a ditch, which would hinder any attack. The foot in the centre were commanded by Major-General Henry Tillier, who had recently joined the prince from Ireland. The right wing of 2,700 horsemen was headed by Lord John Byron, and the left of 2,100 by George Goring, who had won a cavalry victory at Seacroft Moor the previous year. Both were inferior in number to their respective opponents; Oliver Cromwell and David Leslie had 4,700 with which to fight Byron, while Sir Thomas Fairfax and the Earl of Eglinton had 3,000 opposite Goring.

As a summer squall fell, the Parliamentarians and Scots descended the slope to the rattle of thunder; 800 yards separated the two sides. Newcastle was smoking a pipe in his carriage. The time was around 7.00 pm. A surprised Rupert rushed to his command post in the rear, observing and responding to every development. He held his lifeguard of horse, strongly recruited at 140 men, as well as 400 troopers of Sir Edward Widdrington in reserve. Another 600 horsemen under Sir William Blakiston were stationed closer to the infantry centre, to go wherever they might be needed. Against all odds, opening clashes gave the prince hope.

The left wing of horse, led by Goring, smashed their opponents, and chased most from the field. Goring's second line, under Sir Charles Lucas, attacked the now exposed enemy infantry in textbook manner. Although the allied foot had crossed the ditch and engaged the Royalists, they were forced back and soon enough their entire centre except for about two brigades were in retreat. After about one hour, it seemed as if night would fall on a great Royalist victory. The Earl of Leven fled the field, as did Lord Ferdinando Fairfax, leaving the Earl of Manchester as the last of the three senior commanders remaining. His stabilising presence should not be underestimated.

On Rupert's right wing, things were not so well. With Cromwell's renowned horsemen pounding up to them, Lord Byron committed a *faux pas* by leading his troopers forward to receive their charge. By doing so, he masked the fire of his 500 musketeers, rendering them useless, and crossed the ditch, meaning that the enemy no longer had to tackle it. Byron's advance had been against express orders and 'much harm was done' by it.[30] Cromwell broke Byron without even utilising David Leslie's Scottish contingent. On recognising this disaster, Rupert led his reserves straight into the fray.

Some of Byron's men were heartened by Rupert's presence and rallied. 'Swounds, do you run?' the prince had cried, commanding waverers to follow him.[31] Cromwell's well-disciplined men and Rupert's veterans fought a fierce contest until David Leslie committed his troops. When the prince's outnumbered men were finally routed, Rupert was lost in the ensuing chaos. Later pamphlets mockingly portray him hiding in a bean field while his army was systematically destroyed – it probably took him some time to escape his pursuers, but battle accounts do not mention him again. If he did get back to the moor, there would have been little he could physically do apart from oversee the defeat. Scottish infantry reserves had been led up by Major-General James Lumsden, while Cromwell and Leslie's horsemen made short work of the remains of Lord Goring's. The allied victory owed much to the combined efforts of the Earl of Manchester, Lumsden, Cromwell, and Leslie, despite Cromwell being so often singled out.

Though darkness fell on the bloody proceedings, moonlight picked out the final act of the tragedy; Newcastle's Whitecoats clustered together and refused to surrender in the face of unrelenting attacks. Standing resolute behind walls of pikestaffs, they reversed spent muskets and wielded them as clubs. These men proved 'invincible' until finally 'mowed down' by Cromwell's men.[32] Marston Moor's death toll is estimated between 3,000 and 6,000, two-thirds of whom were Royalists.

Chapter 22

Cry, Howl, and Yelp

A Scottish pamphlet called Marston Moor 'one of the greatest acts of Gods great power and mercie manifested to us'.[1] The Royalist Marquess of Ormonde thought it the 'Battle for England'. Decades afterwards, it was also termed England's 'Pharsalian Fight' after the Battle of Pharsalus, a victory for Caesar. Pompey, having supposedly been pressured into fighting it, had fled overseas after his defeat.[2]

When Rupert and Newcastle found each other at York in the early hours of 3 July 1644, the marquess (like Pompey) resolved to leave the kingdom. Newcastle had been an able leader of the northern army, and though he lacked military experience, had made up for it with professionals. He and Eythin had been talked out of quitting the country three months earlier by the king, who had implored them to scorn the tongues and pens of rivals – and ignore idle gossip. Now both men left for Europe. Eight months later, a sickly Eythin would write to Rupert about his departure and the 'multitewd of grieffe' caused by stories that the prince had ordered him not to leave – which tainted him with treason and cowardice.[3]

Newcastle's reason for departing was billed as a refusal to endure the laughter of the court, but there was more to it. Perhaps he felt responsible for stopping Rupert attacking the triple armies before they had fully deployed. The late arrival of his soldiers did not reflect well, but also the imminent loss of the north must have shattered his morale. Patrick Morrah and Brigadier Peter Young criticise Rupert for heeding Newcastle and waiting for the York garrison, rather than following his intuition and attacking on 2 July, either at dawn, or early morning. Frank Kitson takes a more neutral stance. With the benefit of hindsight, I agree with Morrah and Young that Rupert might have enjoyed more success with his own plan, but fully understand his reticence based, crucially, on internal wrangles and his resulting frame of mind. It's hard to criticise Rupert over Marston Moor, as he did his best in the difficult circumstances; it was the culmination of a multi-faceted and challenging campaign that had hitherto been handled with great success.

The prince was unaware of his uncle's victory at Cropredy Bridge. Had he not fought at all, and let the allies continue their march south, this would have simply delayed an inevitable contest. Rupert would have had to evade them to join up with the king, and they may simply have reinvested York. Crucially, the

Parliamentarians had two lots of reinforcements heading to York; Sir John Meldrum from Lancashire and Lord Denbigh from Staffordshire, totalling as many as 12,000 troops. Newcastle's warnings against doing battle are often justified by the defeat. His case is founded on a belief that the commanders of the triple army – Leven, Manchester, and Fairfax – would fall out and go their own ways. As it was, despite being so heavily outnumbered the Royalists fought exceedingly well and Rupert's deployments (including two cavalry reserves) coupled with his timely use, almost clinched a surprise victory.

It's commonly said that Rupert kept the king's letter of 14 June on his person until his dying day as justification for having sought battle. This is a remarkable thing to have done and would suggest Rupert was severely scarred by Marston Moor, even regretful of fighting it. The anecdote stems back to Eliot Warburton, a Victorian author. His source was a hand-written, anonymous note in the margin of James Heath's 1676 *Chronicle of the Late Intestine War in the Three Kingdoms of England, Scotland and Ireland* held in the London Library. Warburton even adds a caveat that the wording is 'as well as I remember'.[4] I have contacted the library, who were very helpful, but they cannot confirm whether they ever held the *Chronicle* – they simply do not have it in their collection today.

C. V. Wedgewood was certainly sceptical about the anecdote of the letter being on Rupert's person until his dying day and felt it was a later embellishment. I entirely agree. It stands at odds with his post-battle activity and behaviour. It affects our perceptions of Marston Moor, Rupert's decisions, and the battle's impact on him. I find no other evidence to suggest he was so haunted by it that he kept that letter on his person.

In 1662, Thomas Fuller does mention the letter in *Worthies of England*. He is more matter of fact, saying that it was 'still safe' in the prince's custody, though there is no source listed as to how he knew that.[5] Note that Fuller is supportive of the Marquess of Newcastle's opposition to doing battle at Marston Moor. The king's letter does indeed survive to this day, but so do reams of civil war correspondence addressed to Rupert, which were all held by his secretary.

In the aftermath of Marston Moor, Rupert did not mope – it was business as usual, and this tells a truer picture. He even interrupted his retreat with a spot of hunting and killed a buck. He met Colonel Clavering and 1,300 reinforcements at Thirsk on 3 July, then the Marquess of Montrose at Richmond next day. Rupert's attitude at this time can be gleaned from a letter he wrote to Sir Philip Musgrove on 7 July from Castle Bolton. In it, the prince references the 'late disaster' and asks for assurances that Musgrove will continue his loyal support, which will help 'sett alle right againe'. By this time, the prince knew that his uncle had 'utterly beaten Waller'.[6] Rupert's determination seems not to have taken too much of a battering – his resolve was to go after the Scots again as soon as could be and make good the defeat. Travelling via Lathom House to Liverpool, he had his foot and dragoons transported to Cheshire by boat. Rupert reached Chester on 25 July.

Though admitting the York defeat to Musgrave, it seems Rupert, with the king's support, engaged in a cover-up to the wider world. Bonfires were lit in Oxford to celebrate a stunning Royalist victory, and the French resident reported seeing a copy of a letter from the prince himself, which gave assurances of success. There would be no other reason for such a letter from Rupert other than to buy time and delay the truth from coming out. Sir Edward Walker also spoke of an express from Newark on 5 July that informed the king his nephew had been victorious. The Earl of Essex, who had marched into the southwest, and whose presence so worried the pregnant queen in Exeter, was scathing over the fake news. So sure was he of the Royalist defeat that he offered a wager; he would hand over Weymouth and Melcombe if proved wrong, though if correct, the Royalists should give Exeter – and the queen. Needless to say, no deal was done. According to Edward Walker, the truth only officially came to the king on 12 July when he reached the Cotswolds.

By the end of that month, gossip in Amsterdam was that the Marquess of Newcastle was much condemned for abandoning his post and that Rupert had been slammed for his rashness. In fact, the king showed much magnanimity. It was said he 'highly caresses' his nephew and acquitted him over the defeat.[7] Politics aside, the king had always been extremely close to Rupert and despite the turmoil and earlier arguments, that core bond remained strong.

Rupert's friends were swift to his defence. Secretary Nicholas praised the prince's 'great diligence' in rallying dispersed men after Marston Moor and assured the Marquess of Ormonde that the prince hoped to soon use them to good account against the rebels.[8] Indeed, despite their victory, the Parliamentarians were not in good shape. The Earl of Manchester complained from Doncaster on 24 July that 'my foote fall dayly sicke' and he could not supply their necessities.[9] Within months, Lord Fairfax's Yorkshire army was reportedly in a very sad condition through want of clothes and money. Following the inevitable fall of York, on 16 July, it was decided that the triple armies should split. With Rupert based in Chester, and furiously recruiting, there was every chance he might avenge his defeat. That was certainly his aim.

Pamphlets continued to attack the prince even if their armies couldn't. 'A Dog's Elegy' jubilantly trumpeted the killing at Marston Moor of Boye, who had slipped his lead during the battle.

> Lament poor *Caevaliers*, cry, howl and yelp
> For the great losse of your *Malignant Whelp*,
> Hee's dead! Hee's dead? No more alas can he
> Protect you *Dammes*, or get Victorie.

The lines allege that Rupert (a 'Son of Blood') tore off his periwig and sword and would fight no more. Boye was a 'Black Water-witch' responsible for the Gunpowder Plot, poisoning King James VI/I, and the country's poor performance when attempting to relieve the Protestants at the Ile de Re. After listing such historic misfortunes, the pamphlet moves to Rupert.

> Now Prince of *Robbers*, Duke of *Plunderland*,
> This Dogs great Master, hath receiv'd command
> To kill, burne, steale, Ravish, nay, any thing,
> And in the end to make himself a King.[10]

Casting Rupert in the guise of a usurper did not lessen King Charles's trust. However, the possibility of ousting the king was one that Parliament did take extremely seriously. It was said that their commanders had orders to seize the monarch as the best means of ending hostilities, but at the beginning of 1644, a new option had reared its head when MPs resolved to put the Archbishop of Canterbury on trial. They accused Laud of having amended the coronation oath to include the upholding of royal prerogatives, leading to discussion over whether the king could be deposed based on the oath's invalidity.

When Leven, Manchester, and Fairfax were besieging York, they were supposedly visited by Henry Vane, termed one of the 'chief directors of the present machine'. This influential player, so it was said, suggested deposing the king should he be taken prisoner or flee the kingdom. The Scots, however, opposed any such notion. Another option was to fabricate allegations of the queen's 'unchastity' and then declare her children 'suspect'. Though professional historians generally reject the report that Vane visited the army, the question of who might replace the king was one that the leadership would no doubt have pondered. In March 1644, at the height of speculation, Charles Louis arrived in England and sent timely congratulations to Parliament and the Scots upon their alliance. His presence was clearly prejudicial to his uncle, not that Charles Louis seemed to care. He judged king and court 'Spanishly inclined' and, as such, of no benefit to him. Gossip was that the elector had been invited to London by a group of MPs, who aimed to establish him in a 'position of dependency' – a puppet king perhaps. Charles Louis even addressed Parliament in person:

> his Wishes were constant for a good Success to that great Work [Parliament] had undertaken, for a Thorough Reformation; and that his Desires were, to be ruled and advised by their grave Counsels: and being ready to serve them, [he] will with Chearfulness embrace their Advice.

The son of Viscount Dunbar wrote that the elector's coming was for no good. The king needed no convincing. A letter of rebuke to his nephew was intercepted.

> your coming at this time into the Kingdom, is in all respects much more strange unto me ... First, Upon what Invitation you are come?

Then, the Design of your coming? Wishing by your Answer I may have the same Cause and Comfort I have heretofore had, to be, Your Loving Unkle, and Faithful Friend.[11]

Arthur Trevor noted that the elector was also offering to take the covenant and that Rupert's mother was also bound for England. It's highly unlikely Charles Louis would ever have done so base a thing as usurp his uncle's throne, which would have forever tainted him. Nadine Akkerman, Elizabeth of Bohemia's biographer, gives a grounded opinion that he was 'less interested in the Stuart monarchy than in recovering his patrimonial lands'.[12]

Blame for the Palatine family split was unfairly attributed to Rupert's eldest sister, Elisabeth – who Henry Jermyn called a '*Donna Imperia*' – most likely for no other reason than she was an intellectual woman in communication with Descartes.[13] The great philosopher was of the opposite opinion; Elisabeth embodied noble modesty, was magnanimous and gentle. A letter to Rupert was also printed, which called on him to give up his work in England and serve the cause of his family instead, alleging that he dishonoured himself by fighting for such men 'who have beene and still are in the number of the greatest enemies of your House'.[14]

Charles Louis aside, the king's attention was taken up by his army's pursuit of the Earl of Essex into the southwest. The Lord General had withdrawn into Cornwall and was now cut off in hostile territory. Rupert's second-in-command, Henry Wilmot, was disillusioned and ever more tired of the war. While in pursuit of Essex, Wilmot was corresponding with him and treating for peace – it was entirely unauthorised communication. When the king found out, Wilmot was arrested. Though there were clear grounds to proceed against him, it was deemed more politic to allow him to flee to France – the king's clemency was based on Wilmot's courageous service and the fact that he was extremely beloved by the rank and file.

Wilmot was accompanied in flight by Henry Percy, General of the Ordnance. The architect of the pair's disgrace was none other than George Digby, who had moved against them after Wilmot called for Digby's removal from the royal council. Thus, in one stroke, two of Rupert's greatest opponents were culled. It was a bitter-sweet occasion because of the subsequent increase in Digby's power, and to make matters worse, it was announced that Wilmot had been removed at Rupert's request. Not only was this designed to placate soldiers and officers, who revered the prince, but it also shifted blame from Digby. Opinion about Wilmot's removal was negative even within the prince's supporters – Sir Arthur Aston declared Wilmot a gallant man, while Dan O'Neale described Rupert as the 'primum mobile' of the affair, having hoped that he might have brought about Digby's downfall in the process.[15]

Not long after giving birth, the queen had also fled England while still in great pain. King Charles had hoped his army might rescue her from Exeter, but she had not waited for him to arrive. That August, when the king christened his newborn daughter, contemplating the loss of the north and the absence of his wife, he was momentarily indisposed with 'mental stress'.[16]

As the king's army encircled the Earl of Essex to 'combate him by Famine', Rupert was kept closely informed.[17] The prince retreated to his base at Bristol in a dark mood. Rumours abounded that his northern officers were disgruntled at not being consulted enough in councils of war. This, and Digby's machinations, had a serious effect on his wellbeing. On 10 September 1644, confiding to Will Legge, Rupert wrote that he and Digby were now 'frends' but neither trusted one another. Digby, he stated, outwardly makes great 'professions and vowes' of friendship, but the prince was categorical that these 'will doe noe good upon him'. Moreover, Rupert remained certain that great factions were 'breedinge' who accused him of being 'the only cause of warr in this kingdome'.[18] Luckily, the Duke of Richmond worked entirely for Rupert's 'safetie & happinesse'. He attempted to reassure the prince that he could find no plots to 'ruine' him and that there was 'litle reason to dispare' because the king retained full confidence. As a result, Richmond explained, it was 'lesse matter to [Rupert] who att courte grow cold to him'.[19] The letter betrays Rupert's paranoid frame of mind – the war with Digby was now a deathly duel.

On 30 August, the king wrote with a 'desyre' that Rupert demonstrate 'a possibilitie' that Digby might recover his favour and that reconciliation was essential 'for my service sake because [Digby] is an usefull Servant'. The monarch asserted that none of his servants could do the prince 'the least prejudice'. Indeed, the king made a stark vow that 'upon the faith of a Christian' he had an 'implicit' trust in Rupert and would always make that good.[20] On the eve of a crucial battle with Essex, when 'a Crown lyes at the stake', the king was again playing peacemaker between Rupert and Digby.[21]

Digby complained to Rupert that his 'Large and punctuall' accounts about the royal army's movements had elicited nothing from the prince in return. It was an issue he had raised before. Rupert was jeopardising the Royalist cause by slighting Digby and thus playing into the man's hands. With some justification, the frustrated Digby asked Rupert to 'command some body to Lett mee know what Dispatches of myne have come to yor Hands', otherwise it would be 'very hard to resolve or conduct any thing with Relation to yor Highnesse'.[22]

Though the prince had been prompted to attack Abingdon, or relieve Basing House, he appears to have struggled to draw together enough men. Attempts to employ Bristol's auxiliaries in such a mission failed when the mayor and populace protested, causing much discontent in the city. The age-old scarcity of gunpowder was also hampering Rupert, with the king issuing a third warrant for his nephew's supply, adding that he would leave the prince to 'punishe' the fault wherever it should lie.

When Essex boarded a fishing boat and abandoned his army in Cornwall, the king claimed a great victory, capturing arms for 10,000 men and thirty-six cannon. Jubilantly, he told Rupert that 'another good Blow, may end our Businesse' and made ready to join his nephew. Their reunion would surely pull the prince from the depths of despondency.[23]

Chapter 23

Vigorouse Remedyes

Rupert languished in Bristol, plotting how best he might combat his growing detractors. Henry Wilmot, now in France, was rumoured to have joined the Marquess of Newcastle, in drawing up a charge against the prince, and it was suggested they would be supported by the Marquess of Hertford and Lord Herbert.

At this most bleak of times, the top job of Royalist Lord General was in the offing. The Earl of Forth and Brentford's impending resignation sparked feverish intrigue, but Rupert's succession seemed the only logical outcome. Arthur Trevor, at Bristol with the prince, complained that he was 'so much given to his ease and pleasures' that every man who saw this was disheartened. The city, Trevor wrote on 13 October, was a 'house of baudry [bawdy]'.[1] This letter is dismissed by Kitson as a 'figment of someone's imagination' because it detailed Lord Forth falling from his horse and breaking his shoulder, which Kitson says occurred at the Battle of Newbury, some two weeks later.[2] This one letter aside, the prince was clearly not himself, and Kitson thinks he was depressed after the physical and mental exertions of two years. How much Rupert indulged in any 'pleasure' is uncertain, though for someone who had subordinated his own needs in favour of his uncle's service, putting himself first for once would naturally have drawn much attention. It has to be said that Rupert was not militarily idle at this time – he attempted to retake a crossing point of the River Severn, and interceded in favour of a Lieutenant Colonel, condemned in Hereford by the governor, Barnabas Scudamore, requesting all of the evidence and details.

As September turned to October, the king requested to hear daily from Rupert, a sure sign of concern. The monarch had promised not to engage the enemy until the prince joined him with reinforcements, but supposedly at Goring's suggestion, the royal army skirmished with Waller and then considered relieving Basing House or Donnington Castle. These contrary decisions were excused on 20 October 1644, when the king wrote that the prince would soon enough see 'more reason for what I have done'.[3] King Charles should never have limited his operations with a promise to avoid fighting, and a military man of Rupert's calibre should never have solicited it.

The second Battle of Newbury took place before uncle and nephew were reunited, on 27 October 1644. It was claimed that Digby wished to see what could be achieved before joining Rupert – to secure another victory without him would demonstrate that the prince was not the key to success, and therefore lessen both his prestige and the certainty of his succession as Lord General. Newbury II also highlighted an equal divide in the Parliamentarian leadership. In the absence of the Earl of Essex, who made a plea of ill-health, command fell upon the Earl of Manchester, who dragged his heels and reluctantly joined forces with William Waller. The latter was also 'weary' of the war and declared he would submit to 'anything that may conduce to the despatch of it'. These lethargic leaders confronted the king, who by comparison was determined 'to conquer or die'.[4] Waller launched a surprise attack, but Manchester hesitated for hours before supporting him. Making the most of this disunity, the king's men rallied and even managed to rout Oliver Cromwell's men. When night finally put an end to proceedings, the Royalists stole away from the field, leaving their enemies to claim a hollow victory. A tell-tale sign of the change in Royalist fortunes came when Sir John Urry, a professional turncoat, defected back to Parliament after sixteen months. Rupert was said to have been horrified when he found out that the king had done battle without him.

When uncle and nephew finally met at Bath, matters came to a head. The tense prince had brought with him 2,200 reinforcements, seven times as many as had been anticipated, and expecting some sign of favour, he sought command of the King's Lifeguard. At Malmesbury, on Digby's intercession, the post was given to Lord Bernard Stuart, with an excuse that it was a 'comand apart'. The prince was left in 'great displeasure' and resolved to resign his commission (just four months since his last threat) but was talked out of it by his friends.[5] Though out of his depth in politics, Rupert recognised his increasing isolation and resorted to attempts to bring George Goring on side. The man was a notorious drinker but had fought well at Marston Moor. Rupert flattered him with assurances that he had a great interest in his welfare.

Then, on 6 November 1644, the prince became Lord General when the old Earl of Forth and Brentford finally stepped down, yet not even this could alleviate his resentment or suspicion. The Venetian ambassador reported a further resignation threat in December 1644, following another 'difference' with the king that was played upon by Digby.[6] This may have been linked to Basing House, where at the end of the year, the Marquess of Winchester attempted to oust the military governor, Marmaduke Rawdon. The governor petitioned the king in person at Oxford, only to find that the monarch was unaware of the marquess's action, which was seen as 'Rupert's doeing' having been done with his approval.[7] The Royalist cause was sinking. Their new general was so extremely dissatisfied that he allowed his personal quarrels to further the division.

Aware of opposition to him, Rupert had unsuccessfully suggested conferring the title of Lord General upon the 14-year-old Prince of Wales. This would have meant Rupert exercising supreme command as Lieutenant General, but with some protection (and enhanced authority) by having his orders rubber stamped by the heir to the throne. Instead, he consolidated his position by promoting close supporters; Maurice was given most of Rupert's old command area of North Wales, Worcestershire, Herefordshire, and Shropshire. The Welsh recruiting grounds were key to Royalist survival. Maurice desired no 'farther latitude' than the same powers his brother had held.[8]

George Goring (also being groomed by Digby) was promoted to General of the Horse and likewise asked for the same freedom that Rupert had enjoyed – of reporting direct to the king. Writing directly to the monarch, Goring complained that his officers were suffering from 'deadnes and backwardnes' and to combat this, receiving orders direct from the king's 'owne hand' would reinforce his authority.[9] When this was granted, Rupert angrily condemned Goring for being 'underhand'.[10] The latter countered, on 22 January 1645, that he had been forced to approach the king because all his requests were 'denyed' by Rupert. The resulting bad blood saw Goring unite with Digby.[11]

Rupert's other duties meant that not only was he responsible for directing the Royalist war effort, but he also had to take a close hand in peace negotiations. Managing the council of war took tact, skill, and diplomacy. Maurice also warned of a dubiously named 'association' in Wales and the borders who were tending to the destruction of 'militare power and discipline'.[12]

Being responsible for hiring and firing commanders, Rupert now had to shoulder displeasure over many decisions. In January 1645, a rift occurred with the Byrons, who had hitherto been his close supporters. Friction with John Byron may have stemmed back to the man's actions at Marston Moor, which had severely hindered the Royalist right wing of cavalry. On 9 January, John denied disrespecting people that the prince 'most favord' – an incident that led him to communicate with Digby over it.[13] At the same time, John's brother Richard (Governor of Newark) foiled a 'damnable plott' to betray the town. When the Byrons' mother, from her lodgings in Oxford's Merton College, heard that Rupert was looking to put Newark's government into a commission, with several men carrying out the duties, she told Richard to resist it and petition the king. Other governors had managed to hang onto their posts 'against Prince Rupert's will', she insisted. Richard duly called on the king to try him by court of war, otherwise being removed for no apparent reason would leave his honour 'much blemisht'. It wasn't long before he was replaced by the prince's man, Sir Richard Willis.[14]

A natural administrator, Rupert was also used to the sheer number of petitions from garrisons and local forces. His no-nonsense decision making gave much-needed clarity, such as when he declined to send Jacob Astley prescriptive orders, and instead empowered him to do the right thing. As Rupert explained, he would be 'loath, by misjudging here' to give directions that would be 'inconvenient there'. The tangle of confusing orders preceding Marston Moor no doubt influenced this.[15]

Being Lord General didn't prevent the prince from leading smaller-scale actions, which he had long since excelled at. However, an attempt to capture Abingdon at the start of 1645, to help safeguard Oxford, brought him into conflict with Digby once again. For the previous three months, the man had exchanged correspondence with Abingdon's Parliamentarian governor, Richard Browne. With the garrison supposedly mutinous over arrears of pay, Digby reckoned he could entice Browne to turn coat and hand the town over. Digby's courting quill flattered and fawned. Polite replies were encouraging, but they never really progressed, leaving the desperate Digby promising all sorts of rewards.

For ten fruitless weeks, letters came to nothing, yet Rupert, who called for military action while the garrison was weak, was muzzled. Digby even revealed to Browne that he was under pressure by Royalist officers to cease his efforts and allow them to decide the matter by force. Eventually, Parliament sent Browne reinforcements, and once securely in Abingdon, he admitted to leading Digby on and let rip 'the poison you vent is worse than spiders'.[16] This was just one of several strongholds Digby tried – and failed – to obtain by secretive means: other more noticeable ones being Hull and Plymouth.

On 11 January 1645, when Rupert finally unleashed his attack on Abingdon, he was outflanked by the strengthened Browne and forced to retreat. The fate of five Irishmen from the prince's force, who were subsequently hanged in Abingdon's marketplace, reignited Rupert's anger over their singling out. Arthur Trevor, a Royalist agent, had written that the prince was 'mightily in love' with the troops sent back from Ireland, who were more and more the lifeblood of the flagging Royalist cause.[17] Naturally, Parliament decried the transfusions of men and painted them all as devilish Irish Papists.

Back in 1644, this had come to a head when thirteen of Rupert's men had been hanged after being captured at Nantwich on account of their supposed nationality and religion. Rupert was quick to respond, and hanged thirteen Parliamentarian prisoners, sending another to MPs with the warning that for every man killed by them, he would hang two. It was a move that drew a scornful reply from Westminster that Englishmen were very different to Irishmen. To prove the point, Parliament passed an Ordinance at the end of 1644, ordering their commanders on land and sea to put to death every Irishman and Catholic born in Ireland in arms against them. Failure to do so would leave the offending commander branded as a supporter of the Catholic Irish Rebellion, and open to just punishment.

It's estimated that around 10,000 soldiers were brought from Ireland to serve the king, and by 1645, Parliament was desperate to stop the flow. On 29 January 1645, after George Goring attacked Parliamentarian Arundel and Aldershot, the Irishmen in his force gave 'noe quarter' to any prisoners, an act that Goring felt he could not condemn considering Parliament's 'inhumane' treatment of their countrymen.[18] Rupert once forbade Jacob Astley to exchange any prisoners with the enemy until Royalist Irish officers were released. When Royalist Shrewsbury was captured at the end of February, and seventeen Irishmen taken prisoner and hanged, Rupert had the same number of Parliamentarian prisoners killed and despatched another strongly worded letter to MPs. He argued that the Irishmen hanged at Shrewsbury were loyal subjects of the king, sent to Ireland to fight the Catholic rebels, and warned that the two sides risked provoking such animosity and cruelty that all elements of 'Charity,

Compassion, and Brotherly Affection' might be entirely extinguished.[19] It can be argued that civil war had done this already, but certainly this was a new depth.

Abingdon, and the latest rivalry with Digby that January of 1645, was the least of Rupert's worries. Wales, the vital Royalist recruiting ground, was in jeopardy. Should it be lost, then the king would be left on borrowed time. Following Marston Moor, one mainstay that bolstered Rupert's confidence was that he could draw fresh strength from the principality. But by 1645, there grew an 'association' of discontented parties that included Clubmen. Rupert's promotion and his departure from Wales was said to have 'cooled the affection of many' there.[20] By February 1645, the rot was taking hold. Shrewsbury (Rupert's former headquarters) was lost to the enemy through the 'treacherie' of the townsfolk. This meant that plundering Parliamentarians now reached within a mile of Royalist Bridgnorth, a place of 'such publick concernment'.[21] The repercussions were feared in Chester, too, where Lord Byron rued that Rupert's absence had 'begott so much dispaire'.[22]

It was felt nobody else but the prince could restore order, and he was summarily despatched to the Welsh border at the end of February. The task was formidable, and the king thanked his nephew for undertaking it so cheerfully. Whilst upon the journey he received another supportive letter from the king, who acknowledged that there was more than one 'kynde of Ennemy you ar to deale with'. Implicit confidence was shown, and Rupert was reassured that if he failed, it would be understandable.[23] Digby also wrote, anticipating the prince's 'timelye and vigorouse remedyes' for these 'distracted countryes'.[24]

From Ludlow, on 8 March 1645, Rupert reported that Wales might soon be in full rebellion if the internal troublemakers were not suppressed. The prince deemed them a 'powerfull enemy' and his task almost impossible, resolving to try and join forces with Maurice.[25] By this point, he had already quelled a mutiny of officers and was impatiently waiting for supplies before he could assess what he might achieve. Wants included powder, as ever, but also clothes for his men, pike staves, and a train of artillery. He complained to Legge about the lack of replies to his letters and stated he would 'faine knowe what [the king] resolves to under take this sumer' – a line which echoes frustration and concern.[26] Rupert had always relished escaping the confines of Oxford, but his detachment left him isolated and out of touch. The fact is, the prince's political failings led to periods of self-exile. Too often he could not conquer his frustrations and employ more effective (and subtle) means of combating his opponents.

If the prince was hampered by lack of equipment and uncertainty, then Parliament did not suspect it. The Parliamentarian Commitee of Both Kingdoms warned that he might try to regain the north. Within weeks, Rupert was on the march to secure Hereford. By then he was in more jovial spirits, not least because he was in action, and reported that the Parliamentarians were 'weake and keep theire holes' – indeed, his focus was entirely taken up with internal division.[27] Soon enough, he joined Jacob Astley, which left courtiers in Oxford pleased with this union of like minds.

'[W]ee all think it a happines to that gallant Prince Rupert in that hee enjoyes your [lordship's] companie.'[28] So wrote Endymion Porter, a groom of the king's bedchamber. He clearly felt as if Rupert could do with Astley's support. But Goring in the West Country was less certain of the prince's movements and wrote not knowing whether the letter would 'find' him at Bristol, or not.[29] Rupert undoubtedly wished he was in that city, for it was also suffering from the internal malaise that gripped the Royalists. He had sent instructions for strengthening the defences, reportedly in a very 'sade contition', and with just 500 men in the garrison, no sentries on the artillery, nor victuals stored in the castle.

There was also suspicion in the prince's mind that Ralph Hopton, now Baron Hopton of Stratton, had a 'chief designe' to gain absolute command of the place.[30] Rupert was sure that Hopton's deputy was a 'rogue' and was gathering evidence to prove it. Sir Charles Lucas, one of the prince's allies, reportedly quarrelled with Hopton. Into this maelstrom stepped the 14-year-old Prince of Wales, who was sent into the west with his own council. The intention was to restore order and authority, but Prince Charles's presence in Bristol simply intensified strife, and factions sought to use him. Rupert, with his few 'shrewd fellows' at Hereford, despaired. He expected 'noething but ill from the west' and didn't care if this opinion became public knowledge.

On 24 March, the prince again lamented Prince Charles's location and did 'pray gode' the boy had been sent to him instead.[31] By 31 March, George Goring had started receiving orders directly from Prince Charles's council and used this as an excuse to ignore Rupert's when they did not suit. Regretting that he did not have 'power' over the Prince of Wales's person, Rupert intended to go to Bristol himself.[32]

First, on 22 April, Rupert saw off Edward Massie at Ledbury. Reporting his success to Will Legge, the prince couldn't help an acid remark that had Goring achieved this, there would have been a 'handsome story' made of it.[33] The Royalist plan had been for the king to help quell unrest in Wales and the borders, relieve Chester, and then reconquer the north. Rupert jokingly warned that the monarch should not bring so many 'scullions and beef eaters' which would prove challenging to accommodate.[34] This humour was short lived and time ticked on without any royal appearance. The problem, Rupert was told, was lack of draught horses. The artillery ('iron work' as Digby called it) could not be transported out of Worcester without them. Ironically in view of such mobility issues, at this very moment, the prince was secretly engaged in discussion over becoming Master of the Horse.

There had been many candidates, such as the Earl of Southampton. Fear was that the current occupant (the imprisoned Duke of Hamilton) might one day return and attempt the 're-cozening' of the king – thus re-establishing his malign influence. King Charles admitted to his wife that he chose Rupert to 'stop other men's grumblings'.[35] It was hardly a ringing endorsement. Anticipating backlash over his appointment, Rupert would only accept the post if it was offered as a favour, so as not to look like he had a hand in Hamilton's 'ruine'.[36] But what he wanted more than anything was the presence of his uncle and his army for a northern campaign.

The king was melancholy and missing Henrietta Maria's company. 'If thou knew what a life I lead,' he had written, lamenting a lack of good conversation like hers, which was the 'chief joy or vexation' in life. People around him, he went on, were either too foolish, busy, reserved, or extreme.[37]

Rupert grew impatient. Admitting to Will Legge he was 'madd att you alle' over the king's continued absence, he insisted that his uncle be ready to march to Chester within a week.[38] He then listed, for his uncle's benefit, the 'inconveniences' of further delays. Confiding to Legge that if the king would not 'heere the souldier [i.e. Rupert]' and heed his advice over civilian counsellors then the prince would 'leaof all' – a fourth known threat of resignation within a year – ironically given on St George's Day.[39]

Chapter 24

Unjust Displeasure

Letters were often written in code for added security, and more so in wartime. Rupert regularly referred to himself in the third person, a practice his mother also employed, as had his father, too. Usually, these codes were made up of numbers (sometimes symbols and pictures) that could be used in place of each letter of the alphabet. Recipients would share ciphers, by which letters could be decoded and understood. During my research, I built up several cipher keys and managed to use them to unlock some coded letters from this point in time to draw fresh insight into the pre-Naseby state of affairs.

One such transcribed letter from Digby, dated 29 April 1645, confirmed general agreement with Rupert's proposal of 'drawing northward as soone as [the king] shall be joined with you' to strengthen the Royalists in those parts. There was also a stark admission that 'Crumwells incursion' and his raids around Oxford 'hath for the present totally disabled the king to move'. Obtaining draught horses was proving an impossibility – 400 were required and the prince was asked to march towards Oxford and gather as many on the way. Crucially, Parliament had just formed the New Model Army, with Sir Thomas Fairfax and Oliver Cromwell in command. Digby warned that 'the reputation of Crumwell's successes is already likely to drawe such swarmes out of London', leaving the king 'in hazard'.[1] The option of sending the 11-year-old Duke of York to Ireland was even raised because of the ever more precarious situation in England. The letter evidences the paralysis within the king's army and his headquarters.

Edward Nicholas, in another de-ciphered letter, validates that Cromwell's work had changed the minds of those who had been 'averse' to take up arms in Parliament's service. These insights show just how devastating Cromwell's operations in Oxfordshire were. He had revealed the king's forces to be impotent and successfully stalled the monarch's plans to regain the north. These are very important considerations in the lead up to the Battle of Naseby; had the king managed to move, a battle might have come about months earlier with a potentially different outcome.[2] So critical was the situation that Rupert was sent five letters over two days from Digby, Nicholas, and the king himself, emphasising the 'wants' of over 400 draught horses. The prince hurried to Burford, arriving on 4 May, before moving to Oxford the following day. Nicholas had hoped Rupert's presence would 'allaye the vayneglorious boasting of ye Rebells uppon Cromwells petty victories' and at the same time correct the want of diligence and vigilance in the Royalist commanders by his good example.³ Goring, having also been summoned, arrived with his troops at the same time as Rupert, finally forcing Cromwell's withdrawal.

A Royalist council of war ensued. The prince successfully argued down proposals that the king march into the southwest to attack Fairfax; instead, it was reiterated that the royal army should join with Rupert and head north. With the Prince of Wales recruiting good numbers and Montrose notching up another victory in Scotland, there was extra hope.

By 11 May 1645, Rupert's flying visit to Bristol, in which he intended to 'rob [the western Royalists] of theyr arms' and equip his own men, also saw him marshal the Prince of Wales's council.⁴ Lord Culpepper, at Rupert's insistence, sent a detailed summary of the Royalist cause in the west, and ended by asking where uncle and nephew might meet to join forces. The report was useful to Rupert, demonstrating that all was hopeful in that sphere, which supported the plan to move north. The Prince of Wales's recruitment was anticipated to create an army of 14,500 under his nominal command with Lord Hopton as Lieutenant General. The force would be independent of Rupert, though Hopton admitted to the king that he feared this would incur the prince's great displeasure.

Harmony was finally restored when uncle and nephew joined forces towards the end of May. The prince also received tidings from Paris, reassuring him of the queen's constant friendship. Word had reached Henrietta Maria that Rupert and Digby had (again) outwardly patched up their differences – Henry Jermyn told Digby that if the news was true to keep it up; but if not, then he should make it happen. Trusty Will Legge was installed as Governor of Oxford, and with internal strife addressed, the royal army pursued Rupert's northern campaign.

As expected, Fairfax moved north and laid siege to Oxford. The royal army nevertheless had Leicester and Stafford in their sights; capturing one of these would cause the New Model Army to end the siege of Oxford and seek battle instead. Legge was instructed to specify how long the headquarters could hold out. He was warned against misrepresenting the situation, and that updates should be in his own hand, otherwise the prince would not believe them. With many Royalists questioning this risky strategy, Rupert needed to know precisely how long he had to achieve his goal.

Just after midnight on 31 May, the Royalists unleashed their fury on Leicester. Henry Bard, an officer loyal to Rupert, was one of the first scaling the walls, despite having lost an arm at Cheriton one year earlier. The royal army lusted for revenge, having been humiliatingly penned in Oxford for so long, while Cromwell had raided all around them. Nobody, therefore, could keep them from plundering the fallen town. Securing Leicester brought financial contributions and recruits from the surrounding area, and prisoners could be exchanged for valuable Royalist POWs such as George Monck, or Henry Tillier, both of whom were on Rupert's wish list. Strategically, the prince was all for keeping the initiative and pushing further north without delay. Goring was ordered to return to the royal army and boost its numbers.

Digby, however, put a spanner in the works. Oxford, he countered, could not be left so vulnerable and they should turn back to its relief. Rupert saw this for what it was – a plot to 'send [the] king to Oxford' – but was too hasty when he reported to Legge from Daventry, on 8 June, that 'it is undoen'.[5] The council of war turned out and backed Digby, who argued it was dishonourable to run any further from the enemy. They should seek out 'a battle of all for all'.[6] Rupert's continued march north was also opposed by all the lords of the council in Oxford, who feared for their own safety. From there, Edward Nicholas sent Rupert a friendly warning to seriously consider the implications of opposing such a unanimous body, which would unleash much 'envy'.[7] With so many ranged against him, Rupert had to back down.

Weakened by leaving a garrison in Leicester, the king's army turned south. A letter from Goring, revealing he was unable to join the king, was intercepted by Fairfax, who did as Rupert had predicted and raised the siege of Oxford. One week later, the New Model Army was just a day's march away from the royal army.

Detachments of the two sides clashed in the village of Naseby on 13 June. News reached the king around 11.00 pm. He hurried to find Rupert at Market Harborough, only to discover the prince was in bed. The king, 'resting himself in a chair in a low room' while he waited, gave immediate order to summon his council of war.[8] Digby and his ally, Jack Ashburnham, treasurer of the army, told the midnight assembly that Fairfax must be sought out. Mocking the 'new noddle army', they gave off an arrogant confidence. Rupert, on the other hand, counselled retreat to Leicester where the garrison could be reabsorbed to increase numbers. Additionally, this might give Goring, or new recruits from Wales under Charles Gerard, time to arrive.

Faced with these conflicting arguments, King Charles had a hard choice. Digby's eternal optimism outshone Rupert's caution, which was easily painted as defeatist. The monarch felt his cause was never in 'so fair and hopeful a way'.[9] Heeding Digby, he thought to 'terrifie' the enemy by going on the offensive.[10]

At Naseby, Royalist scouts reported no sight of the enemy. Disbelieving them, Rupert rode out himself and found them falling back to the village. Knowing that his own reputation and the king's cause rested on this battle, Rupert must have recalled his mistake at Marston Moor, in not attacking the allies at the opportune moment. This time, he was resolved not to abdicate the initiative and instructed the army to advance immediately. Only when the Royalists drew closer did Rupert realise his error – he had seen only a reconnaissance party withdrawing. Much of Fairfax's army had been out of view due to the terrain. Latest estimates in Nick Lipscombe's *Civil War Atlas* put the Royalist strength at 10,000 compared to 13,500 Parliamentarians.

In a decision that is still criticised today, Rupert took charge of the Royalist right wing of horse, rather than remain with the king in overall command. A significant reserve was, however, left with the monarch. Both Royalist cavalry wings were outnumbered, but Rupert felt confident he could despatch the enemy's left wing, which would allow the reserve to be wholly used against Cromwell. As battle commenced, Rupert did indeed sweep most of his opponents from the field, but once again he was unable to control his furious horsemen who hammered off in pursuit. He got as far as the enemy's baggage train where he was mistaken for Fairfax and at first greeted warmly before being shot at.

As at Marston Moor, against all odds it seemed like the Royalists might clinch victory. The resolute veteran infantry, led by Jacob Astley, pushed the Parliamentarians back. Cromwell, however, managed to defeat the Royalist left wing of horse using just a portion of troops under command of his cousin, Edward Whalley. This crucial moment now required the Royalist reserve. The king made ready to lead them into the fray, but his bridle was seized by the Earl of Carnwath, who asked if he would go upon his death. The move instilled confusion, as if the king was turning to withdraw, and the moment rapidly passed. The royal party rode off the field, and the reserve melted away with it. Unchecked, Cromwell turned on the Royalist infantry, and some of his men even came very close to capturing the king, who discharged his pistols and escaped. The baggage train was looted and over 100 female camp followers (by conservative estimates) were killed, with others mutilated, an atrocity excused by attempts to paint them as Irish. In fact, the likelihood is that they were Welsh.

Rupert and the king pelted to Leicester, and after a brief rest rode through the night to Ashby de la Zouch. The prince readied himself for his next battle. On 18 June, just four days after Naseby, Rupert asked Legge (in Oxford) what news had reached them about the defeat – 'doublesse the fault of it will be put upon [me]'. That same day, Digby drafted a letter to the Prince of Wales subtly laying blame on Rupert, having already spread rumours to that effect. Rupert took the letter to the king and threatened that if it was sent, he would resign and join Prince Charles, who had shown him 'more kindnesse then heare'.[11] As the royal party reached Hereford, Digby and Rupert were at each other's throats.

Frank Kitson felt Rupert had 'lost some of his forcefulness' in the Naseby campaign and was even too diplomatic with the council.[12] I think Rupert's force was strong, but it was his impact that was lost. Absences from Oxford, his war with Digby, and the morose edge that swept away his infectious confidence, all played their parts. The embarrassing regularity of threats to resign cannot have helped. No longer was he delivering standout victories.

Rupert and Digby were agreed on one thing – that the Royalist cause could bounce back. The prince ordered his good friend, Sir John Owen, to speed new recruits from Wales and obtain 800 from Lord Byron. Rupert felt that with Charles Gerard's reinforcements set to join them, believed to number 4,000 foot and 1,000 horse, the king would shortly be 'stronger then [sic] ever'.[13] Though laced with overconfidence, it showed he was far from giving up, nor had the enemy pursued them. Instead, Fairfax's army was weakened after detaching twelve troops to escort Royalist prisoners to London. Ten miles outside the city, they turned on their captors and many escaped. The Parliamentarians had an easier job taking back Leicester, because from experience they knew the weakest parts. Many of the Royalist garrison had fled after Naseby, and there was lack of gunpowder and money to pay the troops that remained, therefore Lord Loughborough, the governor, gained permission from the king and Rupert to surrender.

On 26 June, Rupert left Hereford and the king behind, but not before the pair made an agreement (at the king's insistence) to 'deale freely' with one another to avoid misunderstandings.[14] Rupert headed for the Prince of Wales in Barnstaple to assist in defence of the southwest. The move allowed Rupert to put distance between himself and Digby, while the king planned to follow in due course. But the separation of the monarch and his Lord General at this crucial moment was not a good idea and highlights the latter's flaws – it only occurred because Rupert could not deal with Digby. Another letter I decoded informed Rupert that a turncoat colonel in those parts was sending 'all the [king's] designes' to the enemy.[15] Fairfax was hot on Rupert's heels, intending to mop up the southwest.

Writing on 30 June to Will Legge in Oxford, Digby felt certain they would soon be 'in as good a condicon [condition] as ever'. Niceties over, he got to the crux of why he put pen to paper. Explaining that Rupert had little kindness for him, Digby regretted that the prince was not 'gainable' (unwilling to be friends) even though he had attempted it with all industry. He lamented Legge's absence; had the man been present, Digby felt that he might have persuaded Rupert to be better inclined. The prince's misapprehensions, Digby asserted with a twist of the knife, were wounding the prince's honour and the king's.

Digby went on to specify numerous reasons for the defeat at Naseby, all of which by default were laid at Rupert's door, being the Lord General. The artillery was deployed on a hill, meaning they could not 'make use of one peece'.[16] As for the time and place of fighting, no council had been called to debate it – indirectly pointing out that the prince had hastened the army to battle. The reserve was also questioned. Had Legge been there, Digby ventured, he would have queried these tactical issues – a sly suggestion that Rupert was incompetent and relied on his great friend. The letter was typical Digby; critical and derogatory, but subtly so. By contrast, Legge's reply was refreshingly blunt. He called out Digby's deviousness, accusing him of prejudicing Rupert 'not in an open and direct way but obscurely and obliquely'.[17]

Rupert and Digby did not simply dislike each other, they did not understand one another either. Digby's true feelings were expressed in a very different private letter to Henry Jermyn, wherein he claimed to have secured a promise from the king to let Rupert 'content himselfe' with the honour of military action – in other words as a figurehead, merely enacting military tactics decided by a council. '[C]ould it have been sooner obteyned Wee should not have been now putt to such an unhappy after game.'

This bombshell would have put Lord General Rupert on a leash and subordinated him to the authority of a council. After Naseby, Digby complained the prince was showing more 'present emnaty against mee then ever' and ventured the reason was his pre-Naseby advice that the king's army should turn back for Oxford, having trumped Rupert's. Confidently asserting that his own position with the king was secure, despite Rupert's 'anamosityes', Digby implies that the prince's was not. What's more, Digby accuses the prince of placing personal hostility above tactics, thereby bringing Rupert's military judgement into question – before going on to resolve not to do the prince a disservice as long as he was judged capable of serving the monarch. Again, by default, there is a veiled threat in this affirmation of loyalty.[18] Digby certainly had his agents watching William Legge and others in Rupert's circle, who were nicknamed the 'Cumberlanders' after the latter's dukedom.[19]

Rupert's actions at Naseby have haunted his reputation ever since, and an eighteenth-century poem, written by Sir Francis Doyle, furthers the image of a reckless plunderer.

> Oh! Where was Rupert in that hour
> Of danger, toil, and strife:
> It would have been to all brave men
> Worth a hundred years of life,
> To have seen that black and gloomy force, [Cromwell's troopers]
> As it pour'd down in line,
> Met midway by the Royal horse
> And Rupert of the Rhine![20]

When Goring and Fairfax came to blows on 10 July 1645 at Langport, defeat was so disastrous for the Royalists that even Goring admitted it left such 'terror' amongst his men that they could not be brought to fight against 'halfe theire number'.[21] Fuller, in his 1662 *Book of Worthies*, calls the battle a 'flight', rather than a 'fight', and likens it to the Battle of the Spurs. '[H]ence forward the *Sun* of the *Kings cause declined, verging* more & more *Westward,* till at last it *set* in *Cornwal.*'[22]

As July passed, Royalist towns fell like ninepins: Carlisle, Bath, then Bridgwater. After offering women and children passes to leave the latter, Fairfax burned the garrison into submission, refusing to parley until complete surrender was proffered. A very different contest involved Lichfield where Rupert appointed a new governor without the king's approbation. It caused another embarrassing mix-up like that which had occurred when he had appointed himself Governor of Bristol in 1643. Over Lichfield, the king wrote on 13 July 1645 to reveal he had only found out about Rupert's appointment when the new governor told him – something that 'surprysed me alitle this morning'. Attempting to remain unruffled, and not contradicting the man, the king magnanimously played along. Only after the audience did he discreetly write to Rupert and query the decision and lack of notice, generously ascribing it 'meerly out of a hasty forgetfulness'.[23] Once more, he urged Rupert to always speak freely with him – the prince would do just that within the space of a fortnight.

By the time his uncle's letter reached him, Rupert was at plague-ridden Bristol, feverishly preparing it for the siege he knew was coming. Clubmen were an immediate threat. Grouping together to protect their homes from both sides, they more often ended up allying with Parliamentarians. The threat of two groups to Bristol was significant and Rupert was 'put to much trouble' hindering their activity.[24] Much success was gained after meeting with them, and the prince drew up an oath that would keep them in check. The king approved the wording, but wished to exclude a cause about public gatherings, as it would 'needlesly exasperat the Club Men'.[25]

With Bristol in safe hands, the king sent his foot guards to Hereford in a bid to bolster that key town. Digby informed the governor that he should act his part gallantly, pointing out that these were the only armed men the king had left to distribute. Plans for the monarch to cross to Bristol were quickly put on hold, much to Digby's relish, following Fairfax's successes. The king (in Newport) wrote to his nephew of this amendment on 24 July. It was followed by more detailed reasoning from Digby the following day, though both letters seem to have encountered difficulties getting to the prince, who remained oblivious for now. There was expectation that South Wales might rise against the Scots, and the king was staying put to encourage that. But there was also the secret possibility of taking his cavalry, which had survived Naseby, into the north. His decision was said to rest entirely on the actions of the enemy.

Four days later, on 28 July, both Digby and Rupert put pen to paper. Digby extolled the Marquess of Montrose's successes, which would soon mean the king's 'Enemyes' in Scotland would not have 'any man in the field in all [that kingdom].'[26] Rupert, by contrast, wrote to the Duke of Richmond about a 'strange resolution' he had heard that the king intended to head for Scotland to join Montrose. The astounded prince questioned how that would leave Royalists in England and doubted such a journey was even possible. 'If I am now desired to deliver my opinion; which your Lordship may declare to the King. His Majesty hath no way left to preserve his posterity, kingdom, and nobility, but by a treaty. I believe it is a more prudent way to retain something than lose all.'

It was a damning paragraph. The king and queen were negotiating with Catholic Confederates in Ireland, who promised 10,000 men. Rupert also took aim at this pipe dream, telling Richmond that the Irish had not half that number and would cheat the king. Rather, he advocated, his uncle should consider the officers and soldiers who remained in his cause, and their fates, which was most likely 'ruin and slavery'. 'One comfort will be left; we shall all fall together, when this is, remember I have done my duty.'[27]

Rupert waited for Richmond to somehow communicate these opinions. Once again, the prince felt sidelined and discarded, but despite this, resolved that nothing would stop him 'doinge [his] dutie'.[28] On 29 July he told Legge he was not by his uncle's side at this key moment, nor destined to be, because Digby was out to ruin him. Rupert's certainty had been sealed following a recent conference near Cardiff – there, Jack Ashburnham had warned him as much.

When Rupert's recommendation for peace was revealed to the king on 30 July, it was done with 'much care and friendship' by the Duke of Richmond.[29] The king slept on the matter. The following day he set out his thoughts, using Richmond's cipher, and sent the letter to Rupert (who was codenamed 'power' despite it increasingly looking like he was devoid of it). After gravely recapping the issue at stake – 'defence of my religion, crowne, & friends' – the king made a candid admission that showed the clear difference between man and monarch. '[S]peakeing ether as a meere soldier, or statesman, I must say that ther is noe probabillitie but of my ruine yet as a Christian I must tell you that Godd will not suffer rebelles & traitors to prosper, or this cause to bee overthrowne.'

Whatever personal punishments were inflicted on him by God's will, King Charles refused to back down, knowing that offering to negotiate with his enemies would be tantamount to a 'submission'. His cause was God's. Friends were at stake, as well as honour and conscience. This said, the usually sanguine monarch stared defeat in the face, hoping to at least 'end [his] daies with honor & a good conscience'. Next, he set expectations for those who remained in his service; like him, they should expect to die for a good cause, or worse still, live miserably maintaining it against 'the violent rage of insulting rebelles'. Rupert was ordered never again to 'henker after' treaties.[30] The royal letter becomes less coherent at the end – it tells Rupert they had recovered to a pre-Naseby level, and then despairs that his nephew's support for a treaty would simply accelerate defeat. Clearly the king was greatly affected by his nephew's stance.

Digby was jubilant when he read the king's reply. He forwarded a copy to the queen, who was the prime mover in opposing any treaty. Henrietta Maria had counselled her husband not to give up on his friends by making peace lest it reflect weakness – no foreign power would come to his aid were he not willing to fight tooth and nail.

Though uncle and nephew were opposed over policy, the king's love was unchanged, evidenced on 4 August when he wrote to Rupert with the latest council updates. Considering the net was closing on Bristol, the king, with paternal care, offered the prince a get-out. He tentatively suggested Rupert might 'doe so great good' if he joined the Prince of Wales, and though cautioning the danger of the passage, expressed a 'wishe' that Rupert might join his son. The letter had a final tinge of sorrow.

> it will be a long tyme before I see you; I earnestly desire you to have an implicit Faithe in my Frendship & Affection. ...
>
> [I hold myself bound to] protect you as one of my Children; so that you shall share largely with me if ever it shall please God to send happy dayes.[31]

On 5 August, the king left Cardiff and headed north. That same day, Digby wrote to Henry Jermyn in Paris about their 'torrent of misfortunes'. His poisonous pen regretted that if only the king had kept his promise to heed the advice of 'those whose judgements hee was resolved to trust' (i.e. not Rupert's) then they would never have been reduced to this. The crown, he remarked, had 'been absolutly given away to Pr. Ruperts will' on two occasions (presumably Marston Moor and Naseby) with the result that the Royalists were consigned to a 'languishing defense this yeare' and expectation of certain ruin the next. However, there was praise for Montrose – the new miracle-maker – from whom Digby asserted there did 'seeme to portend more wonders'.[32] But for now, King Charles warned Montrose that he could not send anything to assist these wonders other than words of encouragement, which was 'all my song to you'.[33]

The full extent of this fascinating correspondence between Rupert and the king (and Digby) in late July and August 1645 has never been so closely examined and these letters add to the jigsaw. It's likely that Rupert did not receive all these important letters. Between 28 July and 6 August, he certainly did not receive the king's response to his calls for a treaty – indeed, he complains about having written ten times to his uncle without one reply. This communication blackout, coupled with rumours that his uncle had moved north, caused Rupert to pour forth his frustration in a letter to Legge. The king had gone without his knowledge and 'ded send me noe comands'. '[T]o tell you true my humor is to doe noe man seruis [service] against his will.'

Without regret, Rupert justified his letter to the king, which he had 'writt plainely' and deemed it right to 'doe my dutie and speake my minde freely'. Assuming, by the lack of replies, that he'd incurred his uncle's wrath, he expressed a readiness to accept this 'unjust displeasur'.[34] This is dated 6 August by Rupert's hand, but has been misdated in the archive catalogue as 6 May. Bringing it back into the correct place in the chronology adds another key jigsaw piece to the period leading up to the prince's dismissal.

Ten supposedly unanswered letters are concerning, especially when we know of the king's numerous tender responses already quoted. It also seems odd given that Rupert *had* received one reply from the Duke of Richmond, who was with the monarch. The cause might be delays on account of enemy action, interception, a rogue messenger, or deliberate interference by parties who would benefit from preventing the communications.

New understanding of Rupert's frame of mind comes from a critical letter that I deciphered. Dated 9 August, the prince addressed it to the Duke of Richmond and refers to the 28 July call for a treaty. Rupert suggests he had finally received the king's 31 July response and specifies that the reasoning did not 'att alle' alter his opinion. He repeats that the only way the king can preserve his posterity and not forsake his friends was by a treaty.[35]

Morrah thought that Rupert accepted his uncle's reasoning of the 31 July, as does Sir Charles Petrie, in *King Charles, Prince Rupert and the Civil War*. This letter shows Rupert continued to oppose it. The tragedy is that the prince might never have received the king's other letters about strategy, or the touching one of 4 August with its approbation to go to the Prince of Wales. How much the communication breakdown negatively affected Rupert's mindset in the lead up to the siege of Bristol can only be speculated, but it cannot have helped one bit.

Rumours in August had the Marquess of Ormonde due to be called to England to replace Rupert as Lord General. Behind the scenes, Digby persisted in undermining the prince, extracting a fresh promise from the king to take all military direction from his council. Seeing himself as one of four who remained truly loyal to the king, Digby fell out with his former allies, George Goring and Lord Byron. To Rupert, isolated in Bristol, none of this was important anymore. The city was surrounded by the New Model Army.

Chapter 25

Great Error

On 23 August Fairfax arrived before Bristol. Included within his army were six men who would later sign the king's death warrant. When the summons came for Rupert to surrender, it was intensely personal. '[L]et all *England* judge whether the burning of its Towns, ruining its Cities, and destroying its People, be a good Requital from a Person of your Family, which hath had the Prayers, Tears, Purses, and Blood of its Parliament and People.'[1]

The prince kept the messenger overnight in a bid to delay proceedings. Rupert felt Bristol had never been 'in better Condition then now' with his officers and soldiers paid and billeted in town.[2] In preparation for this moment, he had rounded up all surrounding cattle, obtained 2,000 bushels of corn from Wales, and fired nearby villages to prevent them being used as cover by the enemy. Having started with only enough ammunition for three hours of fighting, furious preparation meant that munitions were now stockpiled.

The very first day of the siege dealt a wounding loss. The garrison sallied out to show their resolve, and during the action, Sir Richard Crane – the prince's old friend and commander of his lifeguard – was mortally wounded. The Royalists made aggressive sorties every day for the next week. Another notable casualty was Bernard Astley, son of Rupert's former tutor, Jacob. Such close deaths could not fail to have affected the prince.

Fairfax soon engaged a council of war over whether to storm the place. Lengthy discussions were interrupted by news that Montrose had won yet another victory in Scotland, and that the king, having found it impossible to head north, now considered relieving Bristol with support from George Goring's troops at Exeter. On 1 September, amidst wet and misty weather, Rupert led 1,600 troops out of Bristol's gates and attacked the enemy lines. They inflicted many casualties and captured Colonel John Okey, who had commanded Fairfax's dragoons at Naseby. The unfortunate man had mistaken Rupert's troops for his own side.

The prince's ally in Oxford, Edward Nicholas, praised his attacks. News of them prompted the king at Raglan Castle to write to his nephew promising speedy relief. Worrying over Rupert's safety, he counselled against being at the forefront of such fighting 'in his own person'.[3] But the prince received no letters from anyone during the siege, nor could any relief have been possible due to the king's lack of men.

On 4 September, Rupert was again called upon to surrender, to which he asked leave to obtain the king's opinion. Fairfax recognised this delay tactic. Between 7 and 9 September, the two men continued written exchanges. Then, at 2.00 am on 10 September, the exasperated Fairfax gave orders to storm the city. The signal was the burning of straw and firing of four cannons against Prior's Hill Fort. Though Rupert was ready, having already received a tip-off, he had too few men to cover the vast defences. For three hours the enemy attacked Prior's Hill with roundshot and caseshot, and after finally capturing it, the defenders were put to the sword. Before long, nearly half the Royalists' defensive line, including forts, bulwarks, and ordnance, was lost, leaving their situation hopeless. The prince sent for a parley.

Rupert could have persisted by retreating into the castle, but there seemed no hope of relief. After consulting his officers, the prince agreed to surrender, considering it better to preserve what was left of his garrison. When they came to march out, there were many 'insolencies' from Fairfax's men, prompting Rupert to demand redress.[4] The Royalists were allowed to retain their arms for defensive purposes only, until they made it back to Oxford. After Rupert's death nearly forty years later, *Life and Death of Prince Rupert* would specify he had permission to surrender on honourable terms if he was put to extremities.

On the day that Bristol fell, Digby wrote to Montrose in Scotland praising the man's 'miraculous successes' as a great comfort to the distressed king. It was these victories, he alleged, that had allowed the king to chase the Scottish army out of Wales and raise the siege of Hereford. Far from being chased off, the concerned Scots had left to deal with Montrose and secure their homeland, sending a strong detachment of their cavalry ahead. The deluded Digby, however, asserted that Montrose – along with God – now had the honour of completing the king's 'restauration'. Anything they might achieve in England would pale into insignificance and be nothing but 'battailes of the Cranes and pigonyes'.[5] Sir Philip Warwick put it more realistically when he compared the king at this point to a 'hunted partridge'.[6]

Rupert rode out of Bristol on 11 September impeccably dressed in scarlet, adorned with silver lace, atop a black Arabian. He and his men were escorted by Fairfax and Cromwell. The respect with which Rupert was treated was summed up in a Parliamentarian letter that was intercepted when the messenger was 'made drunke'.[7] In it, Rupert was praised as a person of much honour and desirous of peace, having promised he would intercede with the king in favour of it. On the weight of this, Parliamentarians considered ensuring that nothing be put in print that would reflect negatively on the prince's actions. A faction of Royalists, led by Digby, had no such qualms.

Almost as soon as Rupert made it to Oxford, he set about working on a document defending his conduct at Bristol, knowing that he would be the 'subject of every ones passion, how unjust soever'.[8] Digby went in for the kill, persuading the king that Rupert, who had advocated peace not six weeks earlier, had purposefully rendered Bristol to force the matter. The queen was also said to be highly dissatisfied with

Rupert. In a letter to the 10-year-old Duke of York, the bitter king expressed a wish that the boy be 'knocked on the head' than ever mimic so mean an action as the surrender of Bristol.[9] No sooner had the king relieved Rupert of his offices than Digby played kingmaker. He wrote to the Marquess of Ormonde suggesting that the way had been cleared for the man to take over as Lord General, though Ireland was in no state for this to become a reality.

The Digby propaganda machine was in overdrive. His secretary, Edward Walsingham in Oxford, was described as the man's 'intimate servant' and a 'great babbler' of all secrets.[10] Both master and servant sensed their opportunities. From at least mid-August, Walsingham had been encouraging Digby to strike at the prince and Bristol offered the opportunity. Walsingham incriminated Will Legge and warned of a plot to surrender Oxford too. Rather lamely, he reported that Rupert had addressed Legge in recent letters as 'brother governor' – the prince governing Bristol and Legge Oxford – and used this as evidence of collusion. The fact that Digby referred to Edward Nicholas as his 'brother' secretary was immaterial. When Rupert arrived in Oxford, Walsingham kept his beady eyes on him. He supposedly observed the prince walking in the gardens at Christchurch with Legge, while those around them removed their hats and stood bare headed – in Walsingham's opinion it was as if the king had been present. Digby's wife took aside Lord Hawley, who had been with Rupert at Bristol, and attempted to recruit him to their ends. Hawley craved the king's forgiveness over Bristol, and perhaps thinking the Digbys were best placed to help, told them that Rupert had an intention of inducing the king to a peace. Walsingham went further, hinting that Rupert sought the crown itself. Yet, peace was also called for by the Prince of Wales, who wrote to Fairfax about the kingdom's calamities and offered to become an instrument to bring matters to a close.

Digby convinced the king that he had a dossier of evidence against William Legge, resulting in an order for man's 'clapping upp'.[11] Secretary of State, Edward Nicholas, was left to enact the fateful royal commands, arranging to confine Legge, and serving Rupert with the letter that dismissed him. When writing to confirm all was done, Nicholas added a line of support for Rupert, asserting that the prince had less than £50 in the world.

On 16 September, Digby, in Hereford, redoubled his ascendancy over the forlorn monarch. Writing to Edward Hyde, who was with the Prince of Wales, he rued the loss of Bristol, but confidently fancied that the capitulation might have been divinely ordained – after all, they would now 'gaine more in being ridd of P Rup [Prince Rupert]'.[12] In another letter commenting on Bristol, Digby even amended his description of its 'surrendring' by striking the word out and replacing it with the stronger 'surrendring the fort & castle of Bristoll without a stroake' – despite having previously praised the prince's relentless sorties.[13] To ensure that there would be no chance of Rupert's resurrection, Digby spread rumours that the prince had been in touch with his eldest brother, the Elector Palatine. However false, it was damning, because Charles Louis was lodged in Whitehall Palace, sleeping in his uncle's peacetime bedchamber, and cavorting with MPs at Westminster. With

3,000 cavalry, the king and Digby headed north to Chester, the latter gleefully judging their position to be like a 'Dreame' and predicting it would seem so to 'future Ages'.[14] The king, however, did not shake off thoughts of Rupert as easily. Writing to Prince Maurice from Newtown on 20 September, he touched on Rupert's 'great Error' in the 'unhansom' quitting of Bristol. It had, he said, given him 'more Greefe then any Misfortune since this damnable Rebellion'. He added 'I am most confident [Rupert's action] hath no waise proceeded from his change of Affection to me or my cause, but, meerly, by having his Judgement seduced by some rotten-harted Villaines, making faire pretentions to him.'

True affection for Rupert also shines through with the declaration that 'I am resolved so little to forgett his former services, that, whensoever it shall please God to enable me to looke upon my Frends lyke a King, he shall thanke God for the paines he hath spent in my Armys.'[15]

For his part, Rupert languished in a state of anger and grief with his honour and self-esteem in tatters. As soon as he was informed of his dismissal, he wrote to remind his uncle that he had joined the cause with no other motivation than to do him service. Being censured without a hearing was galling, and the lines barely disguised his raw feeling. He begged permission to attend the king and state his case, or else publish a defence to the world. As for the royal command to dispose of himself beyond the seas, there is a hint of sarcasm when Rupert questions whether the dire situation would make that possible – despite the king's pass.

The spectre of defeat loomed again on 24 September 1645. Rowton Heath was a battle in three parts, the last playing out under the king's nose as he watched from Chester Cathedral. In the chaotic action, his remaining cavalry took a pounding, and his cousin, Bernard Stuart, Earl of Lichfield, and commander of his lifeguard, was slain. The route to Scotland remained blocked. Digby notified Montrose that intentions remained 'to breake through all difficultyes to come to you' and dismissed any notion that the Royalists had been 'much worsted' at Rowton, declaring the enemy to have suffered the same losses.[16] Pinning his hopes to news that Montrose had marched into England, he assured the Scotsman that Ormonde could send him reinforcements from Ireland. The truth was that just two weeks before Rowton, Montrose's troops had been trounced at Philiphaugh, at the Scottish border. The king's options were dwindling as fast as his remaining garrisons. Attempting to prevent his master from going to Oxford (and Rupert), Digby advocated taking the remaining troops to Newark and then striking north through Yorkshire.

A gloating Parliamentarian pamphlet was published in a final riposte to Prince Rupert, written as if his last will and testament. It decrees a desire to 'see my Body decently carried beyond Sea', poking fun at the king's orders for him to leave the kingdom.[17] He leaves towns, castles and forts to Parliament and decrees that all money and plunder should be restored to its true owners. Rupert, however, was very much alive and kicking. While Digby implored Ormonde to travel to England and take command, explaining they were more in want of a general than an army, Rupert felt certain he could regain favour if his arguments were heard.

Welbeck Abbey was the furthest north the king and Digby reached. The bygone world of the monks had been linked to the current owners, the courtly Cavendish family. William Cavendish, Marquess of Newcastle, had left England after Marston Moor and remained on the continent. A famed equestrian, his Welbeck riding houses, where extraordinary feats had been performed, were now empty. As the king reviewed his few remaining horsemen, he prayed they might achieve a miracle for him. The subsequent shock appointment of Lord Digby as Lieutenant General north of the Trent took aback this last band of brothers. The 2,000 cavalrymen were top-heavy with officers, many of whom were better qualified than the political pariah. Then word finally reached them of Montrose's defeat one month earlier at Philiphaugh.

Deciding to remain in Newark, the king delegated to Digby the task of leading half his cavalry north, but at Sherburn-in-Elmet, on 15 October 1645, Digby met with disaster only days into his journey. His force limped on to Annan Moor, southern Scotland, where they were vanquished. The Royalists paid the price for Digby's inept leadership. When the king's private papers had been captured at Naseby, Digby had condemned those who had left such precious items in the royal carriage. At Sherburn, his own coach was taken, along with sixty-nine personal letters and a cache of ciphers, which were all embarrassingly scrutinised.

With his hopes dashed, the king remained cut off in Newark. Plague stalked the streets. Prince Rupert, too, was heading directly for his uncle. Unable to put up with fresh slurs over Bristol, one stemming from the queen's circle that he had 'sold the towne for money', the prince set off on a cross-country march to exonerate himself.[18] Eighty volunteers from Oxford accompanied him, including his devoted brother, Maurice. An enemy force harried them, and one rider (a Royalist deserter) rode up to Rupert and shot at point-blank range, though the weapon misfired. The king forbade his nephews entry to Newark, but they were nevertheless given a ceremonial welcome by the governor, Sir Richard Willis.

Upon entering the royal presence on 16 October, Rupert was said to have employed little formality or respect. Maintaining a dignified front, King Charles responded with a few words to Maurice and stomached their presence all through supper. Succumbing to Rupert's persistence, the king eventually granted a court martial, which found in Rupert's favour and exonerated him from cowardice or treachery. Unfortunately, it did not draw a line under matters. The vulnerable monarch, on the verge of defeat, now had little left but his dignity. Sir Richard Willis's provocative greeting of Rupert, after the king had forbidden entry, could not go unpunished – Willis was removed from the governorship and appointed to command the royal lifeguard. Although in effect a promotion, it reflected poorly on the man's honour to have been removed from the governorship under such circumstances. Willis, like Rupert, now demanded a court martial.

Newark was no haven. Secretary-at-War, Sir Edward Walker, noted that Digby had insisted upon taking the king there for the sole purpose of keeping uncle and nephew apart. Plague and the enemy lurked. When, amidst these disputes, a window of opportunity arose, the king made ready to take it and hurry back to Oxford. As he prepared to leave, Rupert and Willis, along with Charles Gerard, burst into his presence after church on Sunday, 26 October. The prince was aggrieved at Willis's removal for being his 'faithfull friend' and complained it was a slur on them both. The king defended his decision. When Gerard interceded in their support, raising his own grievances over losing command in Wales, the king countered that the superiority of the Scottish army had meant Gerard could not subsist there.

Gerard	I was able to make good Army and Garrisons against the Scots.
King	[You] Tell me I lie.
Rupert	I beseech your Majesty let not Sir *Richard* suffer for being my freind.
King	By God he doth not.

The prince then spoke for everyone when he named Digby as the creator of all this bad blood. When Gerard agreed, the king accused them of suggesting he was 'but a child' led 'by the nose' by Digby and angrily defended him as an honest man – any who disagreed were traitors. Gerard, making a cutting retort, suggested in that case they all must be traitors.

King	Perhaps you have spoke the words: otherwise you would never have come and raised such mutinies, and that publickly.

Both Gerard and Willis realised they had stepped out of line and attempted to make amends. The king expostulated that he hazarded his life for them all and the good of his people, at which point Rupert – unmoved – insisted that Willis be restored to his former position.

Willis	I am disgraced every where, boyes point at me; I have nothing to live upon but my reputation, and thats now gone, for no cause given to your Majesty.
King	What have I left to me [?] I am sure the Rebels have possessed themselves of all my goods, Towns, Magazines

The quarrel ended abruptly when Rupert asked for a pass to leave the kingdom, whereupon the king sighed and replied, 'O' nephew.'[19] Matters were so bad that the king offered passes to any who wanted them. Soon enough Rupert, Willis, and Gerard, together with between 200 and 400 men, took up the offer and left Newark. The king was said to have watched his nephew go with tears in his eyes. It's hard not to sympathise with King Charles at this point of low ebb, and certainly Rupert was being arrogant and uncaring, as well as self-absorbed. Maurice supported his brother but showed more discretion and restraint.

The prince and his party did not go far, however. They reached Belvoir, a Royalist garrison that stood like an island amidst enemy territory. From there he wrote to Parliament asking for leave to depart the kingdom and for an escort to convey him safely to Banbury. On 30 October he received warning that Sydenham Poyntz, Parliament's commander in the north, was drawing close and might disturb them. After Rupert's petition for a pass had been before the House of Lords, he was informed that there was overwhelming support – 'they are fearefull that you should returne againe to the kings service'. What's more, within the letters captured after Digby's defeat in Yorkshire was a copy of the king's response to Rupert's call for peace. The discovery of this letter did Rupert a 'greate deale of right' and elicited him much support at Westminster.[20]

From Belvoir the disgruntled Royalists put affairs in order after their 'late unhappy difference' with the king, arranging for their houses to be cleared and horses sold. News of Digby's hat-trick of defeats reached them, prompting Gerard to mock that the fallen secretary-cum-commander did not even have 100 pens (scribes) nor 100 soldiers left. Rupert, considering the king's cause to be 'totally lost', wrote to Will Legge on 3 November and afforded just three words about Digby – 'Alas! poor man.'[21]

In Newark, King Charles turned to one of the last commanders he had. The Marquess of Montrose's stunning successes had shored the king up after Naseby, and in these gloomy November days, he expressed affliction that he could send him no succour. Instead, he praised Montrose's 'eminent fidelity and generosity' and assured the marquess that his last defeat had far from lessened royal esteem. In his lonely moment, King Charles opened his heart to this fellow Scotsman. Employing a Scottish phrase, he asserted his affection for Montrose would 'kythe the cleerlier' – or would be clearly shown in due course.[22]

In London, MPs became more 'insolent' in the wake of Digby's defeat, and though agreeing that Rupert could depart the kingdom, they warned he should not come anywhere near the capital. Now having permission from both king and Parliament to leave, Rupert dragged his heels. He travelled to Banbury and then Worcester, where he remained for weeks, prompting the king to write to the governor to query this 'long abode'. The monarch then commanded the prince and his followers to go by 1 December, to prevent the 'eating out of Our quarters' by those who had abandoned his cause.[23] At the end of November, Rupert's band went to Woodstock, where their continued delay perplexed both sides.

Rupert's reticence was encouraged by many. The Earl of Dorset hoped the prince did not 'have the hart to leave us all in our saddest times' nor abandon his uncle. Sink or swim with the king, Dorset urged, calling on God to inspire Rupert.[24] Will Legge pointed out, as only he could, that King Charles was 'a Kinge, [your] unkle, and in effect a parent to you'. He counselled Rupert to submit himself, adding that 'in Civillity you ought to doe it'.[25] An anonymous entreaty from someone who valued Rupert 'above all the world besyds' and whose heart was faithful to his service revealed that they had heard the king express sorrow over the finality of Rupert's parting. The anonymous correspondent begged the prince to make 'sume hansume applycation' to the king, reminding him that he had many friends at court – his enemies could only 'barcke' at him and not 'fytt' (fight).[26] Morrah guessed the author was the Duchess of Richmond. The lobbying paid off.

Rupert's first attempt to make amends was a letter stating the great 'vallew' he placed in his uncle's favour and affection, which had such 'rule' over his thoughts. '[M]y havinge beene now som tyme as I am from you is [too] great an Evidence to perswade a beleefe of my failing of that respect and dutye I owe you.'

Underlying resentment over his treatment was still apparent. The letter did not go far enough, and the king signified as much to Legge, after granting the latter's freedom. Rupert's second letter did 'freely acknowledge my errours' and entreated the king to judge him by his better and more lasting expressions of zeal and affection.[27] Still, much was left to be desired. It has been related that Rupert next sent the king a blank sheet of paper with his signature at the bottom, implying that he would write anything required. This, King Charles received with much emotion. By 9 December, Rupert was in Oxford, where the king embraced him and 'repented much' his nephew's ill usage.[28]

Chapter 26

Prejudicial to Monarchie

As 1645 came to an end, there was little Rupert could do other than wait on the last throws of the Royalist dice. From Dudley Castle, the Royalist governor warned that the king's soldiers everywhere were discontented and laying down their arms. The monarch tried in vain to weld governors, commanders, and commissioners together, issuing orders that 'all opinions bee layd aside that breed misunderstandings' to focus better efforts against the enemy.[1] This, along with his subsequent complaints about 'the generall defection of comon honnesty' fell mostly on deaf ears.[2] Chester and its lifeline to Ireland, from where the king hoped to receive reinforcements, surrendered on 3 February 1646. On 16 February, the army in the southwest, led by Lord Hopton, was defeated at Torrington. Then, on 21 March, the last Royalist field army in England, commanded by Lord Astley, put up a courageous fight at Stow-on-the-Wold. When the Parliamentarians clinched victory, Astley is said to have sat on a drum in the market square and told the enemy, 'You have done your work and may go play, unless you fall out among yourselves.'[3]

As Fairfax encircled Oxford, the king planned his final move, unwilling to be checkmated. There was talk of him going to London, where his presence might provoke an uprising, or at least give him more control of the endgame. The queen warned that unless he went to the capital at the head of an army, then he was lost. Rupert, however, was said to believe that if his uncle could get to the capital with 300 men, then within three hours he would have ten times that number – the prince was also credited with a vow to 'cut all the Throats of the Roundheaded Rogues that sit in the Parliament'.[4] MPs made it known that if the king came to the capital uninvited, he would be placed under restraint in the Tower. The French were also meddling, attempting to prevent a clear victory by either side, so that internal dispute kept the three kingdoms neutered. Their ambassador extraordinaire recommended the king surrender to the Scottish army at Newark, who had hinted they might support his restoration.

Short of leaving his kingdoms, which the king would never do, throwing himself upon the flimsy promises of the Scots was his best option. He consulted Rupert about gathering troops to escort him to the Scottish army near Newark but eventually settled on disguising himself and making his way with just a few followers. Warning against the plan, the prince nevertheless offered to accompany his uncle, though this was declined on account of his 'tallnesse' which would give the game away.[5] On 10 April, Rupert requested that his objections be confirmed in writing, considering the plan 'of such eminent danger' to his uncle's person. King Charles complied, but insisted that Rupert 'must conceale this, untill the Action be over; & in the meane tyme, assist me, as hartely, in it, as if you fully concurred with me'.[6]

Accordingly, on 27 April 1646, at 3.00 am, the king rode out of Oxford. His hair and beard had been cut short, no longer looking like the divine monarch glorified by van Dyck's brushes. His final court artist, William Dobson, was just finishing a portrait of the king, which captured the vulnerable man so often hidden behind the veneer of monarchy, replete with a haunting look of defeat. Little was heard of the king for eight days. On 5 May 1646, he finally surrendered to the Scots at Southwell, only to discover that they had repudiated previous discussions with the French envoy. This left the monarch livid over the 'relapsed perfidiousness' of the Scots.[7]

With Royalists left to fend for themselves, Rupert made overtures to Fairfax, whose New Model Army 'came so thick' around Oxford. Three days before the king turned up at Southwell, Rupert enquired whether Fairfax might offer the prince 'some place of liberty and safty'.[8] Despite this communication, Rupert had not given over the fight. On 12 May, he rode out of Oxford without riding boots, instead wearing 'shooes and stockings'.[9] Accompanied by 100 horsemen, they were fired on by the Parliamentarians, one shot piercing Rupert's shoulder but missing the bone. In the final days of the civil war, the legendary figure had been proved mortal – his wound was symptomatic of the fallen cause. But the prince's miraculous luck had not entirely vanished, for as he dropped his pistol, it was said to have fired as it hit the ground and shot his opponent's horse. Dispensing with riding boots suggests an unplanned act, or perhaps a way of covering his intention to mount up and lead an attack. Whether attempting to break through the besieger's lines and escape, perhaps even with a resolve to rescue the king, or simply taking part in a sortie against the besiegers, Rupert's motives are unclear.

May 1646 had the Palatine family scattered across Europe in an even more hopeless position than ever. King Charles's surrender prompted hope that a peaceful settlement would improve the family's fortunes. They might also come back together as a result. While Rupert and Maurice were in beleaguered Oxford, Charles Louis remained in London, where a citizen attempted to arrest him at a city feast. When Edward committed the ultimate sin and converted to Catholicism in 1645, a religious divide split the siblings. It had stemmed from living in Paris, where he met Anne, daughter of the Duke of Nevers. The pair were married soon after. Sir Kenelm Digby mused that nobody could refuse such a 'sweete and winning' prince.[10] Henry Jermyn called it a true 'Romance story'.

Union and conversion had been kept secret from the groom's family – though his aunt, Henrietta Maria, had played matchmaker. In her eyes, Edward would

Prince Rupert as a boy, by Jan Lievens. Circa 1631. (Creative Commons)

A young Rupert, by Gerrit van Honthorst. Unknown date. (Creative Commins)

Prince Rupert in Combat Dress, copy after Anthony van Dyck. Circa 1645. (Rijksmuseum)

Princess Elisabeth (1618–1680) Rupert's sister, by Alexander Cooper, after Gerrit van Honthorst. Circa 1640–50. (Rijksmuseum)

Prince Maurice (1621–1652) Rupert's brother, by Gerrit van Honthorst. 1643. (Creative Commons)

Princess Louise (1622–1709) by Gerrit van Honthorst. 1648. (Creative Commons)

Prince Edward (1625–1663), Rupert's brother, after Gerrit van Honthorst. Seventeenth century. (Creative Commons)

Rupert's Standard at Marston Moor, by Abraham Cooper. Circa 1824. (Tate Images)

Prince Rupert by Wallerant Vaillant. Circa 1658. It almost certainly portrays Rupert during his time in Frankfurt, when he produced many engravings of his own. (© The Trustees of the British Museum)

The Beheading of John the Baptist, by Prince Rupert. 1658. (Rijksmuseum)

The Magdalen, by Prince Rupert. 1659. (Creative Commons)

The Standard Bearer, by Prince Rupert. 1658. (Rijksmuseum)

The *Constant Reformation*, by William van de Velde the Elder. 1648. (Creative Commons)

Prince Rupert, by Sir Peter Lely. Commissioned by James, Duke of York in 1665, following naval victory over the Dutch at Lowestoft. One of a set of 13 portraits of the naval commanders. Circa 1665–1668. (Creative Commons)

Frances Bard (c.1646–1708), by Sir Peter Lely. Seventeenth century. (Creative Commons)

George Monck, Duke of Albermarle (1608–1670), by Sir Peter Lely. Seventeenth century. (Rijksmuseum)

Prince Rupert, by Nicholas Dixon. Circa 1665–1708. (The Portland Collection, Harley Gallery, Welbeck Estate, Nottinghamshire / Bridgeman Images)

Ruperta (1673–1741) daughter of Prince Rupert, by John Keyse Sherwin. 1787. (Creative Commons)

Margaret (Peg) Hughes (Unknown–1719), Prince Rupert's partner and mother of Ruperta, by Sir Peter Lely. 1672. (Creative Commons)

Left: Monument mentioning Henry Harcourt, who married Sarah Frances Bard, the niece of Rupert's mistress, Frances Bard. Installed in St John the Baptist, Aldbury, decades after Frances Bard's death, it details that Persiana had been 'sister to Princess Rupert'. As shown in this image, attempts have since been made to erase the reference to Frances Bard as 'Princess Rupert'. 2024. (Kind permission of Rev. Michelle Grace)

Below: Closer image of the reference to 'Princess Rupert'.

receive a stable income, position at court, and prospects that eluded the other penniless, Protestant Palatines. Anne was a beautiful and 'very riche' heiress in her own right with an income estimated at £6–7,000 per annum.[11] Anticipating the family fall-out, Edward had considered joining Rupert in England fighting for their uncle. The latter had put in a good word. Although a gentleman had duly been despatched to collect Edward, the prince was not destined for war-torn England. His mother found out and, after expressing a wish to die at the news, demanded in vain that Edward go to her. Nor could Edward be talked out of his 'sopperies'.[12] Rumours abounded that he would head to Rome for the Pope's blessing, whereupon he would be made Elector Palatine and supplant his brother. The eldest sister, Elisabeth, was equally upset over it all and received extra doses of philosophical advice from Descartes.

Charles Louis, pressing for an extra gentleman to attend his younger brother Philip, hoped to prevent any similar folly, though it was decided the army would offer suitable distraction. A posting in Venetian service seemed heaven-sent. As Philip made ready to depart, Charles Louis bid their mother to lay her 'curse' upon him, that warned against any temptation to change religion.[13] Of a similar character to Rupert, it was murder that would taint the 18-year-old. Jaques, Count L'Epinay, a young Frenchman in exile, had attached himself to Philip's mother, the Queen of Bohemia. For her part, the queen relished his attention – adored by many men, she was the epitome of a damsel in distress. A cult of courtly adoration surrounded her, with L'Epinay playing a full part. In June 1646, Philip flew into a rage upon hearing that L'Epinay was claiming to have slept with both his mother and sister, Louise. It was even said that the latter had given birth to his love child.

Attempts to bar L'Epinay from the queen's presence on 15 June proved unsuccessful. That night, Philip was assaulted – he claimed by L'Epinay – and they duelled. Tensions spilled over to the following day, when Philip and his friends chased L'Epinay, culminating in the prince stabbing the man with his hunting knife. As a result, Philip fled Holland, leaving his mother split between rage and sorrow. Rupert intervened in his defence, supported by Charles Louis, who said that had Philip not sought satisfaction, the 'blemish' would have been a lifelong stain on his honour.[14] Princess Elisabeth's support of Philip resulted in her mother sending her to live at the court of the Elector of Brandenburg – exile in all but name.

Morrah puts the date of L'Epinay's murder as 20 June 1646. As Philip's knife severed the Frenchman from the Queen of Bohemia's side, Oxford surrendered on King Charles's orders and civil war in England and Scotland came to an uneasy end after nearly four years. Rupert and Maurice were permitted to leave the kingdom within six months, though forbidden from coming within 20 miles of London. Initially they went to Oatlands Palace, in Surrey, and there must have met their cousin, baby Henrietta – King Charles and Queen Henrietta Maria's last child, who had been born in 1644. From here, word reached the two brothers that Charles Louis wished to meet them. On 1 July, the three siblings met in Guildford. There was much to discuss; Edward, Philip, and the prospect that at least the lower part of the Palatinate might be restored to Charles Louis as the Thirty Years' War came to an end. For reasons that remain unclear, Parliament suddenly gave Rupert and Maurice ten days to leave England, therefore they made their way straight to Dover. On 5 July, Rupert sailed for Calais, and three days later Maurice left for Holland. A pamphlet celebrated their departure.

> All I can say is to you Prince Rupert, England is heartily glad to see you so neere to be gone, and her doth wish you never to come againe ... And for you Prince Maurice, [pray] never think of comming into Wales againe, for if you do, all [the] plunder'd Cows-bobby, all [the] Onions, Leeks, and Oat-Cakes in Wales will muster themselves together, and rise up in Judgement against you.[15]

After disembarking at Calais on 10 July 1646, Rupert travelled to the exiled court of Queen Henrietta Maria at Saint-Germain. There he was given a cold shoulder by his aunt. Not only was he still tainted by his surrender of Bristol, but the queen was surrounded by many of his enemies, too. As a result, the prince was 'ill entertained' by his aunt until the Queen Regent of France intervened.[16] Rupert was then offered a military post, so eager was France to secure his talent. He accepted, as ever having little money, but obtained permission to re-enter King Charles I's service whenever required. His uncle, held prisoner by the Scottish army at Newcastle, wrote to Henrietta Maria in favour of him on 5 August. 'If thou see Pr. Rupert tell him I have recommend him to thee, for albeit his passions may sometimes make him mistake, yet I am confident of his honest constancy and courage, having at least [last?] behaved himself very well.'[17]

The Prince of Wales welcomed Rupert and asked him to act as an interpreter during meetings with a prospective wife. Prince Charles was not a willing groom, and Rupert most likely also found such trifles quite tedious. But the young prince relished having his famous cousin by his side, who was an antidote to the stuffy French court. Rupert was not distracted from the business of war for long, recruiting displaced Royalists and soon enough amassing 2,000 men.

By 10 April 1647, with 'comand of all the english, wch are or shall bee brought in this kingdome [France]', Rupert searched for officers that he knew and trusted. One man he entreated to join him was his friend, Sir John Owen, to whom he offered 'much better conditions, then other princes give'.[18] The Welshman was instructed to raise men in England, Scotland, or Ireland and ship them to Calais. Eager to serve under the prince, he replied 'thinking one worthy of your commands, so farr engages me'.[19] The unreliable George Goring's application to the prince was, by comparison, refused out of hand.

With Scotland torn over its loyalties, and a significant faction building in support of King Charles I, Rupert kept one eye on developments. The Scots had handed the king to the English in exchange for £400,000 but seeing the New Model Army was increasingly dominated by Puritans, they now recognised them as the greater threat. By May, Rupert was being mooted as leader of a Scottish Royalist force, subordinate to the titular command of the Prince of Wales. As the English Parliament and their army came to loggerheads, they each made separate attempts to negotiate a favourable peace settlement with the king, despite the army having no legal position to do so.

Wartime loyalty had been split between king or Parliament, but the burning question was now Independent or Presbyterian? MPs sympathising with the latter, seen as more moderate, took control of London's trained bands. Thus threatened, the New Model Army entered London to restore order and suppressed the Presbyterian coup.

Meanwhile, Rupert's brigade was tasked with the relief of Armentières, under siege by a Spanish army of 20,000, and despatched to the border of the Spanish Netherlands. The French army of 7,000 that he joined was – like a job share – commanded on alternate days by two very different men. The Comte de Gassion was a young Frenchman, while the other, Marshal Rantzau, was an aged Dane. Neither respected the other. What's more, Gassion was reckless with his own safety and so had even less regard for anyone else's. On one occasion he went alone to carry out reconnaissance of the enemy and only escaped with his life due to Rupert's timely assistance. Tempting fate, Gassion did the same again, though this time requested Rupert accompany him. The prince did so but took his servant Mortaigne and page Robert Holmes along, but were soon spotted by a party of Spanish horsemen who rounded on them. Though Rupert and Gassion got away, Mortaigne and Holmes were both wounded, the latter in the leg. Gassion and his attendants fled. Unwilling to leave Holmes to his fate, Rupert risked his life and courageously got the man onto the back of his horse, whereupon the trio escaped.

Gassion's reckless behaviour can be criticised, but he was no different to the young Rupert, who had crept through the trenches towards Breda at great personal risk. It was the abandonment of the prince and his followers that was entirely disgraceful. The growing discord between Rupert and Gassion finally reached breaking point when the prince beat back 6,000 Spanish troops whilst covering the French retreat. At a suitable point, Rupert made ready to fall back too, but Gassion instructed him to stand firm against overwhelming odds. Perhaps jealousy on the comte's part accounted for his behaviour. Refusing to hold this untenable position – it was not even Gassion's day to command – Rupert retreated regardless. If left unchecked, such games would consume one or both men.

When Rupert captured the town of La Bassee without French assistance, rivalry inevitable increased. Ironically, the Spanish defenders had included a contingent commanded by none other than George Goring, the civil war thorn in Rupert's side. Shortly afterwards, when Rupert and Gassion led a foraging party, the prince noticed a dog looking intently into the distance. Before he could signal his suspicions, they were ambushed. Gassion dismounted and passed order to attack on foot, though when Rupert and his attendants followed suit, the Frenchman remounted and made off with all the horses. Rupert eventually escaped, but not before taking a bullet to the head, which necessitated his return to Saint-Germain in delicate stages. A matter of weeks later, Gassion was killed. An anonymous contemporary document, referred to by historians as Rupert's diary, gave details of the prince's movements at this time. It recounts in understated terms that he was not 'well us'd' by the French commander.[20] Interestingly, Rupert's 1677 library (he was aged 58 at that time) included a copy of *La Vie du Mareshall de Gassion* so both this critical moment in his life, and the man who nearly caused his untimely end, were never forgotten.

A Parliamentarian news sheet described Rupert's wound as a brush to the head. From his captivity at Hampton Court, on 17 September 1647, King Charles wrote to his nephew and apologised for not being in touch sooner. He sent the despatch via the Duke of Richmond, the prince's great friend.

> Nepueu, amongst many Misfortunes wch are not my Falt, one is, that you have mist those expressions of kyndness I meant you, wch I belive was occasioned by your being in the Army it being lykewais [likewise] the reason that made me wryte so few letters to you; besydes, the truth is, as my Condition is yet, I cannot say any thing to you as I would, not being able to second words with dides [deeds]; wherfore excuse me if I only say this to you now, that since I saw you all you[r] Actions hath more then confirmed the good opinion I have of you, asseuring you that next my Children (I say, Next) I shall have most care of you, & shall take the first oportunity eather to imploy you, or to have your Company.

A loving postscript: 'I [heard] not of your hurt, before I was asseured of your recovery, for wch, nobody without Complyment, is glader then my selfe.'[21] Rupert was soon fighting fit in the fullest sense. Without employment to distract him, at Henrietta Maria's court he rubbed alongside many Royalists who he had quarrelled with during the civil war, such as Henry Percy. They were soon joined by George Digby, whose antics had offended so many people that there was a queue of revenge-seekers. Henry Wilmot issued the first challenge to Digby, closely followed by Rupert. Though Digby tried to exonerate his past actions, suggesting they were simply the by-product of his role as Secretary of State, Rupert was having none of it. He waited, sword in hand, in a forest at the Cross of Poissy.

When Digby warned he would be late on account of having no horses, the prince sent some of his own, but word of the duel reached Henrietta Maria. The queen sent her close confidante, Henry Jermyn (a friend of Rupert's) to stop the contest, but Digby tried to recruit the man as his second. An outraged Jermyn declared that if he did disregard the queen's orders, then he would be of Rupert's party. The encounter was only prevented by the arrival of the queen's guards and the Prince of Wales. By October, Prince Charles was mediating between Rupert and Digby and a full reconciliation was affected, Rupert declaring that he was 'far from making a quarrel with the Lord Digby upon any thing he had done against him as Secretary of State, tho' of never so much prejudice'.[22] Next Digby prepared to face Wilmot. He did so in feigned defence of Rupert's honour, claiming that Wilmot had cast a slur on the prince. No doubt Rupert found this irony amusing as two of his opponents did battle. Digby would emerge victorious, wounding Wilmot in the hand.

On 11 November 1647, King Charles escaped confinement at Hampton Court with Will Legge and two other men, and rode into the night. Just prior to this, the royal captor, Colonel Edward Whalley (a cousin of Oliver Cromwell) had shown the king a letter that warned of plots against his life. It had been written by Cromwell and may have been designed to scare the king to flight or into complete submission to the army's peace terms. His disappearance can't have been unexpected, for in light of other threats to his person, he had withdrawn his promise not to escape.

No sooner did news of the escape break than the previously fractured New Model Army reunited in the face of a common threat – very good news for Fairfax and Cromwell. Prior to this, it had been in a state of mutiny, with army commanders struggling to control the more radical elements and suppress the Levellers, who pushed for male suffrage for men over 21 years of age, regardless of property and wealth – something Fairfax and Cromwell both branded as anarchic. At a series of sessions in Putney, representatives had lobbied the army grandees about their desires for a peaceable settlement, but with the king at large, these damaging sessions were closed down. Then, at Corkbush Fields on 15 November, while attempting to reimpose authority, a mutiny occurred. Three Levellers were made to roll dice. Private Richard Arnold, after securing the lowest number, was shot dead.

Meanwhile, the fugitive king had no clear idea where to go, which suggests his flight was an unplanned gamble. Several destinations were considered: the West Country, Channel Islands, France, or a wild card – the Isle of Wight. The last was adopted. The Governor, Robert Hammond, was related to Charles's chaplain, but was also yet another cousin of Oliver Cromwell. There, King Charles found himself in closer confinement than ever.

Charles Louis had waited on his uncle during his sojourn at Hampton Court. When the king's whereabouts became known, he wrote on 24 November 1647 asking for permission to do so again. The letter betrays a troubled relationship. Acknowledging the 'dislike you expressed of my wayes & of my reasons for them', Charles Louis nevertheless proclaimed relief over the safety of his uncle's person, professing a wish that king and Parliament might come together in a good understanding. He would never forget the respect due to his uncle, no matter the outcome, nor whatever the king 'may thinke' of him.[23]

King Charles held his eldest nephew at arm's length but embraced Scottish commissioners who sought him out at his island prison. These men were very different to Parliament's allies, the Covenanters. Termed 'Engagers', they felt royal restoration would be the best way of establishing Presbyterianism in England, and after gaining a majority in the Scottish Parliament they sought a secret alliance with the king. On 26 December 1647, this was signed and sealed. They promised military aid in exchange for the king's commitment to establish Presbyterianism for a defined period. Rupert was kept closely informed. He was advised to befriend the Duke of Hamilton, leader of the Engagers, and told that Scotland would have a 'great stroake' in settling the king's affairs.[24] A new civil war was in the brewing. Lord Craven, the Palatine family's generous supporter, felt matters were becoming 'prejudicial to monarchie and absolutely distructive to episcopacy'. He half-expected the king to be taken to the Tower of London at any moment.[25]

As a long-expected Scottish army gathered, there was one old score to settle before Rupert felt he could leave the past behind him. Henry Percy, former General of Ordnance, had given the prince many personal jibes and hindered his military operations. During a hunting expedition, Rupert seized Percy's bridle, and demanded satisfaction over a more recently perceived slight. Both men dismounted and fought immediately. Rupert wounded Percy in the 'fleshie part' of his right side and hurt his hand.[26] James Fen, a Scotsman in Paris, reported home about this 'very new a publick quarrell'. Despite his non-serious wounds, Percy had 'performed his parte with all the gallantrye can bee imagined'.[27]

While Rupert and Percy fought like dogs, Commonwealth England turned on itself. The commander of Pembroke Castle declared for the king, ostensibly as a protest over lack of wages and against Parliament's intentions to disband the New Model Army. It was a spark that soon had all South Wales in revolt. Rioters at Norwich declared their support of the king, as did a 30,000-strong petition sent in from the county of Essex. Then, on 28 April 1648, Royalist Sir Marmaduke Langdale secured Berwick and a day later Carlisle Castle was taken. These two strongholds opened communication and supply lines for the Scottish army. The month of May saw scenes of riot at Bury St Edmunds, while the 14-year-old Duke of York escaped from captivity in London during a tactical game of hide and seek. Before the month was out, Kentish Royalists took Dartford and Deptford, as well as numerous other towns and fortresses. Such revolts were not confined to land; nine ships of the Royal Navy declared for the king and for the first time the Royalists had men-of-war at their disposal instead of mere armed merchantmen. Rumours were rife that the Prince of Wales was to land in England.

Chapter 27

Heavie Tye

On 20 May, the Town Clerk of Sandwich was called out of his bed at 3.00 am with news that Prince Charles was in the Bell Tavern. The clerk roused a sea captain and went immediately to investigate. As the stranger slept, the pair resolved it was not the prince on account of his flaxen-coloured hair but respectfully waited until he awoke before questioning him. When the man asserted that he was, indeed, Prince Charles, the mayor was called, and messengers urgently sent to Parliament. Having enjoyed chicken dinners and a comfortable bed, the 'prince' was sent to Parliament where he admitted to being one Cornelius Evans from London.

The real prince was itching to get to Scotland rather than Sandwich. There he wanted to take command of the army being mobilised in support of his father, and the Scots were equally impatient for his presence, writing to both the king and queen to advocate it. Henrietta Maria had other plans. Instead, she sent her son to Holland, where he might take command of the squadron of vessels that had defected. Accordingly, Prince Charles left for Calais on 29 June 1648, accompanied by Rupert and the aged Earl of Forth and Brentford, both previous Royalist Lord Generals, along with a posse of civilian advisors. One Scottish observer commented that 'all industre was usid' to try to prevent Rupert from being of the party.[1]

Despite these machinations, Rupert was noted to be of cheery disposition and 'a strangely changed man in his carriage'. Temperance was noted, a quality not often associated with the prince. Lord Hatton was 'overjoyed' to see the transformation 'both for the publicke and [Prince Charles's] happiness in his company'.[2]

When the royal party arrived in Holland, they found the little fleet at Hellevoetsluis enthusiastic in its support. The Duke of York, having escaped London dressed as a woman, had been the first royal on the scene. As titular Lord High Admiral, the duke's advisors (namely Joseph Bampfield, a prime player in his escape) had Lord Willoughby of Parnham, a former Parliamentarian, appointed as vice-admiral. The boy and his confidantes were ousted when the Prince of Wales arrived and took command, though Parnham was retained.

Attempts to separate Rupert from Prince Charles, as advocated by Lord Dunsmore and other Royalists in England, continued unabated. To this effect, one of their envoys headed to Prince Charles 'with all speed'. The reasoning was that a significant number of Royalists and moderate Parliamentarians were so 'unsatisfied' with Rupert that his very presence would prevent them engaging for the king. Bampfield summed this up in a letter to Rupert, warning that any peaceful overtures might be voided by his very name, which 'carryes a warr with it'.[3] But, Bampfield added, the underlying reason of attempts to remove Rupert was jealousy of his influence with the Prince of Wales. There was no question of them being separated, for Prince Charles would not entertain it, instead harbouring much 'kindness' for his heroic cousin.[4]

Quarrels aside, time was of the essence. The Kentish Royalists had marched towards London but were defeated by Sir Thomas Fairfax. The remnants fled to Colchester and holed up in the town, which was then besieged. Cromwell had also restored order in South Wales, meaning that England was all but subdued by 8 July when a Scottish Engager army of 14,000 finally crossed the border.[5]

Two weeks after the Scots entered England, Prince Charles boarded his flagship and made ready to sail. He issued an appealing and moderate declaration, stating his intent to assist the Scots in restoring his father, but promising to maintain the freedom and privileges of Parliament, and disband the New Model Army to free the country from its cost. An act of indemnity was put forward to facilitate a peaceful reconciliation. With such proclamations heralding his arrival, the ships sailed to the Kent coast. There William Batten, Parliamentarian vice-admiral, defected – he was in turn knighted and given the same rank in the Royalist fleet. It was important that the prince was kept as close to the action as possible, either Kent and Essex, or with the Scots, who were marching down the north-west coast. A wildcard option was to free the king from the Isle of Wight and convey him to London, where his presence might secure suitable terms.

In the end, the fleet remained stagnant off the coast, attempting landings to support besieged Royalists in Deal and Sandown, though without success. Each merchant ship they intercepted, using the proceeds to fund their fleet, gradually eroded support from the traders and people of the capital. Representatives of the Engagers boarded Prince Charles's flagship and urged him to go directly to Scotland or their army.

Though 'Most pairt' of the English courtiers about Prince Charles had an aversion to him joining the Scots, he was all in favour. Unlike his father, the Prince of Wales was willing to be entirely flexible with his principles – the Scots insisted that if he was in Scotland, he should worship according to Presbyterian form, and despite significant disagreement from his advisors, he agreed.

While there was rivalry between Scottish and English councillors, it was observed that Rupert 'doeth moir suay [sway] the princis [prince's] humor then all about him'. A motion was proposed to make Rupert 'generalisimo' over the Royalist forces, which would have been detrimental to the Scots, but it was noted that he did not seem 'much tekn [taken]' by it.[6] Instead, Rupert favoured befriending the Scottish emissaries and avoiding friction. When Prince Charles was informed that Rupert and Maurice would not be welcome to accompany him to Scotland, the young man struck out the article. Rupert, displaying perfect diplomacy, promised not to go with his cousin if the point was not specified in writing and this impressed the Scots.

As matters progressed, King Charles, on the Isle of Wight, was under close guard and all escape attempts had come to nought. Cut off from events, receiving only sporadic letters from his family, he became increasingly frustrated. On 31 July, to encourage the Scottish army as best he could, he declared it was 'no small comfort to me, that my native countrey hath so true a sense of my present condition'. He backed this up with the belief that nothing but a 'Free Personal Treaty' with him could settle the unhappy distractions of these 'distressed kingdoms'.[7] In General Fairfax's words, the king was a golden ball; each faction – Scots, Parliament, and New Model Army – attempted to use him to achieve their own respective goal at the expense of the others. The following day, a letter to the Prince of Wales hinted at the stresses the king faced when he explained he would have put pen to paper sooner 'had I knowen where you had been'. He begged his son to write back, warning that he would 'take it unkindly if you doe not answer this, & write me [numerous] other letters'.

> I comand you to doe nothing whether it concernes War or Peace but with the Advice of your Councell: & that you be constant to those grounds of Religion & Honor wch heertofore I have given you.[8]

The Scottish army duly joined with English Royalists led by Sir Marmaduke Langdale and this combined force was intercepted by Cromwell at Preston, on 17 August 1648. Having just restored order in Wales, 'Old Ironside's' speedy arrival struck like a lightning bolt. Battered by rain and believing this could not possibly be the enemy commander himself with his whole army, who they believed was still in Wales, the Scots gave precious little support to Langdale's men, who were trounced. Cromwell then led his troops in pursuit of the Scots, and utterly defeated them at Winwick two days later. On the back of this double defeat, Colchester was starved into submission and surrendered on 28 August. The Prince of Wales's fleet was also running short of supplies and made ready to sail back to Holland, but first he had to deal with a mutiny. Prince Charles faced the troubled men on deck and calmed tempers, assisted by the timely appearance of the Parliamentarian fleet. With acclamations of joy and 'throwing up their capps', the mutineers instead focused their efforts against the enemy.

William Batten appeared nervous as his former comrades drew closer. Wiping sweat from his chin with a 'napkin' or cloth, Rupert took it as a secret signal to the Parliamentarians. Impatiently pacing the deck and 'swearing bloodily', Rupert threatened 'if things go ill, the first thing I will do is to shoot [Batten]'.[9] A great wind kept the two fleets apart and threatened to blow the Royalists on to the sand banks, which along with lack of victuals, made them turn for Holland. The Earl of Warwick, leading the Parliamentarian ships, followed in their wake with another detachment on its way to reinforce him. Sailing through the night, Rupert remained on deck, but when a light was spotted, assuming it to be the second enemy fleet, he gave orders to engage. Batten hurried to the Prince of Wales, persuading him they were merely colliers, and overrode Rupert. It's unlikely they were colliers, but to have engaged would have been risky in the extreme as the Royalists may have been caught between both enemy fleets. So, Batten perhaps correctly erred on the side of caution.

The Royalist ships arrived at Hellevoetsluis on 4 September 1648. Their greatest achievement was making it to the safe inner harbour, narrowly beating Warwick, who was left to anchor in the outer one. The Dutch, conscious of the animosity on their doorstep, placed a fleet of their own between the two. Both parties took their quarrels to the taverns. A bigger threat facing the Royalists was their resupply and repair whilst keeping the seamen disciplined. The Prince of Wales journeyed to The Hague. With Batten and Lord Willoughby reluctant to expend their energies, command of the fleet devolved upon Rupert, who threw himself into the role with gusto.

There was much to do. Rupert recognised the importance of paying the men and keeping them fed with beef, pork, biscuit, bread, and cheese. To this end his mother pawned some of her jewels to assist and men such as Sir William Vavasour obtained credit. Discipline was the counterbalance, which Rupert maintained with a fair, but iron, fist. When the *Constant Reformation* needed re-rigging, and a party of men from the *Antelope* refused to come aboard, he and ten officers confronted them. The order was repeated. As the men moved menacingly closer to the prince, a ringleader called out 'one and all' at which Rupert picked him up and held him over the side of the ship.[10] After due warning, the rest fell into line and the man was released. Morale was constantly tested by the Earl of Warwick, who offered an amnesty to the Royalist sailors. He even sent a small party to surreptitiously board the second largest vessel in Rupert's fleet, but the prince got wind of the plan. Royalist sailors lay in wait on the decks with pikes and swords at the ready, but spotted at the last minute, Warwick called off the operation.

Moulding this desperate band of men and securing their loyalty by force of character and personal example again proved Rupert's qualities of leadership. The Prince of Wales, recognising his cousin as the man of the hour, appointed him Lord High Admiral. Through this office, Rupert was able to counter the authority of the Earl of Warwick, who held the same post courtesy of Parliament. As was his wont, Rupert offered to have the Duke of York as titular figurehead to help see off factionalism, but this was declined – better Rupert accept all the jurisdiction he could, for jealousy and intrigue could erupt over the most minor of decisions. When a cargo of sugar was captured, Rupert appointed his friend Sir Robert Walsh to oversee the sale. Lord Culpepper, a hot-headed opponent of the prince, disagreed; Walsh, he asserted, was a known cheat. Rupert took exception and replied with words to the effect that he would defend the man's honour and almost immediately, Culpepper accepted the tacit challenge as a duel. Far from itching to fight, Rupert gingerly attempted to play down the matter, and another friend, Sir Edward Herbert, facilitated a reconciliation with Culpepper. The last laugh was Rupert's however, when he appointed Walsh vice-admiral.

When William Batten took up the Parliamentarian amnesty, and Lord Willoughby was sent to the Royalist West Indies, Rupert must have breathed a sigh of relief. The Dutch ships also left the harbour, unwilling to be pinned there as winter approached. In their absence, Rupert made extra efforts to defend his vessels, erecting batteries, and fortifications around the harbour, and putting the *Convertine* across the entrance. The Dutch baulked, but Rupert was unabashed, pointing out he had no option but to look to his own defence. Unfortunately, the *Constant Warwick*, *Hind*, *Love*, and *Satisfaction* turned themselves over to Warwick, leading Rupert to re-examine his remaining officers and put them all 'to the test'.[11] Where any faint hearts were identified, he 'putt in good men' to replace them.

The presence of his beloved brother, Maurice, who made occasional visits, must have been reassuring. Another man wishing to join Rupert and secure a place in the fleet was the Marquess of Montrose. He and Rupert were kindred spirits in terms of their military fame, implicit love and respect for the king, and disregard for courtly politics. Montrose was also blacklisted by the Scottish Engagers, being a contentious figure and having previously trounced numerous Covenanter armies. With no other desire than to fight on for the king, the inactive Montrose was reported as being 'discontent' and was held at arm's length by Prince Charles and Henrietta Maria, who feared alienating their Engager allies. Detractors spread rumours that there existed 'coraspondence twixt the parlament and [Montrose]'.[12] With his letters to Prince Charles going unanswered, Montrose had considered French service, before turning to Rupert.

The prince and marquess exchanged many letters. Rupert remained realistic about his own constraints and priorities, while encouraging and respecting Montrose; 'this imployment will not give me leave to stirr from it'.[13] Rupert's regard for the man was evident and he promised to meet the marquess when he had time, the fleet currently being a 'heavie tye'. '[T]ruly sr I shall be glad to untertake any service [with] you wch you shall be pleased to propose for wch reason & having both the same ends the kings service I must wish infinetly to see you and conferr wth [your lordship] about it.'[14]

In another, Rupert attempts to further reassure Montrose – 'the noble kindness I see [your lordship] still preserves for the King maks me much to covet that we may bee happy to serve him together'.[15]

Above all, Rupert sympathised. He understood what it was like to be ostracised by those to whom he had given everything and attacked by supposed comrades-in-the-cause. Perhaps recalling his experiences after Bristol, Rupert warned that their correspondence might draw negative attention from certain people. '[I] shall not by any want of care faile to prevent any ill use that may be made of the knowledge of it ... there are some such [people] to be taken heed of.'[16]

At the end of November, Warwick departed Hellevoetsluis with his fleet – his reputation did not survive his failure to deal with the Royalists. Rupert's vessels were freed as a result. Meanwhile, from his gaol on the Isle of Wight, King Charles was in desperate straits. During Rupert's frenetic activity, a messenger from his uncle had verbally imparted a request of 'great importance for my service' that took priority over everything else.[17] The king, involved in meticulous negotiations with Parliament's representatives, had requested a ship to facilitate his escape. The request was most secret, proving the great trust between uncle and nephew, and only the Prince of Orange was to be told about it. Rupert would have undertaken this himself had his presence not been so vital to the fleet. As he revealed to Montrose at the time, 'whilst I am severing the goates from the sheepe I dare not absent my self wth out Hazarding all our hopes here'.[18] A ship was duly sent to the king, but he made no use of it and resolved to remain on the island. While tense negotiations continued, commissioners hectored the monarch into making his most significant concessions yet, leading King Charles to liken himself to a garrison commander, holding out with no chance of relief. He resolved to stand fast and 'make some stone in this building my tombstone'.[19] Watching proceedings with increasing concern was the New Model Army. King and Parliament were on the brink of an agreement that would be detrimental to the revolutionary political and religious ideologies of many in the army.

On 1 December, the army leadership made their move and sent detachments of troops to seize the king and spirit him away from Carisbrooke Castle – and thus out of Parliament's control. King Charles's new destination was Hurst Castle, a tiny Tudor fortress perched on a shingle spit, battered by rain and gales. Making the best of it, he laid out his silver bell, gold watch and the silver basin for his wax nightlight – candles struggled all day to light the dank rooms. Hurst, Charles was certain, was the place where regicide was to be committed, but the army leaders had more public plans. Rupert gave his all to readying the fleet for sea and his uncle's aid, and as Henry Jermyn acknowledged, the prince's 'great paynes and labor' were paying off.[20] So immersed was Rupert in the task at hand that Lord Craven felt the need to remind him to 'have a thought of writinge [to] your fameley'.[21] Princess Elisabeth, ill with smallpox, was 'persecuted' by her 'wretched illness' and, unable to use her hands or eyes, was fed like a child.[22]

Much hope was pinned on Ireland, where the Marquess of Ormonde fought on in the king's name. At such a crossroads, even with King Charles's life hanging in the balance, Digby was quick to stir bad blood between Rupert and Ormonde. Writing to the latter, he accused the prince of doing everything to get command of the fleet, adding, 'I hope his aim is only at the honour of carrying the Fleet thither [to Ireland] ... if he have any further design of continuing to command the Fleet, or of remaining in that Kingdom, I fear the consequence of it.'[23] Jermyn, however, on behalf of Henrietta Maria, asked Ormonde to stay on good terms with Rupert. This request was hardly necessary. Earlier that year, Ormonde had unequivocally declared to Will Legge (whom he humorously nicknamed William Wicked) 'keepe mee in Prince Rupert's good opinion, & dam your self if I bee not a very perfect lover of his person, & will bee a ready obeyer of his comands'.[24]

A huge blow came on 6 December 1648, when a relatively obscure army officer named Colonel Thomas Pride arrived at Westminster with an armed guard. As MPs and peers turned up, Pride, aided by Lord Grey of Groby, checked their names and had those deemed Royalists or moderates either arrested or turned away. In total, 231 men were excluded, leaving a rump who were entirely in tune with the radical aims of the army. Pride had bigger backers for such a pivotal move, including Cromwell and Ireton, leaving the more conservative General Fairfax to opt for discretion over valour. The purged remnant voted to end negotiations with the king and repudiated everything that had just been agreed.

Many exiled Royalists saw the writing on the wall. On 20 January, Edward Hyde, struggling to find material to make clothes for himself, wrote to Rupert of a rumour that the king had been 'carryed' to Saint James's Palace.[25] Will Legge was in no doubt that the king would 'eare long perish in the hands of Murderers' and was ready to leave England and 'follow [Rupert] into any other [kingdom] where you may imploy [me]'.[26] Lord Craven received more detailed news that the king was to face a public trial. Craven's agent, Thomas Webb, had little hope for the king's life and predicted that proceedings would be 'resolved to ye contrary' especially if the king refused to acknowledge the authority of his handpicked judges – almost half of whom refused to turn up when the court assembled. Webb had spoken to 'some greate [ones] of ye Army' to get a feel for whether they would have the king ousted, or killed, and found most favoured death.[27] This is a fascinating revelation, that adds much to debate as to whether the king's death was inevitable, or not. Descartes lamented the cruelty of fate that relentlessly persecuted Princess Elisabeth's family.

Chapter 28

Arch-Traytors

In Westminster Hall, on 20 January 1649, King Charles began his finest ever performance. This dignified defence attracted much sympathy and respect. Refusing to acknowledge the jurisdiction of the court, he countered that he now stood as a last bastion of his people's liberties, compared to the rump of handpicked MPs or militant judges that sat before him. A masked Lady Fairfax yelled from the gallery that Oliver Cromwell was a traitor, and the court later broke up in turmoil. Next day, Rupert sailed from Hellevoetsluis. With him went Maurice as his vice-admiral and Sir John Mennes as rear-admiral. Also on board the six ships (*Constant Reformation, Convertine, Swallow, Guinea, Thomas, James*) were Mortaigne, the prince's Master of the Horse; Choqueaux, his surgeon; and Robert Holmes. Three Dutch East India ships provided an escort. Rupert had sent the *Roebuck*, and *Blackamoor Lady*, ahead to seize prizes off the Scilly Isles. Most of his vessels arrived at Kinsale, on the south coast of Ireland, by 26 January, though Rupert in the *Constant Reformation* was separated. He made it five days later.

Unbeknown to Rupert, on 30 January his uncle had been escorted to a scaffold in front of Whitehall Palace in central London. The capital had been locked down, all post stayed, and ports closed. The king had lain down and placed his neck on a six-inch-high block. Crowds were held back by the military, and though unseen, the courage of how he faced his end became a lasting epitaph. Stretching forth his arms to signal his readiness, the axe then struck a clean blow through the fourth cervical vertebra. The assistant, after holding the decapitated head aloft by the hair, supposedly threw it to the floor, leaving the face bruised.

Rupert's brother, Edward, declared he would die without regret when he had 'dipped' his hands in the blood of 'these murderers'. He also called for all the 'weapons of Christianity' to be turned on England, which had dared 'sacrifice its king to its rage'.[1] The execution was enough to prompt Charles Louis to sever ties with the Parliamentarians. Once back in Holland, Sophia noted with perhaps some relief that her brother 'cares no more for those cursed people'.[2] Henrietta Maria, as initially oblivious to the king's fate as Rupert, was anxious for news from the latter. So too was the exiled court of the new king. Edward Hyde wrote to Rupert about the 'horrid wickedness' that was committed in the 'light of the sunn'.[3] He implored the prince to 'vouchsafe two or three lines to Charles II, who will be much encouraged by it'.[4] One of the new king's first acts shows the respect he had for Rupert and the Palatines when he earmarked the Order of the Garter for princes Maurice and Edward.

Word of his uncle's death took two weeks to reach Rupert, on 12 February 1649. He resolved to take vengeance upon those 'Arch-Traytors, pretending the name of Parliament, and keeping a perpetuall Sessions, of blood-thirstinesse and murthering Massacre at Westminster'. The New Model Army was branded a 'Rebellious Army of Sectarian Murtherers'.[5] Taking the opportunity to dismiss the scandalous propaganda levelled at him during the civil war, he made it clear he was ready to do all he could to restore his cousin.

Now that the fleet had reached Ireland, the question was what could it do to aid the new king? Options were severely limited due to a shortage of skilled mariners, as well as the immense work involved in its upkeep. Every day was taken up training, recruiting, and resupplying, and the most that could be done was to send out a few vessels to capture prizes. One lucky haul involved a ship worth £40,000. Robert Mansell took the opportunity to present Rupert with ideas for a 'sea petar' – a form of explosive, perhaps akin to a limpet mine.[6]

On the mainland, the Marquess of Ormonde moulded various factions together to form a workable government; a coalition of Royalists and Catholic Confederates, which appealed to the Scots in Ulster. The late king's countrymen had been given no say in his fate and had opposed his trial. The two Parliamentarian armies in Ireland were hard pressed by this united front. One, in Ulster, was commanded by George Monck, a Royalist who had turned coat after being captured in 1644. The other was holding out in Dublin. Ormonde wanted the new king to come to Ireland and bless his government with legitimacy. He also wanted Rupert to blockade Dublin, which was protected by just two enemy warships that could be 'surprised with little difficultie'.[7] The town reportedly had only ten days' bread left.

Restricted by lack of resources, Rupert resorted to improving the seaward defences of Kinsale whilst recruiting. He might have broken free of Hellevoetsluis, but herculean efforts were required to move his ships once more – thirsting for revenge on his uncle's murderers, he would have done more if he could have done. Neither could he assist Montrose, who continued to write. In April, he lost two ships, but took a prize which he seems to have appropriately named *Charles*. Soon enough, the *James*, *Charles*, *Roebuck*, and *Thomas* were sent to Scilly to look for more prizes. One month later, four Parliamentarian warships arrived to protect Dublin, followed by more under the command of Robert Blake, who blockaded Kinsale. Pinned to their port, Rupert's crews often became mutinous. He executed some, which 'somewhat startled the rest & kept them in better order'. Richard Blakemore and Elaine Murphy state in *The British Civil Wars at Sea* that records of the fleet show that the seamen 'receieved regular wages, and large sums of money were spent on food and other supplies' which is testament to Rupert's administrative skills.[8] By the end of June, after enlisting 260 sailors, a council of war met and resolved against doing battle with Blake. The prince, meanwhile, considered the Scilly Isles as a suitable alternative base, or even Portugal, where King John IV was sympathetic.

Keeping one eye on his back and the other on Ormonde's progress, Rupert must have welcomed news of the defeat of one Parliamentarian army in Ireland (Monck's). Cromwell, however, was poised to depart England with 11,000 men. When a storm forced Blake's ships away from Kinsale and to Milford Haven, Rupert failed to capitalise on the opportunity to escape. As such, he consigned the fleet to another four months at Kinsale, during which time Cromwell landed and unleashed his bloody campaign. The Royalist Governor of Cork, 17 miles away, made repeated invitations for Rupert to join him in a hunting party, though luckily to no avail – his intention had been to trap the prince and then turn both him and Cork over to the enemy. Waterford was also vulnerable to plotting. When the commander of Kinsale's fort also tried to turn coat, the prince foiled the attempt and had him hanged. Despite this precarious situation, the new king was on his way to Ireland, stopping off in Jersey at the end of September. Passage, however, stalled through lack of funds and in vain he called upon Rupert to alleviate this 'great necessity and streights'.[9] There the king was forced to stay until early 1650, watching helplessly as Ireland became the second of his kingdoms to be entirely lost.

When Blake and his ships were scattered again by tempests, Rupert's fleet of seven stole out of Kinsale on 20 October. Nine months had borne nothing of significance. Judging this period, Morrah considered that Rupert 'could hardly have put up more than a token resistance'.[10] Kitson concurs: 'It is easy to feel that Rupert should have taken firmer control of the campaign, but it is unlikely that he would have saved Ireland for the King and he might well have lost the fleet in the process.'[11] What use is a fleet that secures no advantage? The only thing that can be said is that by persevering, the naval threat diverted the English Commonwealth and cost them, while also giving Royalists an illusion of power and a small income from prizes. Its continued existence was Rupert's achievement.

Leading his ships across the Bay of Biscay, Rupert sailed towards Lisbon and the mouth of the River Tagus, where he captured several prizes. Two were kept and renamed *Second Charles* and *Henry*, and he bought a Dutch ship named *Black Prince*. Now with nine vessels, he laid up the *Convertine*, not having men or guns enough to spare for them all. Support from King John IV of Portugal, nicknamed 'John the Restorer', was a welcome change of fortune. Proclaimed king in 1640, John had led the Portuguese revolt against Spain, and during the civil wars, had discussed marrying one of his daughters to the Prince of Wales. As a fledgling state with Spain at its back, Portugal relied on foreign support, therefore his ministers warned against entertaining Rupert and offending the English Commonwealth. John was not to be moved.

From the Tagus, Rupert made the most of his royal welcome. King John certainly seemed to admire his efforts and the two formed a strong friendship. Rupert's position was one of contradiction; despite being King Charles II's Lord High Admiral, serving the royal House of Stuart, it was now a family without power or crown. As more nations recognised the Commonwealth, Rupert's legitimacy lessened, and his status moved from admiral to pirate. To maintain authority, he demanded all foreign ships salute his flag – a courtesy that had long been given to the Royal Navy. John allowed the Royalists to move upriver to Oeiras Bay and from there, Rupert and Maurice took part in the social life of the Portuguese court.

On 17 January, Blake was ordered by the Commonwealth to destroy Rupert once and for all. To avoid a third lengthy blockade, he was permitted to attack any foreign ships that gave aid to the prince, leaving officials in London believing that success could be achieved 'without much difficulty'.[12] Another of Rupert's key supporters was Antonio de Sousa, who had been Portuguese ambassador in England during the civil wars. De Sousa had secretly conveyed letters between Charles I and Henrietta Maria which brought threats of 'violence to his house' from the Parliamentarians. Knowing that his correspondence was being opened, the bold ambassador had pranked MPs by preparing a dummy packet that included some spectacles and a note that the gift might assist with their spying. The late king had so valued de Sousa's loyalty that he had declared 'the memory of [it] ought to bee deare even to his posterity'. Now, in January 1650, de Sousa acted as a go-between for Rupert, making necessary representations to King John and his council. The man's work did 'greatly help' matters.[13]

Notwithstanding this assistance, Rupert had to stay alert. Most Portuguese ministers worked against him, such as Secretary of State, De Silva, who attempted to prevent the sale of prize ships and cargo. The royal council contested one ship, insisting that it was not Rupert's to profit from, but Portugal's, though King John resolved matters by declaring that he had gifted it to Rupert. There was similar division around King Charles II. Rupert received a letter dated 28 February 1650, from Edward Hyde, reporting 'many designes and some troubles amongst us'.[14] Hyde complained that the exiles had 'not yet heard [one] worde from your Highnesse' since leaving Hellevoetsluis.[15]

King Charles had made repeated requests of Rupert to convey him to Ireland. Instead, Rupert continued to prey on Commonwealth shipping, sending any spare proceeds to his cousin along with gripping reports of his adventures, which must have been a welcome diversion for the young king. Engaging in bouts of nautical hunting, Rupert led his vessels in pursuit of many quarries, sometimes chasing them all day. On one occasion the targeted ships turned out to be his own. When a Newfoundland vessel full of fish was captured, the cargo was taken, and the craft fired against a moonlit backdrop. Robert Blake's arrival soon put paid to this activity.

The Commonwealth admiral rather arrogantly assumed he could sail upriver and destroy Rupert right under the noses of the Portuguese. Entering the Tagus without so much as asking, he was fired on by the forts – a thorough shot across the bows – and quickly withdrew. When King John decreed that no English ships were permitted to reinforce Blake, the man resorted to other means. A plot was hatched whereby Rupert and Maurice, hunting with the royal court, were to be ambushed and killed by some English mariners, who had gone ashore to collect water. When this was foiled, Rupert retaliated in kind with a plan to attack the ship of Blake's vice-admiral with a firebomb – a double-headed barrel filled with explosives and disguised as a cask of oil. The plot failed when the man detailed to plant the device, disguised in Portuguese clothes, cursed in suspiciously fluent English.

Exasperated, Blake sought permission from King John to attack Rupert. Unsurprisingly declined, he sailed out to sea, in a manner of summoning Rupert to a duel, though to no avail. When Blake was reinforced by four ships, King John banned him from re-entering the river or taking water from the mainland, thereby forcing Blake to send squadrons to Cadiz for supplies. With no such difficulties, Rupert was emboldened. When two French ships arrived to support him on 5 April 1650, they anchored among Blake's fleet by mistake and were seized. Rupert had the *Constant Reformation* fire a warning shot across Blake's bows, and again the following day, which put out one of his topsails. Diplomatic pressure combined with the prince's cannonballs resulted in the Frenchmen (which included two Knights of Malta) being freed after three days.

Attempting to resolve the standoffs, the Portuguese offered to place a fleet between the two opponents so that Rupert might escape, but this only resulted in a series of cat-and-mouse chases that failed to provide the anticipated outcome. Try as he might, the prince could not get away from Blake and instead returned to Oeiras Bay that July. King Charles II had better luck, however, and, placing all his eggs in the Covenanters' basket, left for Scotland. There he was encouraged by a desire to crown him, but as equally dismayed to find that the price of this would be his religious subjugation. With no real alternative but to accept Presbyterianism, attempts were made to brainwash the 19-year-old with its doctrine. While treating with the Covenanters, the king also commissioned Montrose to invade Scotland and fight against them. This hedged his bets but bound his hands. When Montrose was defeated and captured, the king could not avoid condemnation of the marquess, who was then hanged, drawn, and quartered in Edinburgh. It was a tragic end for such a towering figure, and the inexperienced king was left with blood on his hands.

The king's move to Scotland brought some relief for Rupert. Reducing Blake's numbers, the Commonwealth's priority turned to subjugating the Scots. Refusing to play any part in this, and perhaps using it as a means of escaping from his controlling and radical subordinates, General Thomas Fairfax resigned. No more would he be the army's figurehead. No more did they need him. Instead, Oliver Cromwell, well-connected and with family in numerous key places, took over supreme command of the army. Though political power was outwardly handled by a Council of State to give collective responsibility, Cromwell, wielding the sword, was its de facto head.

On 3 September 1650, the day that Cromwell spectacularly defeated the Scottish army at Dunbar, almost half of Blake's force left him. Rupert seized his chance. Under cover of fog, a condition he used numerous times to his advantage on land, he slipped past his enemies. Four days later, Rupert in the *Constant Reformation* became detached from his ships, and was shocked when the *George*, Blake's flagship, emerged from the fog and almost collided with him. Luckily the *Constant Reformation* escaped with only its topmast shot away. On 12 October, Blake was forced to call off the chase and go to Cádiz for supplies. Rupert escaped with six ships into the Mediterranean, reaching the Balearics on 4 November. Not one to be put off, the indefatigable Blake was quick to resume his pursuit, driving the Royalist *Black Prince* ashore, whereupon the crew set her ablaze. He chased the other four to Cartagena in mid-November, and though they managed to survive Blake, storms dashed these ships to pieces, leaving Rupert's strength severely diminished.

Not long afterwards, Blake was recalled to England, and another great storm dispersed the princes – Rupert to Sicily and Maurice (with a new prize vessel called *Marmaduke*) to Toulon. Concerned that his brother might have been lost at sea, Maurice did not venture ashore. Weeks later, perhaps just days into 1651, Rupert's surprise arrival gave much relief. Henry Jermyn, from Henrietta Maria's court, wrote with joy on 6 February 1651 – no man, he exclaimed, could have been more concerned than he. By this time, King Charles had been crowned by the Scots, meaning Rupert was now serving an anointed monarch. With renewed determination, he renamed the *Marmaduke* the *Revenge of Whitehall*, which summed up his *raison d'être*. News of his exploits spread as far as Exeter gaol, where Will Legge had languished having been captured at sea while Rupert was at Kinsale. From 'The jayle', he wrote on behalf of a man who owned some of the goods taken with the *Revenge* and appealed for their restitution.[16] John Bilton, a shipwright from Deptford, had been captured with the vessel and according to him, Rupert kept him prisoner in an attempt to force him to defect. In the end, the resolute Bilton escaped and claimed to have travelled 600 miles on foot back to England.

At Toulon, Rupert incurred great debts on account of repairing and resupplying his few ships, which by April had increased to five. With renewed determination to deal with the piratical prince, the Commonwealth despatched eight ships under command of William Penn, sailing in the *Fairfax*. Dubbing his opponent the 'bloody wretch', Penn abounded with confidence.[17] The wily prince prepared to sally forth from Toulon. Potential destinations included the West Indies (and Royalist-held islands of St Kitts, Nevis, Antigua, Barbados, and Montserrat), or the Portuguese Cape Verde Islands, which was a stepping point to the latter. A third option was the Azores. Keeping his cards close, Rupert gave it about that he was intending to sail to the eastern Mediterranean, and when he did leave Toulon on 17 May 1651, he stuck to this pretext, heading east until out of sight. After this, he turned about and headed out of the Mediterranean altogether. The ruse worked. It was two months before Penn realised he had been foiled, and the frustrated commander took a further two months to reach Gibraltar, admitting he had missed the grand end of his design.

With the wind in his sails, Rupert made for Madeira and a very friendly reception from the governor. There they took refreshments and sold as much of a cargo of corn, taken in a captured Genoese ship, as they could, but the island was too poor to purchase it all. By 1 July 1651, having laden his ships with provisions, the prince made a strike towards the Canary Islands in the hope of increasing his numbers with more prize ships. A bigger fleet would strengthen his hand in arguing for the West Indies as his preferred destination. Finding no English ships at the Canaries, being too early in the year, many started to question their plans – and the prince. Rupert ventured that prizes could be taken on the way to the Indies, but his officers stood fast in opposition apart from Captain Fearnes, who Kitson describes as the prince's flag officer.

They insisted that such a voyage to the Indies would not be possible, 'alleageing the leake that began (three dayes before we went from Maderas) in the [*Constant Reformation*], made the ship in too badd a Condition to be carryed soe long a Voyage'.[18] This 'passionate carryadge' caused disorder and put doubts into Fearnes's head about the seaworthiness of the flagship.[19] Unwilling to shoulder responsibility for any miscarriages that might occur, which would see him 'left to sattisfie private mens malice', it was Fearnes's subsequent reluctance that forced a frustrated Rupert to call a full council of war. This crucial juncture is explored in more detail after close examination of Rupert's own account in the Bodleian Library.

On 7 July, the officers duly debated where to go in search of prizes and make suitable repairs to the flagship. The West Indies was struck off on account of an assumption there was 'noe provisions was to bee gott' there and that the *Constant Reformation* could not survive the journey. This argument was put with 'such vyolence' that 'their oppinions could not beene altered'. Even Rupert's reluctant proposal of the Cape Verde Islands was declined because it was seen as merely a stop-off point to the Indies. Consensus was for the Azores. Though Fearnes argued that this would prove ruinous to the fleet, it must be said that Rupert did not seem to personally back the man up or intervene.

Writing retrospectively, the prince felt that had Fearnes 'spoken plainly' and assured him that the flagship could have dealt with a longer voyage, or proposed to repair her elsewhere, then he would have taken a firmer hand. Rather unfairly, the prince also declared that Fearnes 'wanted more resolution [strength of conviction] then knowledge'.[20] It sounds very much like Fearnes was shamefully used as Rupert's fall-guy in recriminations over the consequences of this fateful decision. The Azores it was.

As they departed, the flagship seemed to take on less water, giving Rupert momentary second thoughts. These were soon put out of his head when the *Honest Seaman* was left behind to repair a topmast, leaving no alternative but to go on with the plan and meet it at the Azores. On 25 July they reached their destination and spent over a month at Terceira resupplying. Through various gains and losses, his fleet was now six-strong. What's not been noted before is that his fleet helped the Portuguese Governor of Terceira fend off an insurrection. Gunpowder was donated, and Royalist merchants (William Serchfield, John Malorey, and Richard

Dorington) helped 'force the Castle' to King John's obedience.[21] This act prompted Rupert to petition the king for restoration of the three men's estates – which had been seized, along with those of all English merchants, following Blake's attack on a Portuguese fleet in 1650. This was all the calm before the storm; Emanuel de Faria y Sousa, writing a history of Portugal fifty years later, would reflect that 1650 'proved unfortunate at sea' and that storms cast away several Portuguese vessels at Terceira.[22] The prince and his fleet found 1651 no better.

Rupert would later regret 'we spent more time then we should have done' in the Azores. The stay dragged on from 25 July to 7 December 1651. Those who had favoured this destination had argued that they might intercept East India Company ships on their return to England, but as the prince wrote with bitter hindsight, they had already reached the Thames. Having missed their prizes, neither could the leaky *Constant Reformation* be repaired at the Azores, because of the renowned 'Ill wether'. Food was also in short supply. Feeling vindicated, the prince reflected that the Cape Verde Islands were abundant in 'Goates' while the Indies were rich in flesh and bread.[23] Then, amidst these frustrations, Captain Goulding of *St Michael the Archangel* defected and sailed to England. While storm clouds swirled around the Azores, events of enormous importance were unfolding in England.

Chapter 29

Unhappily Cast Away

On 3 September 1651, a Scottish army with the king at its head was defeated by Cromwell's forces at Worcester. The encounter created an infinite number of widows, and fatherless children all of 'excessive affliction'. Those that were not killed were taken prisoner and subjected to 'unexpressible calamities'.[1] Scotland was mortally wounded.

King Charles had escaped Worcester with a small party that included Lord Henry Wilmot (Rupert's civil war adversary) and a moss trooper who was good with directions. Numerous accounts of this remarkable episode vary slightly as to what happened next. One was later related by Lady Wood, one of Henrietta Maria's household, who heard King Charles recount the tale to his mother. At some point in the ensuing flight, the king felt it best to send the well-known Wilmot and others away. Eventually, after stopping at a house near the Boscobel estate, moss trooper and monarch, now alone, abandoned their horses and took refuge in a hollow tree around 10 yards from the roadside, narrowly avoiding some enemy cavalrymen who raced by. The pair 'quaked & shak't' so much that the king worried the rustling leaves would betray them. After dusk fell, they left their hideout and met associates in a forest – whereupon it was agreed they would scout for food while the king returned to his tree, a precursor to the Royal Oak.

The route of the king's escape took him to Boscobel House, where he hid in (or up) the famous oak tree to avoid enemy soldiers, and on to Moseley Old Hall, where he met Wilmot once more. It was said that during Wilmot's conversation with a blacksmith, a Jane Lane arrived, and it was recognised that her brother had served as a Royalist officer. Immediately they fetched the king and took him to Mr Lane's home near Walsall, after which he was 'shav'd [and] dy'd' then dressed as a park keeper. Suitably apparelled, he could ride as Jane's servant with Wilmot following at a discreet distance. Whilst travelling with Jane, the king pretended to be sick of a fever, which was a good excuse to lie low at the inns they stayed at and keep to his bed. To further this, she would purposefully lament the illness, declaring that the boy 'will never recover'.[2] One night a foot soldier overheard and unwittingly encouraged the disguised monarch to drink a health to King Charles, which would surely cure him. Finally, the king made his way to Shoreham, in Sussex, and though there was a price of £1,000 on his head, he succeeded in taking ship to France.

In the Azores, Rupert's vessels were not going anywhere – the *Constant Reformation*'s leak worsened, yet the source could not be discovered. Bad feeling intensified when a mid-September order called on all officers to put their individual views in writing as to their next destination. With Rupert now hell-bent on the West Indies, clandestine meetings were prohibited, cabins pulled down to reduce privacy, and candles forbidden to be lit between decks. It's difficult to understand how the *Constant Reformation* could get anywhere except the seabed – it was a disaster in the making.

On 26 September 1651, the elements intervened. Storms blew the ships from Terceira and for three days the tempest battered them. Pumps worked hard to save the *Constant Reformation*, cannons were thrown overboard, and raw meat forced into the gaps between planking. Casks swirled around the hold as it filled. The other vessels unsuccessfully fought the waves attempting to get alongside, and then Dr Hart, Rupert's chaplain, gave the stricken mariners a final service. Around 10.00 pm, flaming torches erected on the doomed flagship were extinguished when the turbulent sea swallowed it. Rupert had been persuaded or forced to leave the vessel, but over 300 of his best sailors, together with numerous officers and friends, all perished. Gone too was treasure, ciphers, and papers.

They had been blown over 200 miles from Terceira. Now aboard the forty-two-gun *Swallow*, Rupert and Maurice, together with the forty-gun *Honest Seaman*, made it back to the Azores on 19 October. There they found the forty-gun *Revenge of Whitehall* but discovered that the *Loyal Subject* had been wrecked near Faial. Rupert would attempt to recover the latter's guns (something that would drag on for nearly ten years) but for now, he could not bring himself to contemplate anything. With the devastated prince laid low, his brother took command. Rupert fell into a dark place of recriminations and vulnerability, mulling over all the lost opportunities that might have prevented this situation, assessing what and who was to blame, and preparing long narratives in defence of himself. Closeted in his cabin, he now considered, 'how misserably we have bene misguided and Ruin'd' by five months in the Azores. This had put the fleet in a worse state than if they had faced 'any strenth that ever the Rebells could have sent [against] us'.[3] The situation is reminiscent of his condition in the latter stages of the civil war, when depressed and undermined by poisonous intrigues.

With nothing to lose, the way to the West Indies was now clear. Nobody had the heart to object. There would be better pickings and opportunities, such as the chance to 'anger if not undoe' the King of Spain. Santo Domingo, for example, was said to be defended by only 200 soldiers and such considerations helped Rupert gradually regain spirit and purpose. He looked forward to going 'handsomely' there.[4] 'God Almighty Guid [guide] us,' he declared.[5] On 7 December 1651, they set out, calling at Cape Blanco on the African coast for refitting, where Rupert made contact with local peoples. Attempts to trade went badly. He lost two men after an aggressive and confused standoff but gained a 3-year-old African child who became separated from his family and supposedly clung to the prince's leg.

A prize ship was also despatched to King Charles full of cargo to be sold, though Rupert punctually specified the monarch could take the profits but only 'after the debts I made att Toulon ar satisfyed'.[6]

The prince's voyage came too late for any Royalists in the West Indies. On 11 January 1652, Barbados surrendered and the king's cause in this far-flung corner was snuffed out. Rupert had moved his flag to the *Swallow* while Maurice shifted onto the *Revenge*. On 1 February, they arrived at the Cape Verde Islands, where grey sand mixed with red, all peppered with shells, and where they found English ships trading from the mouth of the River Gambia.

The Guinea Company, formed by merchants and given a monopoly by Kings James and Charles, was likewise embraced by the Commonwealth for their advantage. Now directed by Parliamentarians, it continued to trade people, as well as hides, wax, teeth (tusks), and gold. The company also hoped to discover fabled 'Mountains of gold'.[7] Four months earlier, in September 1651, it had despatched the *Friendship*, *John*, and *Supply* with orders to obtain fifteen to twenty 'young lusty Negers' of about 15 years of age.[8] By December, they provided thirty pairs of shackles and bolts to secure any that became rebellious and desired 200 more. The Portuguese had resented these English traders, and in a bid to shut down competition, murdered seven of the *Friendship*'s crew. The Portuguese Governor of St Jago then suggested Rupert and Maurice seek out the remaining English traders, being in both their interests, and provided pilots to assist.

After precariously navigating the shelves and sands of the River Gambia in February 1652, Rupert found the English and captured their vessel *Friendship* along with the enslaved people on board. All those taken were, without distinction, distributed across the Royalist fleet to shore up numbers and the *Friendship* was promptly renamed *Defiance*. One former English captain, who was now forced to serve on the *Revenge*, named the princes and their cohorts 'pests and plagues of human society'. He alleged that Rupert and his men expressed a wish that London should be 'altogether in flames', the Tower of London 'sunk as far below as it is above the ground', and that Cromwell's 'heart's blood were out'. A very small band of mutineers formed on the *Revenge*, and after biding their time, overpowered Captain Marshall and sailed it back to England. Their account gave an interesting glimpse of the crew, which included 'English with French and negroes' alike.[9]

Gambia proved lucrative for the Royalists, who captured several prizes, one of which held an African interpreter named Captain Jacques, whom Rupert subsequently released. The brother of a local king was also entertained by Rupert and Maurice on board their flagship. When the fleet anchored off another native village one of the seamen, having lived there, was permitted to go ashore to visit. This suggests the prince treated his mariners, on the whole, with decency, regardless of background, and not as prisoners shackled to his boats. The sailor granted shore leave was subsequently prevented from returning and, unwilling to give up on any of his men, Rupert despatched a party to intervene. The small craft overturned as it neared the beach, leaving the mariners surrounded by hostile African villagers.

The same happened to a second party led by Robert Holmes, but luckily Captain Jacques arrived and used his influence to calm matters. A third boat collected most of Rupert's men, but in the process took an African canoe, shooting dead one of the men in it. Holmes and his escort were seized again.

Taking personal charge, Rupert moved in close, while Jacques continued to negotiate. Upon agreement, the prince signalled to release the canoe, but only one of the hostages was freed – Holmes was retained contrary to terms. The Africans fired arrows, ran down the beach, and dived into the water, then Rupert was struck above his left breast. Calling for a knife, he promptly cut out the arrow and prepared to swim out with a rescue party, though Jacques managed to grab Holmes and took him to a spot where he could be rescued.

Eventually making his escape, Rupert and his six ships continued their journey to the West Indies on 9 May 1652 and in the Virgin Islands they carried out repairs. There was little food to be had and everyone – princes included – suffered reduced rations. They put to sea again on 29 August and within a fortnight a hurricane hit them, almost one year after the *Constant Reformation*'s loss. Tossed and scattered for four days, the leaky *Swallow* often had up to 4 foot of water in the hold. Its sails were torn away, leaving the ship to the mercy of the storm, but miraculously it was not wrecked.

When conditions improved, the carpenter was sent to determine the source of a major leak, quickly finding it when a splash of water struck his face. A bailing party was sent below, but had little effect, and when Rupert went into the hold to investigate, he discovered the men instead groping for fish that had come in through the hole. As was often the case, Rupert's vessel had been separated from the rest, so there was nothing to do but wait and pray that Maurice had also survived. He captured some ships at Antigua and hunted daily with dogs, but the weeks passed without any news. It became painfully clear that his was the only vessel to have survived.

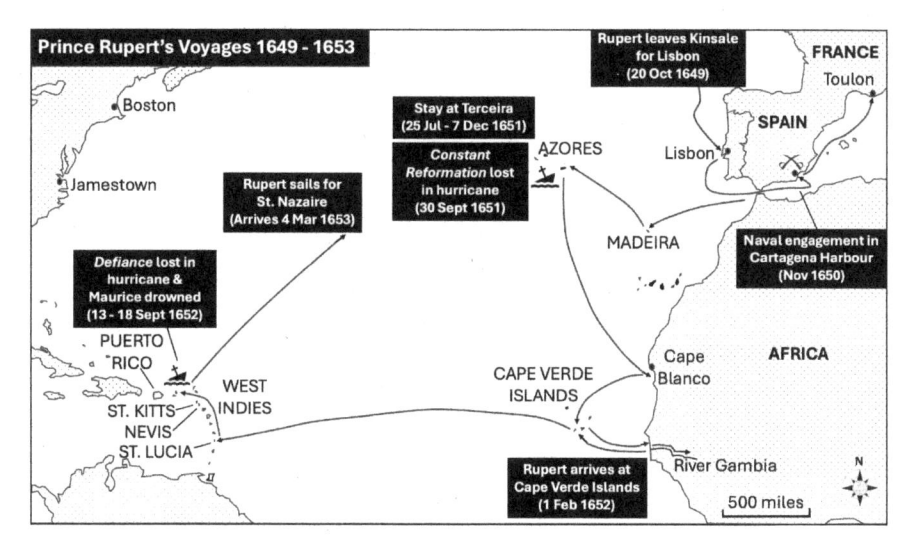

Maurice was thought to have been 'unhappily cast away' between the islands of St Christopher and Tortuga.[10] But for Rupert, the loss of his beloved brother was far from clear-cut. Overwhelmed by the very thought, he simply could not believe it. Numerous times his 'lost' ships miraculously reappeared, and reports that Maurice was 'taken up' by the Spanish and detained in the castle at Puerto Rico or captured by Algerian pirates complicated everything.[11] The deafening silence continued – not one of Maurice's 200 crew was heard of again and Rupert was forced to consider the unthinkable. After sailing aimlessly, praying for some sign, the broken prince was stricken with a tropical disease. On 12 December, the *Swallow* sailed forlornly for France.

Chapter 30

Dark and Deep

When the *Swallow* limped up the Loire and anchored off St Nazaire, an epic four-year chapter in Rupert's life ended. It was 4 March 1653. Gripped by a 'dangerous fit of sickness', the prince could barely disembark.[1] The few possessions he brought back were indicative of his lonely and bereaved existence, the *Swallow* itself being the item of most monetary value. What might be raised from its sale could not in any way represent the trials and tribulations he had experienced.

The hand-to-mouth existence of the exiled royal court had, although sporadically, financially benefitted from Rupert's exploits. He had cost the Commonwealth, embarrassed them, and kept the Royalist pennant flying against all odds, but the price had been devastating. The fact must not be overlooked that apart from very brief spells, the last eleven years of Rupert's life had been exhaustively spent fighting for the Royalist cause.

Rupert returned a changed man, having experienced human weakness in the face of all-powerful natural elements. Though extremely ill, his will was not broken, and this is testament to his strength of character. Developing a great understanding of naval logistics, supply, upkeep, and tactics had tested and enhanced his powers of leadership. Living day to day on the edge, dealing with lack of news, and exercising life-and-death decisions, he had motivated a diverse band of men under the harshest of conditions. Though propaganda had made him super-human – even non-human – these exploits well and truly proved his substance as a courageous action man.

Well-wishes poured in. Henry Jermyn wrote on 22 March, assuring the prince of Henrietta Maria's enduring affection, and urging him to have a care for his health, suggesting his old apothecary might provide necessary drugs. King Louis XIV sent a coach to fetch Rupert to Paris, where he arrived in April, lodging at the Palais Royal. The prince fascinated the fashionistas of French society, who veered between adulation and intense curiosity. Here, Kitson suggests, he experimented with herbal treatments and was understandably withdrawn, though spending time with his brother, Edward. That summer, whilst swimming in the Seine and nearly drowning, he was rescued by his 'blackamoors' (who had been with him since Africa) when one, called Hamilton, grasped the prince's hair, pulled him back to the surface, and swam ashore with him. This near-death experience must have stirred thoughts of Maurice, and the hundreds of souls lost when his ships had foundered. Being in the Africans' company, including the 5-year-old boy who had lost his family, friends, and homeland, shows Rupert had a respect for them. He might even have reflected how fortunate he was compared to the child.

By January 1654, he joined King Charles's council and was appointed Master of the Horse. Involvement ranged from adjudging slanders against Edward Hyde, now Lord Chancellor, to furthering an assassination attempt on Cromwell, who in April 1653 had established himself as Lord Protector at the head of what was, in effect, a military dictatorship. This plotting against Cromwell caused indirect collaboration between Rupert and Digby. The prince's surgeon, Choqueaux, was a key contact, alongside Digby's secretary, Edward Walsingham, who had been instrumental in Rupert's 1645 downfall.

The sale of the *Swallow*'s guns and other materials was coordinated by Robert Holmes and overseen by Rupert, who was harried by King Charles and his desperate need for money. The matter would cause an underlying rift because the king refused to pay Rupert half the proceeds and had not settled the Toulon debts that the prince had insisted upon. More important matters took precedence when France made overtures to Cromwell, leaving King Charles (and his courtiers) *persona non grata*. Rupert's presence in Paris was also resented by some gentlemen on account of his liaisons with their ladies, one of which was the Count of Mongiron, who attempted to kill the prince.

In the middle of 1654, King Charles left for Cologne. Rupert resigned as Master of the Horse and went to Heidelberg to stay with Charles Louis and Sophia. He sent his secretary to his sister, Elisabeth, who also joined them. There they discussed Maurice's fate and rumours of his captivity. Ten years later, one inhabitant of St John's Island, Puerto Rico, would state that pipestaves marked 'MP' (Maurice Princeps) had been washed up, along with a carved golden lion from his ship.

Discussion also centred on granting Rupert an estate whereby he might settle down. Lands at Langessel were earmarked, along with a house that needed restoration – specifically a paddock as large as the highways would allow. Charles Louis had been restored as Elector Palatine under the terms of the treaty that ended the Thirty Years' War, but only to the lower half of the Palatinate. The upper remained in the hands of the Catholic Elector of Bavaria. Now re-established in Heidelberg, Charles Louis offered Rupert and Edward an income of roughly £375 per annum, rising to £600 after five years. The Palatine siblings had dwindled in number, only six remaining at this point out of thirteen, following the deaths of Henrietta Maria (1651) and Philip (1650).

Vienna beckoned in August. Rupert's intention was to lay claim to his share of the financial compensation (£15,000) allotted to the family for the loss of the Upper Palatinate. Emperor Ferdinand III was his old friend, who had so supported him after his release from Linz in 1641. Charles Louis was careful to help his brother look the part, and he arranged for a 'George' (Order of the Garter medal) to be made for him – though commiserating that the goldsmith was a drunkard, and his work quite crude, it was good enough. Charles Louis, Elisabeth, and Sophia also sent a special note to Rupert in verse. These sibling bonds were important in balancing Rupert, who was prone to be austere and fierce. He delighted in reading the work, written in their three different hands, even replying with his own rhyming couplets. These told how he passed his time in 'so many fruitful vices', prizing one thing, then another, and desiring to possess what a moment later 'I forgot to dream of'.[2] Freed from the burden of command, the prince was adjusting to a more mundane pace of life.

The Spanish ambassador assisted Rupert, arranging introductions, but business took much longer than expected. Perseverance paid off when the prince accepted the emperor's offer of repayment by instalments, with interest, and a down payment equating to £2,700 allowed Rupert to finance his new life. He also negotiated on behalf of King Charles II, securing some financial assistance for him too. On 7 October 1654, Rupert's secretary, Toby Holder, confirmed that owing to Cromwell's subjugation of Scotland, any notion of Rupert commanding a Scottish army of Royalists was at an end. Even whilst establishing himself in the Palatinate, Rupert had retained a preference to serve King Charles.

Feeling flush with his first payment, Rupert treated himself to fifteen pairs of dogs which were despatched to Heidelberg. He arrived there in November, and his relationship with Charles Louis was very cordial, perhaps at its highest point. But the prince's employment soon got in the way. The Duke of Modena had asked Rupert to raise an army to help defend the small state from Papal forces, and though agreeing, the prince ran into a multitude of entanglements. The French contingent of these troops would not be led by anyone other than the duke, whose agreement resulted in Rupert becoming his subordinate, which was contrary to the prince's commission. Underhandedly, the duke intended to actually use the troops to wrest Milan from the Spanish.

In the New Year of 1655, King Charles, in Cologne, still hopeful for a Scottish uprising, called on Rupert to withdraw from the Duke of Modena's service. This the prince did, considering the duke's duplicity as just cause. France, however, condemned Rupert. Charles Louis, who had allowed some of his brother's recruits to be quartered in his lands, found himself warned for unwittingly hosting soldiers that were to be used against Spain and the matter caused much discontent all round. As Rupert moved between Cologne, Heidelberg, and The Hague, he waited on events, tactfully declining an invitation by Queen Anne of France and Henrietta Maria to visit Paris. Though Modena harassed Rupert, claiming that the prince was bound to him by honour, Rupert scarcely troubled himself over it. Instead, on 24 October 1655, he set out for Vienna on behalf of King Charles, to encourage further Imperial aid. On the eve of departure, the king requested use of Rupert's 'Calasse' – a type of carriage drawn on two wheels for more comfortable journeys. Unwilling to give up his prestigious transport, his royal cousin was told to approach the manufacturer, who would 'in a little tyme make such anothir'.[3]

The four-month Viennese interlude produced nothing noteworthy for King Charles, though Rupert did discover 'wispered att viena before my departur' that the Spanish were 'tempering for a Peace wth Cromwell'.[4] Confident that nothing would come of it, he felt enough 'bowldnesse' to counsel King Charles against paying court to Spain. When such peace moves failed, Spain would surely by default approach the king. Cromwellian England did, however, agree a treaty with France in November 1655, leaving Henrietta Maria watching the celebratory bonfires in Paris, noting with dismay that they were so great she feared the city might be burned down by them. King Charles was sick with 'greefe'. His affairs in Scotland and England were in pieces – 'all the fatt is in the fire'.[5]

A consolation – as Rupert had predicted – came when Spain offered to support King Charles's restoration in exchange for certain concessions. But first, the king was told to capture a port for troops to land, and to that end, he based himself in Bruges and started recruiting an army. Rupert's offer to assist was declined on 15 June; the Duke of York would be in command. In England, Rupert was not altogether forgotten, and popular songs played at the time included 'Prince Rupert's March' and 'Rupert's Retreat', all harking back to his civil war days.

Now without employment, and spending increasingly more time in Heidelberg, Rupert's frustrations mounted, foremost amongst them being lack of agreement with Charles Louis about lands and income. To make matters worse, in this down-time, Rupert became attracted to Louise von Degenfeld, a maid of Charles Louis's wife, Electress Charlotte. Louise ignored the attention, but one of Rupert's love notes was found by Charlotte, who promptly assumed it was for her. Rather embarrassingly, the electress certainly did have feelings for Rupert, and he was forced to reveal the truth. The love triangle was further complicated by the discovery that Charles Louis was already having an affair with the maid, which led to the breakdown of his marriage. Quarrels between the brothers intensified, and reports mention the palace door being shut in Charles Louis's face. Rupert, termed 'dark and deep', departed to visit his friend, the Archbishop Elector of Mainz.[6]

Throughout the first half of 1657, the brothers battled it out despite their mother imploring them to resolve matters. When Rupert reluctantly returned to Heidelberg to attempt it, Charles Louis warned against his coming until summoned and promptly departed for his country residence. The Governor of Heidelberg was told to bar the prince entry. Rupert's arrival, and subsequent snubbing was the final straw – hurt and outraged, he swore a solemn oath never to return to the Palatinate and went back to Mainz. Towards the end of the year, he moved to Frankfurt to await the election of a new emperor, whose aid he could solicit, Ferdinand III having died in April.

Before the troublesome year of 1657 was out, one last crisis struck the Palatines. Rupert's sister, Louise, was the last child remaining with their mother in The Hague. She had once been the subject of discussions over a Polish marriage, though these fell through on account of their desire for her to embrace Catholicism. The Elector of Brandenburg had also unsuccessfully sought her hand. In 1655, Christina of

Sweden visited The Hague. The only child of Gustavus II Adolphus, she had decided never to marry and had recently abdicated the throne. The former queen, like Rupert's eldest sister, Elisabeth, became close to philosopher Rene Descartes. Christina no doubt saw Louise, too, and there was something akin between the two. Christina, caring little for her appearance, was renowned for not attending to her hair and Louise was no different – her siblings often made jibes that it seemed she had used her paintbrushes as combs. When Christina departed The Hague, rumours that she had converted to Catholicism were to prove correct and this became another similarity when Louise secretly converted in December 1657.

Not only did Louise convert, but she also absconded. It soon became clear that the Princess of Hohenzollern had been closely involved, and the woman incurred Elizabeth of Bohemia's worst wrath as a result. She branded Hohenzollern a criminal and, in a bid to shun the truth, suggested that her daughter had been kidnapped. Hohenzollern, upset at the slander, wrote to Elizabeth with regret over the anger and upset, but acquitted herself of any guilt. Yes, Louise had confided her intentions, but Hohenzollern contributed nothing other than what assistance she felt she could not refuse. The French ambassador also found himself embroiled – in his opinion, Hohenzollern had contrived and managed it all.

Louise travelled to Brabant and then Antwerp as her mother was consumed by anger and fear. King Charles and his sister, Mary, Princess of Orange, condemned Louise for leaving her mother 'so unhandsomly'.[7] In response, Louise declared she was 'very well satisfied' with her actions, only sorry for the upset; she was not without her supporters, such as the Bishop of Antwerp, and her brother, Edward, who had converted over ten years earlier. When Louise reached her destination – France – Edward welcomed her, as did Henrietta Maria, who promised to 'have a care of her as of her own daughter'. News of the latter likely enhanced the bitterness of Louise's mother.[8]

Fearing that her own reputation might be compromised, Elizabeth of Bohemia approached the Dutch States General in January 1658. She begged the assembly to remain her friend and sent them the Princess Hohenzollern's letter to prove there was a plot. Elizabeth steadfastly refused to see Hohenzollern and the States General duly removed the princess's right to appoint magistrates in Bergen-op-Zoom as punishment.

In this moment of despair, the Queen of Bohemia turned to Rupert. From Frankfurt, sympathetic to her upset, he also wrote to the States General and admitted to being afflicted by his sister's action. Thanking them for their kindness towards his mother, the prince termed the matter a kidnapping. He also wrote to his cousin, the Elector of Hesse-Cassel, lamenting that had Charles Louis allowed Louise to enter the Lutheran convent at Herford (with her sister, Elisabeth) then matters would not have followed this course. One consolation was that Rupert and his mother were brought closer – he expressed a happiness that she had opened up to him, which was a mark of her confidence.

Louise's motives remain uncertain to this day. It's often speculated that she had fallen in love with the Marquess of Montrose and never recovered from his death. Nadine Akkerman wrote that Montrose had been led to believe that if he helped King Charles II regain his throne, he might have had Louise's hand. But Montrose's brutal death, after being defeated by the Covenanters, was seven years prior to Louise's flight. Princess Hohenzollern tried to excuse her assistance of Louise on account of the latter being pregnant (the second occasion of such a rumour), though Elizabeth of Bohemia refused to believe this. It was, she retorted, a 'monstrous base lye'.[9]

Louise was most likely tired of the humdrum of her mother's court and the tedious life she led as a princess without prospects. Perhaps Christina of Sweden proved an inspiration? In a letter, Louise put it down to an awakening that Catholicism was the only way to salvation and as such, she looked for a tranquil retreat where she could have 'full leisure for the service of God'.[10]

The British Library holds a very special (undated) letter from Louise. It was a joy to examine, not least because it was written mostly with rebuses – Louise had sketched images to represent words or phrases, that formed a cipher of sorts, with a line of French at the end. This letter, addressed to George Goring, might have been behind Morrah's very brief reference to the man's rumoured 'flirtation' with Louise, but neither the beauty and form of the letter, nor its content, was described.[11] Louise ends affectionately: 'I remain your [drawings of Cupid poised with an arrow, followed by a star]'. This, it seems certain, was Louise ending the letter referring to herself as Goring's shooting star. This is interesting, because her father referred to himself as Celadon and her mother as Astraea, two lovers from the play *L'Astree*. Astraea translates as 'star-maiden'. Louise opened the letter playfully, by confirming receipt of Goring's, which libelled upon her person, and cryptically continued. At the top is sketched a man playing a cello asking 'what shall wee singa' and a woman replying 'up, up my heart'.[12]

It appears by this letter that Louise and Goring were once very close, though he was married. Frustratingly, there is no date, and he was in The Hague at several different times. In 1647, when Rupert refused to give him a commission, Goring entered Spanish service. After a four-year hiatus in communication with the Royalists, the man wrote to King Charles II in 1655 from Spain to offer his services. On 25 July 1657, Goring died in Madrid after having converted to Catholicism. Five months later, Louise fled The Hague. There has never been a suggestion that Louise's conversion was anything to do with Goring's death, but it is as plausible a cause as Montrose's demise.

Rupert's self-imposed exile in Frankfurt gave him freedom from politics and court life. One of the few interruptions came when Joseph Bampfield, the man who had helped the Duke of York escape custody in 1648, sought Rupert's favour and protection. Bampfield, who intended to seek a 'livelyhood where soever he can find it' appealed to Rupert via Henry Jermyn, a most influential person in Henrietta Maria's circle. Jermyn endorsed Bampfield, noting the man's sufferings entitled him to all the 'releefs' and support he could get.[13] A suspicious Rupert forwarded the letter to his old friend, Secretary of State Edward Nicholas, who showed King Charles. The monarch was 'much astonished' that Jermyn should have endorsed any such request, Bampfield being a turncoat employed by Cromwell.

Without employment, Rupert indulged his passions of art and science. The African lad was sent to the Elector of Hesse-Cassel, who baptised and educated him, though tragically he did not long survive. Rupert's two 'moors' (as Charles Louis termed them) fought and killed one other in July 1658. One man who remained in the prince's intimate circle was Valentine Pyne, his secretary, who had voluntarily joined him after the execution of Charles I. When Pyne was summoned to leave Frankfurt, Rupert intervened and urged King Charles to rescind the instruction, telling him that Pyne was able to 'observe and study such things as are in these parts'.[14] It's a rather cryptic phrase that hints at a targeted design in this period of supposed artistic repose. During this time Rupert invented a quadrant for measuring altitude at sea, a device for raising water, and explored how gunpowder might be produced with a greater explosive effect. He had always been keen on military engineering and advances that might bring tactical advantages. John Mansell, who had discussed naval explosives with him in Kinsale, had made contact again over how all sorts of fireworks might be fired from ordnance like an ordinary bullet. Perhaps it was military experimentation that Pyne was involved with.

There was also engraving – the so called the 'black art'. Rupert threw himself into it, developing not only his own skills, but also furthering the process and designing instruments, which were hard to come by, having had to send to Vienna for them. The principle he pioneered was treating the surface of a copper plate to darken it, and then scratching out a lightened image. This was the opposite to the regular light-to-dark method. In his lifetime, Rupert was credited with inventing this process, though Colonel Louis von Siegen, in the household of the Elector of Hesse-Cassel, was also experimenting with it. Wallerant Vaillant was another pioneer, and he spent much time with Rupert in Frankfurt that year. Both von Siegen and Vaillant have since been named the creator, but Rupert, at very least, introduced it to England and demonstrated it to John Evelyn in 1661.

Plenty of Rupert's work survives as testament to his talent. He considered an artist could achieve as much with this method as with a paintbrush. The prince's works have a focus on ordinary people, such as a woman looking downwards (much like Titian's *Christ and the Adultress*), a peasant carrying a bag, another with a stick and reed basket, a beggar with a staff and rosary, and a boy holding a basket with fish. Even his landscapes tended to contain people going about their day-to-day business, one including a man driving a horse-drawn waggon. These fit with Rupert's happiness to mix with any level of society, especially those with trades or skills that he might learn from. It's easy to imagine Rupert's tormented mind being gradually eased by this day-to-day creativity as he sat and observed people come and go. There was also a portrait of Mary Magdalen. His most well-known are the *Standard Bearer* and *The Great Executioner with the Head of Saint*

John the Baptist, the latter having a strong parallel with the execution of Charles I. Eighteenth-century antiquary, George Vertue, noted a rumour that when William Dobson painted a similar work in 1645, during the civil war, the head of Saint John had been based on Rupert's features.

Vaillant also produced an engraving at this time, said to be of Rupert, wearing a feathered hat with his head leaning casually against one hand. He looks very much at ease but slightly too young and innocent. Vaillant completed another with chalks, which is definitely Rupert in armour, appearing much more weather-beaten and thoughtful.

Morrah suggests that this period also saw the beginnings of an idea for Rupert's biography, and that notes were duly made. After twenty years of tragedies, trials, and tribulations, this inactivity was the rest Rupert's body and mind craved. By coming to terms with the past, he might now consider his future.

Chapter 31

Brotherly Trick

His Highness, Lord Protector Oliver Cromwell, died in his plush bed at the heart of Whitehall Palace on 3 September 1658. He's often referred to as a king in all but name. Though he wore no crown, Cromwell did have a sword – control of the army – which was infinitely more powerful. Armed also with the doctrine of Puritan Predestination, it imbued him with a passionate belief that he was God's instrument, and therefore his actions were by default the Lord's. Such belief had driven him on as much as belief in divine right had driven the late king. Cromwell had played his part in ending the monarchy and seeing off the Levellers and their anarchic desire for people power, but had failed to bequeath a stable government. The protector died haunted by the shadow of monarchy.

His demise resurrected hopes for the king's restoration. Though the protector's son, Richard, had for some time been designated his successor, there was much uncertainty. King Charles issued the Declaration of Breda, promising a pardon for all those who had fought against the crown, except for the regicides. Matters moved slowly and with much caution – Richard Cromwell was not half the politician of his sire. Renowned republican Henry Marten, smelling danger, left England in 1659. Before he departed, he was said to have seen George Monck, military commander in Scotland, and asked whether the man would support a king or a Commonwealth. Despite Monck answering the latter, Marten dismissed the reply and told a tale of a man with a saw, pickaxe, and hatchet, who when asked what he was going to do, replied, 'Take measure of a gentleman and make him a suit of clothes.'[1] Monck was told to apply the story to himself – he was just as unlikely to set up a Commonwealth.

Monck played a pivotal role. On 15 November 1659, he announced he'd had a call from God to march into England and maintain the liberty of Parliament, though didn't elaborate on what that might mean. Affairs seemed 'wholly doubtfull' to many as they waited for Monck to 'unmaske himselfe'.[2] Princess Louise, from her French convent, told King Charles she was praying for his success. Courted by both king and Commonwealth, Monck reached the capital and called for a free Parliament, which invited the king to return to his three kingdoms. Rupert received a prompt invitation to accompany his cousin.

In August 1658, Rupert had been offered employment by the new Emperor Leopold I and had travelled to Vienna. After being appointed Lieutenant-Field-Marshal in the

Imperial army, he secured a victory against the Swedes at Wismar in Mecklenburg, in April 1660. Because of this commitment, he was unable to join King Charles. Instead, on 29 May, Rupert arrived at The Hague just as the king entered London amidst outpourings of joy. This 'Hapy restoration' was deemed by Elizabeth, Viscountess Mordaunt, to be a 'merecol [miracle] past expectation'. She poured out her joy in a diary entry, declaring that it was the beginning of the church's settlement and praising God's mercy.[3] Henrietta Maria continuously reminded her son to reward his father's old servants and remember that this was all God's providence.

When King Charles II stepped foot on English soil in 1660, he had duly knelt and given thanks to God, before embracing and kissing General Monck and addressing the man with 'ye title of Father'.[4] It was a tender mark of great respect for the architect of the restoration. Monck was not just kingmaker, but monarchy-maker. The Duke of York had followed suit and kissed the general several times, and amidst the cries of God Save the King, the Duke of Gloucester had thrown up his hat and called for the Almighty to bless Monck.

Rupert's mother was anxious to go to England and share the joy. The Hague had never been a real home, and Charles Louis was not enthusiastic about her settling in the Palatinate. Word from England was to stay put for now, but swept up by the excitement, she argued that she had taken farewell of everyone and did not have 'any handsome excuse to stay'. To Rupert, she explained that delay would be taken as 'disaffection' and make her 'despised' in all places, nevertheless, she did delay for another year.[5] Rupert, too, had to return to his troops and obtain his discharge. At this most inopportune moment, he was also stricken by the illness picked up during his sea voyages.

Finally making it to London in September 1660, Rupert found the celebrations tinged by sadness. King Charles's brother, Henry, had succumbed to smallpox. He was a prince of great hopes said to have had virtues beyond others of his age. In November, Henrietta Maria brought her youngest child, Henrietta Anne, but no sooner had one sibling arrived than yet another departed when the king's sister, Mary, died of smallpox on 29 December. The tragic dwindling of the royal family left Rupert taking precedence over everyone except the king and Duke of York. Plans were made to provide him with a pension of £4,000 per annum and his old position as Lord President of Wales was considered. But the prince did not intend to commit at this stage, considering himself beholden to Emperor Leopold, who was facing war with the Ottoman Empire. If conflict broke out, Rupert was expected to take part. If not, he would settle in London, where he was already 'very fond of living'.[6]

Those early months of 1661 gave Rupert the chance to meet old acquaintances and get a feel for the political landscape, as well as show John Evelyn his mezzotint techniques. Despite the short spell, it was not without drama when one of the prince's attendants searched for gunpowder in the cellar of the cockpit at Whitehall Palace, the lodgings of George Monck, now Duke of Albemarle. This resulted in the duke cudgelling the man until he maimed him. Rupert, having much respect for the duke, dismissed the offending servant and then offered to fight anyone who had been behind rumours that had led to the search. Within months, a further incident occurred over a 'fier balle' (fireball) caused by a small barrel of powder that Rupert's staff had left in his quarters, which he angrily hoped might not be mistaken for any 'plott'.

Granting the faithful Will Legge power of attorney over his affairs, Rupert prepared to visit Vienna to explore his options. In April, he sailed to Holland, suffering seasickness on the first day and making an 'offer to Neptune'.[7] Behind him, King Charles II was crowned on St George's Day. At The Hague, he met his mother, finding the 'poore woman' very dejected at still not having received any invitation to London.[8] Rupert urged Legge to push her case with Edward Hyde, the Lord Chancellor, who was now Earl of Clarendon, after his daughter married the Duke of York. Surprisingly, the Earl of Craven, who had bankrolled the Palatine family for decades, came in for criticism when Rupert declared that the man 'hath not done very well' in assisting his mother's case. Elizabeth of Bohemia had by now firmly closed the door on Charles Louis, refusing to live in the Palatinate on account of the breakdown in their relations. He had quibbled over her pension (for six months she had not received it) and even claimed that had she moved to Heidelberg, his marriage would not have collapsed.

Despite delays, Rupert travelled through Cleves in May, where he met with great 'alarums and preparatcons of warr'. The Turks were threatening Hungary, and the Princes of Germany were called by the emperor to combat them. Sweden was arming itself, while Holland postured over the herring trade, threatening that they would 'mantaine it wth the sword'. It was timely that here Rupert met an 'Ingenir' (engineer) called De Rues. Considering him the ablest in his profession, the prince waxed lyrical over his skills and advocated his employment upon the fortifications of Portsmouth – as nobody does it 'soe well and soe cheap & fast as he'.[9]

From Cleves, he went to Cassell, and then on to Mainz. Here he heard that his mother had finally departed for England. In his relief, he encouraged Legge (now a groom of the king's bedchamber) to secure a cargo of Rhenish wine that he had sent and 'drink it in remembrerance of your freinds'.[10] On 4 June 1661, Rupert reached Vienna. There he found obstacles to his becoming General of the Horse – first and foremost he was not Catholic. Noting that there were 'soe smale preparatcons' being made for war and realising that any Imperial army would simply roast inactively in the sun and develop the feverish 'hungaria sickness', Rupert stomached the quibbles over his posting. Meanwhile, he continued negotiating for his portion of reparations following the Treaty of Münster, which by the 1690s was estimated to be 150,000 Rixdollars. A financial backup came in the form of wine (Hungarian, Rhenish, and muscadine) which he hoped to trade, and which might also supply the court in London and serve as gifts for friends. After chiding Legge for not writing 'one silable' to him of late, he admitted 'the hunting retards much businesse', having lent his greyhounds to the emperor.[11]

Sport aside, Rupert's social activities allowed him to be King Charles's eyes and ears. Conversations with the former Spanish ambassador over Charles's proposed marriage to a princess of Portugal allowed Rupert to report back that the matter 'extreamly troubles' Spain. The Imperials, so closely related to the Spanish, were also perturbed, and because of the prospect, ministers avoided visiting Rupert – though the empress and archduke showed every courtesy. As a result, Rupert exhorted Legge 'for god sake' to give notice if war with Spain became likely.[12] However, a conflict with his brother, Charles Louis, would break out before any other. On 25 August 1661, Rupert exploded over a 'stori' that 'doth troble me in the highest degree'. Charles Louis had written to an Imperial Privy Counsellor expressing uncertainty over King Charles II's intent against the House of Austria, and pointed out Rupert's intimacy with the monarch, which in effect raised mistrust of the prince and undermined him. '[A]lle this is a Brotherly trick youl say but I thank [God] they heere doe little beleeve what he sais.'[13] Luckily the emperor retained a lifelong 'great regard' for Rupert.[14]

A book also came to Rupert's notice, which used 'most base' language about his civil war actions and must have added salt to the wounds. Dedicated to Rupert's good friend, Colonel John Russell, the prince exclaimed that had Honest Jack read the book, he would have 'broken the translators head' over its contents.[15] Rupert now intended to return to London, likely considering his mother's homeland to be the most fitting place to establishing himself. He had vowed some years past never to return to the Palatinate and his brother's 'barbaros intentions' now reinforced that decision.[16] In the days following there was no let-up in his anger at Charles Louis. Rupert declared in another letter to Legge 'by heven I am in such a humor that I dare not write to any'.[17] To cap it all, one of his greyhounds, called Royall, was dying. 'I would rather loose the best horse in my stable.'[18]

On 22 September 1661, Rupert was back at Frankfurt. The journey was tedious, and he made as much haste as he could. 'I shall shacke [shake] of[f] my shackles [and] be gon in one breath to Rotterdam.'[19]

At Cassell, he met his eldest sister, Elisabeth, now abbess of the Lutheran convent at Herford. He also sent reminders to King Charles, over transporting his wine from Rotterdam, and for having his lodgings prepared. Rupert's principal home was Whitehall Palace, where his quarters led off the stone gallery. Here, his rooms would eventually sport mohair hangings and contain twenty-four cane chairs, along with a pendulum clock – it was, after all, an office, too. In the bedchamber he slept in a blue damask bed. Shortly after his return, two new rooms were built that overlooked the privy garden. Additionally, he was given rooms at Windsor Castle.

Rupert's mother, however, was not granted any official residence and was housed by Lord Craven, and then forced to rent from the Earl of Leicester. Charles Louis badgered his mother over her possessions, attempting to stake his claim, but she was out of his clutches. She and Rupert had long since realised their similarities and he was now her favourite son. Sophia was happy that they had been reunited but complained that Rupert barely wrote to her – she knew not if he was still in the world. Tragically, it was her mother who would soon be gone from it.

Chapter 32

Surgery & Phisick

If Helen of Troy's beauty was enough to launch a thousand ships, then Elizabeth Stuart's charm and sufferings had led to the deployment of many thousands of soldiers. She had been indomitable throughout all her trials and tribulations. But after forty-nine years on the continent, she lasted barely nine months in London, dying on the eve of her forty-ninth wedding anniversary at the age of 65. Apart from a few specific items, her belongings were in the main left to Rupert – thus Charles Louis was spurned, which bequeathed another brotherly feud.

At the time of his mother's death, Rupert had already received a promise of suitable employment from King Charles and had been made a Privy Counsellor. Following this, he had resigned his Imperial posts. Back in 1638, when visiting his uncle, Rupert had declared a wish to bury his bones in England. He now pledged life and service to his cousin and the three kingdoms.

In August, when Queen Henrietta Maria returned once more to England, she brought with her Rupert's brother, Edward. The old queen landed at Dover to find a quarrel between King Charles and his new Portuguese wife, Catherine of Braganza, over the latter's mistress, and it was hoped Henrietta Maria might restore order. The royal journey from Dover was soon interrupted by another dispute. Rupert found fault with the Duke of Buckingham, a dissolute favourite of King Charles II, over a horse and challenged him to a duel. Buckingham declined to fight because of a hunting injury to his arm and instead promised satisfaction when he was recovered, but Rupert pulled the man from his mount in the public street. Luckily several people intervened, and the prince was held back. The quarrelsome royal family was then feasted and entertained. Rupert and Edward had much to talk about, including their mother's will – Charles Louis was outraged by it, and he enjoyed at least tacit support from his siblings. Rupert was unapologetic and made that abundantly clear, which subsequently strained relations with Edward up until the latter's death in March 1663.

As Duke of Cumberland, Rupert sat in the House of Lords and was part of standing committees, as well as the Privy Council. He did his best to champion the plight of many civil war Royalists, such as Sir John Heydon, the late king's General of Ordnance, though with varying success. He enthusiastically backed his friend Robert Holmes (describing himself as the man's 'owld master') when Holmes was despatched to Guinea to find the fabled mountains of gold that Rupert had heard about ten years earlier.[1] Holmes, by retracing parts of the prince's epic voyage, must have given Rupert hours of scintillating updates. Another expedition went to recover the fifty guns of the *Loyal Subject*, wrecked off the Azores in 1651, and the prince even designed a way of raising sunken objects by which to help. Then in the middle of 1663, a packet of letters arrived courtesy of Lord Windsor, from a diplomat at Puerto Rico, which included an attestation about Prince Maurice. Witnesses told of a vessel that was wrecked off the south coast of the island.

By 1664, the Dutch were accelerating their shipbuilding. Three new warships were being hurried out from Amsterdam as a trade war brewed with England. Rupert sensed an opportunity to prove his dedication to his new country and put his naval experience to good use. During this sabre-rattling, King Charles was also called to mediate between Rupert and Charles Louis, though brotherly peace was not to be found for many more years. No more fruitful were clandestine negotiations over Rupert's marriage.

The Duke of Richmond, Rupert's great friend during the civil wars, had died in 1655. Gossip suggested that his widow was destined to marry Rupert, though as years passed, nothing materialised. In 1664, Rupert communicated with a woman in Nantes over his matrimonial prospects, a woman who herself admitted she had a lot of respect for the prince. Frustratingly, her letters are anonymous. She was acting as an intermediary for yet another anonymous lady. In one, the middle-woman remarks on news that the prince was committed to a duchess from a long time past. Most likely this was the Duchess of Richmond. It if was, then Rupert paid the price for dallying, for the duchess married Colonel Thomas Howard that same year.

Madame Nantes, as I term her, complained at one point about Rupert's lack of contact, though the suitor did not give up and still wished to convey a thousand compliments to the prince. Though the identities of these two ladies remain a mystery, it was around this time that Rupert struck up a relationship with Frances (or Francesca), daughter of courageous Royalist officer, Sir Henry Bard. The man had travelled on foot through France, Italy, Turkey, Palestine, and Egypt prior to the civil war. Described as 'a compact body of vanity and ambition, yet proper, robust and comely', his courage was undeniable.[2] Having lost an arm at Cheriton in 1644, he had gained an Irish peerage as Viscount Bellamont the following year.

In 1660, Bellamont had been sent as envoy to the Shah of Persia. After being robbed, his wanderings with interpreter, John Belle, finally ended when he was consumed by a sandstorm on his way to India, somewhere between Agra and Delhi. He had left a destitute widow, Anne, and four children (Anne, Charles Rupert, Frances, and Persiana). Widow Bellamont petitioned Charles II in September 1660, concerned that she might have to admit herself to a gaol and leave her children to the charity of others, noting that Charles Rupert was King Charles II's godson. Their family losses ran into thousands of pounds from the civil war, and her husband's death ended his income of £5,000 per annum. It's inconceivable that

Rupert wouldn't have assisted the family of one of his most trusted officers in some way. Frances was young; her year of birth is placed at 1646, therefore she is thought to have been aged around 18 when linked to the prince. Precisely how their relationship came about is unknown, but in July 1664, Rupert was in the middle of preparations for war, having volunteered to lead a fleet to Guinea and strike the Dutch.

By September, a royal progress to the New Forest was planned by the king, from which Rupert would break away and join the fleet at Portsmouth. A surgeon was appointed for the prince, though Rupert promptly wrote a list of additional medicines that the man should obtain. Preparing to put his life in the Almighty's hands, Rupert's naval prospects brought him into close contact with William Batten, who he had threatened to shoot in 1648, and William Penn, the Commonwealth admiral who had pursued him in the Mediterranean. The close ally of these men, diarist Samuel Pepys, took an almost obsessive dislike to Rupert. Political manoeuvring also meant Rupert had to reluctantly share command with the Earl of Sandwich, another patron of Pepys.

King Charles II's sister, Henrietta Anne, had married the Duke of Orléans, brother to King Louis. Charles wrote to her that there was scarcely one Englishman who did not passionately desire a war with Holland. In hastening out Rupert and the fleet, the king confidently blamed the Dutch for any 'mischife' that might subsequently occur to them.[3] On 4 October 1664, Rupert boarded the *Henrietta* after having dined with the king and Duke of York. The latter had been eager to command himself, and so from London he followed events with a keen interest, firing off numerous missives to Rupert. Immediate orders were to sail to Portsmouth and wait – the fleet included at least 500 Scottish volunteers, so was not solely an English affair. As Holmes took Dutch forts and trading posts in Guinea, Holland recovered from the plague, but spotted fever then broke out in London. With a Dutch fleet now despatched to Guinea, Rupert was finally ordered to sail, though not to Holmes's support. Instead, he was instructed to join another fleet that had been assembled for the Duke of York to command.

With Rupert putting his trust in God, the parson on board suffered some sort of breakdown, or as the prince put it 'the spirit of mutiny' entered him. The man babbled into the night, abusing the captain, while Rupert 'strained' his patience because the man had come recommended by the Archbishop of Canterbury.[4] In the end, Parson Levit was sent ashore, and while he waited for another, Rupert admitted he had not 'troubled' the Almighty much with prayers.[5] No sooner had the ship quietened than a block, or piece of a yard-arm, struck Rupert's head, aggravating the gunshot wound he had suffered in 1647. He wrote to Legge of the incident, who notified the Duke of York, whereupon Rupert's old surgeon, Choqueaux, was hastily despatched. More than anything, Rupert was 'extremely impatient' over the thought he might not be able to go to sea after all.[6] Charles II's diplomat at The Hague, George Downing, certainly felt that the incapacitated prince should not 'goe out wth this fleet' and said so to ministers.[7]

On 4 November 1664, Rupert was trepanned on board ship – a horrific operation where a small segment of skull is drilled through so that corrupt matter can be released. While Choqueaux was unwilling to 'let him stir', the fleet scoured the channel for Dutch prizes.[8] Scurrilous rumours, in which Pepys indulged, would later paint Rupert's illness as the pox. By 4 December, he remained seriously ill, and the Duke of York prevailed on him to return to London. The prince had hoped the long-anticipated voyage to West Africa, and the warmer climate, might have aided his recovery, but this was not to be. From France, the king's sister Henrietta Anne warned that the Dutch were delaying sending out more ships in the hope that this might lead to the English exhausting their supplies while they waited.

When the fleet returned to port, Elizabeth, Viscountess Mordaunt, thanked God for her husband's safety, writing in her diary that the Lord had held the man's soul and 'hathe not suffered his feet to slip'.[9] By February, 100 Dutch prizes had been taken, leading to King Charles declaring war on 4 March 1665 and nineteen days later, Rupert, in better health, joined the fleet.

As the vessels were made ready, the prince intervened over Choqueaux's wages – the Frenchman had petitioned the king for arrears and complained that false rumours alleged he had been selling items to make back the money. The matter came to the attention of navy commissioner Sir William Coventry, who warned ministers that the surgeon was on his way to the capital to pursue his grievances and was threatening them with Prince Rupert's anger over the matter. Though Choqueaux evidently had cause for complaint, it was the prince who suffered.

> Choqueux is in such whrath [wrath] that he hath not his desirs, that he hath not sent any medcins for my head and refuses to come him selfe soe that I am destitute of alle but gods merci ... I gave him out of my owne [money] beforee [£40] but for alle this he sent me word that he could not stirr.

Without relief, Rupert complained, 'I doubt not to doe well wth out such a surgane [surgeon].' As such, he turned his mind to attempts to discover 'a new way and more charitable Kind of surgery & phisick' which he might employ to ease his suffering.[10]

On 21 April 1665, the fleet got underway for Holland. It was arranged in three squadrons – White, Red, and Blue. Rupert commanded the first, which led, with the Duke of York in the centre, and the Earl of Sandwich's Blue squadron at the rear. The intention was either to do battle or seize the East India merchantmen who were returning home. Rupert warned that the fleet did not have enough provisions to wait off the coast if the Dutch did not come out to fight, but he was overruled. All attempts to provoke the enemy into action failed – the fleet blockaded the Zuider Zee, capturing eight merchantmen, but after three weeks were forced to return home. Whilst resupplying, gentlemen volunteers arrived and were divided between the squadrons. Rupert took the opportunity to visit a friend, and on return to the flagship, the boat carrying him encountered a difficult passage. Alongside the prince were the Duke of Buckingham and Lord Blaney. Rupert was reminded of his beloved brother and expressed a hope they might not be similarly drowned, prompting Buckingham to remark that his grandfather and three great-uncles had also been lost at sea. Blaney humorously assured that though he liked their company, he wished he was out of it, lest their history curse him too.

On 1 June, a lookout in the *Royal James* spotted the Dutch who had finally put to sea. As dawn broke two days later, the enemy was barely 40 miles away, and the English had the weather gauge (were upwind of the enemy). Rupert led the vanguard with his White squadron and 'received the charge of their fleet', not discharging again till close and then 'firing through and through the enemy with great success'.[11] A diagram in the Bodleian Library shows the prince's ships arrayed like an arrowhead pointing straight at the Dutch with the words 'Prince Robt Broake through' written in the centre of the enemy position.[12] Rupert divided the enemy. To carry off this feat, his vessels had withheld fire until amongst the Dutch, something which must have tested many a man's nerve (the same orders he had given his cavalry). It is noted that his ships took 100 shots from the enemy before giving off a return salvo.

For nearly six hours the two sides, at the mercy of the elements, sailed close and fired their cannons when opportunity presented itself. Their numbers were almost equal. After passing each other by, the fleets had to tack (or come about by turning through the wind) to bring about another encounter. The breathtaking line of vessels – over 100 men-of-war on each side – pumping out shot must have been a powerful sight, especially considering Rupert's seafaring exploits had involved only a tiny number of ships. Shot could splash short or rip through sails. The way naval battles unfolded at slow speed might lull new recruits into assuming the danger was lessened, but direct hits would send splintering shards across a deck. Anyone in the way of this wooden spray might be impaled or cut to pieces as if by a hundred knives. For five more hours battle raged.

The Duke of York had the *Royal Charles* target the Dutch commander's flagship, the *Eendracht*. Chainshot killed the Earl of Falmouth, while the son of the Earl of Burlington had his head torn off and the same shot went on to kill Lord Muskerry. These men were standing with the duke – second in line to the throne – who was covered by their blood and wounded in the hand by a piece of skull. As the *Royal Charles* seemed ready to be boarded, the *Eendracht* suddenly exploded, the force shattering windows at The Hague. After fourteen hours, the Dutch raced for home.

They had lost between 6,000 and 10,000 men and seventeen ships, and the English just 700 and one respectively. Rupert was reported to have done wonders – 'none excelled him in valour and success' – and he had been in the fray several times.[13] The Duke of York also behaved extremely courageously, and as Lord High Admiral must take the laurels of victory – he, Rupert, and Sandwich worked well together. Granted a gift of £200 from the king, Rupert modestly declared that his greatest joy was to have been a small instrument in 'chastising so high an insolency'.[14] He wrote this from his bed on board ship, excusing his handwriting and revealing the issue to be an accident of the surgeon. It appeared he had sustained an injury to his leg. Such dangerous near misses, however, wounded the Duke of York's active naval career; being next in line to the throne, his death would have been devastating, therefore he was recalled.

As the Great Plague ravished London, the stoic Duke of Albemarle remained in the capital and directed government. The royal court decamped and headed first to Salisbury and then to Oxford. King Charles asked Rupert to accompany him, leaving Sandwich in command of the fleet. Though the Dutch had opened negotiations after the late battle, Sandwich was instructed to intercept either De Ruyter, who was bringing back nineteen ships from West Africa, or any enemy merchantmen. This would increase pressure and secure more advantageous terms. Though De Ruyter gave Sandwich the slip, the latter captured several prize ships, which encouraged Parliament to vote for subsidies to continue the war in 1666.

When Sandwich authorised his flag officers to take their share of the prize money in advance of formal procedures, the fleet returned in September 1665 amidst a furore. Albemarle condemned Sandwich's decision. The Duke of York, from behind the scenes, also stirred trouble and Parliament caught a whiff of financial irregularity. When Sandwich raced to court to explain himself, he was supported by Rupert, who well understood the challenges commanders faced at sea.

The witch-hunt saw Sandwich sent as ambassador to Spain to remove him from the situation. Rupert and Albemarle were then named joint commanders of the fleet, but they would face a second enemy in 1666. At the end of January, France declared war on England. One month later, Denmark added itself to the anti-English alliance.

Nearly thirty years earlier, the teenage Rupert had been attached to the then George Monck's company at the assault on Breda. Now, the two men complemented one another well in personal style and character – the duke was respectful of Rupert's royal status and neither harboured personal rivalries. On 13 February, several naval commanders hosted a dinner for Rupert, and cheerfully anticipated the next bout of warfare, while a new third-rate ship of the line named *Rupert* was launched at Harwich. On 29 April the two commanders boarded their flagship, the *Royal Charles*, after considering strategy; the French and Dutch should be prevented from joining. Rupert's preference, which he made clear to the king, was that if the fleet should be divided to fight both enemies, then he wished to engage the French.

On 14 May, Privy Counsellors arrived on the flagship and discussed intelligence with Albemarle (Rupert having gone ashore) and asserted the Dutch were unlikely to have their fleet sailing within six weeks. Albemarle agreed to release twenty ships to hunt the French, which Rupert approved of when he returned. On 29 May, after impatiently chasing orders from the king and Duke of York, Rupert finally received them and set sail with his detachment. He instructed the Privy Council to dispense with frilly formalities in their letters and instead keep them brief and to the point.

No sooner had Rupert arrived at St Helens on 1 June than he received orders to return to Albemarle – the Dutch fleet had been sighted. But that same day the duke had engaged them, considering it dishonourable not to have done so. Given the odds, Albemarle's men fought with valour for three days and two nights. Rupert's arrival 'much incouraged the fleete' though at one moment the prince's ships came precariously close to shallow waters and were prevented from running aground only after swift warning from Albemarle.[15] Their combined number was sixty ships against De Ruyter's sixty-four.

When battle with the Dutch opened on Monday, 4 June 1666, Rupert, with around thirty ships, bore the brunt. The Dutch showed equal courage. The action lasted from six o'clock that morning until seven o'clock in the evening and Rupert was 'environed with as many dangers as the enemy could apply unto him'. '[T]hey raked him fore and aft, plyed him on both sides, and to all that, were just clapping two Fireships upon him, but two of our Fireships that attended the Prince, got betwixt that danger and him, and bravely burnt the bold Assaylants.'[16]

When both fleets were sailing parallel to one another, Rupert pulled off a brilliant manoeuvre by cutting right through the Dutch line and putting his ships on the larboard (left) side of Admiral de Ruyter's flagship. Albemarle managed to bring his vessels up quickly to the starboard (right) and put De Ruyter in a deadly sandwich. This saw Rupert and Albemarle voraciously targeted, and their flagships put out of action, both losing their topmasts. Albemarle had to shift his flag to a different vessel twice, but reportedly still 'rode on'.[17] As Rupert explained later, they were 'in a posture to strike a great stroke, but [were] forced off, not having so many ships to [transfer to] as his Spitzbroder Trump'.[18] Luckily for the two commanders, the Dutch broke off the fight and retreated, aided by an opportune mist.

Rupert's conduct was praised as 'incomparable, if the Generall [Albemarle] had not beene his competitor for ye honor of that day'. It was judged that they both did 'equally [well] to the amazemt of their friends and enemies'.[19] During the four days, the Venetian ambassador in Paris reckoned that ten English ships were lost. The *Royal Prince* ran aground and was burned by the crew with the loss of ninety-two brass guns; the *Swiftsure*, *Essex*, and *Convertine*, along with the *Loyal George*, a merchantman, were taken, along with four former Dutch prizes, many of which were destroyed by their own crews. The frigate *Henry* was assailed by seven Dutch men-of-war and three fireships, but survived, though the forecastle was badly burned.

There were many acts of heroism on both sides. Albemarle was wounded by a splinter to the thigh, but kept to the deck to inspire his men, 'giving them new life and spiritt'.[20] His 'faithful and indefatigable' secretary, Sir William Clarke, lost a leg and died.[21] Six of Prince Rupert's staff were killed as they stood right by him. George Hillson lost the use of an arm when saving the prince's life, and Rupert gratefully interceded to secure him a gunner's place. Sir Christopher Myngs, shot in the neck, pressed his finger against the wound in a bid to carry on, though a second shot finished him. A bullet also lodged in the throat of William Reeves,

Rupert's former page, rendering him silent as blood poured from it. When Reeves's ship was boarded, he hauled himself to the powder store, intending to blow it up, but was captured before it could be done. Having been stripped and denied medical attention, Reeves threw himself overboard twice to escape or die but was fished out on both occasions. He eventually found his way home at the end of the war. At least another six captains died, while others lost an array of arms or legs.

Devastatingly, 5,000 of King Charles's seamen had perished with 3,000 more captured – while the Dutch lost only 2,000 killed and wounded. Nevertheless, poems lauded the two commanders' 'meraculus suckses' (miraculous success).

> Tho' we were sinfull, pouwerles, and distrest
> Thou hast vs wonce agane, with victre [victory] blest
> And safely hath, our generals preser[v]ed
> Such mercis Lord, we neuer haue deser[v]ed.[22]

The Venetian ambassador in Paris claimed the English kept their vessels at sea longer than necessary to cover up their vast losses. Though their courage had impressed the Dutch, the death toll was sure to be baulked at in England – Rupert and Albemarle had to retain the confidence of the king, political leaders, and the people at large. News of the battle spread fast. In Florence, Dutch and English inhabitants clashed, competing to outdo one another in a three-day festival. They attempted to erect stages in the same place, interfered with each other's flags, and derided one another. A pamphlet was printed accusing Rupert of being 'ye first yt fled' in the late sea battle, resulting in an English official making complaint to the Grand Duke of Florence. '[A] Prince of ye Blood, A Prince of the most undaunted Personall Valour and tryd Courage ye World ever knew to be so infamously libell'd in his Presse' was unforgivable, he insisted.[23]

Soon enough, the offending printer was clapped up in a dungeon. These accusations, no matter how distant, were extremely damaging. James Hayes, Rupert's secretary, documented what he had observed of the prince's conduct and tactfully suggested it be included in official reports – Rupert had brought new courage to his friends and terror to the enemy. Hayes pointed out that he could not imagine any greater courage, conduct, or presence of mind than that shown by the prince, who was showered by cannonballs all day. Rupert assured the king that the damage to the fleet was general and could be repaired in fourteen days – which was just as well, because it was clear that the Dutch were looking for a renewed contest. Rupert's letter ended with a remark that a parson aboard a ship that was on fire had asked the boatswain how best to be saved. Upon being told to leap overboard, he did so, and was drowned. Rupert's dry sense of humour had clearly survived the battle.

Albemarle came in for the greatest criticism over engaging the enemy whilst numerically inferior. The two commanders then did battle with navy officials over the resupplying of the fleet – Rupert railed at their 'intolerable neglect'.[24] In the meantime, the prince issued additional instructions for flag officers to capitalise on tactics, said to be 'Very severe and ample'. By 17 July, the Dutch were in English waters. Next day, Rupert sent for the Dean of Westminster 'to preparre for the last hazards of the world resolveing itt seemes to retorne a glorious Victor or to dye like a good christian'. He must have known that after their heavy losses, everything hung on this next encounter.

Six days later, while Queen Catherine took the waters under care of her doctor, Rupert and Albemarle set sail from the Nore with ninety vessels and seventeen fireships, stocked with 'fire workes' which they had made trial of before the king. The pair were rough and demanding with their pilots. Sir William Penn was ordered to man fifteen more ships and follow as soon as can be. George Hamilton, a commander of the royal guard, also 'stole downe' to the fleet and attempted to board but was ordered back by the king despite it being short of manpower.[25] Plague was partly to account.

In the early hours of St James's Day, 25 July 1666, Rupert and Albemarle intercepted their enemy. Each of the three squadrons engaged the Dutch within an hour of one another from 10.00 am. The rear squadron of the Dutch, led by Tromp, cut off the English equivalent and the two fought separately. With the fire-eating Albemarle chewing on tobacco and urging immediate action, Rupert stuck to a more concerted plan, while Robert Holmes, now a vice-admiral, engaged with Admiral de Ruyter's flagship. On board Holmes's ship was a volunteer who had 'severall dreames' that he should kill De Ruyter – purposefully placed with Holmes, who would boldly do all he could to make that dream a reality.[26] After near eight hours, the main Dutch fleet disengaged and hastened away.

Holmes's ship was out of action, while Rupert and Albemarle's flagship, the *Royal Charles*, had taken a beating. De Ruyter had survived but he lost 4,000 men to the English 300. The Earl of Clarendon described it as 'soe glorious a Sunshyne of victory'.[27] All through the night Rupert and Albemarle led the 'Chace' after the Dutch and next morning were in great hope of taking De Ruyter's flagship.[28] The Dutchman's plight was doubly threatened when Rupert sent his newly made pinnace, *FanFan*, after the enemy like a hunting dog. Its ten oars rowed the craft to De Ruyter, stricken by the lack of wind, and fired salvo after salvo from her two guns. For an hour the immobile Dutch had to endure this bombardment, which was a cause of much English merriment.

Though De Ruyter escaped once more, Vice-Admiral Adrian Bankaert's vessel of sixty guns and another of sixty-six guns were taken and set alight to avoid slowing the English pursuit. The two fleets' rear squadrons fought it out until midnight, whereupon Tromp escaped. Rupert and Albemarle reported themselves masters of the sea on 27 July, with the loss of just one ship, and now lay off the Dutch coast. For eleven days they searched for prizes and then, on 8 August, Sir Robert Holmes was ordered to land 500 men on the island of Vlieland and 400 on Terschelling. The next day, plumes of black smoke proved Holmes's success, but he had in fact amended his plan on sight of a better opportunity. What became known as 'Holmes' Bonfire' consumed up to 170 ships that had lain in an anchorage. On 10 August, the attack on Terschelling went ahead and destroyed 1,000 houses; damage on both days was said to amount to £1,000,000.

When the fleet arrived back in England on 15 August, Holmes, now ill, earned Rupert's high praise, describing the man's success as the greatest blow the Dutch had received since the war was declared. For reasons unspecified, the prince seemed less content with his co-commander, Albemarle. Rupert's unease was addressed by the Earl of Clarendon, who wrote to him on 5 August, and extolled the 'greate satisfacion and delight' the fleet's victories had brought the king. Rupert's part, Clarendon emphasised, had brought him 'another kind of reputation then you have had in all the other brave Actions of [your] life'. The prince had shown 'greate Judgment, greate Temper, greate Composure of mind'. Clarendon had, during the civil war years, criticised the prince numerous times, especially over his temperament, yet in 1666, he doled out praise to pacify Rupert. It was an attempt to plaster over cracks in the prince and duke's relationship. Quick to assert that Albemarle was also complimentary, Clarendon reassured Rupert that the duke had 'magnified yor courage, your good humour, your very civill, and gratious way of liveing wth him' imploring that harmony between the commanders should not be broken.[29] After all, Clarendon added, there was barely one month left of their joint command. Though the king intended to separate the pair, nobody could foresee the devastating act that would bring it about.

Chapter 33

Desdemona

In mid-August 1666, on board the *Royal James*, Albemarle laid a wager with Rupert that the Dutch would not be able to fight again that year. On 26 August, the prince won the bet when the enemy put to sea in search of their French allies. Between 31 August and 2 September, all engagement was prevented by foul weather and storms, which had Rupert and Albemarle holed up at St Helens on the Isle of Wight. Repairs took ten days, during which time an oven fire in Pudding Lane went on to consume London, making it appear like divine retribution over Holmes's Bonfire. Viscountess Mordaunt called the inferno a 'destroying Angel'.[1]

Albemarle was called to take charge in the capital, and he left the fleet on 6 September, which given Clarendon's earlier letter, would not have concerned Rupert. There then occurred many near misses between the Dutch and English, which convinced the French that their allies were deliberately evading battle. The Dutch retired to Ostend but set out again, and on 25 September met Rupert's fleet, only for a strong wind to intervene. Three days later, they sailed home and stood down for the winter. After being buffeted by storms, his attempts to do battle frustrated, a ruffled Rupert arrived in the charred capital. When Samuel Pepys told the Navy Board that a fleet so great had been brought home in as bad a state as ever due to both weather and the enemy, Rupert flew into a towering rage. He denied the ships were in any such condition, causing the terrified Pepys to blame subordinates for telling him so.

The year 1666 was a dramatic one even in Rupert's personal life; Frances Bard had given birth to a son whilst he was away. The prince acknowledged the boy, who was named Dudley in honour of his maternal great-grandmother, Susan Bard, née Dudley. Frances was said to dislike the court and shunned it. In January 1667, however, Rupert was confined to his quarters at Whitehall Palace by a resurgence of his old head injury and it was even reported at the exchange that he had died. On 28 January he agreed to be trepanned again, and underwent the procedure on 3 February, though it did not go deep enough to achieve full success. As a result, a repeat took place on 21 February, which released a 'great quantity of corrupt matter'.[2] The prince started sleeping better and diverted himself in his purpose-built workhouse, by designing instruments that might make the process easier.

Pepys greased the rumour mill by furthering stories of Rupert being pox-ridden. The Earl of Sandwich, who had served as an envoy to Spain for two years, received a letter from one of his agents reporting Rupert's 'deplorable illness'. That, and Albemarle 'being grown [so stout] to be thought necessary at land & fitter [there] then for ye sea', increased chances of the earl's recall to the navy.[3] As Rupert recuperated, he would have heard that an expedition had built a fort at Hudson's Bay, called Fort Charles, and the territory was named Prince Rupert's Land (now part of Canada). The prince, forever passionate about trade and exploration, fitted out two vessels to capitalise on the fur trade and subsequently became Governor of the Hudson Bay Company. Beaver House, their aptly named London headquarters, had Rupert's coat of arms proudly engraved above one of its windows.

Though these two trading ships were being readied, at the same time there was great debate over how many ships of the Royal Navy should put to sea that year. King Charles had already sent peace feelers to the Dutch and French, pinning his hopes on these coming to fruition. That would mean there would be no need for a full war fleet and the expense it would incur. Coupled with that, huge debts still remained outstanding to navy suppliers and the seamen themselves. The best that could be done in the circumstances, despite the Dutch not being inclined to any peace, was to safeguard ports and coasts with smaller vessels. The larger ships of the line were not put into commission. The country, in effect, took on a dangerously defensive stance.

When eighty Dutch ships, filled with 4,000 soldiers, arrived off England's east coast on 7 June 1666, there were few English ships to counter them. Two days later, a squadron of lighter Dutch ships entered the Thames. Matters were exceedingly desperate and the Dutch landed 800 men who captured a fort at Sheerness. Luckily, the elements (winds and tides) combined to delay them. Rupert was also recovered enough to play his part. On 13 June, the desperate king ordered him to Woolwich. The prince, whose head dressing was discernible under his wig, instructed city officials to be furnished with 'Boates, men and materialls'.[4] He raged at Sir William Coventry that ships had been sent away from Woolwich, prompting a caveat that if Rupert ever thought 'fitt to countermand' any instructions, then his wishes should take precedence.[5]

Albemarle was despatched to oversee defences at Chatham. Chains were erected and ships sunk to keep the Dutch from sailing further upriver, while fireships were readied and land batteries erected. The national emergency lasted until 26 July, when the Dutch finally headed back out to sea. Nevertheless, the *Royal Charles* was humiliatingly towed away, eventually taken on to Holland, where her stern carving still exists in the Rijksmuseum. Rupert moved to Sheerness and fortified shore defences, drawing on his experiences of being pinned into various harbours in the 1640s and 50s. Finally, on 31 July 1667, a treaty brought an end to hostilities.

Peace was welcome to Rupert. He did nothing but smile politely at the Venetian ambassador's later suggestion that he command their fleet against the Turks. Indeed, without war, he could focus on his hobbies, as well as Frances

Bard and his son, often referred to as Dudley Rupert. The prince remained a close companion to the king and a trusted counsellor, following the court to Bagshot for hunting, or horse racing at Newmarket. On 2 September 1667, partnered with a Captain Cooke, he took part in a tennis match against two other courtiers, the four being deemed the best players in the country. Drama could still rear its head. In November 1667, when Rupert was travelling through King Street to Parliament in his sedan, the prince's footmen were set upon and wounded by two men, who were later apprehended.

Fall-out from the humiliating end to hostilities rumbled on, however, and the Earl of Clarendon, who was Lord Chancellor, came under increasing pressure. The fact that he was the Duke of York's father-in-law did not help him. Many joined the attack on Clarendon for political reasons, while others searched for a scapegoat to take the blame for the financial crisis. The king was also tired of the old man's nagging advice. He plumped for Clarendon's retirement, after twenty-five years of loyal service to the Stuarts. Instead, the man clung on as MPs, baying for his blood, prepared to reassemble amidst talk of impeachment. Shockingly, the king let it be known that he would sacrifice Clarendon, and the very threat was enough to provoke the man to flee the kingdom. Something akin to the dislike between Henry VIII's chief minister, Thomas Cromwell, and Anne Boleyn, existed between Clarendon and King Charles II's mistress, Barbara Villiers. The latter was reportedly very jolly over the old man's fall. Rupert seems to have taken a more neutral stance, as he would in many such political seesaws to come. Age brought him more wisdom and reflection. He did, though, take Cranborne Lodge from the exiled Clarendon, located in Windsor Great Park.

In September 1668, Rupert was appointed Constable of Windsor Castle, a post that would keep him close to the king. He went on to repair and improve the fortress, especially the round tower, and erected numerous platforms, batteries, and bridges. A major was appointed to open and close the main gate. Visitors to Rupert's quarters would enter via a steep staircase that led up to a hall. Both were hung with all manner of martial equipment, from pikes, muskets, pistols, bandoliers, holsters, drums, back, breast, and headpieces – the haul numbered thirty-four assorted firearms and there was even a mortar piece present. This gleaming array was a warlike shell that reflected the prince's outward character.

Yet the bedchamber, with its crimson damask bed, was very different, hung with tapestries and 'effeminate' paintings.[6] The rooms were spacious and ample, containing four tables and thirty chairs. There was also a forge, where he could lock himself away in scientific study, and a library stocked with hundreds of books. On 19 September 1668, his sister Elisabeth gave her judgement that Windsor 'will keep him away [from] londen'.[7] Also at Windsor he kept his pack of hounds, and a stable including twenty-seven horses of varying sorts, including two goldings called 'Hodge' and 'Punch'. A plush coach, drawn by grey or black horses, would convey him wherever needed. There must have been numerous visits to St George's Chapel, knowing his late uncle's final resting place was somewhere beneath the floor. Windsor was a comfortable home with most of his possessions and entertainments.

There was also four acres of land in the 'wilderness' that Rupert leased in 1668, known as Upper Spring Garden, and located within the verges of Saint James's Palace. The rent was 13 shillings and 4 pence per annum, and he was given permission to pull down the current house and build a new one. This parcel of land was enclosed by a brick wall and contained coach houses, a stable, and garden. Accounts from 1704 suggest it abutted, or was very close to, the road that ran from Charing Cross to Pall Mall, site of today's Carlton House Terrace. South of Rupert's house was a grove of elm trees. Elisabeth was quick to give more advice, warning that his putting his house in order meant putting away his dogs to preserve the furniture. But by next post she reconsidered, explaining that she loved her brother's contentment 'more then a cleane housse'. The new house at Spring Gardens contained a dining room, drawing room, bedchamber, replete with gilt-leather wall hangings and couch, and housed six servants.

If the new place at Spring Garden was for Frances, who disliked the court, then she didn't benefit. The pair split around 1668. The prince's sister, Sophia, hinted at Frances having given offence, which suggests a less than amicable parting. Elisabeth also wrote to Lord Craven that year, describing Rupert as 'noe frend to his owne good'. Her letter intriguingly reveals further personal thoughts about her brother and his relationships.

> he [that] is noe frend to his owne good [therefore] very well canot be so to any other but I think [Rupert too far] gone in his way to be amendable by misfortune ... I am rather of opinion yt a greate misfortun would make him desperat either over turne his braines or put him to some strange & rash resolution for hee will feare lese falling as he did in his mariage & never beleve that he can finde a friend because he never was a frend at any body living.

Though the language is somewhat confusing in parts, this remarkable letter specifically comments on marriage. Referring to Rupert 'falling as he did in his mariage' is too vague in its precise meaning (failing or falling?) leaving many connotations to guess at. Written in 1668, it lends support to that year being the one in which Rupert and Frances split. Elizabeth says that Rupert would struggle to be a 'frend' to any other, as he did not value himself enough – this also suggests her brother struggled to commit, which would make any marriage unlikely.[8] Perhaps Elisabeth's meaning was commiseration that the prince had failed to marry.

Investigating the enigmatic Frances Bard poses many problems. Though the daughter of a viscount, she was far from wealthy, which does not bode well. Financial transactions cause historical footprints. Another contributing factor is her sex – women's legal positions at this time meant that money was usually controlled by men. I've always harboured many questions about Frances.

Her ardent assertion that she had been married to Rupert centres around the strange slip of paper (like a retrospective affidavit) purporting to prove it, which only surfaced in the nineteenth century.

> July ye 30th, 1664.
> These are to certifie whom it may concerne that Prince Rupert and the lady Frances Bard were lawfully married at Petersham in Surrey by me.[9]

Rupert denied the marriage claims. The church records are incomplete, with many pages having been removed, including the period in question. Henry Bignall, who signed the scrap of paper, certainly was curate at Petersham prior to the Restoration, but he seems not to have been there by 1664. The church did house high-profile marriages, such as the Duke of Lauderdale and Countess of Dysart, but the Bignall note is highly likely a fake, produced much later with an intention of bolstering Frances's claim.

It's extremely doubtful Frances and Rupert married. Far more likely they had discussed it, and perhaps he made some sort of promise, which went by the wayside when their relationship broke down. Certainly, the prince's sister Louise thought so. Judging from a reply she penned to Rupert, it's clear he had enquired about Frances (who had left England) and the claims she was making in Europe. Louise had heard rumours about 'some sort of promise of marriage' but confirmed Frances mentioned nothing of it on their meeting – 'she made it clear to me that she has always held you in all the respect and esteem that she ought to do'. More tellingly, Louise stated her belief that 'these ladies are quicker to tell lies than you would be to engage yourself to marry', a phrase that suggests Frances's claim was not the first.[10]

Though Frances's exact whereabouts after the split are unknown, Dudley Bard was sent by Rupert to Eton (where the boy's maternal grandfather had also studied). He was then taken under the tutorage of Sir Jonas Moore at the Tower of London, who was Surveyor of the Ordnance, mathematician, author, and cartographer. Moore had once reputedly boiled his buttock to cure sciatica. He could also be a wit. When the Duke of York once declared that mathematicians and physicians had no religion, Moore replied with a wish that the duke had been such a man, considering the latter's conversion to Catholicism. Rupert would have visited Dudley frequently, not least because his long-time friends Will Legge and Valentine Pyne were there, being Treasurer of the Ordnance, and Master Gunner of England respectively. The prince and his blond-haired son were also captured on canvas by Sir Peter Lely.

Though Rupert much preferred experimenting in his forge, thinking up inventions, or scratching out mezzotints, he enjoyed the theatre. In 1671, Elizabeth Polewheele would dedicate her comedy play, 'The Frolicks' or 'The Lawyer Cheated' to Rupert and his bright and glorious mind. The prince also had the works of Margaret Cavendish, Duchess of Newcastle, in his library. When, also, Queen Catherine called for a masquerade, at which guests would choose a nationality and then dress appropriately, Rupert morphed into Alexander the Great. In doing so, he competed head-to-head with Lord Thanet, as Caesar. A royal trip to Tunbridge Wells, believed to have been in the summer of 1668, included dancing, drinking and plays – the usual gaieties associated with Charles II's court. Rupert was part of this progress. Anthony Hamilton, who wrote a memoir, records events at Tunbridge and gives an observation of Rupert at the time.

> The prince was brave and courageous, even to rashness; but cross-grained and incorrigibly obstinate: his genius was fertile in mathematical experiments, and he possessed some knowledge of chemistry: he was polite even to excess, unseasonably; but haughty, and even brutal, when he ought to have been gentle and courteous: he was tall, and his manners were ungracious: he had a dry, hard-favoured visage, and a stern look, even when he wished to please; but, when he was out of humour, he was the true picture of reproof.

Tunbridge changed Rupert's life forever. There, actresses Margaret Hughes caught his eye. He was immediately besotted with her, but the attention was not at first reciprocated – Peg, as she was known, rejected him – or at least feigned it. Hamilton termed her an 'impertinent gipsy' and accused her of doing so to sell her favours more dearly.[11] The prince was not to be put off. Peg brought down and greatly subdued his natural fierceness, to the point where he acted the wooer, which was so unnatural that he no longer seemed the same man.

Peg seems to have exploded onto the scene. One of the first female actresses on stage – if not the first – playing Desdemona at Drury Lane in 1663, it's often said she was Sir Charles Sedley's mistress, a thoroughly debauched character. The link to Sedley is somewhat tenuous. It's based on Pepys having met Sedley's mistress at the theatre in May 1668, who he said was new to town and called Pegg. Pepys kissed her, ogled her beauty, but controlled his abusive, wandering hands and sourly remarked that she seemed modest, but wasn't so. Peg Hughes had, by that time, been on the stage for some years so was hardly new to town.

Courted by the formidable prince from the summer of 1668, it's unclear when Peg Hughes finally accepted his advances. For Rupert's part, she took precedence over everyone and everything. Gone were alembics, crucibles, furnaces, and all the black furniture of the forges; mathematical instruments and chemical speculations now took a back seat, leaving sweet powder and essences as the only matters occupying his attention. The king, of course, was greatly amused by it all. Rupert enticed Peg to leave the stage and live with him. He gave her a splendid house in Hammersmith, once the home of Sir Nicholas Crispe, a dedicated Royalist whose heart had been entombed in a monument adorned with a bust of King Charles I. The brick house overlooked the river and much later became home to Queen Caroline, wife of George IV.

By 1668, only four out of twelve of Rupert's siblings were living. Charles Louis was suffering from 'ye goute' in his right hand, while Elisabeth was often confined to bed with a sore leg, which had troubled her for four years. It stemmed, she thought, from an ignorant surgeon who had once applied plasters that her leg could not endure.[12] This did not entirely stop her boar hunting, many such heads going as gifts to Lord Craven. From her sickbed she had few regrets, declaring she would rather keep her humble abode than be wife to any king. But she struggled to make ends meet, lacking ready money and having only two large rubies (one white) to sell. In her bedchamber hung a portrait of the Earl of Craven, along with one of Rupert.

Sophia, the youngest sibling, was married to the Prince-Bishop of Osnabruck, the only sister to have legitimate children. Rupert was godfather to her daughter, Sophia Charlotte. On receiving a painting of Rupert, Sophia complained his face did not look martial enough, but was overjoyed by the sporadic letters he wrote, frequently urging him to have the good nature to do so more often. Both Sophia and Elisabeth quarrelled with Charles Louis over payment of their allowances. Louise, by comparison, was relatively comfortable, having been appointed Abbess of Maubuisson in 1664, a Catholic convent in France worth £40,000 per annum. After her conversion, she had been cut off from the family but remained extremely close to her brother Edward. His death in 1663 served as a catalyst for reconciliation with Charles Louis. Edward's widow remained one of Louise's closest confidantes for the next twenty years.

Chapter 34

Albion's Patron

As Rupert forged a relationship with Peg, another partnership came to an end. Three days into 1670, George Monck, Duke of Albemarle, died.

> These Glorious Actions prov'd that You cou'd be,
> Great Albion's Patron both at Land and Sea;
> And with more Justice may that Title Clame,
> Than he who England does for Patron Name.[1]

Sophia wrote to Lord Craven extolling Albemarle's fame and virtues. Ever the pragmatist, a very Palatine trait, she was happy that Craven had been given two offices of the late general's. A state funeral was arranged. Albemarle's body wound its way from Somerset House to Westminster Abbey, with the king declaring that the send-off should be adorned with all circumstances of honour for such a great subject. The funeral effigy wore a periwig, its hands and head made of wax and painted lifelike. Rupert must have rued the passing of such a greatly respected friend and comrade; poignantly, his library in 1677 retained an Oxford University tribute to Albemarle published at his death. Further recognition that Albemarle had been central to the restoration of the monarchy came when, filling the vacancy created by the duke's demise, his son was almost immediately given the Order of the Garter.

The loss of the architect of the monarchy's restoration was significant. That January, when the French ambassador put on a play for the king and queen, it seemed as if Albemarle's death had temporarily destabilised everything. The royal couple were dressed in masquerade, Queen Catherine reputedly wearing £300,000 worth of jewels, when the stage 'broke as they were dancing'. The fiddler 'tumbled' but the King was 'nimble Enough to avoyde it'.[2]

In April 1670, Rupert's sisters, Sophia and Elisabeth, united over his health. Sophia wrote to Craven about her brother's trepanning some years earlier, and it appears the sisters' fresh concern was prompted by another bout of ill-health. It opened the question of Rupert's belongings – specifically the family jewels in his possession. By May, the prince's health had improved, but the presence of Peg Hughes unnerved Sophia, who didn't entirely trust her. She openly admitted her fear that if Rupert should die, those jewels might be lost, and urged Craven to intercede with the prince to draw up a will.

One month later, Peg's brother (who was employed in Rupert's household) was killed in a fight with one of the king's servants over an argument whether his sister or Nell Gwyn was prettiest. That month, Sophia heard with some relief that Rupert had made a will in favour of his two sisters. Louise, the third, had long ago given up earthly possessions. Perhaps Albemarle's loss brought home the fragility of life to the ageing Rupert, still troubled by both his head and leg wounds.

Sophia received more good news in September, when Rupert and Charles Louis came to an agreement. It followed King Charles's intercession, warning Charles Louis that if he had to take sides, then it would be Rupert's – it was said the king had not forgotten Charles Louis's dubious antics during the civil wars. James Hayes, Rupert's Secretary, had gone to the Palatinate with the offer that Rupert would drop his request for an apanage in that territory (worth £6,000 per annum) in favour of retaining their mother's possessions already in his hands, and £3,000 per annum – quite specifically, only if he did not go on to have lawful children. This last point is telling, and by default opposes Frances Bard's claims of an earlier marriage. It also means that the possibility of future lawful issue, though remote, was not ruled out and that Rupert might still take a wife.

I wonder how much Rupert's willingness to patch things up with his brother might have stemmed from the contentedness Peg provided. For Sophia, it was long overdue, especially considering Charles Louis's only legitimate son (a handsome young man said to resemble his Uncle Rupert) had fallen ill with smallpox whilst touring in Geneva. This gave a timely reminder that if he should die, Rupert would become his brother's heir, a fact that might have encouraged Frances's claims of marriage, considering the benefits it would bring to their son, Dudley. Though Rupert suffered health concerns in 1670, his romance with Peg gave him a new lease of life. Added to this, he was also made Lord-Lieutenant of Berkshire.

In May 1670, the king's sister, Henrietta Anne, sailed to Dover. The court, including Rupert, met her amidst joyful scenes of reunion. Little did Rupert suspect that the purpose was to iron out the details of an alliance between King Charles II and King Louis XIV, and what's more, a secret agreement for the former's conversion to Catholicism. All through 1669 and 1670, Rupert had advocated an alliance with the Dutch and Swedes against France, even working on the Elector of Brandenburg to favour such a union. The King of Sweden – a Protestant champion – was also awarded the Order of the Garter, with Rupert ceremoniously dressing his representatives in the robes. Furthermore, the prince had helped secure a trade deal with Denmark, which was to France's detriment. So, when in May 1671 he got wind of a French alliance his outrage can only be imagined, yet outwardly he reluctantly made the best of it.

By this time, King Charles II's financial affairs were dire and all pensions had been stopped. As a result, the £150,000 sweetener that Louis XIV offered in support of King Charles's conversion was a tempting sum. Rupert was one of many that now faced a barrage of financial pleas, which tested his conscience; 'the poore workmen of windsor', improving the castle under the prince's direction, were left in great necessity. Their desperate cries for money haunted Rupert so badly that he tried to stay away from the castle. But he chased officials for their payment, obtaining a little money from the queen's jointure that alleviated their 'deplorable' condition – enough to keep them alive, he declared.[3]

Another petitioner was Roland Laugharne. A Parliamentarian in the civil wars, he had eventually turned coat in 1648 and subsequently lost his whole estate because of it. Now he recalled that event in pleas for Rupert's support. That same year, it was noted that a Captain Lawrence van Heemskercke, who had contracted debts in the king's service, was struggling to feed his family for want of his annual £200 pension. It was noted that he would have perished, had it not been for the goodness of Prince Rupert, who assisted him. The prince was especially happy to further the families of his old comrades, such as Rupert Billingsley, a godson, endorsing his 'Antient and Loyall Family' and recommending him for command of a company of foot. On 5 April 1671, Rupert carried out the solemn duty of being chief mourner at the funeral of the Duchess of York, who had died five days earlier.[4]

War with the Dutch brought hope of spoils and further trade that might alleviate the financial crisis. The usual question of leadership arose, with the Duke of York itching to command. When the matter was laid before the king, the duke was not averse to using Rupert's anti-French sentiments against him – a man with such opinions, who lacked gentleness and diplomatic sensitivity, would not be best placed to maintain unity between the allies. The king prudently opted for the duke over the prince. Rupert, however, would take charge of the Admiralty at home and wage war with officialdom over maintaining and supplying the fleet.

Apart from leading his adoptive country in wartime, Rupert used his scientific interests to search for an advantageous military development – a gamechanger. He landed on metallurgy in a bid to improve gunnery. The Venetian ambassador attempted in vain to wheedle out information but was only able to report that it involved casting iron to the calibre of 50 pounds and upwards. This would make lighter, cheaper, and more manoeuvrable guns, which could even be coloured brass to retain a smart appearance. The prince took oaths of secrecy from workmen involved, though one person who was privy was Anthony Ashley Cooper, Earl of Shaftesbury, with whom Rupert became great friends. Unfortunately, nothing came of the guns in time for the fresh war with Holland, which was declared on 17 March 1672.

This time Brandenburg allied with the Dutch, while England, France, and Sweden teamed up. The Habsburg emperor remained neutral so long as Spanish territory was not attacked. King Louis was to mobilise 120,000 troops, while England oversaw the war at sea with thirty-six French ships provided. As the English fleet readied itself, Rupert summoned the Navy Board to his Whitehall lodgings at 9.00 am prompt on Monday, 9 May 1672. Delegates were warned to be thoroughly prepared with lists of the ships in the fleet, their stations, stores, and conditions, along with what stores and victuals remained on land. Amidst rumours that the Dutch were at sea, 100 men were ordered to fortify Sheerness. Rupert and his colleagues also warned the king that as the Duke of York had taken his ships to sea, the Thames was acutely vulnerable.

Five days later, with the English fleet off Dover, it rapidly became apparent that the Dutch were nearing the Gunfleet and threatening the mouth of the river. The king ordered Rupert to the scene. The prince went immediately to Gravesend that evening, Chatham next morning, and then Sheerness by noon. He wrote in his report on 15 May that he could see the Dutch and set off in a yacht the next day to observe more closely. Luckily, the combined English and French fleet had a friendly wind in their sails and their presence caused the Dutch to fall back out to sea. Across the Channel, the French army neared Holland, but were stopped in their tracks when the Dutch opened their sluices. The resulting four-foot-deep moat, many miles wide, gave superb defence.

Anxious to deal with the allied fleet first, the Dutch actively sought them out. With sixty-two ships to the allies' seventy-four, De Ruyter hoped his aggressive stance might make up for his lower numbers. The *Royal James* was blown up in the ensuing encounter and the Earl of Sandwich killed as he attempted to get to another ship. It was the only allied loss, compared to three Dutch ships, but the allies suffered 900 deaths, whereas the Dutch lost 600. Rupert had done everything to assist the Duke of York, gathering intelligence from forts and ships and forwarding it on. Despite his numerous responsibilities, he had also furthered tests on a wooden frame, which could fit around a ship's hull and offer it extra protection – to make it cannon-proof. Though both sides postured, no further naval battle occurred, and by September, it was deemed too late in the year.

One month later, Will Legge died, perhaps the closest friend Rupert ever had. Legge had been devoted to Rupert's interests for thirty years. In the man's last year, he had fallen foul of auditors and was put out as Treasurer of the Ordnance after not handing in accounts for eight years. He had been so ill when he made his will that he couldn't even utter the names of the numerous 'poore kindred' to which he wished to make bequests. Instead, before his spirit became 'spent and faint' he recalled how his wife, Elizabeth, had been so kind and loving.[5]

Chapter 35

God Zounds

When a body was found bobbing in the sea off Harwich, it was fished out. Pinned on the waterlogged clothing was the sparkling star of the Garter. The Earl of Sandwich's corpse was taken aboard Rupert's yacht *FanFan* and sent to Deptford, and then on to Westminster Abbey for interment. The post of Vice-Admiral of England was conferred upon the prince. A decision was also taken that the Duke of York should not risk his life the following year, and therefore the fleet was to be assigned to Rupert.

The matter was significantly influenced when the Treaty of Dover came to light, though not the secret clause in which the king had promised to convert to Catholicism, backed by French troops. King Charles II was a consummate survivor. A Parliamentary backlash saw him restore harsh persecution of Catholics, as well as agree to the Test Act in March 1673. By its terms, anyone holding government or military office was obliged to take the sacrament in an Anglican church to weed out closet Catholics. The Duke of York, a secret convert, knew his position would soon be untenable.

The English and French fleets should have joined together at Portsmouth in April 1673. Instead, the French only left Brest in May. Calling for 'expeditious acting', Rupert rounded up as many hands as he could, such as riggers and carpenters from Chatham and soldiers from Sheerness.[1] He also tested iron shot filled with explosives, much like grenades, which could be fired from naval cannons, though the trial did not go well.

On 2 May 1673, the Dutch made full sail for the mouth of the Thames in a bid to blockade it. Having anticipated this, Rupert had deployed enough ships to see off the threat. On 13 May, he boarded the *Royal Charles*, and three days later, the French contingent arrived under the command of the Marquis d'Estrées. After one week, the allies set off in search of the Dutch, with Rupert chased by complaints from the Duke of York, who felt he was not receiving enough updates. The allies had nearly 2,000 more guns and commanded seventy-six ships to fifty-two of the Dutch. A verse of hope praised Rupert and the fleet.

> Man'd with stout Seamen yielding to no stroke;
> For (like their Ships) their *Hearts* are *Trusty Oke* [oak].[2]

On 28 May, the Battle of Schooneveld commenced. The encounter was not a decisive one, with low casualties on both sides, though Colonel James Hamilton, son of the Duke of Ormonde's sister, had his leg blown off by a cannonball and later died. His proximity to Rupert had made some think the prince had been hit. The incorrigible Sir William Reeves, Rupert's former page, took a fireship and attempted to destroy Admiral Tromp, but was foiled. The following day, King Charles II's 43rd birthday, London was in festival mood and the court celebrated with the 'greatest Galantry imaginable' and plenty of fireworks.[3] From the coast of Holland, Rupert wrote a report about the battle, praising his commanders and the French, but condemning some captains of fireships, one of which prevented Reeves's success. He ended wishing the king many happy returns.

From the start, the Dutch employed fake news in a bid to destabilise the English. They claimed to have taken St Helens on the Isle of Wight, and that Rupert had been killed at Schooneveld. Such prolific reports caused English officials in Hamburg much anxiety, and even reached Rupert's sister, Elisabeth. The prince was forced to send a letter reassuring her that he was very much alive, which arrived at the same time as official condolences.

King Charles was amused by the many lies. He was also happy with Rupert's performance, despite the latter being frustrated over not delivering a grander success. The prince was not on particularly good terms with Sir Edward Spragge, his second-in-command, even though the man was brother-in-law to the late William Legge. Itching for a second battle, Rupert did not sleep on the evening of 3 June, expecting the Dutch to launch a night attack. Instead, it was near 11.00 am next morning when they sailed from their anchorage, the same time that Spragge chose to leave his ship and seek conference with Rupert. When the man finally arrived on the flagship, with the Dutch in sight, he was immediately ordered back to his post. Unfortunately, his absence caused his squadron to remain stationary, and because of that, so too did the French.

A tired and furious Rupert sailed his own squadron through the two stationary ones and took the vanguard, much as he would have done in his younger years, when leaping onto a horse and galloping into the fray. What followed was an insignificant skirmish that expended much gunpowder and achieved little. The frustrated prince led the fleet home.

King Charles called for any Englishmen that had served in Dutch ships, and who had been subsequently captured by Rupert's fleet, to be sent home to be hanged – pending witnesses of their treason. For all this tough stance, the king joked that he expected a chiding from his cousin and sent letters ahead in a bid to soften him. Reserving his vitriol for the navy commissioners over lack of supplies, Rupert threatened them with his cane and harried officials over the wounded, insisting they be sent back to their ships as soon as they were cleared by the surgeon. Six years earlier, he had reportedly assaulted Henry Bennett, later Earl of Arlington, at the council table in a dispute over naval matters.

On 15 June, the Duke of York resigned as Lord High Admiral, doing so before the Test Act came into force; though the office was put into commission (exercised by a group of men), Rupert was first named and became the duke's de facto replacement. To the relief of officials, the prince was soon back on board the *Royal Sovereign*.

On 17 July, he commanded 200 ships, amidst which were sailing 8,000 soldiers on hired vessel. These were led by the 57-year-old Count Frederick Schomberg, whose father had been Master of the Household to Rupert's parents. Schomberg had been born in Heidelberg, and having studied at Leiden, and fought at Rheinberg, he would have been very well acquainted with Rupert. Direction was for the entire fleet to do battle with the Dutch in the open sea. At the mouth of the Thames, Schomberg had one of his military colours hoisted up the mast of his frigate *Greyhound*. Considering use of flags was strictly regulated, being key to communicating messages throughout the fleet, Rupert had the *Royal Sovereign* fire two shots across Schomberg's bows. A lieutenant was then sent to demand the lowering of the colour. Meanwhile, a messenger from Schomberg arrived on Rupert's deck to find the prince apoplectic with rage. Observing his lieutenant returning, and the offending standard still fluttering, Rupert promptly imprisoned Schomberg's man. Not only that, but he also passed order that the *Greyhound* should be sunk if the flag was not removed.

The Earl of Carlisle pacified Rupert and clarified the matter to Schomberg. The prince would later offer a half-hearted apology to the king, but the count never forgave Rupert for his insulting and violent passion. When he and his soldiers left the fleet a week later and landed at Yarmouth, Schomberg fired off letters to the Earl of Arlington complaining that Rupert did not take advice and was dominated by Sir William Reeves. The latter was now master of the *Royal Sovereign*, the prince's Deputy Governor of Windsor Castle, and a captain-lieutenant in his foot company stationed there. Reeves and Rupert made for a determined duo, but the prince had no puppet-master.

The fleet sighted the Dutch on Sunday, 10 August and attempted to draw them into the open sea. The weather was close and hazy. Although the Dutch avoided battle, Rupert continued to shadow them as night fell. The cautious French squadron stopped numerous times during the nocturnal chase and were kept going only by Rupert's persistent demands. At daylight next morning, Rupert hoisted the union flag at his mizzen, thus giving command for the fleet to move to battle order. At 7.00 am he placed a union flag at his mizzen topmast and foretop mast, signalling the fleet should tack. The English and French were in a very good line formation.

Now things started to go awry; there was a fog and light rain, and Spragge's rivalry with the Dutch Admiral Tromp saw the pair detach from their respective fleets and begin their own battle. Approaching midday, the French under d'Estrées stood off from the action despite having advantage of the wind, leaving Rupert's squadron to bear the brunt of the enemy. Devoid of his vanguard and rearguard, one astounded officer asked if the prince could see the inactive French – 'Yes, God zounds, doe I' was the exasperated response.[4]

> Arms, Bowells, Legs, and gastly Heads are spread'
> Throughout the Decks, all cover'd with the dead.[5]

Spragge's *Royal Prince* was disabled, so he took to a boat, which was narrowly missed by falling masts. When his new flagship was put out of action, Spragge boarded his boat and was making for the *Royal Charles*. At that point, an enemy shot punched through the *St George*, destroying Spragge's skiff in turn, and he drowned. Sir William Reeves was also struck in the face by a cannon shot, but this time there was no miraculous survival, and the hero died from his wounds. Rupert, increasingly concerned for Spragge's absent and now leaderless squadron, extricated his own and joined them. This saved the situation.

As another victory evaded Rupert, he reflected that it was 'ye plainest & greatest oppertunity yt was ever lost at sea'. At sunset, Rupert 'edged off wth an easy sail' carrying the damaged ships with him. Count d'Estrées sought orders and queried the signal given during the battle while his ships were idle. To Rupert, the instruction was plain; 'it wanted neither signal nor Instructions to tell him [what] he should have done then'. The prince was much relieved when the Dutch did not offer a renewal of the contest – 'I thinke it ye greatest providense [that] ever befell me in my life [that] I brought off [his majesty's] Fleet'.[6] With so many ships holed under the waterline (Rupert called them lame geese) and provisions short, they headed home.

Reeves's loss saddened Rupert, who wrote that he was a very good and brave officer, whereas remarks about Spragge's death were more formal. The latter made way for good old Robert Holmes to become admiral in his stead, who had been previously blackballed by the king. Public rumours of a rift with the French dismayed King Charles. Rupert had reportedly been so disgusted by his allies that he had threatened to lay down his commission. Tellingly, d'Estrées's second-in-command, de Martel, was in full agreement with Rupert's account of the battle and the lack of French support at the crucial moment. For 'agreeinge much' with Rupert, de Martel was sent to the Bastille. Both King Charles and King Louis wished to preserve the veneer of unity to keep up pressure on the Dutch, and Rupert was forced to declare d'Estrées a brave man and cover up French failings.[7] King Charles told the prince that nothing would produce a good peace better than appearing ready to continue the war.

This became Rupert's last military venture after forty years. Back in 1633 he had fought with the Dutch at Rheinberg. Now his military career ended with his name being 'as terrible to the Hollander as ever the Name of Drake was to the Spaniards'.[8]

Chapter 36

Popish Plot

There had been reports that the Duke of York and Prince Rupert had drawn swords in front of the king in July 1673, after the duke had called the prince a coward, and the prince retorted that the duke was a traitor. When Rupert returned home from sea in September 1673, relations were further strained by rumours that friends of the duke were whispering against the prince. Nevertheless, Rupert received a hero's welcome by the populace, who recognised his anti-French sentiments in a moment when many, including the king and Duke of York, were seen as far too pro-Catholic.

Though peace was agreed in February 1674, Rupert retained his posts and continued to further defences, inspecting the new fort at Sheerness. He also remained a key figure at court, attending Privy Council and Navy Board meetings, the House of Lords, and functions such as the goldsmiths' pageant in 1674. He was also made Lord-Lieutenant of Surrey, adding to his like role in Berkshire. As a Fellow of the Royal Society, his accidental discovery of 'Prince Rupert's Drops' were demonstrated – having dripped molten glass into warm water, it caused a tadpole-shaped drop. The head was as strong as could be, whereas the tail, if pressured, would cause the whole thing to shatter. Other more practical inventions included permanently colouring marble, a noiseless musket, means to measure altitude at sea, blowing up rocks to assist mining, methods of healing an incision to a pig's gut, and a recipe for treating burns. Rupert developed medicines and potions and frequently used them or prescribed them to family.

His personal opposition to a French alliance had not prevented him from fighting alongside them. Another event that opened contradictions in his private and public opinions came when the king dismissed the troublesome Earl of Shaftesbury (Rupert's good friend) from the post of Lord Chancellor. The prince continued his personal friendship with the man, no matter their political differences. Rupert's patented guns was a shared interest with Shaftesbury. There was also trade and exploration of Prince Rupert's Land, both he and Shaftesbury being key shareholders in the Hudson Bay Company. In September 1675, two ships aptly named after each of them docked at the Downs. On board was an 'Indian' described as 'a very lusty man' who was presented to Rupert.[1] The Guinea Company, which had profited the Commonwealth and Oliver Cromwell's Protectorate through trading enslaved people and goods, was superseded at the Restoration by various companies that culminated to form the Royal African Company. This, led by the Duke of York and Prince Rupert, continued to ship higher numbers of enslaved people from Africa to the New World.

Politically, Shaftesbury was agitating against the Duke of York, whose marriage to the Catholic Mary of Modena was deeply contentious, lest it produce a male heir – a boy would take precedence over the duke's two Protestant daughters from his first marriage. Dismay ensued when the new Duchess of York became 'very bigg wth child' while Queen Catherine (having suffered numerous miscarriages) did 'continue little'.[2]

Rupert and Peg had received their own bundle of joy after she gave birth to a baby girl, named Ruperta, in 1673 – most likely the end of May, or early June. On 9 June, between the two naval battles of Schooneveld and Texel, Rupert had begged leave to 'steal' to London on 'very private' business, which is most likely linked to this.[3] He duly arrived in London, according to the *Gazette,* on 14 June, and two days later royal household accounts reference a warrant that four silver bottles (which were used to feed babies at the time) should be delivered to the prince. His happiness with Peg, Ruperta, and Dudley offered Rupert a family life that became a blessing to his last decade.

Age aside, he was as forthright as ever. Two years later, he had some quibble about an overpayment made to him, which was to be written off as a gift from the king. Rupert objected to the wording and the term of gift was removed. In council he also opposed the lengthy prorogation of Parliament between February 1674 and April 1675, though personal relations with the king remained as strong as ever. After suffering a fall in 1675, he was kept company in his convalescence by an old civil war friend, Henry Jermyn, Earl of St Albans.

One anecdote revealed that the king's illegitimate son, the Duke of Monmouth, also visited Rupert. There he found the prince, St Albans, and a sailor. Rupert asked Monmouth to endorse the sailor's petition, and as the young man sat to write, the seaman clapped his hands on Monmouth's shoulder. After three repeats, Monmouth sprang up and declared, 'If it were not for the respect that I owe to the Prince I would teach thee who I am!'[4] The men were reduced to fits of laughter when the sailor revealed himself to be the Duke of Buckingham, a master of practical jokes and disguises. Reminiscing about the past, Rupert asked Buckingham to recount a tale of how the man had supposedly disguised himself to woo Cromwell's daughter and gain state secrets. The episode ended when Buckingham took his leave, anxious to search out a particular lady to whom he had taken a fancy. To this, Rupert replied, 'Were you eighteen, we might excuse you, but at our age it is as well to have a little moderation.'[5] The delightful interlude shows Rupert at his ease, happy with his life and loves, and a prominent figure with King Charles's favourites, despite differences in age and personal tastes.

In the last years of his life, Rupert indulged his artistic and scientific interests with 'more seriousness & attention that ever'. Even the most unpleasing aspects were sweet and pleasant to him as he performed the most difficult and laborious operations amidst the 'sooty and unpleasant' workshop.[6] This toil was interrupted on one occasion when some of the king's courtiers 'drunke away all reason' and rampaged around Windsor Castle.[7] They broke into Rupert's laboratory and smashed up his chemical instruments, and by 3.00 am, fell upon each other, resulting in one being stabbed to death. This occurred in the room next to the king, who, at the Duke of York's urging, left immediately for London.

The Duke of York would not always be there to save his brother. Opposition to his religion bubbled beneath the surface. There was continued mistrust of the king, to the degree that Parliament blocked the building of more warships in case the king misappropriated the finances. The outspoken Shaftesbury, incurring royal displeasure once more, was sent to the Tower of London in 1677. Behind the scenes, the king attempted to cajole further money and deals out of King Louis, something that became a ticking time bomb.

Outwardly the monarch went along with MPs' desires and opened negotiations to marry the Duke of York's eldest daughter to the Dutch Prince of Orange. Rupert, who was Mary's godfather, was overjoyed, but she was tearful at the prospect. The prince's attempts to steer the king away from Catholic France seemed, on the surface, to be working. King Charles, however, still hankered after an Anglo-French union, and in accordance with the Treaty of Dover's secret terms, he prorogued Parliament, expecting Louis to send him a large sum of money for doing so. Instead, the furious French king refused to pay up on account of Princess Mary's match. The king's love affair with France had caused so much damage and mistrust that when a 'Popish Plot' erupted in August 1678, it spread like wildfire.

At first, the whole plot seemed no more than a tall tale; the king was to be assassinated and the French would take control of the kingdom. The informant introduced two witnesses. One was Titus Oates, an Anglican who had turned Jesuit, before reverting to his original faith. The sceptical king handed the whole matter over to the Earl of Danby and went off to Windsor for a spree of hunting and fishing. Oates implicated one of the queen's household, and Danby, perhaps erring on the side of caution (or simply out of his own dislike of France) took the matter very seriously. When Oates was examined by the council, he spewed out names like a scattergun. The queen's physician, and the Duchess of York's secretary, were named to strike at the real bullseyes – the two royal women themselves, being the most prominent Catholic females in the land. Accusing the physician, who was adept in the use of poisons, was ideal as that was said to have been intended as the king's fate. It appeared as if the aim of the plot was to discredit the queen and effect her removal, bar the Duke of York from the throne, and have King Charles marry anew and produce legitimate Protestant heirs – failing that, to legitimise his Protestant son, the Duke of Monmouth.

Oates and his crew struck lucky by naming the Duchess of York's secretary, because investigators soon discovered dubious letters he had written to King Louis XIV. These fanned the flames. Next, a relatively minor magistrate, Sir Edmund

Popish Plot

Berry-Godfrey, was found dead on Primrose Hill in October 1678. Having recently taken Oates's deposition, his murder was swept into the plot, and this first blood sent London into a panic-stricken furore. Oates became famous, hailed as a saviour, while his words and image spread around the capital. He preached sermons and basked in his new fame. Those who realised the absurdity of his claims were too scared to contradict them out of fear he might implicate them in return. The noise of nocturnal digging around Parliament saw Sir Christopher Wren and Sir Jonas Moore despatched to investigate out of fear of a new Gunpowder Plot. The cellars of nearby houses were cleared, and a passage knocked through them with sentries parading day and night.

In December 1678, details surfaced of the king's continued negotiations with France during Dutch marriage discussions. Having been handled on the monarch's behalf by the Earl of Danby, snarling MPs prepared to tear the minister down. The king quickly dissolved Parliament, despite Rupert's warning to the contrary. Two months later, the Duke of York was sent abroad to avoid being an incendiary. Next, the Privy Council was dissolved and a new one constituted, with Rupert topping the list as the most senior member, given the Duke of York's absence. The atmosphere was so tense that a 3-year-old child, reputedly speaking a number of foreign languages, caused many to excitedly hail him as a 'Prophett', though it turned out he had simply been taught Latin and Greek from the moment he could speak.[7] Another rumoured attempt on the king's life in July 1679, coupled with being (genuinely) taken ill in August, prompted the Duke of York to return to England without permission. He feared that if his brother should die, Monmouth might claim the crown while the cushioned throne was still warm.

At such moments, Rupert must have breathed a sigh of relief that he had no legitimate male heir to be consumed by this mess; if he had, the boy would almost certainly have been thrust into the breach as an alternative to the Duke of York. Perhaps herein lies the answer to Frances Bard's claims of marriage. Rupert had never seemed seriously open to marriage, perhaps concerned that any offspring might become embroiled in terminal wars of succession as claimants. This was ample reason to stress that he never married Frances. For her part, she would not want Dudley to be destitute, as her family had been, and surely recognised that legitimacy would have transformed the boy's (and her own) standing and influence.

When Oates preached a sermon in London, published by Rupert's bookbinder along with a dedication to the prince, the political crisis became quite personal. Realising that this storm needed to blow over, Rupert intervened to get the Duke of Monmouth out of the kingdom, lending his house at Rhenen. The Duke of York was held in such scorn that at Cheapside 'ye multitude gazed at him' without putting off their hats. He was quickly sent to Scotland. Reports abounded of the populace calling on God to bless the Protestant duke, while imploring the devil to take the Catholic one, yet Rupert supported the embattled Duke of York on account of his legitimate claim to the throne.[8] Rupert continued taking Parliament's Oath of Supremacy and Allegiance, as well as the Protestant sacrament.

These were tense times when everything was at risk. Rupert put off a visit to his ailing sister, Elisabeth, sending instead some special drops that both she and Sophia might use. The tricks of the trade, as he termed the recipe, was despatched after Elisabeth's physician failed to make it correctly. For the prince who feared physicians that 'lett blode and dye' (bleeding their patients until they were too weak to survive) he much favoured his own remedies.[9] Household accounts for 1679 show payments to a chemist. Alas, the prince's drops were no use to Elisabeth, and she died on 12 February 1680, leaving what little she had to the Elector of Brandenburg, who had financially assisted her abbey. Excusing this to her 'dear and faithful brother', she assured Rupert she would ever pray for his temporal and eternal welfare.[10] Charles Louis followed her to the grave six months later, succeeded in the Palatinate by his sickly son and namesake.

England's body politic was also continuing to ail. Shaftesbury, once more committed to the Tower and now seriously ill, was transferred to the cool lodgings of Sir Jonas Moore, Dudley's tutor. A summer heatwave had combined with the hot political crisis. In December 1679, Rupert presented the king with a petition on behalf of Shaftesbury's party, arguing that Parliament should not be prorogued, though he did not personally sign it. By September 1680, Shaftesbury was back at his home in Aldersgate Street, and though Rupert suffered much with his leg, it did not prevent him from visiting.

The Popish Plot, which had been like a rampant plague, finally started to ease. The last victim was the Catholic Viscount Stafford, who was tried on account of Oates's ever more ludicrous allegations. The House of Lords voted 32–54 in favour of Stafford's death – Rupert supported it, but his old adversary, the Duke of Newcastle, was one of the few who courageously stood firm against. The Lord High Steward made a tearful speech before Stafford was given over to the axeman.

Chapter 37

Great Rupert

Sophia's son, George Louis, visited England in December 1680. Though King Charles II was not the best of hosts, and George's arrival at Greenwich was devoid of any official welcome, Uncle Rupert soon stepped in. He intervened with the king over lodgings for the young man and then met him at Whitehall. George was in regular contact with Rupert, noting that his uncle was often confined to bed on account of his leg. On 29 December, George remarked that the execution of Viscount Stafford prompted little more noise than if a chicken had just had its head lopped off. The populace, having come to their senses, now tired of Oates, and no longer took him seriously.

Rupert recognised the potential in George. A union with the Duke of York's second daughter, Anne, would unite the lines of King Charles I and his sister, Elizabeth of Bohemia, to produce a Protestant super-heir. He proposed the plan to Sophia and, while George was in England, furthered it at every opportunity. My research has revealed that Peg was also a key part of diplomatic manoeuvring, striking up a very good friendship with George, which was exciting to discover. It adds much colour to her character and shows how trusted she was. Peg was not treated as a mere mistress by Rupert, but rather a respected, intimate, and central part of his family and politics. He committed to her as his life partner.

George was not exactly a born wooer, having inherited little of the Stuart charm. Born the day before King Charles II had triumphantly entered London in 1660, George was a plain and dour 20-year-old who seemed much older. His younger brother was, in their mother's opinion, much more like Rupert in looks. Princess Anne did not take a liking to George, nor did the Duke of York, who must have felt increasingly vulnerable about his place in the line of succession. Not to be put off, after George returned home, Rupert and Peg continued to further the match and kept in touch with him.

In April 1681, Rupert was reportedly 'very ill at windsor of a feaver, in so much that there is some feare of him'.[1] He even had a hand in building an invalid chair to help him get around. By July, when Shaftesbury was arrested once more, this time in council, Rupert was permitted to withdraw beforehand to disassociate himself from the action. The next day he dined privately with his friend. At the same time, he was also preparing for a jaunt on his personal yacht, ordering it to be 'well ffitted' and purchased a new silk union flag 5 yards long by 3 yards wide.[2] This is most likely the vessel listed in an inventory after his death, described as a 36-foot, two-masted shallop, and if not the *FanFan* itself, built in the 1660s, it was very much like it. The desire to get out and about remained strong. Indeed, household accounts show payments to a tennis player, betraying Rupert's long-term love for the sport in spite of his ailments.

The king seemed perpetually engaged in a back and forth game with Parliament over the line of succession, attempting to de-rail the plans of Shaftesbury and his party, who wished to bar the Duke of York. Rupert continued pushing for Princess Anne's marriage to his nephew, despite her negative reaction. On 4 December 1681, he wrote to Sophia to say that George was once more on his feet (in the running) for her hand. The following year, Peg was exchanging letters with Sophia and sending her gifts – perhaps jewellery on one occasion as the latter remarked on wearing it. George, too, wrote directly to Peg, expressing himself very much obliged for her sage advice, and pleased that she had not forgotten him. In that same letter, he expressed frustration at Peg's sister, 'mistris Judit' (Judith was two years younger than George), for not having paid him any compliments. The omission made him think she had 'galens' (gallants – or a male suitor) in mind and is highly suggestive that something more than flirtation passed between George and Judith while he had been in England.[3] This again demonstrates Peg's very significant influence in the family, especially as George would later become the first Hanoverian monarch.

On 26 October 1682, George wrote again to Peg, thanking her for her continued advice, but with an air of finality lamented he had never known the true intentions of Princess Anne. The match with his cousin was now dead in the water. Nevertheless, George assured Peg that he would reward her support; Rupert would have taken great comfort in his family's acceptance of her.

Praising Peg for taking 'great care of me during my illness' Rupert added that he was 'obliged to her for many things'. As for little Ruperta, her father dotingly observed that she 'already rules the whole house and sometimes argues with her mother, which makes us all laugh'.[4] Peg sent a portrait of their daughter to Sophia, who remarked that she was the prettiest in the world. In 1682, Ruperta was aged 9, and Dudley Bard 16.

Rupert employed a housemaid in April 1682, perhaps to help Peg care for him. Entries also show purchases of bread for the prince, denoting his decline, and which lasted for one month. In May 1682, he was at Windsor, where representatives of the King of Bantam presented the prince with two ceremonial umbrellas, which had acted as canopies to protect their letters of credence. The maid was eventually dispensed with in September. Eight weeks later, on 20 November 1682, Rupert signed his will.

This was done in the presence of seven men. These included Edmund Andros, whose aunt had been a courtier to Rupert's mother. More recently, Andros had been an officer in the Barbados Regiment until his appointment as Governor of

New York in 1674, and had also married a distant relative of the Earl of Craven. There was Ralph Marshall, a secretary of Lord Craven's, William Dutton-Colt, who would later become an envoy to Hanover, and George Kirke, likely related to the Groom of the King's Bedchamber of the same name, if not the man himself. There was also Francis Hawley. This may be the same man who had fought with Rupert in the civil wars and had been with him during the 1645 siege of Bristol (who died in 1684) or a relative. Certainly, Peg's sister, Judith, went on to marry a Francis Hawley, which all suggests that Rupert maintained a long friendship with the Hawleys.

Whether Rupert had an inkling that the end was near or not, he continued to fight it, enjoying one last trip to the theatre four days after signing his will. If it was with Peg, that would have been a fitting last outing. The following day, 25 November, he took to his crimson velvet bed at Spring Gardens with fever and a cough that turned to pleurisy. The Hudson Bay Company held its annual meeting in the other room. It's said that Rupert sent his Garter back to the king with a last request that Ruperta might marry the monarch's illegitimate son, the Earl of Burford.

Between 5.00 am and 6.00 am on Wednesday, 29 November 1682, before dawn lit the red serge curtains in his bedroom, the prince died like a 'ripened Fruit, that being arrived at its perfect maturity, drops of its own accord'.

> Nor is thy Memory here onely crown'd,
> But lives in Arts, as well as Arms renown'd;
> Though Prideless Thunderer, that stoop'd so low,
> To forge the very Bolts thy Arm should throw,
> Whilst the same Eyes Great Rupert did admire
> Shining in Fields, and sooty at the Fire:
> Perceiving thee advanc'd in feats of Arms so far,
> At once the Mars and Vulcan of the War,
> Till Dancing Cyclops shall thy praise repeat,
> And on their Anvils thy tun'd Glories beat.[5]

Chapter 38

Ruperta and Dudley

That November of 1682, as Rupert's life came to a close, a mob in the capital chanted support for the Duke of Monmouth over the Duke of York, attacking houses in the city. The prince had been spared sight of the inevitable succession crisis that would destroy Monmouth and topple York.

Within a day of his death, Rupert's titles were carved up and new recipients earmarked. That same day, his body was opened and a stone the size of a goose egg discovered in his kidney – it would have stopped the passage of urine had there not been a hole right through it. In the skin covering his brain was found a bone, and another in his heart, which was given to the king. This is a coincidence, as a bone had also been found in the heart of Rupert's comrade-in-arms, the Duke of Albemarle. The prince's corpse was embalmed using 20 yards of crimson taffeta, 15 yards of Florence, 30 ells each of superfine Holland, fine Holland, and coarse Holland linen.

On 6 December, Rupert's body was taken from the painted chamber at Westminster, where it had been flanked by six large candlesticks. It was carried under a black velvet pall 7 yards long lined with taffeta, borne by eight staves, to Westminster Abbey. The coffin displayed a copper plate meticulously bearing all his titles and offices. A cushion of black velvet lay on top, bearing a crimson velvet cap and coronet. There he was interred. Lord Craven was, fittingly, chief mourner with the Duke of Monmouth and other Knights of the Garter following. A vast crowd of mournful spectators lined the route.

His will, naming Lord Craven executor, made provision for Peg and Ruperta, who inherited much jewellery (including twenty-one assorted table diamonds, nine pairs of pendant pearls, and three pearl necklaces, one valued at £5,000, likely the same that was later purchased by Nell Gwyn for £4,520). There is no mention of a house at Hammersmith (which Rupert bought for Peg soon after their meeting) and this suggests it had been entirely given over to her. Just before Rupert died, a Viscount Granard wrote to Peg from Dublin; she had asked the man to investigate her ancestry. The result, after speaking to several in Ireland, was an attested pedigree (which unfortunately seems not to have survived) showing the O'Hughes line (linked to the O'Neills). Granard even put Peg in touch with her Irish relations for more details. This is new and tantalising insight into Peg's heritage and might one day be elaborated upon.

Peg may have retained the prince's house at Spring Gardens for a couple of years. In 1686, Charles II's former mistress, Barbara Villiers, looked to sub-let it, but was hindered when a squatter took possession and ran a tavern from the place. By 1704, it was in a state of ruin. In later life, Peg lobbied for £20,000 that had been due to Rupert for his patented guns, though Queen Anne frowned upon the petition. The suggestion is that Peg gambled away much of her inheritance and died at Eltham in 1719. Her sister, Judith, married Francis Hawley, who became a colonel and was killed in action in 1692. Sir Walter Scott suggested Judith's eldest son, Henry Hawley, was actually an illegitimate child of King George II – though the latter was only an infant when Henry was born. But could Scott have meant George Louis (who would become King George I), Rupert's nephew, who evidently had an association with Judith after his 1680/1 visit? Judith had four children and died in 1737.

Ruperta did not marry Lord Burford, as her father had reportedly wished. Instead, she made a happy match with Emanuel Scrope Howe and had six children, though sadly only one lived to any great age. Ruperta's descendants survive to this day as the Bromleys – baronets who regularly call their sons Rupert or Charles. Ruperta became a dedicated Ranger of Alice Holt and Woolmer Forests, living in a small house that went with the job. There she planted a tree in memory of her renowned father and fought against illegal hunters. She also had a less than grandiose apartment in Somerset House.

Dudley Bard (specifically named so in Rupert's will to emphasise his non-legitimacy) was bequeathed the prince's house at Rhenen and all his Palatinate interests, such as the outstanding money owed by the emperor. Dudley also received a bounty of £100 from King Charles II. In 1684, he was commissioned as a captain in the Coldstream regiment of guards, the colonel being Lord Craven, who must have kept a paternal eye. Dudley was everything in the world to his mother, Frances. She was a staunch Catholic and Jacobite, proud that her son fought for King James VII/II at Sedgemoor in 1685, against the army of the Duke of Monmouth, who had laid claim to the throne. Dudley's father would also have approved. After Monmouth's defeat and execution, Dudley returned to Germany and the estate left him by Rupert. He was killed whilst scaling the walls at Buda in August 1686, serving with English volunteers against the Turks. Sophia described her nephew as a noble young man. She interceded to have his possessions and claims transferred to his mother so that the bereaved woman could enter a convent. Frances, however, had no intention of doing that.

In 1688, when King James VII/II was overthrown by the invasion of his son-in-law, William of Orange, Frances left England in disgust. She went to the only place she might find support and financial assistance: the court of Rupert's sister, Sophia, at Hanover. Frances became extremely close to Electress Sophia who praised her good and virtuous nature. From here, Frances sought to further the Jacobite cause and also indefatigably pushed her claim to have married Rupert. Though Sophia remained quietly sceptical, she supported Frances's attempts to extract the money owed to Rupert from the emperor, which amounted to 75,000 rixdollars. In 1693, after travelling to Vienna, Frances was offered 10,000 and a pension of 1,000 per year. Her claims of marriage were directly beneficial to such business and Frances's family were as convinced as she was of the union.

After Dudley's death, Frances took two of her sister Persiana's daughters (both Protestants) under her wing – thus clipping theirs. Whether they liked it or not, Aunt

Frances worked upon her nieces' conversion to Catholicism. The matter caused a scandal. Frances was not alone in this work – her other sister, Anne lived with her. One of the girls is said to have died whereas the other, Sarah Frances – named after her aunt – would eventually return to England. It has been assumed that Frances Bard's use of the title 'Lady Bellamont' suggested she was the eldest of her sisters, but Anne and Persiana also styled themselves in that way. On the death of their mother, presumably in 1668 when administration of her effects was approved, the grant went to Anne – much more likely the eldest.

British diplomats, exasperated by Frances's Jacobite intriguing, dismissed her as Prince Rupert's 'old popish strumpet'.[1] A new envoy to Hanover was appointed in the shape of Emanuel Scrope Howe, Ruperta's husband, in 1705. It wasn't long before he was also writing of Frances's malicious manner. Ruperta would have no doubt seen the woman claiming to be her father's widow. At Frances's death, in 1708, a Latin epitaph described her as 'Serrenissimo Principi Roberto Palatine quondam matrimonio juncta'.[2]

Persiana's descendants called Frances Bard 'Princess Rupert' – this is carved into a monument in the church of St John the Baptist, Aldbury. It was put in place decades after Frances Bard's death and shows how deep-rooted the marriage claim was with the family. Fascinatingly, attempts were later made to erase the words, showing an equally deep-rooted disbelief. Rowland Gwynne, a Welsh correspondent in Hanover, once reported home that Sophia indulged Frances because she believed the woman had been married to her brother. The unconvinced Gwynne, however, made a good point when he added if that was the case, then Frances would surely have laid claim to the title Duchess of Cumberland, rather than that of Lady Bellamont. The fact she never did is evidence that she was unwilling to stake her claim and move it beyond gossip and hearsay. Rather she pushed it just enough to secure a modest income and a home at Hanover, motivations that further erode her position.

Of Frances Bard's siblings, a brother, Charles Rupert, died childless in 1667. Her sister, Anne (born c.1639) married a Shrewsbury draper called Daniel Jevon at Saint Clement Danes, London, on 10 July 1671. She was listed as 32 years old; he was 56 and a widower. It seems the couple did not have children.

Frances's other sister, Persiana, married their cousin, Nathaniel Bard, whose father was a wealthy city merchant. The pair had numerous children, including the aforementioned Sarah Frances, who went on to marry Henry Harcourt. Persiana also had a son, called William. In 1711, one traveller noted seeing William and Sarah Frances with their Aunt Anne Jevon at Aix-la-Chapelle, in Westphalia. He observed that both siblings were extremely (and equally) pretty. It appears that William passed away before his mother.

Rupert's sister, Sophia, used to say that she would die while slumbering. In fact, she expired quite suddenly on 8 June 1714, after being caught in a rain shower. Her cousin, Queen Anne, followed her to the grave on 1 August. Sophia missed out on becoming Queen of Great Britain by seven weeks. Her son, George Louis, once proposed by Rupert as a match for Anne, then acceded to the throne as King George I.

Chapter 39

Lady Katherine Goring

Late 1644 had been a point of Rupert's lowest ebb though it ended with his promotion to Lord General. Early the following year, despatched to save Wales from internal strife, he was isolated, frustrated, and inactive, and perhaps this combined to prompt him to write a telling, and personal, line in his correspondence with Will Legge. The extremely rare glimpse into his personal life is a gem of information, yet at first glance seems nothing. Almost tongue-in-cheek, on 11 March 1645 from Ludlow, Rupert remarks that George Goring had 'shew a discontent' recently. He went on to hint at the reason for this, noting that he could 'tell a story of [Goring's] sister'.[1] These few words do not give us any juicy details, and I initially overlooked them, until reading more about Lady Katherine Goring. Unsubstantiated rumours in the 1660s, that Katherine's son was Rupert's child, revealed just how important these words of 1645 were.

Katherine was in Oxford during the civil wars. Her presence was mired in rumour and scandal, which further strained her difficult marriage. She had married Edward Scott around 1632. Marital life had seemed promising, with Katherine's mother, Mary Goring, initially complimenting her new son-in-law's family for the 'tender love and true respects you are plesed to shew unto my poore Daughter'. Lady Goring specifically remarks upon 'my childs hapines'.[2] But after living together for one year, Edward later alleged that Katherine began to abandon the home; on one occasion paying a visit to friends in London and staying three years, and another, when her brother George had a sore foot (perhaps his wound at Breda), a visit to him resulted in another three-year absence.

Katherine had wished to escape what she termed the 'suspitions and jealousies which I see are naturall to Scotts Hall' – Edward's family home. It appears she returned to her own family. Though admitting her actions subjected her to 'many tounges [tongues/gossip]' she was quick to point out she was not miserable.[3] In 1637, Katherine attempted to coax Edward from Scotts Hall, telling him he was 'heartely wellcome hether' and asking for his portrait.[4] The more he employed her, the more he would oblige her, she reasoned. It seems there were genuine attempts on her part to establish common ground and interests.

On 20 January 1642, Katherine addressed Edward's mother after hearing of her husband's illness, begging for weekly updates on his condition. At this point she was close to the royal court, as Edward had asked her to find someone who might present a petition to the king on behalf of Kent. With king and Parliament at dangerous loggerheads, Katherine was happy to oblige with the petition, stating she knew 'many that will be ready to [present] it'. She also mentions having met some 'Parlament men' who wanted Edward's father to be Lord-Lieutenant of Kent and proposed that her brother, George Goring (with many contacts in Westminster), might support that.[5] She also shared gossip; the queen was due to go to Portsmouth in a bid to flee the kingdom; the Marquess of Hamilton wanted to marry Lucy, Countess of Carlisle and make her Queen of Scotland; and the king had made provision to seize Hull.

In this, we see Katherine at the forefront of politics, very much aware of her influence, and she even asks if her parents-in-law would like her to do them any service. That letter is couched in submissive terms, and though she describes herself as a 'weake instrument' this does nothing to disguise her steely resolve and confidence. She was unwilling to be shut away in the Scotts' small Kentish estate.

Soon after this, however, Katherine began hearing from many sources that her husband did 'despise' her. That prompted her to write to Edward – a blunt letter that sparked further rift. The purpose of her despatch, she reflected, was to privately 'breath out the discontent of my soule' but her father-in-law got wind of the letter and was angered by it. Immediately writing to her mother-in-law, Katherine asserted that her words 'did avoyde all sharpnese' towards Edward, which she candidly acknowledges she could be prone, it being 'noe stranger' to her disposition. This letter also sheds crucial light on the reasons for the couple living apart when Katherine urges her in-laws to let her husband 'travell for a while' with her. She was clearly trying to broaden her husband's horizons in a bid to make their marriage work – 'a little sight of the world would doe him so much good', she ventured. Very tellingly, she even promises that if this was granted, upon their return she would leave all her friends and 'live where he will have me to live'. Katherine and Edward were two very different people – she a confident socialite that thrived on being at the centre of events, while he was a quiet, rather passive man (with over-protective parents). On the eve of civil war, Katherine acknowledged that she and Edward were both 'most unhappy'.[6]

A third three-year gap followed when she raced to civil war Oxford. Edward Scott was a Parliamentarian, serving the cause as a captain (though his precise military exposure is uncertain), while Katherine's family were staunch Royalists and her father a great favourite of Henrietta Maria. None of Katherine's previous absences seem to have been accompanied by specific accusations of loose living and morals, though it was scandalous. The third occasion would prove different, in light of remarkable new evidence I found in the Kent Archives.

Within the Royalists' war-torn court, it was reported that Katherine was 'very much taken notice of in reguard her lodgings were soe often frequented by Prince Rupert & others'. Lord Wentworth (son of the Earl of Cleveland) was supposedly one of these 'others' and had a 'great familiarty' with her, which involved him giving many gifts, such as a coach and four horses. As the Royalist cause crumbled, the Prince of Wales's physician, Dr John Hinton, revealed that he was led blindfolded by a lady to her chamber and there required to 'doe his office'. He delivered her of a child. Hinton maintained a professional silence and 'noe intreaties could bring the partie [name] to light' but he revealed the birth was at Cardiff.[7] When the Prince of Wales moved to Bristol in 1645, Hinton had joined him. By July 1645, king and court were at Cardiff and spent nearly two months there, so it's most likely the birth occurred around this time. Katherine would have had reason to be at Cardiff and Hinton would have been near at hand.

Amidst bickering Royalists in their death throes, rumours were rife that Katherine was the woman who had given birth, and soon they spread around Oxford. Katherine was sitting on a powder keg. It was only a matter of time before Edward would hear. Realising her precarious position, and the dishonour it would invariably bring to both her and her husband, Katherine made a bold move. Having spent so many years away from her husband, she now changed tack and made every effort to get to his side as the war ended. Perhaps this was to admit her situation, save their marriage and honour, and have him acknowledge the child. Another factor might have been the death of Edward's father at the start of 1646.

Edward, however, refused to entertain any reunion. In February 1646, Katherine resorted to barricading herself inside Nettlestead House, one of the Scott's properties, which resulted in a siege. Water supplies were cut off, leaving Katherine 'prittie hard driven' and estimates were that she could not hold out more than three further days. Nevertheless, attempts to relieve her came in the form of the Earl and Countess of Westmoreland, who tried sending two butts of wine, two hens, and other provisions. These were all seized by the besieging soldiers, who also had to deal with several poor women that in a 'tumultuous way' arrived to support Katherine. This astounding episode came to an end when she was forced to escape through a window.[8] Katherine's desperation was clear. It lends vast weight to rumours she had given birth to an illegitimate child.

Later that year, Katherine submitted a petition to Parliament for maintenance, desiring that she be received back into her husband's house. With Prince Rupert on the verge of leaving England, King Charles now a prisoner, and the Royalist Gorings classed as delinquents, she had little means of support. Not surprisingly, this was brushed aside by MPs. Edward, for good measure, took the Covenant, keeping himself firmly aligned with the victors. Refusing to be ignored, Katherine swore the Negative Oath, repudiating her Royalist past, and then promptly turned up at Scotts Hall on 3 May 1646. She sent a youth to request keys to the park gate.

Edward, fearing another siege, refused to receive her. Within half an hour, Katherine approached the hall on foot with three women, one of whom argued that Katherine would have returned home one and a half years earlier, had not Edward's father refused her request. The Scotts' aged servant, Timothy Rookes, was blunt by way of reply – there was good cause to turn her away. Uttering 'harsh words' against her dead father-in-law, Katherine demanded to see Edward, presenting an order from Parliament that advocated such a meeting. Rookes dismissed her pass, caustically telling her that MPs might have ordered her to go to her husband, but they had not instructed him to see her. Defeated, Katherine's parting shot was that when she was 'happy' again, she hoped to see those working against her 'begg'.[9]

By this time, Edward Scott was fully aware of rumours about his wife. When Oxford was besieged and on the brink of capitulation in 1646, Anthony St Leger was within the university town, having served the king. His family had a 'neere Alliance and Relation' with the Scotts. Being in the right place at the right time, Edward asked St Leger about rumours of the hasty childbirth and the remarkable reply confirmed everything; liaisons with Rupert, the birth in Cardiff, and John Hinton. St Leger told Edward that he could 'vouch uppon knowledge' of it all and he does, indeed, seem like a trustworthy witness who had spoken to Dr Hinton.[10] Armed with this stinging news, Edward must have confronted his wife about it at some point, as he would claim that she seemed to be 'well pleased' with the rumours and did not dispute 'either the place or occasions'. To him, it was a violation of marriage vows, and their divorce was unavoidable. 'I cannot re-admit her without mine owne ruine, & the ruine of my family.'[11]

Katherine's desire was much the opposite – separation from her husband was something 'shee utterly protests against'. Through the office of several peers, who wrote to Edward on her behalf on 29 June 1646, Katherine laid herself at his feet, offering to give Edward 'such satisfaction in all particulars'.[12]

She left no stone unturned. Desperately writing to Colonel John Browne, the husband of Edward's sister, Katherine expressed frustration at being 'kept both from my husband, and from all meanes of subsistance' and complained that she was being treated with 'abuse and dishonnour'.[13] Her opinion was that unnamed third parties, to serve their own ends, were keeping her and Edward apart. Browne rapidly drafted a reply, which denied Edward was in anyone's power, together with a list (in the latter's hand) of the reasons why he refused to see her. Katherine even put it about that Edward was held captive to prevent any reconciliation – a lie he branded a 'foule calumny'. But there does seem some foundation to Katherine's suspicions. Edward was subject to a stream of advice from family friend, Sir Anthony Weldon, a fierce Parliamentarian who urged him to prevent any illegitimate child inheriting his estate. Most correspondence over the stormy marriage also seemed to go via Colonel John Browne, who became a middle-man. But Edward, in his own words, could not be clearer. 'When I shall shew any desire of [Katherine's] society, I shall bee contented to bee esteemed, a foole or a mad:man; her departure from mee manifesting her alienation of affection.'[14]

By 1649, Katherine had gone to France with, amongst others, the diarist John Evelyn, who lauded her merits and perfections, as well as her entertaining and graceful conversation. There is no detail to explain her child's location. Matters appear to have gone silent for six years, until 1656, when Edward took a drastic step and sued for divorce, declaring all Katherine's children had been 'begotten in adultery' – the only hint that there were more than one.[15] She was branded a wicked wife. One of the committee members appointed to investigate the divorce noted that he would have hanged her. The greater part of the male commissioners were against her, already having written her off as a common whore. Over a hundred people were present at the sittings, where opportunist pickpockets operated, while the sordid details of the couple's lives were exposed. Yet Katherine appeared dressed in black, with a long patch on her forehead, which might suggest a battle with smallpox, or simply a fashionable adornment. Formidable in the face of such male opposition, she confidently greeted her husband, 'How do you do, Mr Scot' (she had addressed him formally since at least 1637), but he gave little reply.[16]

Some members of the committee judged Katherine deserved no more alimony than a dog, but Lord Strickland was sympathetic and prevented the hearing from being entirely one-sided. She wanted £145 per annum, together with arrears. Many long debates, including witnesses, delved into Edward's allegations that Katherine had given birth to several children, fathered by many different men, and his wish to bar them from succession to his estate. A (biased) Parliamentarian soldier claimed that one lover had been King Charles I's chaplain, while a maid reported seeing Katherine in bed with a Colonel Thomas Howard. The divorce does not seem to have reached a conclusion, despite efforts from Katherine's father, the Earl of Norwich, to mediate. It's uncertain if Katherine and Edward did live together again, but she did at least receive a payout of £240 and more ad hoc sums in the years that followed. An uneasy truce settled.

One name that was not mentioned in divorce proceedings was that of Prince Rupert – though within seven years, after the Restoration of the Monarchy, that all changed. Rumours resurfaced that he had been one of Katherine's lovers, and some (including diarist John Evelyn) directly speculated that he was the father of Thomas Scott, Katherine's son. Samuel Pepys noted that Thomas was illegitimate in his diary entry for 14 January 1664. Edward Scott had certainly claimed Thomas was not his son, but by 1663, he changed his mind and declared in his will that the boy was legitimate, in spite of the 'malice and Suggestion of evil affected persons to the contrary.'[17]

Rupert never acknowledged Thomas as his son – something he did when it came to children of his later relationships. If Katherine had taken several lovers, then Rupert may not have been certain of paternity. Additionally, Thomas was in line to inherit a family estate, and his mother was a woman of means in her own right. Rupert's acknowledgement of the boy would have further jeopardised all of this, cast a proven slur on Katherine, and by default Thomas. It would have certainly ended the Scotts' marriage and left Katherine and young Thomas in a bad situation. The mercenary prince had no riches, home, nor influence of any sort that might have helped, before 1660.

Rupert's letter to Will Legge, in March 1645, is clear evidence that directly links the prince to Katherine and is straight from the prince's own pen. It records an intimacy of phrase, at least, which very likely stemmed from an intimate encounter(s) which gossip, twenty years later, alluded to. Then, St Leger's extraordinary letter shines startling light into the entire affair, finally bringing the real Katherine Scott and her story out from the shadows. Prior to this, she was known only for her absences from her husband, not for her fascinating character, or the reasons behind her actions. Naming people and places, St Leger's letter further strengthens the possibility that Rupert was Thomas's father, not least because it was the Prince of Wales's own physician who was called upon to deliver the child.

Thomas Scott went on to become an officer in King Charles II's lifeguard, was given a pension, and knighted in 1663. He married that same year to a daughter of Royalist Sir George Carteret. By some accounts, Carteret pulled this off against competition from Henry Bennett, later Earl of Arlington. Though Thomas's true paternity remains unresolved, the preferment he enjoyed, despite his dubious parentage, supports Prince Rupert. This new evidence strongly suggests Rupert did have an affair with Katherine in late 1644 or 1645, which Morrah had previously discounted: 'The evidence for Prince Rupert's association with Lady Catherine is tenuous in the extreme.'[18]

Katherine Scott was not the only woman in Oxford to attract attention. Lady Isabella Thynne (née Rich) was daughter of the Parliamentarian Earl of Holland and travelled to the university town in 1643. She was married to Sir James Thynne, owner of Longleat, described in 1662 as the biggest house in Wiltshire. The beautiful Isabella reportedly lodged in Balliol College and frequented the wooded grove at Trinity College, where she would often play the lute, much to the chagrin of the ageing president. Dr Ralph Kettle waged a personal war on uncouth manners, pouncing on students with scissors and cutting their long locks. So, the sirenesque Isabella attracted the wrath of Kettle and others, but she also had her admirers. Poet Edmund Waller captured her allure.

> The trembling strings about her fingers crowd,
> And tell their joy for every kiss aloud:
> Small force there needs to make them tremble so;
> Toucht by that hand who would not tremble too?[19]

John Aubrey notes a story that Isabella and Lady Anne Fanshaw used to go to chapel half-dressed like angels, deliberately seeking out and antagonising Dr Kettle, who on one occasion gave Anne a stern talk about her behaviour. Isabella did not escape censure, and reputedly earned a 'box on the ear' from Henrietta Maria.[20]

One pamphlet, more than all others, focused on Rupert's civil war private life. It was extremely graphic in its wild allegations against him and his pet 'She-Monkey', who is clearly based on a woman in Oxford. *The Humerous Tricks and Conceits of Prince Robert's Malignant She-Monkey* describes the 'animal' as having 'bad looks' and 'deformed' visage due to the 'mad malignant tricks' played in her youth. She despairs of finding a husband, not being able to 'keep her legs together' and was riddled with the pox. Aside from eating the 'longest whitest sugar plums' which she would suck the juice out of, she was said to have been instructed in the art of plunder by Rupert. Despite luring scholars from their books and sapping the strength of many a cavalier, the pamphlet tells how the monkey was married at Oxford only to cuckold her husband within three days.

> Prince Roberts Monkey is a toy,
> That doth exceed his dog cal'd Boy,
> Which through dogged folly,
> Both barkes and bites,
> But this delights
> The Prince when's melancholy.[21]

The real identity of the monkey is not apparent. Aside from Katherine, Isabella, and Anne, much gossip in Royalist circles alluded to the close relationship between Rupert and Mary Villiers, Duchess of Richmond and Lennox. Vivacious and outgoing, she clearly got on well with Rupert, and this attracted much attention, not least because of the support she showed him during the civil war. Mary and her husband were Rupert's biggest advocates, and both extremely close to him. The proud duke – King Charles's cousin – was Rupert's eyes and ears at court, keeping him abreast of every occurrence. In Ireland, Viscount Taafe and Dan O'Neale, one of Rupert's close officers, engaged in loose talk about the prince's rumoured 'amours' with the duchess, only for Taafe to then reveal the conversation to Rupert himself. As a result, the prince understandably became estranged from O'Neale. Kitson says, 'The likelihood is that Rupert was in love [with the duchess] but managed to control himself.'[22]

While Rupert and the Richmonds remained tight-lipped on this gossip, Parliament used it in a mocking post-war pamphlet from 1647. I would concur with Morrah, Kitson, and Spencer that it's unlikely the relationship between the prince and duchess was anything more than platonic. When the duke died in 1655, there was much expectation that he might marry her – expectations that came from as close a person as Rupert's sister, Louise. She remarked in 1667 that had Mary married Rupert, her brother 'would not have kept her company so faithfully'.[22] Louise, an abbess, penned this observation after meeting the duchess, noting how Mary was fretful when her new husband, Colonel Thomas Howard, was away from her side. It's interesting to speculate if this man was the same Colonel Thomas Howard that was noted as having been seen in the bed of Katherine Scott in Oxford.

Katherine Scott, Frances Bard, and Margaret Hughes played a profound part in Rupert's life. I'm extremely pleased to be able to enhance our knowledge of their lives more than ever before. Knowing more about them transforms understanding of the prince.

Conclusion

History has not been favourable to the overshadowed seventeenth century; Whigs preferred to demonise aspects, rewrite it, and leave other parts firmly buried in the past. Rupert's remarkable legacy is that he stirs debate, passion, and interest nearly 400 years after his death – indeed, his sparkling and action-packed existence embodies so many aspects of the seventeenth century.

Rupert failed as Royalist Lord General because he was not politically adept, nor a unifying force. His years at sea whilst the cause collapsed left little to show for it. As an admiral at the Restoration, he was very competent and, on the whole, did well. These aspects of his life might be what he is best known for, but they do not define him. Nor do they explain why, of thirteen children born to Frederick and Elizabeth, he endures as the most famous.

He is as contentious now as he was in his day – a hero and a villain, as well as a pin-up, still adored for his looks and exploits. His herculean efforts and charisma united and inspired people of all ages, beliefs, nationalities, and sexes, and today they are still very much part of his appeal. Performing best when operating at local levels, by targeted campaigns or guerrilla tactics, he very nearly won the civil war for King Charles I.

A forward thinker, curious, innovative, and naturally courageous. These attributes thrived in the progressive seventeenth century and Rupert used them to good effect. Brought up as an exile with no home or prospects, he ended his days settled and secure, with a family about him, serving his adoptive country and leaving his mark in numerous fields.

His greatest success was surviving the adversity and gut-wrenching tragedies of a 'world turned upside down' and becoming a stabilising influence following the Restoration. Rupert has many hallmarks of a hero, albeit a very human one. Despite frailties and faults, he lived life to the full and did his very best; something that timelessly resonates with people across the centuries.

Notes

Introduction

1. BoL: MSFairfax 37/f94
2. BL: Harley MS 991/71/f36r
3. BoL: MS Fairfax 37/f94
4. BL: Harley MS 991/71/f36r

Chapter 1

1. CSPV, December 1617
2. BL: Add MS 7002/ff404
3. CSPV, December 1619
4. BL: Lansdowne MS 817/13
5. Nadine Akkerman, *The Correspondence of Elizabeth Stuart*, Vol. I (2011), pp. 253–254
6. Nadine Akkerman, *Correspondence*, Vol. I, p. 274
7. Nadine Akkerman, *Elizabeth Stuart, Queen of Hearts* (2021), p. 145
8. BL: Add MS 22959
9. Nadine Akkerman, *Queen of Hearts*, p. 150

Chapter 2

1. Nadine Akkerman, *Correspondence*, Vol. I, p. 279–280
2. BL: Lansdowne MS 817/13
3. Mark Turnbull, *Charles I's Private Life* (2023), p. 11
4. BL: Lansdowne MS 817/13
5. BL: Lansdowne MS 817/13
6. Nadine Akkerman, *Correspondence*, Vol. I, p. 327
7. CSPV, May 1612
8. Patrick Morrah, *Prince Rupert of the Rhine* (1976), p. 22
9. Patrick Morrah, *Prince Rupert*, p. 23
10. BL: Lansdowne MS 817/13
11. Ibid.
12. Ibid.
13. TNA: SP16/523/f.59r
14. TNA: SP84/138/f.20v

15. Mark Turnbull, *Charles I's Private Life*, p. 60
16. Mark Turnbull, *Charles I's Private Life*, p. 76
17. TNA: SP84/138/f.20v

Chapter 3

1. Nadine Akkerman, *Correspondence*, Vol. I, p. 719
2. TNA: SP81/40/276
3. Mark Turnbull, *Charles I's Private Life*, p. 79
4. Nadine Akkerman, *Correspondence*, Vol. I, p. 750
5. Nadine Akkerman, *Queen of Hearts*, p. 254
6. TNA: SP81/36/81

Chapter 4

1. BL: Lansdowne MS 817/13
2. BL: Egerton MS 1818 f.78r
3. TNA: SP81/36/34
4. TNA: SP81/36/81
5. Ibid.
6. CSPD, August 1641
7. CSPV, January 1632
8. Patrick Morrah, *Prince Rupert*, p. 29
9. Nadine Akkerman, *Correspondence*, Vol. II, p. 134

Chapter 5

1. Nadine Akkerman, *Queen of Hearts*, p. 267
2. TNA: SP16/534/f.12
3. Nadine Akkerman, *Correspondence*, Vol. II, p. 147
4. BL: Harley MS7000/ff.344r
5. TNA: SP81/40/f.72
6. NAS: GD406/1/10468
7. Nadine Akkerman, *Correspondence*, Vol. II, p. 164
8. Patrick Morrah, *Prince Rupert*, p. 30
9. *Historical Memoires of the Life and Death of Prince Rupert* (London, 1683)
10. BL: Lansdowne MS 817/13
11. Ibid.
12. CSPD, August 1635
13. BL: Lansdowne MS 817/13
14. Ibid.

Chapter 6

1. Nadine Akkerman, *Correspondence*, Vol. II, p. 361
2. Nadine Akkerman, *Correspondence*, Vol. II, p. 343
3. George Bromley, *A Collection of Original Royal Letters* (1787), p. 89

Notes

4. Nadine Akkerman, *Correspondence*, Vol. II, p. 388
5. Ibid.
6. George Bromley, *Royal Letters*, p. 86
7. Ibid.
8. CSPD, March 1636
9. TNA: SP16/318/f.154
10. Nadine Akkerman, *Correspondence*, Vol. II, p. 453
11. BL: Harley MS 7000 ff.359v
12. Nadine Akkerman, *Correspondence*, Vol. II, p. 442
13. Nadine Akkerman, *Correspondence*, Vol. II, p. 490
14. BL: Add MS 70499/f.218 & 218v
15. https://hab.bodleian.ox.ac.uk/en/collections/bodleian

Chapter 7

1. Christchurch Library, Oxford: MS 540
2. TNA: SP 16/361/f.68
3. Nadine Akkerman, *Correspondence*, Vol. II, p. 614
4. Nadine Akkerman, *Correspondence*, Vol. II, p. 453
5. TNA: SP 16/346/f.83
6. Charles Spencer, *Prince Rupert, The Last Cavalier* (2007), p. 35
7. BL: Lansdowne MS 817/13
8. Siobhan Keenan, *The Progresses, Processions, and Royal Entries of King Charles I* (2020), p. 117
9. Sir George Radcliffe, *Earl of Strafford's Letters*, Vol. II (1739), p. 85
10. Mark Turnbull, *Charles I's Private Life*, (2023), p. 89
11. BL: Harley MS 7000/ff.464v

Chapter 8

1. BL: Lansdowne MS 817/13
2. Ibid.
3. Nick Page, *Lord Minimus* (2001), p. 119
4. Nadine Akkerman, *Correspondence*, Vol. II, p. 625
5. CSPD, August 1637
6. NAS: GD406/1/9281
7. Nadine Akkerman, *Correspondence*, Vol. II, p. 650
8. Sir George Radcliffe, *Strafford's Letters*, Vol. II, p. 115
9. Nadine Akkerman, *Correspondence*, Vol. II, p. 694
10. BL: Lansdowne MS 817/13
11. Frank Kitson, *Prince Rupert, Portrait of a Soldier* (1996), p. 57
12. Charles Spencer, *Prince Rupert*, p. 37
13. Nadine Akkerman, *Correspondence*, Vol. II, p. 718
14. Ibid., p. 720
15. BL: Lansdowne MS 817/13
16. Ibid.
17. Ibid.

Chapter 9

1. *The History of this Iron Age: Wherein is Set Down the True State of Europe, as it was in the Year 1500* (London, 1656), p. 182
2. Steve Murdoch and Kathrin Zickermann, *The Battle of Lemgo, 17 October 1638: An Empirical Reevaluation* (Miltärhistorisk Tidskrift, 2024), p. 89
3. Patrick Morrah, *Prince Rupert*, p. 51

Chapter 10

1. Nadine Akkerman, *Correspondence*, Vol. II, p. 780
2. Nadine Akkerman, *Correspondence*, Vol. II, p. 726
3. Nadine Akkerman, *Queen of Hearts*, p. 338
4. Charles Spencer, *Prince Rupert*, p. 40
5. BL: Add MS 62084/f.1-63
6. BL: Lansdowne MS 817/13
7. Nadine Akkerman, *Correspondence*, Vol. II, p. 732
8. Charles Spencer, *Prince Rupert*, p. 41
9. BL: Lansdowne MS 817/13
10. Metropolitan Museum of Art website: www.metmuseum.org/toah/hd/durr/hd_durr.htm
11. BL: Lansdowne MS 817/13
12. BL: Add MS 62084/f.1-63
13. BL: Lansdowne MS 817/13
14. Ibid.
15. TNA: SP16/461/f.65.
16. BL: Add MS 62084/f.1-63
17. BL: Lansdowne MS 817/13
18. Ibid.
19. CSPV, June 1641
20. TNA: SP16/483/f.27
21. TNA: SP81/51/f.186
22. Nadine Akkerman, *Queen of Hearts*, p. 336
23. CSPD, August 1641
24. Frank Kitson, *Portrait of a Soldier*, p. 67
25. TNA: SP 16/485/f.8
26. TNA: SP81/52/207
27. CSPD, October 1641
28. TNA: SP16/484/f.148
29. TNA: SP16/484/f.135
30. CSPV, November 1641
31. TNA: SP16/485/f.8.
32. BL: Lansdowne MS 817/13

Chapter 11

1. TNA: SP16/486/f.51
2. Nadine Akkerman, *Queen of Hearts*, p. 338

3. BL: Lansdowne MS 817/13
4. CSPD, December 1641
5. BL: Lansdowne MS 817/13
6. CSPD, December 1641
7. Nadine Akkerman, *Correspondence*, Vol. II, p. 1015
8. TNA: SP16/485/f.226
9. Mark Turnbull, *Charles I*, p. 111
10. Ibid., p. 113
11. Ibid.
12. Ibid.
13. Mark Turnbull, *Charles I*, p. 114
14. Ibid.
15. Mark Turnbull, *Charles I*, p. 115
16. Nadine Akkerman, *Correspondence*, Vol. II, p. 1020
17. Mark Turnbull, *Charles I*, p. 115

Chapter 12

1. BL: Lansdowne MS 817/13
2. HOLJ, Vol. 4, 17 February 1642
3. Mark Turnbull, *Charles I*, p. 115
4. BL: Lansdowne MS 817/13
5. Mark Turnbull, *Charles I*, p. 119
6. Ibid., p. 117
7. Ibid., p. 118
8. Nadine Akkerman, *Correspondence*, Vol. II, p. 1031
9. Mark Turnbull, *Charles I*, p. 118
10. Ibid., p. 119
11. Nadine Akkerman, *Correspondence*, Vol. II, p. 1045
12. Nadine Akkerman, *Queen of Hearts*, p. 348
13. Nadine Akkerman, *Correspondence*, Vol. II, p. 1045

Chapter 13

1. HOLJ, Vol. 5, 11 July 1642
2. *Autobiography of Sir Simonds D'Ewes*, ed. James Orchard Halliwell (1845), p. 300
3. BL: Lansdowne MS 817/13
4. TNA: SP16/491/f.237
5. Halliwell-Phillipps, *D'Ewes*, p. 300
6. CSPV, August 1642
7. BL: Lansdowne MS 817/13
8. CSPV, September 1642
9. Patrick Morrah, *Prince Rupert*, p. 70
10. BL: ADD MS 18980
11. BL: Lansdowne MS 817/13
12. CSPD, July 1636
13. BL: Lansdowne MS 817/13

14. Ibid.
15. HOLJ, Vol. 5, 2 August 1642
16. J. Sears McGee, *An Industrious Mind* (2023), p. 373
17. Conrad Russell, *The Fall of the British Monarchies* (1991), p. 519
18. Patrick Morrah, *Prince Rupert*, p. 77
19. Charles Spencer, *Prince Rupert*, p. 57
20. Mark Turnbull, *Charles I*, p. 147
21. Jonathan Healey, *The Blazing World* (2023), p. 171
22. CSPV, September 1642
23. BL: Add MS 62084/f.1-63
24. BL: Lansdowne MS 817/13
25. CSPV, September 1642

Chapter 14

1. Henry Ellis, *Letters from a Subaltern Officer of the Earl of Essex's Army* (1854), p. 15
2. Ibid., p. 5
3. BL: ADD MS 18980
4. BL: ADD MS 62085
5. Henry Ellis, *Subaltern Officer*, p. 16
6. Ibid., p. 18
7. Ibid., p. 19
8. BL: ADD MS 62084/f.1-63
9. *Life and Death of Prince Rupert* (1683)
10. John Spiller, 'Where England's Sorrows Began', *Midland History*, Vol. 47 (2022), p. 21–37
11. Henry Ellis, *Subaltern Officer*, p. 22
12. John Spiller, 'England's Sorrows', p. 21–37
13. Henry Ellis, *Subaltern Officer*, p. 22
14. Edward Hyde, *History of the Rebellion* (1843), p. 299
15. CSPV, October 1642
16. John Spiller, 'England's Sorrows', p. 21–37

Chapter 15

1. Henry Ellis, *Subaltern Officer*, p. 19
2. BL: ADD MS 62085
3. S: MS/559
4. BL: Harley MS 6988
5. Patrick Morrah, *Prince Rupert*, p. 83
6. Frank Kitson, *Portrait of a Soldier*, p. 90
7. Henry Ellis, *Subaltern Officer*, p. 13
8. 'Prince Robert's Declaration' (1642)
9. BL: ADD MS 62084/f.1-63
10. Patrick Morrah, *Prince Rupert*, p. 85
11. Nick Lipscombe, *Civil War Atlas* (2021), p. 70
12. Philip Warwick, *Memoirs of the Reign of King Charles the First* (1702), p. 249
13. Charles Spencer, *Prince Rupert*, p. 69

14. Mark Turnbull, *Charles I*, p. 124
15. Ibid., p. 126
16. CSPV, October 1642
17. Mark Turnbull, *Charles I*, p. 124–125
18. NAS: GD16/35/3
19. Mark Turnbull, *Charles I*, p. 124–125
20. Charles Spencer, *Prince Rupert*, p. 71
21. NAS: GD16/35/3
22. Mark Turnbull, *Charles I*, p. 125
23. NAS: GD16/35/3
24. Mark Turnbull, *Charles I*, p. 126
25. NAS: GD16/35/3
26. BL: Add MS 62083/f.13
27. BL: Add MS 22959
28. NAS: GD160/530

Chapter 16

1. CSPV, November 1642
2. *Speciall Passages and Certain Informations*, 8–15 November 1642
3. CSPV, November 1642
4. Mark Turnbull, *Charles I*, p. 127
5. BL: Harley Add MS 6988
6. Ibid.
7. CSPV, September 1642
8. 'Two speeches of the Lord Wharton, spoken in Guild-Hall' (27 October 1642)
9. BoL: MS Fairfax 37/82
10. 'Prince Rupert his Declaration' (London 1642)
11. 'A Speech Spoken by His Excellence Prince Rupert … at his returne from Redding to Oxford' (1642)
12. Ibid.
13. Lincs: 2/ANC/14/22

Chapter 17

1. Cornish: T/1608/6
2. BL: Add MS 18980
3. 'A True relation of the approach of Prince Rupert to that good towne of Marlborow' (1642)
4. Ronald Hutton, *The Royalist War Effort* (1999), p. 34
5. BL: Add MS 18980
6. Nadine Akkerman, *Correspondence*, Vol. II, p. 1051
7. CSPD, October 1642
8. Mark Turnbull, *Charles I*, p. 128
9. Nadine Akkerman, *Queen of Hearts*, p. 350
10. Patrick Morrah, *Prince Rupert*, p. 108
11. 'A chaleng sent from Prince Rupert and the Lord Grandison, to Sir William Belford' (1643)

12. Eliot Warburton, *Memoirs of Prince Rupert and the Cavaliers*, Vol. II, (1849), p. 109
13. John Washbourn, *Bibliotheca Gloucestrensis* (1825), p. 21
14. BL: Add MS 18980
15. Thomas Carte, *The Life of James Duke of Ormonde*, Vol. V (1851), p. 400
16. BL: Add MS/62083/ff.1
17. 'A looking-glasse, wherein His Majesty may see his nephews love' (1643)
18. 'Observations vpon Prince Rvperts white dog called Boy' (1642)
19. CSPV, February 1643
20. TNA: SP116/529/4
21. Staffs: MS/571
22. BL: Add MS/18980
23. William Dugdale, *Life, Diary and Correspondence of Sir William Dugdale* (1827), p. 96
24. BL: Add MS 18980
25. Staffs: MS/568
26. TNA: Add MS/19893
27. BL: Harley Add MS/6988
28. CSPV, February 1643
29. TNA: SP116/529/4
30. Mark Turnbull, *Charles I*, p. 128–129
31. Ibid.
32. TNA: SP116/529/4
33. BL: Add MS/18980
34. Ronald Hutton, *Royalist War Effort*, p. 20

Chapter 18

1. *Prince Rupert's Burning Love to England Discovered in Birmingham's Flames*, London, 1643
2. Patrick Morrah, *Prince Rupert*, p. 111–112
3. John Rushworth, *Historical Collections of Private Passages of State*, Vol. V (1721), p. 148–154
4. BL: Add MS/18980
5. BL: Add MS/18983
6. BL: Add MS/18980
7. Staffs: LD/262/11/2
8. BL: Add MS/18980
9. Ibid.
10. BL: Add MS/18983
11. Ibid.
12. BL: Add MS/18980
13. Ibid.
14. Patrick Morrah, *Prince Rupert*, p. 114
15. BL: Add MS/18980
16. Patrick Morrah, *Prince Rupert*, p. 117
17. CSPV, July 1643
18. BL: Add MS/62084/f.1-63
19. BL: Add MS/18980

20. Ibid.
21. Ibid.
22. BL: Add MS/62084/f.1-63
23. BL: Harley Add MS/6988
24. Ibid.

Chapter 19

1. Charles Spencer, *Prince Rupert*, p. 94
2. Patrick Morrah, *Prince Rupert*, p. 122
3. Ibid., p. 124
4. BL: Add MS/18980
5. BL: Add MS/62083/f.26
6. Charles Spencer, *Prince Rupert*, p. 100
7. Philip Warwick, *Memoirs*, p. 249
8. BL: Add MS/18983
9. Staffs: MS/477/8
10. BL: Add MS/18980
11. Mark Turnbull, *Charles I*, p. 131
12. BL: Add MS/62084/f.1-63
13. William Ansell Day, *The Pythouse Papers* (1879), p. 16
14. NAS: GD/406/1/1915
15. *Life and Death of Rupert* (1683)
16. Thomas Fuller, *History of the Worthies of England* (1662)
17. Charles Spencer, *Prince Rupert*, p. 105
18. BL: Add MS/21506
19. BL: Add MS/18980
20. Nadine Akkerman, *Correspondence*, Vol. I, p. 795
21. BL: Add MS/18980

Chapter 20

1. BL: Add MS/62083
2. William Ansell Day, *Pythouse Papers*, p. 17
3. Charles Spencer, *Prince Rupert*, p. 111
4. BL: Add MS/18980
5. BL: Add MS/62083
6. BL: Add MS/62084
7. BL: Add MS/18980
8. Mark Turnbull, *Charles I*, p. 132
9. BL: Add MS/18980
10. BL: Add MS/18981
11. Thomas Carte, *Ormonde*, Vol. III, p. 230
12. Patrick Morrah, *Prince Rupert*, p. 135
13. BL: Add MS/18981
14. BL: Add MS/18981/f.42
15. BL: Add MS/21506

16. BL: Sloane MS/1519/f.30
17. BL: Add MS/18981
18. State Library Victoria, Melbourne RAREEMM 222/20
19. BL: Add MS/62083/f.5
20. Staffs: D(w)1778/I/i/36
21. *Life and Death of Prince Rupert* (1683)
22. Ibid.
23. BL: Add MS/62083/f.60
24. BL: Add MS/18981/f.105
25. BL: Add MS/18983

Chapter 21

1. BL: Add MS/18981/f.104
2. Mark Turnbull, *Charles I*, p. 135
3. BL: Add MS/18981/f.81
4. BL: Add MS/18981/f.109
5. Thomas Carte, *Ormonde*, Vol. III, p. 278
6. BL: Add MS/6988
7. BL: Add MS/18981/f.126
8. Worcs: 899:749/8782/68/53
9. BL: Add MS/18981/f.132
10. BL: Add MS/62083/f.7
11. This crucial letter was sold by Christie's auctioneers, in November 2012. Unfortunately, its present whereabouts is unclear. The king wrote it from Oxford and it has a postscript 'Charles Garret is only angrie because my L: Wentworth (as he cals it) is put over his head, to be Major Generall of the Horse, being satisfied concerning his Brigade, so that indeed, but for your sake I could be hartely angry at him.'
12. BL: Add MS/18981/f.138
13. Mark Turnbull, *Charles I*, p. 136
14. BL: Add MS/18981/f.182
15. BL: Add MS/18983
16. NAS: GD/3/5/339
17. BL: Add MS/62084/f.1-63
18. Liv: 920 MOO/1371
19. Thomas Carte, *Ormonde*, Vol. III, p. 319
20. Ibid., p. 329
21. Mark Turnbull, *Charles I*, p. 136
22. V&A: NRA/38887
23. Wanklyn and Jones, *A Military History of the English Civil War* (2005), p. 179
24. Mark Turnbull, *Charles I*, p. 137
25. NAS: GD/16/50/21
26. BL: Add MS/62083/f.61
27. *History of this Iron Age* (1656), p. 211
28. BL: Add MS/62084/f.1-63
29. Patrick Morrah, *Prince Rupert*, p. 157
30. Ibid., p. 158

31. Ibid.
32. Thomas Fuller, *Worthies* (1662)

Chapter 22

1. NAS: GD/16/50/21
2. Thomas Fuller, *Worthies* (1662)
3. BL: Add MS/62083/f.66
4. Eliot Warburton, *Memoirs*, Vol. II, p. 437
5. Thomas Fuller, *Worthies* (1662)
6. Cumb: DMUS/5/5/4/11
7. BL: Add MS/62085
8. Thomas Carte, *Ormonde*, Vol. III, p. 340
9. BL: Harley Add MS/7001/f.170r
10. 'A Dog's Elegy' (1644)
11. Mark Turnbull, *Charles I*, p. 138–139
12. Nadine Akkerman, *Queen of Hearts*, p. 356
13. Thomas Carte, *Ormonde*, Vol. III, p. 259
14. 'A copie of a letter sent to the most illustrious and high borne Prince Rupert' (1644)
15. Thomas Carte, *Ormonde*, Vol. III, p. 353
16. Mark Turnbull, *Charles I*, p. 141
17. Cornish: RS/1/1058
18. Staffs: D(W)1778/I/i/39
19. Cornish: RS/1/1054
20. BL: Add MS/18983
21. 'The accusation given by His Maiestie against the Lord Wilmot' (1644)
22. Cornish: RS/1/1058
23. BL: Add MS/18983

Chapter 23

1. Thomas Carte, *Ormonde*, Vol. III, p. 355
2. Frank Kitson, *Portrait of a Soldier*, p. 212
3. V&A: NRA 13466
4. Mark Turnbull, *Charles I*, p. 142
5. BL: Add MS/62084
6. CSPV, December 1644
7. Herts: DE/X985/79959X
8. BL: Add MS/18982
9. Ibid.
10. Ibid.
11. Ibid.
12. Ibid.
13. Ibid.
14. Ibid.
15. CSPD, January 1645
16. John Rushworth, *Historical Collections*, Vol. V, p. 748–787

17. Thomas Carte, *Ormonde*, Vol. III, p. 278
18. BL: Add MS/18982
19. HOLJ, Vol. 7, 22 April 1645
20. BL: Add MS/18982
21. Ibid.
22. BL: Add MS/1519/f.76
23. BL: Add MS/62083/f.10
24. BL: Add MS/18982
25. Staffs: D(W)1778/I/i/41
26. Staffs: D(W)1778/I/i/42
27. Staffs: D(W)1778/I/i/44
28. BL: Add MS/1519/f.47
29. BL: Add MS/1519/f.23
30. Staffs: D(W)1778/I/i/43
31. Staffs: D(W)1778/I/i/44
32. Staffs: D(W)1778/I/i/45a
33. Staffs: D(W)1778/I/i/37
34. Staffs: D(W)1778/I/i/45a
35. James Orchard Halliwell, *Letters of the Kings of England* (1848), p. 379
36. Staffs: D(W)1778/I/i/47
37. Mark Turnbull, *Charles I*, p. 144
38. Staffs: D(W)1778/I/i/48
39. Staffs: D(W)1778/I/i/37

Chapter 24

1. BL: Add MS/18982/f.46
2. BL: Add MS/18982/f.48
3. BL: Add MS/18982/f.50
4. Staffs: D(W)1778/I/i/45b
5. Staffs: D(W)1778/I/i/54
6. Mark Turnbull, *Charles I*, p. 146
7. BL: Add MS/18982
8. *Life and Death of Prince Rupert* (1683)
9. James Orchard Halliwell, *Letters*, p. 382
10. *Life and Death of Prince Rupert* (1683)
11. Staffs: D(W)1778/I/i/55
12. Frank Kitson, *Portrait of a Soldier*, p. 249
13. Staffs: D(W)1778/I/i/55
14. Staffs: S/MS/497
15. BL: Add MS/18982/f.65
16. BL: Add MS/18982
17. Frank Kitson, *Portrait of a Soldier*, p. 252
18. BL: Add MS/33596/f.9
19. Mark Turnbull, *Charles I*, p. 154
20. *Sun* (London Newspaper) Monday, 28 May 1849

21. BL: Add MS/18982/f.69
22. Thomas Fuller, *Worthies* (1662)
23. Staffs: S/MS/497
24. BL: Add MS/62084/f.1-63
25. BL: Add MS/18983
26. BL: Add MS/18982
27. Charles Petrie, *King Charles, Prince Rupert and the Civil War* (1974), p. 9
28. Staffs: D(W)1778/I/i/57
29. BL: Add MS/18982
30. BL: Add MS/18983
31. Ibid.
32. Ibid.
33. NAS: GD/220/3/90
34. Staffs: D(W)1778/I/i/50
35. Staffs: D(W)1778/I/i/59

Chapter 25

1. John Rushworth, *Historical Collections*, Vol. VI, p. 23–89
2. Staffs: D(W)1778/I/i/50
3. BL: Add MS/62085
4. John Rushworth, *Historical Collections*, Vol. VI, p. 23–89
5. BL: Add MS/33596/ff.13r-14v
6. Mark Turnbull, *Charles I*, p. 152
7. TNA: SP16/497/f.224
8. 'A declaration of His Highness Prince Rupert' (1645)
9. Mark Turnbull, *Charles I*, p. 155
10. Thomas Carte, *Ormonde*, Vol. I, (1739) p. 207
11. BL: Add MS/33596
12. BL: Add MS/33596/ff.15r-16v
13. BL: Add MS/33596
14. BL: Add MS/33596/ff.17r-v
15. BL: Harley Add MS/6988
16. BL: Add MS/33596
17. 'The Last Will and Testament of Prince Rupert' (1645)
18. BL: Add MS/18982
19. 'The Bloody Treatie' (1645)
20. BL: Add MS/18982
21. Mark Turnbull, *Charles I*, p. 157
22. NAS: GD/220/3/91
23. 'The humble desires of Prince Rupert, Prince Maurice, and others' (1645)
24. BL: Add MS/18982
25. Staffs: S/MS/543
26. BL: Add MS/62083/f.77
27. BL: Add MS/18982
28. BL: Add MS/62084/f.1-63

Chapter 26

1. BL: Add MS/33596
2. BL: Add MS/1988
3. Frank Kitson, *Portrait of a Soldier*, p. 267
4. HOLJ, Vol. 8, 7 January 1646
5. BL: Add MS/62084/f.1-63
6. V&A: NRA/13466
7. Mark Turnbull, *Charles I*, p. 159
8. BL: Add MS/1519/f.69
9. John Rushworth, *Historical Collections*, Vol. VI, p. 276–298
10. E. W. Bligh, *Kenelm Digby and His Venetia* (1932), p. 249
11. BL: Add MS/18982
12. George Bromley, *Royal Letters*, p. 127–128
13. Ibid., p. 131–132
14. Ibid., p. 133–134
15. 'A true copy of the Welch sermon preached before the two princes' (1646)
16. BL: Add MS/62084/f.1-63
17. John Bruce, *Charles I in 1646* (1856), p. 58
18. Glam: NRA/5885
19. NLW: Clenennau Letters & Papers, 627
20. BL: Add MS/62084/f.1-63
21. V&A: NRA/13466
22. Patrick Morrah, *Prince Rupert*, p. 220
23. BL: Harley Add MS/1988
24. BL: Add MS/18982
25. BL: Harley Add MS/7001/f.207r
26. Patrick Morrah, *Prince Rupert*, p. 221
27. NAS: GD/406/1/2472

Chapter 27

1. NAS: GD/406/1/2427
2. Patrick Morrah, *Prince Rupert*, p. 227
3. BL: Add MS/18982
4. Ibid.
5. Army size: Nick Lipscombe, *Civil War Atlas*
6. NAS: GD/406/1/2427
7. BL: Harley Add MS/6988
8. BL: Harley Add MS/6988/f.208
9. Patrick Morrah, *Prince Rupert*, p. 229
10. Ibid., p. 232
11. BL: Add MS/18982
12. NAS: GD/406/1/2450
13. NAS: GD/220/3/142
14. NAS: GD/220/3/143

Notes

15. NAS: GD/220/3/140
16. NAS: GD/220/3/144
17. V&A: NRA/13466
18. NAS: GD/220/3/143
19. Mark Turnbull, *Charles I*, p. 173
20. BL: Add MS/18982
21. BL: Add MS/18982
22. Charles Spencer, *Prince Rupert*, p. 199
23. Thomas Carte, *Ormonde*, Vol. III, p. 595
24. Staffs: D(W)1778/I/i/67
25. BL: Add MS/18982
26. Staffs: S/MS/544
27. BL: Add MS/63743

Chapter 28

1. George Bromley, *Royal Letters*, p. 295–296
2. Patrick Morrah, *Prince Rupert*, p. 239
3. BL: Add MS/18982/f.177
4. Patrick Morrah, *Prince Rupert*, p. 239
5. 'The declaration of His Highnesse Prince Rupert' (1649)
6. BL: Add MS/18982
7. Richard Blakemore and Elaine Murphy, *The British Civil Wars at Sea* (2018), p. 156
8. Ibid., p. 117
9. Staffs: D(w)1778/i/i/73
10. Patrick Morrah, *Prince Rupert*, p. 241
11. Frank Kitson, *Prince Rupert: Admiral and General at Sea* (2002), p. 68
12. British History Online: www.british-history.ac.uk/thurloe-papers/vol1/pp132-139
13. TNA: SP/89/4/f.211
14. BL: Add MS/18982
15. BL: Add MS/21506
16. BL: Add MS/18982
17. Frank Kitson, *Admiral*, p. 102
18. BoL: MS/Fairfax/37/f.95
19. BoL: MS/Fairfax/37/f.96
20. BoL: MS/Fairfax/37/f.97
21. BoL: MS/Fairfax/37/f.75
22. Emanuel de Faria y Sousa, *The History of Portugal* (1698), p. 459
23. BoL: MS/Fairfax/37/f.98

Chapter 29

1. *History of this Iron Age* (1656), p. 259
2. BL: Harley MS/991/f.44v-45
3. BoL: MS/Fairfax/37/f.99

4. BoL: MS/Fairfax/37/f.72
5. BoL: MS/Fairfax/37/f.100
6. BoL: MS/Fairfax/37/f.72
7. BL: Add MS/62085
8. BL: Add MS/70518
9. CSPD Interregnum, June 1652
10. 'Life and Death of Prince Rupert' (1683)
11. BL: Add MS/62085

Chapter 30

1. 'Life and Death of Prince Rupert' (1683)
2. Patrick Morrah, *Prince Rupert*, p. 290
3. Surrey: G52/2/19/103b
4. LPL: MS/646
5. BL: Add MS/18827/f.1
6. CSPV, December 1656
7. George Bromley, *Royal Letters*, p. 288
8. Ibid.
9. Nadine Akkerman, *Queen of Hearts*, p. 395
10. Patrick Morrah, *Prince Rupert*, p. 297
11. Ibid., p. 102
12. BL: Add MS/18738/f.99
13. TNA: SP77/32/129
14. TNA: SP77/32/12

Chapter 31

1. BL: Harley MS 991
2. BL: Add MS/62081
3. *The Diarie of the Viscountess Mordaunt* (1856), p. 60
4. Kendal Archive Centre, WDRY/5/385
5. George Bromley, *Royal Letters*, p. 188
6. CSPV, December 1660
7. Staffs: D(w)1778/I/i/83
8. Staffs: D(w)1778/I/i/84
9. Staffs: D(W)1778/i/i/85
10. Staffs: D(W)1778/i/i/86
11. Staffs: D(W)1778/i/i/87
12. Staffs: D(W)1778/i/i/88
13. Staffs: D(W)1778/i/i/92
14. BoL: MS/Carte/104/f.64
15. Staffs: D(W)1778/i/i/87
16. Staffs: D(W)1778/i/i/93
17. Staffs: D(W)1778/i/i/92
18. Staffs: D(W)1778/i/i/94
19. Staffs: D(W)1778/i/i/99

Chapter 32

1. Staffs: D(W)1778/I/i/94
2. Laurence Lockhart, 'The Diplomatic Missions of Henry Bard', *IRAN*, Vol. 4 (1966), p. 97
3. BL: Add MS/18738/f.115
4. CSPD, October 1664
5. Ibid.
6. *The Flemings in Oxford*, Vol. I (1913), p. 150
7. TNA: SP/84/173/8
8. CSPD, November 1664
9. *Diarie of the Viscountess Mordaunt*, p. 73
10. Staffs: D(W)1778-V-762
11. CSPD, June 1665
12. BoL: MS/Carte/79/f.12
13. CSPD, June 1665
14. Ibid.
15. Lancs: DDKE/acc7840/HMC/245
16. *A True narrative of the engagement between His Majesties fleet and that of Holland*, London 1666
17. Lancs: DDKE/acc7840/HMC/245
18. CSPD, June 1666
19. Cornish: T/1727
20. Ibid.
21. Charles Harding Firth, *The Clarke Papers*, Vol. I (1891), p. ix
22. *Diarie of the Viscountess Mordaunt*, p. 87
23. BoL: MS/Carte/35/f.551-552
24. Frank Kitson, *Admiral*, p. 232
25. BoL: MS/Carte/222/f.108
26. Ibid.
27. Durham University Library, Add MSS 1100
28. TNA: SP/116/348
29. Durham University Library, Add MSS 1100

Chapter 33

1. *Diarie of the Viscountess Mordaunt*, p. 91
2. CSPD, February 1667
3. BoL: MS/Carte/223/f.305
4. TNA: SP/46/136/534A
5. TNA: SP/46/136/505
6. Christopher Hibbert, *The Court at Windsor* (1964), p. 75
7. BL: Add MS/63743
8. Ibid.
9. *English Historical Review*, Vol. 15 (1900), p. 761
10. Patrick Morrah, *Prince Rupert*, p. 412–413
11. Count Grammont, *Memoirs of the Court of Charles II* (1846), p. 269
12. BL: Add MS/63743

Chapter 34

1. 'On the death of his grace the Duke of Albemarle' (1670)
2. NAS: NRAS/2177/Bundle4225
3. BL: Add MS/62083/f.88
4. BL: Stowe MS/204/f.320
5. TNA: PROB/11/335/286

Chapter 35

1. TNA: SP/46/137/420A
2. 'A Panegyrick to His Highness Prince Rupert' (1673)
3. NAS: NRAS/2177/Bundle4465
4. Patrick Morrah, *Prince Rupert*, p. 374
5. TNA: SP/116/388
6. BoL: MS/Carte/80/f.776r-v
7. TNA: SP/82/12/80
8. 'Life and Death of Prince Rupert' (1683)

Chapter 36

1. CSPD, September 1675
2. NAS: NRAS/2177/Bundle4461
3. Patrick Morrah, *Prince Rupert*, p. 416
4. Count Grammont, *Memoirs*, p. 106
5. Ibid., p. 115
6. 'Life and Death of Prince Rupert' (1683)
7. BL: Add MS/62081
8. Ibid.
9. Staffs: D(W)1778/i/i/91
10. Patrick Morrah, *Prince Rupert*, p. 423

Chapter 37

1. BoL: MS/Carte/222/f.280
2. TNA: ADM/106/360/375
3. BL: Add MS/38091/ff.242
4. Patrick Morrah, *Prince Rupert*, p. 425
5. 'Life and Death of Prince Rupert' (1683)

Chapter 38

1. *The English Historical Review*, Vol. XI (Oct 1896), p. 527–530
2. Patrick Morrah, *Prince Rupert*, p. 412

Chapter 39

1. Staffs: D(W)1778/I/i/42
2. Kent: U1115/C34
3. Kent: U1255/C1/1
4. Kent: U1115/C42
5. Kent: U1115/C41/1
6. Kent: U1115/C41/2
7. Kent: U1255/C2
8. Kent: U1115/C43
9. Kent: U1115/C4
10. Kent: U1255/C2
11. Kent: U1255/C8
12. Kent: U1255/C5
13. Kent: U1255/C1
14. Kent: U1255/C8
15. British History Online: www.british-history.ac.uk/burton-diaries/vol1/pp297-298
16. British History Online: www.british-history.ac.uk/burton-diaries/vol1/pp259-266
17. TNA: PROB 11/312/448
18. Patrick Morrah, *Prince Rupert*, p. 408
19. Beriah Botfield, *Stemmata Botevilliana* (1858), p. cccl
20. Mary Boyle, *Biographical Catalogue of the Portraits at Longleat* (1881), p. 91
21. 'The humerous tricks and conceits of Prince Roberts malignant she-monkey' (1643)
22. Frank Kitson, *Portrait of a Soldier*, p. 162
23. Patrick Morrah, *Prince Rupert*, p. 404

Bibliography

Manuscripts

Bodleian Library (BoL)
MS Carte 222, 104, 35, relating to Rupert's life
MS Carte 33, 38, 72, 79, 80, 222, 223, Rupert & naval matters
MS Fairfax 37, relating to Rupert's fleet c.1650–51

British Library (BL)
Egerton MS 1818, Letters & Papers chiefly relating to Scottish Affairs
ADD MS 22959, writing of John Rous, Rector of Stanton Downham
ADD MS 24195, sonnets of King James VI/I
ADD MS 18980–83, civil war letters
ADD MS 33596, miscellaneous Royalist correspondence
ADD MS 35331, Autograph Diary of Walter Yonge
Harley MS 6988, Royal letters and warrants 1625–1655
ADD MS 72438, Trumbull correspondence
Harley MS 986, Richard Symonds notes 1643–44
Thomason Tracts, Vol. I 1640–1652
ADD MS 18827, Civil War letters
ADD MS 63743, Earl of Craven's correspondence
ADD MS 63744, post-Civil War letters
ADD MS 70518, miscellaneous letters and papers
ADD MS 34727, letters concerning naval matters
Sloane MS 555, Rupert's library catalogue
Sloane MS 1030, regarding Rupert's heart
Sloane MS 1519, civil war letters
Lansdowne MS 817, memorandum about Rupert's early years
ADD MS 38091, letters relating to Margaret Hughes
ADD MS 62081 & 62083–5, Benett family papers
ADD MS 29873, Mayor of Worcester's memorandum book
ADD MS 21506, letters from Rupert's sister, Sophia
ADD MS 29767, Rupert's household accounts
Harley MS 6986 & 7000–7003, Letters & State Papers
Harley MS 991, *Constant Reformation* & Charles II's escape from Worcester
Stowe MS 204, Rupert's recommendation of his Godson

Bibliography

Kings MS 140, Palatine family letters
ADD MS 4158, State Papers, John Thurloe
ADD MS 18738, Family letters

Cheshire Archives
ZA/B/2/68, preparations surrounding Rupert's visit in 1644

Cornish Studies Centre
RS/1/1054, 1055, 1058, 1061, letters written to Prince Rupert from various Royalists during the Lostwithiel campaign
T/127, relating to naval engagement with the Dutch

Cumbria Archive Centre
D MUS 5/5/4/11, letter to Prince Rupert (not mentioned)

Durham University Library
Add MSS 1100, letter from Clarendon to Rupert 5 August 1666.

Glamorgan Archives (Glam)
NRA 5885, letters from Charles I and Rupert

Gloucester Archives
D7115/2 & D7348/1/3, letters relating to Rupert and the civil war (not mentioned)

Hertfordshire Archives
DE/X985/79959X, A Brief Relation of ye Antient famely of the Rawdons

Kendal Archive Centre
WDRY/5/385, Letter to Daniel Fleming reporting on the king's landing.

Kent Archives
U1118/T12
U1255/C1–10
U1115/A4
U1115/A3 Bills and Receipts of Sir Thomas Scott
U1115/C34 From Lady Goring
U1115/C41–47 Scott Family Letters

Lambeth Palace Library (LPL)
MS 645, family correspondence of Charles II
MS 646, letter from Prince Rupert to Charles II

Lancashire Archives (Lancs)
QSP 22/12, QSP 84/6, QSB 1/288/38 & DDKE/acc 7840 HMC/199, relating to Rupert's activities in Lancashire, June 1644
DDKE/acc 7840 HMC/245, account of 1666 naval engagement against the Dutch
DDKE/acc 7840 HMC/354, relating to the condemnation of Lord Stafford in 1680

Lincolnshire Archives (Lincs)
2ANC14/22, Rupert's degree at Oxford

Liverpool Record Office (Liv)
920 MOO/1371 & 72, relating to Rupert's activities in Lancashire, June 1644

Melbourne State Library
RAREEMM 222/20, letter from King Charles I to Rupert. Viewed online (https://beyondthebook.slv.vic.gov.au)

National Library of Wales (NLW)
Clenennau Letters & Papers 627

National Records of Scotland (NAS)
GD406/1, GD223/3 & GD40/9, GD406/1/2450, GD3/5/339, GD406/1/1940, civil war letters
GD16/50/21, D1/53/52, JC38/4 & 5, accounts relating to Marston Moor
NRAS 2177/Bundle 4465, 1673 Dutch war
NRAS 2177/Bundle 4225, 1670 celebrations
NAS: GD406/1/10468, Frederick's death

Nottingham University Library
PW 1/530, letter from the Marquis of Newcastle (not mentioned)

Staffordshire Record Office (Staffs)
D(W)1778, letters between Rupert and Will Legge
D262/11/2, news sheet relating to Lichfield, 1643
D948/4/6/5, S/MS/497–571, civil war letters

Suffolk Archives
HD 36/A/304, mentions Rupert's activities with the fleet in 1664

Surrey History Centre
G52/2/19/103b, letter from Rupert's secretary, 1655

The National Archives (TNA)
SP 16, 20, 46, 77, 78, 81, 82, 84, 89, 105 & 116, Calendar of State Papers
ADM 106, Admiralty papers
LC 2, Rupert's funeral
PRO 30/24, papers of the Earl of Shaftesbury
C 115/98, civil war letter
PROB 11/312/448, Will of Edward Scott
PROB/11/335/286, Will of William Legge

V&A Museum
NRA 13466 & NRA 38887, letters to Prince Rupert

Bibliography

Wiltshire & Swindon
413/407, Siege of Newark 1643

Worcestershire Archives (Worcs)
899:749/8782/68/46 & 53, civil war letters to Rupert

Yale University Libraries: Beinecke Library
Osborn FB190 & FB191, correspondence of William Legge

Pamphlets

'The two speeches of the Lord Wharton, spoken in Guild-Hall' (1642)
'A Speech Spoken by His Excellence Prince Rupert … at his returne from Redding' (1642)
'A True narrative of the engagement between His Majesties fleet and that of Holland' (1666)
'A Trve relation of the approach of Prince Rvpert to that good towne of Marlborow' (1642)
'A chaleng sent from Prince Rupert and the Lord Grandison' (1643)
'A looking-glasse, wherein His Majesty may see his nephews love' (1643)
'Prince Rupert's Burning Love to England Discovered in Birmingham's Flames' (1643)
'His Highnesse Prince Ruperts raising of the siege at Newarke upon Trent' (1644)
'A particular relation of the action before Cyrencester (or Cycester) in Glocestershire' 1643)
'An exact relation of the bloody and barbarous massacre at Bolton' (1644)
'A Dog's Elegy' (1644)
'A copie of a letter sent to the most illustrious and high borne Prince Rupert' (1642)
'The accusation given by His Maiestie against the Lord Wilmot' (1644)
'The Last Will and Testament of Prince Rupert' (1645)
'The Bloody Treatie' (1645)
'A true copy of the Welch sermon preached before the two princes' (1646)
'The declaration of His Highnesse Prince Rupert' (1649)
'The humerous tricks and conceits of Prince Roberts malignant she-monkey' (1643)
'The humble desires of Prince Rupert, Prince Maurice, and others' (1645)
'Observations vpon Prince Rvperts white dog called Boy' (1642)
'Prince Robert's Declaration' (1642)
'Three Tracts Relative To The Battle of Birmingham' (1643)
'A Panegyrick to His Highness Prince Rupert' (1673)
'On the Death of his grace the Duke of Albemarle' (1670)
'His Highness Prince *Rupert*'s Letter to the Earl of *Arlington* ... from on Board the *Royal Charles*, off of the *Oster-bank*' (1673)

Books

Akkerman, Nadine, *The Correspondence of Elizabeth Stuart*, Vol. I & II (OUP, 2015)
Akkerman, Nadine, *Elizabeth Stuart, Queen of Hearts* (OUP, 2021)
Barter Bailey, Sarah, *Prince Rupert's Patent Guns* (Trustees of the Royal Armouries, 2000)
Bligh, E.W., *Sir Kenelm Digby & His Venetia* (London, 1932)
Blakemore, Richard J., and Murphy, Elaine, *The British Civil Wars at Sea* (Boydell Press, 2018)

Botfield, Beriah, *Stemmata Botevilliana, Memorials of the Families De Boteville, Thynne, and Botfield* (London, 1858)

Boyle, Mary Louisa, *Biographical Catalogue of the Portraits at Longleat in the County of Wilts the Seat of the Marquis of Bath* (London, 1881)

Bromley, Sir George, *A Collection of Original Royal Letters* (London, 1787)

Bruce, John, *Charles I in 1646* (Camden Society, 1856)

Bury, Baroness Blaze de, *Memoirs of The Princess Palatine* (London, 1853)

Carte, Thomas, *An History of the Life of James Duke of Ormonde*, Vol. I & II (London, 1736)

Cavendish, Francis William Henry, *Society, Politics and Diplomacy 1820–1864* (London, 1913)

Clarendon, Earl of, *The History of the Rebellion and Civil Wars in England*, Vol. II (Oxford, 1888)

Cooper, Susan Margaret, *Actresses of the Restoration Period* (Pen and Sword, 2023)

D'Aulnoy, Baronne, Marie Catherine, *Memoirs of the Court of England in 1675* (London, 1927)

Day, William Ansell, *The Pythouse Papers* (London, 1879)

De Lisle, Leanda, *Henrietta Maria: Phoenix Queen* (Chatto & Windus, 2023)

Dugdale, William, *The Life, Diary and Correspondence of Sir William Dugdale*, ed. William Hamper (London, 1827)

Ellis, Sir Henry, *Original Letters, Illustrative of English History*, Vol. IV (London, 1846)

Ellis, Sir Henry, *Letters from a Subaltern Officer of the Earl of Essex's Army* (London, 1854)

Faria y Sousa, Emanuel de, *The History of Portugal* (translated by John Stevens, London, 1698)

Fox, Frank, *The Four Days' Battle of 1666* (Seaforth, 2009)

Fuller, Thomas, *The History of the Worthies of England* (London, 1662)

Godfrey, Elizabeth, *A Sister of Prince Rupert* (London, 1909)

Grammont, Count, *Memoirs of the Court of Charles II* (London, 1846)

Grosjean, Alexia and Murdoch, Steve, *Alexander Leslie and the Scottish Generals of the Thirty Years War, 1618–1648* (Pickering & Chatto, 2014)

Halliwell-Phillipps, James, *Autobiography of Sir Simonds D'Ewes* (London, 1845)

Healey, Jonathan, *The Blazing World* (Bloomsbury Publishing, 2023)

Hibbert, Christopher, *The Court at Windsor* (Longmans, 1964)

Historical Memoires of the Life and Death of that Wise and Valiant Prince Rupert (London, 1683)

Hutton, Ronald, *The Royalist War Effort 1642–1646*, Second Edition (Routledge, 1999)

Kitson, Frank, *Prince Rupert: Portrait of a Soldier* (Constable, 1996)

Kitson, Frank, *Prince Rupert: Admiral and General at Sea* (Constable, 2002)

Lockhart, Laurence, 'The Diplomatic Missions of Henry Bard', published in *IRAN*, Vol. IV (Taylor & Francis, 1966)

McGee, J. Sears, *An Industrious Mind* (Stanford University Press, 2015)

Morrah, Patrick, *Prince Rupert of the Rhine* (Constable, 1976)

Murdoch, Steve and Zickermann, Kathrin, *The Battle of Lemgo, 17 October 1638: An Empirical Reevaluation* (Miltärhistorisk Tidskrift, 2024)

Newman, P. R. and Roberts, P. R., *Marston Moor – 1644: The Battle of the Five Armies* (Blackthorn Press, 2003)

Page, Nick, *Lord Minimus* (HarperCollins, 2001)

Pendlebury, Graham, *Aspects of the English Civil War in Bolton and its Neighbourhood 1640–1660* (Neil Richardson, 1983)

Bibliography

Petrie, Charles, *King Charles, Prince Rupert and the Civil War* (Routledge & Kegan Paul, 1974)
Rushworth, John, *Historical Collections of Private Passages of State*, Vol. V (1721)
Russell, Conrad, *The Fall of the British Monarchies* (Clarendon Press, 1991)
Scott, Eva, *Rupert, Prince Palatine* (New York, 1899)
Shapiro, Lisa, *Princess Elisabeth of Bohemia and Rene Descartes* (University of Chicago Press, 2007)
Spencer, Charles, *Prince Rupert, The Last Cavalier* (Weidenfeld & Nicolson, 2007)
Spiller, John, '"Where England's Sorrows Began": A Reassessment of the Battle of Powick Bridge, 1642', *Midland History*, Vol. 47 (2022)
The Clarke Papers, Vol. I (Camden Society, 1891)
The English Historical Review, Volume XV, Issue LX, October 1900
The English Historical Review, Volume XI, Issue 44, October 1896
The History of this Iron Age: Wherein is Set Down the True State of Europe, as it was in the Year 1500 (London, 1656)
The Flemings in Oxford, Vol. I (Clarendon Press, 1913)
The Private Diary of Elizabeth, Viscountess Mordaunt (Duncairn, 1856)
Thurley, Simon, *Palaces of Revolution* (William Collins, 2021)
Tibbutt, H. G., *The Life and Letters of Sir Lewis Dyve* (Bedfordshire Historical Record Society, 1948)
Turnbull, Mark, *Charles I's Private Life* (Pen and Sword, 2023)
Townsend, Dorothea, *Life and Letters of Mr Endymion Porter* (London, 1897)
Walker, Edward, *Historical Discourses Upon Several Occasions* (London, 1705)
Wanklyn, Malcolm and Jones, Frank, *A Military History of the English Civil War* (Pearson, 2005)
Warburton, Eliot, *Memoirs of Prince Rupert and the Cavaliers*, Vol. I, II & III (London, 1849)
Warner, George F., *The Nicholas Papers* (Camden Society, 1886)
Warwick, Sir Philip, *Memoirs of the Reign of King Charles the First* (1702)
Washbourn, John, *Bibliotheca Gloucestrensis* (1825)
Waylen, James, *A History Military and Municipal of the Town of Marlborough* (London, 1854)
Young, Peter, *Marston Moor 1644, The Campaign and the Battle* (Windrush Press, 1997)

Index

Abingdon, England, 59, 77, 89, 107, 121, 124–6
Adwalton Moor, Battle of, 90
Africa/African, 171–3, 175–6, 181, 190, 192, 213
Albemarle, Duke of, *see* George Monck
Aldbourne Chase, 96
Alnwick, Baron Percy of, *see* Henry Percy
Amsterdam, Holland, 10, 118, 188
Andros, Edmund (Governor of New York), 218–9
Annan Moor, Battle of, 143
Anne, Princess (the Duke of York's daughter & later Queen Anne), 217–8, 221–2
Antelope (ship), 158
Antigua, 167, 173
Arlington, Earl of, *see* Henry Bennett
Arundel, Earl of, 18–9, 28, 41, 125
Ashburnham, Jack, 131, 136
Ashby de la Zouch, England, 81, 103, 132
Astley, Bernard (son of Sir Jacob Astley), 139
Astley, Sergeant-Major-General Sir Jacob (Bernard Astley's father and Prince Rupert's tutor), 7, 11, 30–1, 55, 69, 124–7, 132, 139, 147
Aston, Sir Arthur (Governor of Reading), 79, 87–8, 95, 100, 120
Aylesbury, England, 77
Azores, 167–9, 171, 188

Balfour, Sir William, 69
Bampfield, Joseph, 155–6, 180–1
Banbury, England, 70, 78, 107, 145
Banér, Johan, 38
Bankaert, Vice-Admiral Adrian, 195
Barbados, 167, 172, 218
Bard, Anne Jr (Anne and Henry Bard's daughter, Frances Bard's sister and Daniel Jevon's wife), 188, 222
Bard, Anne Sr (Henry Bard's wife), 188
Bard, Charles Rupert (Anne and Henry Bard's son, and Frances Bard's brother), 188, 222
Bard, Dudley Rupert, (Frances Bard and Rupert's son), 197, 199, 201, 205, 213, 215, 218, 220–2
Bard, Frances/Francesca (Prince Rupert's partner), 188–9, 197–201, 205, 215, 221–2, 229
Bard, Nathaniel (Frances Bard's cousin and Persiana's cousin/husband), 222
Bard, Persiana (Anne and Sir Henry Bard's daughter, Frances Bard's sister and Nathaniel Bard's cousin/wife), 188, 221–2
Bard, Sarah Frances, (Frances Bard's niece, Nathaniel and Persiana Bard's daughter, and Henry Harcourt's wife), 222
Bard, Henry (Viscount Bellamont), 130, 188, 247, 254
Bard, Susan (née Dudley) (Frances Bard's grandmother and Dudley Bard's maternal great-grandmother), 197
Bard, William (Frances Bard's nephew, and Nathaniel and Persiana Bard's son), 222
Barnstaple, England, 133

Index

Basing House, England, 121–3
Bath, England, 123, 134, 254
Batten, William, 156–9, 189
Bedford, Earl of, 98
Bedfordshire, England, 74, 255
Belford, Sir William, 79, 237
Bellamont, Lady, *see* Frances Bard
Bellamont, Viscount, *see* Henry Bard
Bennett, Henry (Earl of Arlington), 209–10, 228, 253
Berkeley Castle, England, 80
Berlin, Germany, 6
Bignall, Henry, 201
Billingsley, Rupert (Prince Rupert's godson), 206
Birmingham, England, 84–6, 93, 238, 253
Bishops Wars, 68
Black Prince (ship), 164, 167
Blackamoor Lady (ship), 162
Blake, Robert, 163–7, 169
Blakemore, Richard, 163, 245, 253
Blakiston, Sir William, 114
Bohemia, King of, *see* King Frederick V of Bohemia
Bohemia, Queen of, *see* Queen Elizabeth of Bohemia
Bohemia/Bohemian, 1–4, 6–8, 15, 23, 28, 33, 36–8, 41, 43–4, 46, 49, 53, 55, 120, 149, 179–80, 185, 217, 255
Bois le Duc, *see* s-Hertogenbosch
Bolton, England, 108, 253–4
Bonaventure (ship), 49
Boscobel House, England, 170
Boye (Rupert's dog), 41, 53, 71, 80–1, 118
Boyle, Mary Louisa, 249, 254
Brandenburg, Elector of, 6, 149, 178, 205, 216
Breda, Declaration of, 183
Breda, Holland, 8, 30–1, 40, 75, 151, 183, 192, 223
Breitenfeld, Battle of, 14
Brentford, Earl of, *see* Patrick Ruthven
Brentford, England, 71–4, 94, 122–3, 155
Bridgnorth, England, 104, 126
Bridgwater, England, 134
Bridlington, 83

Bristol, Earl of (George Digby's father), 54, 70, 75, 92–4
Bristol, England, 54, 70, 75, 82, 91–5, 102, 121–2, 127, 130, 134–6, 138–43, 150, 159, 219, 225
Bromley, Sir George, 232–3, 244–6, 254
Brooke, Lord, 65, 72, 82
Browne, Colonel John, 60–2, 226
Buckingham, Duke of (George Villiers), 1, 3, 9, 11, 26, 187, 191, 213
Bulstrode, Richard, 60, 62
Burford, England, 129, 219, 221
Burton-on-Trent, England, 90
Bury St Edmunds, England, 154
Byron, Baron John, 59–61, 64, 91, 97, 100–101, 103, 114–5, 124, 126, 132, 138
Byron, Richard (Governor of Newark) (Baron John Byron's brother), 124

Cádiz, Spain, 166–7
Calais, France, 150, 155
Canterbury, Archbishop of, *see* William Laud
Canterbury, England, 22, 49, 64, 119, 189
Cape Verde Islands, 167–9, 172
Cardiff, Wales, 136–7, 225–6
Carisbrooke Castle, England, 160
Carlisle, Countess of, 48, 224
Carlisle, Earl of, 11, 19, 24, 210
Carlisle, England, 134, 154
Carnwath, Earl of, 132
Castle Bolton, England, 117
Catherine, Queen, 187, 195, 202, 204, 213
Catholics, 1, 3, 5, 8–9, 11, 13–5, 19, 23, 25, 28–9, 32–3, 39, 42, 47–9, 65, 73, 79, 108, 125, 135, 148, 163, 176, 178–80, 185, 201, 203, 205, 208, 212–6, 221–2 *see also* Confederates
Cave, Sir Richard, 32, 44, 88
Cavendish, Margaret, 202
Cavendish, William (Duke of Newcastle), 25, 64–5, 73, 77, 83, 90, 93, 98, 101–102, 106–107, 111–112, 116, 118, 122, 143, 150, 216, 252
Chalgrove, England, 89–90

Charles (ship), 163
Charles I, King, 7, 9, 11–24, 26–8, 31–2, 40, 42–51, 53, 56–8, 65–6, 68–70, 75, 78, 80, 82–3, 87, 90–1, 94, 96, 100, 104–105, 120, 122, 127, 131, 136–7, 143–6, 148–50, 153, 157, 159–60, 162, 165, 167, 170, 172, 176–84, 186–8, 190, 192, 198, 203, 209, 211, 214, 217, 225, 227, 230–3, 235–45, 251–2, 254–5
Charles II, King, 90, 162, 164–6, 177, 180, 184–9, 199, 202, 205, 208–209, 217, 220–1, 228, 247, 250–1, 254
Charles Louis, Elector (Prince Rupert's brother), 3, 6, 9, 11, 13–4, 17–9, 21–6, 28, 30–2, 34, 36–8, 42–4, 46, 48–9, 51–2, 78–9, 119–20, 141, 148–50, 153, 162, 176–9, 181, 184–8, 203, 205, 216
Charles, Prince of Wales, 2–3, 8, 13, 52, 69, 75, 88, 90, 96, 100, 123, 127, 130, 132–3, 136, 138, 141, 150–2, 154–9, 164, 225, 228
Charlotte, Countess of Derby (Prince Rupert's cousin), 108
Chatham, England, 198, 207–208
Cheriton, Battle of, England, 188
Cheshire, England, 74, 86, 88, 101, 105, 117, 251
Chester, England, 103, 109, 117–8, 126–8, 142, 147
Choqueaux (Prince Rupert's surgeon), 162, 176, 189–90
Christchurch, England, 141, 233
Cirencester, England, 79–81
Clarendon, Earl of, *see* Edward Hyde
Colchester, England, 156–7
Cologne, Germany, 176–7
Commonwealth, 154, 164–5, 166–7, 172, 175, 183, 189, 212
Confederates, 135, 163
  see also Catholics
Constant Reformation (ship), 158, 162, 166–9, 171, 173, 250
Constant Warwick (ship), 159
Convertine (ship), 159, 162, 164, 193
Cooper, Anthony Ashley (Earl of Shaftesbury), 206, 212–4, 216–8, 252

Cork, Ireland, 164
Cornwall, England, 91, 120–1
Coventry, England, 54–5, 95
Coventry, Sir William, 190, 198
Crane, Sir Richard, 33, 39–40, 53, 64, 99, 139
Craven, Earl of, 28, 32–4, 39, 154, 160–1, 185–6, 200, 203–205, 219–21, 250
Cromwell, Oliver (Lord Protector), 80, 114–5, 123, 129–30, 132, 134, 140, 153, 156–7, 161–2, 164, 166, 170, 172, 176–8, 181, 183, 212–3
Cromwell, Richard, 183
Cropredy Bridge, England, 111, 116
Culpepper, Lord John, 70, 109, 130, 158
Czech Republic, 1–3, 6, 15, 45

d'Estrées, Marquis, 208
Dartmouth, England, 98–9
Davenant, Sir William, 23–4, 111
de Gassion, Comte, 151–2
de Gomme, Bernard, 53, 89
de la Roche, Monsieur Bartholomew, 53, 82, 87, 102
de Rohan, Marguerite, 23, 91
de Ruyter, 192–3, 195, 207
de Sousa, Antonio, 165
Deal, England, 156
Deddington, England, 77–8
Defiance (ship), *see Friendship*
Degenfeld, Louise von, *see* von Degenfeld
Deptford, England, 154, 167, 208
Derby, Countess of, *see* Charlotte, Countess of Derby
Derby, Earl of, 74, 105
Derbyshire, England, 58, 74
Descartes, Rene, 120, 149, 161, 179, 255
Devizes, England, 80, 91
Devon, England, 27
Digby, Lord George, 54–5, 64, 66, 70, 77, 81, 84–5, 87, 97, 100–102, 104–107, 109, 120–7, 129–38, 140–5, 152–3, 160, 176
Digby, Sir Kenelm, 148, 244, 253
Dobson, William, (artist – according to Waldemar Januszczak 'the lost genius of British art') 148, 182

Index

Donnington Castle, England, 122
Dover, England, 21, 49–50, 150, 187, 205, 207
Dover, Treaty of, 208, 214
Dublin, Ireland, 163, 220
Dudley Castle, England, 106, 147
Dunsmore Heath, England, 59, 65
Durdham Down, England, 82
Durham, England, 77, 247, 251
Dyck, Sir Anthony van, *see* Anthony van Dyck
Dyve, Sir Lewis, 59, 63, 107, 255

East India Company, 169
Edgehill, Battle of, 66–7, 70–4, 76, 78, 86, 91, 95
Edinburgh, Scotland, 5, 68, 166
Edinburgh Castle, Scotland, 68
Edward, Prince (Prince Rupert's brother), 7, 18, 32, 43, 148–9, 162–3, 175–6, 179, 187, 203
Elisabeth, Princess (Prince Rupert's sister), 3, 6, 8, 14, 19, 21, 43, 46, 70, 120, 149, 160, 176–7, 179, 186, 199–200, 203–204, 209, 216
Elizabeth of Bohemia, Queen (Prince Rupert's mother, King James I's daughter, King Charles I's sister and King Frederick V's wife), 2–13, 15–8, 22–5, 28, 30–3, 36–9, 43–4, 46, 49, 51–3, 55, 66, 78–9, 120, 149, 179–80, 185, 187, 200, 217, 230–1, 253, 255
Elizabeth, Viscountess Mordaunt, 184, 190, 197, 246–7, 255
England/English, 1–9, 11–5, 17–28, 30–2, 33–4, 36–8, 40–1, 43–75, 77–170, 172, 178, 180–1, 183–210, 212–29, 232–4, 236–40, 242, 247–8, 250–5
    north of, 73
Essex (ship), 193
Essex, Earl of, 56–9, 61–3, 65–70, 72–3, 84, 87, 89–90, 95–7, 109–10, 118, 120–1, 123, 236, 254
Essex, England, 56–9, 61–3, 65–70, 72–3, 84, 87, 89, 95–7, 109–10, 118, 120–1, 123, 154, 156, 236, 254

Evelyn, John (diarist), 181, 184, 226–7
Exeter, England, 98, 110, 118, 120, 139, 167
Expedition (ship), 50
Eythin, Baron, *see* James King

Fairfax, General Sir Thomas, 80, 84, 105–106, 108, 114, 117, 119, 129–35, 139–41, 147–8, 153, 156–7, 161, 166
Fairfax, Lord Ferdinando (General Sir Thomas Fairfax's father), 105, 108, 115, 118
Fearnes, Flag Captain, 168
Ferdinand III, Emperor, 39–41, 44, 51, 176, 178
Ferentz, Sir Thomas, 32, 34, 37, 39
Fiennes, Captain Nathaniel, 60, 62, 92–3, 95
Forth and Brentford, Earl of, *see* Patrick Ruthven
France/French, 7–9, 11–2, 14, 19–20, 28, 30–2, 42–3, 49, 54, 91, 104, 109, 118, 120, 122, 130, 137, 147–8, 150–5, 159, 166–7, 170, 172, 174–80, 183, 188, 190, 192–4, 197–8, 203–215, 226
Frankfurt, Germany, 16, 178–81, 186
Frederick Henry, Prince (Prince Rupert's brother), 3, 6, 8–10, 18, 20, 31, 53
Frederick V of Bohemia, King (Prince Rupert's father), 1–7, 9–10, 12–8, 44, 230
Friendship (ship), 172
Fuller, Thomas, 97, 117, 134, 239, 241, 243, 254

Gassion (de), Comte, *see* de Gassion
George Louis (Princess Sophia's son and Prince Rupert's nephew), 217, 221–2
Gerard, Charles, 30, 131, 144–5
Germany/German, 1, 6–8, 14–9, 32–4, 36–43, 45, 73, 90, 114, 149, 176–81, 184–6, 205–206, 210, 216, 219 221–2, 234, 254
Gloucester, Duke of, 184
Gloucester, England, 79–80, 82, 95–8, 251
Gloucester, Siege of, 97
Gloucestershire, 184, 253

259

Goring, Lady Katherine (married Edward Scott), 223–9, 251
Goring, George (Lady Katherine Goring's brother), 24, 30–1, 56, 84, 88, 112, 114, 123–5, 127, 130–1, 134, 138–9, 150–1, 180, 223–4
Grandison, Lord/Viscount, 30, 79, 237, 253
Greenwich, England, 12, 49, 217
Greyhound (ship), 23, 210
Guinea, 188–9
Guinea (ship), 162
Gunpowder Plot, 9, 23, 118, 215
Gustavus II Adolphus of Sweden, King, 13–8, 23, 66, 68, 179, 205
Gustavus, Prince (Prince Rupert's brother), 7, 14
Gwyn, Nell, 90, 205, 220

Hague, The, Holland, 6–7, 9–10, 13, 16, 18, 46, 49, 78, 158, 177–80, 184–5, 189, 191
Hamilton, Duke of, 50, 98, 100, 127, 154, 224
Hammersmith, England, 202, 220
Hampden, John (MP), 48, 90
Hampshire, England, 28
Hampton Court, England, 49, 152–3
Hanover, Germany, 219, 221–2
Harcourt, Henry (Sarah Frances' husband), 222
Harcourt, Sarah Frances, *see* Sarah Frances Bard
Haselrig MP, Sir Arthur, 48, 92
Hastings, Henry, 58, 81–2, 86, 106, 133
Hatzfeldt, Melchior von, *see* von Hatzfeldt
Hawley, Francis, 219, 221
Hawley, Judith (née Hughes) (Margaret 'Peg' Hughes's sister and Francis Hawley's wife), 218–9, 221
Hawley, Lord Henry, 141, 221
Heidelberg, Germany, 176–8, 185, 210
Hellevoetsluis, Holland, 53, 155, 158–9, 162–3, 165
Henrietta (ship), 189
Henrietta Anne (Charles II's sister, wife of Duke of Orléans and sister-in-law of King Louis XIV), 189–90, 205

Henrietta Maria, Queen (Charles I's wife), 12–3, 17, 21, 23–5, 30–1, 49–52, 54–5, 71, 73, 78, 83, 86, 90, 94–5, 98, 106, 128, 130, 136, 148–50, 152, 155, 159–60, 162, 165, 167, 170, 175–80, 184, 187, 224, 228, 254
Henrietta, Princess (Prince Rupert's sister), 7
Henry (ship), 164, 193
Henry VIII of England, King, 1, 199
Herbert, Lady, *see* Mary, Lady Herbert
Herbert, Lord, *see* Lord Herbert of Raglan
Herbert, Sir Edward (Attorney General), 47, 158
Hereford, England, 88, 122, 126–7, 132–3, 135, 140–1
Hereford, Siege of, 140
Hertford, Marquess of, 81, 92, 94, 122
Hesse-Cassel, Elector of, 179, 181
Highnam, Battle of, 83
Hind (ship), 159
Hohenzollern, Princess, 179–80
Holland/Dutch, 3, 6–10, 12–4, 16, 18–21, 27–31, 36, 40, 44–6, 49, 51–5, 66, 68, 71, 73, 75, 78, 81, 83, 98–9, 118, 149–51, 155, 157–9, 162, 164–5, 177–80, 183–5, 188–92, 197–8, 205–11, 214, 220–1, 223, 228, 247, 251–3
Holland, Earl of, 24, 81, 98, 228
Hollandine, Louise (Prince Rupert's sister), *see* Princess Louise
Holles MP, Denzil, 48, 72–3
Holmes, Robert, 151, 162, 173, 176, 187–9, 195–7, 211
Hopton Heath, Battle of, England, 82
Hopton, Lieutenant General Sir Ralph, 4, 91, 94–5, 106, 127, 130, 147
Hotham, Captain Sir John, 52, 73, 77
House of Commons, 48
  see also Houses of Parliament and Parliament
House of Lords, 47, 53, 73, 145, 187, 212, 216
  see also Houses of Parliament and Parliament
Howard, Colonel Thomas, 188, 227, 229

Index

Howe, Emanuel Scrope, 221–2
Hudson Bay Company, 198, 212, 219
Hughes, Judith, *see* Judith Hawley
Hughes, Margaret 'Peg' (Prince Rupert's partner), 202, 204, 229, 250
Hull, England, 52, 54–5, 81, 83, 90, 95, 98, 105, 125, 207, 224
Hurry, Sir John, *see* Sir John Urry
Hyde, Edward (Earl of Clarendon), 57, 60, 62, 65, 94, 141, 161–2, 165, 176, 185, 236

Ireland, Lord Deputy of, *see* Thomas Wentworth
Ireland/Irish, 4, 22, 39–40, 46–7, 51, 54–5, 101, 103, 108–109, 114–5, 117, 125, 129, 132, 135, 141–2, 147, 150, 160, 162–5, 167, 181, 188, 220, 229
   south coast of, 162
Isle of Wight, 153, 156–7, 159, 197, 209
Italy/Italian, 7, 43, 47, 51, 149, 177, 188

James (ship), 162–3
James VI/I, King, 1–2, 5–9, 32–4, 36–8, 75, 96, 114, 118, 172, 250
James VII/II, King, 221
Jermyn, Henry (Earl of St Albans), 24, 91, 102, 105, 120, 130, 133, 137, 148, 152, 160, 167, 175, 180, 213
Jevon, Daniel (Anne's husband and Frances Bard's brother-in-law), 222
John (ship), 172
John IV of Portugal, King, 164

Kent, England, 156, 224, 249, 251
Kineton, England, 66–7
King, Lieutenant General James (Baron Eythin), 32–4, 36–8, 114
Kinsale, Ireland, 162–4, 167, 181
Knaresborough, England, 111
Königsmarck, Count Hans Christoff von, *see* von Königsmarck
Kuffstein, Count von, *see* von Kuffstein
Kuffstein, Susanne Marie von, *see* von Kuffstein
Küstrin, Germany, 6

Lancashire, England, 74, 90, 95, 101, 105–106, 109, 111, 117, 251–2
Lane, Jane, 170
Langdale, Sir Marmaduke, 154, 157
Lathom House, England, 105, 108, 117
Laud, William (Archbishop of Canterbury), 22, 25, 27, 29, 119, 189
Legge, Captain William 'Will' (Treasurer of the Ordnance), 76, 81, 87–9, 94–5, 103, 108, 121, 126–8, 130–5, 137, 141, 145–6, 153, 160–1, 167, 185–6, 189, 201, 207, 209, 223, 227, 252–3
Leicester, England, 55, 57, 59, 130–3, 186
Leiden, Holland, 7, 13–4, 20, 210
Lemgo, Battle of, 32, 234, 254
Lemgo, Germany, 32–4, 36, 38, 40
Leopold I, Archduke/Emperor (Emperor Ferdinand III's brother), 41–2, 45, 183–4
Leslie, David, 114–5
Leuven, Belgium *see* Louvain
Leven, Earl of, 115, 117, 119
Lichfield, Earl of, *see* Lord Bernard Stuart
Lichfield, England, 82–4, 86–8, 95–6, 103, 106, 134, 142, 252
Lincolnshire, England, 25, 28, 74, 77, 113, 252
Lindsey, Earl of, 67–9, 71, 76
Linz Castle, Austria, 40
Lion (ship), 53
Liverpool, England, 109, 117, 252
London (ship), 54
London, England, 1–2, 12–3, 25, 41, 46–9, 70, 72–5, 81, 83, 87–8, 90, 95–6, 99, 117, 119, 129, 133, 145, 147–9, 151, 154–6, 162, 165, 172, 184–7, 189–90, 192, 197–8, 201, 209, 213–7, 222–3, 232, 234, 237–8, 242, 247
London, Tower of, England, 147, 154, 172, 201, 214, 216
Longleat, England, 228, 249, 254
Louis XIV, King, 175, 189, 205–206, 211, 214
Louis (Prince Rupert's brother), 7, 10
Louise Juliana (Prince Rupert's grandmother, Frederick V's mother and Maurice, Prince of Orange's sister), 6

Louise, Princess (Abbess of Maubuisson) (Prince Rupert's sister), 7–8, 44, 149, 178–80, 183, 201, 203, 205, 229
Louvain, Siege of, 19, 40
Love (ship), 159
Lower Palatinate, *see* Palatinate
Loyal George (ship), 193
Loyal Subject (ship), 171, 188
Lucas, Sir Charles, 30, 69, 102, 114, 127
Lützen, Germany, 17

Maastricht (Spanish fortress), 18
Madagascar, 23, 28
Madeira, 167
Madrid, Spain, 42, 180
Magdeburg, Germany, 14, 73
Mainz, Germany, 14, 16, 178, 185
Manchester, Earl of, 47, 74, 106, 108, 115, 117–9, 123
Mansfeld, Count Ernst von, *see* von Mansfeld
Market Harborough, England, 59, 131
Marlborough, England, 77, 255
Marmaduke (ship), 167
Marston Moor, Battle of, 38, 111–3, 115–8, 123–4, 126, 131–2, 137, 143, 252, 254–5
Mary, Princess of Orange (King Charles's daughter), 71, 99, 179
Mary, Queen of Scots, 5
  see also Queen of Scotland
Massie, Edward, 95, 127
Maurice, Prince (Prince Rupert's brother), 6, 18, 30–2, 43, 51, 53, 56, 58, 63, 83, 87, 91–4, 98–9, 107, 124, 126, 142–4, 148–50, 156, 159, 162–3, 165, 167, 171–4, 176, 188, 243, 253
Maurice, Prince of Orange (Prince Rupert's great-uncle), 6, 8
Maximilian, Duke of Bavaria, 6, 15, 39, 42–3, 45
Meldrum, Sir John, 104, 117
Meppen, Germany, 32
Merton College, 25, 124
  see also Oxford University
Midlands, England, 56, 59, 82, 84

Minden, Germany, 32–4, 36, 38
Modena, Mary of, 213
Monck, George (Duke of Albemarle), 30–1, 130, 163, 183–4, 192–8, 204, 220, 248, 253
Montrose, Marquess of, 98, 117, 130, 135, 137, 139–40, 142, 145, 159–60, 163, 166, 179, 180
Moore, Sir Jonas (Surveyor of the Ordnance), 201, 215–6
Mortaigne (Prince Rupert's Master of the Horse), 104, 151, 162
Münster, Germany, 33, 39, 185
Myngs, Sir Christopher, 193

Naseby, Battle of, 129, 131–7, 139, 143, 145
Nassau, Prince Maurice of, *see* Maurice, Prince of Orange
Navy, *see* Royal Navy
Navy Board, 197, 206, 212
  see also Royal Navy
Netherlands, The, *see* Holland/Dutch
New Model Army, 80, 129–31, 138, 148, 150–1, 153–4, 156–7, 160, 163
Newark, England, 74, 81, 90, 103–105, 118, 124, 142–5, 147, 253
Newbury, Second Battle of, 122–3
Newbury, England, 96–8, 102, 122
Newcastle, Duchess of, *see* Margaret Cavendish
Newcastle, England, 53, 74, 105, 111–4, 202
Newport Pagnell, England, 99–100
Nicholas, Sir Edward (Secretary of State), 40, 47, 80, 86, 89, 97, 106, 118, 129, 131, 139, 141, 180, 255
Northampton, Earl of, 30, 66, 81–2
Northumberland, Earl of, 81, 98, 105
Northumberland, England, 54, 77
  coast of, 54
Norwich, Earl of (Katherine Goring's father), 227
Nottingham, England, 54–6, 67, 74, 252

O'Neale, Lieutenant Colonel/Mr Daniel 'Dan', 53, 55, 81, 89, 120, 229
Oates, Titus, 214–7

Index

Orange, Prince of, *see* Maurice, Prince of Orange and William, Prince of Orange
Orange, Princess of, *see* Mary, Princess of Orange
Order of the Garter, 18, 52, 163, 176, 204–205
Ormonde, James Butler, Duke of, 101, 116, 118, 138, 141–2, 160, 163, 238–43, 245, 254
Oxford University, 25, 59, 65, 204, 252
Oxford, England, 70, 73, 75, 77–83, 85–92, 95, 97, 100, 106–107, 109, 118, 123–4, 126, 129–34, 139–44, 146–9, 192, 223–6, 228–9, 233, 237, 240, 247, 254–5
Oxfordshire, England, 111, 129

Palatinate, 3, 6, 11–6, 22, 24, 30–2, 39, 42–5, 49, 51, 75, 78, 150, 176–8, 184–6, 205, 216, 221
  Lower, 3, 6, 43
  Upper, 6, 39, 42, 176
Paris, France, 43, 130, 137, 148, 154, 175–8, 193–4
Parliament, 1, 11, 15, 23, 46–9, 51–3, 56–7, 59, 62, 65, 68, 70, 72, 78, 80, 83–4, 98, 107, 109, 119, 123, 125–6, 129, 139, 142, 145, 147, 150–1, 153, 155–8, 160, 163, 183, 192, 199, 213–6, 218, 224–6, 229
  see also Houses of Parliament and Scottish Parliament
Parliamentarians, 49, 51, 54, 57–8, 60–7, 69–74, 77–8, 80–4, 89–92, 95–7, 101, 103–109, 114, 117–8, 126, 131–3, 135, 140, 142, 147–8, 152, 155–7, 159, 162–5, 172, 206, 224, 226–8
Pembroke, Earl of, 27, 81
Pembroke, Wales, 154
Pepys, Samuel, 189–90, 197–8, 202, 227
Percy, Henry (Baron Percy of Alnwick) (General of the Ordnance), 24, 88, 93–4, 96, 102–104, 109, 120, 152, 154
Philip, Prince (Prince Rupert's brother), 7, 17, 43, 149, 176
Plessen, Count Volrad von, *see* von Plessen

Plessen, Sybille von, *see* von Plessen
Plymouth, England, 98–9, 125
Porter, Endymion (Groom of the Bedchamber), 23, 49, 100, 126, 255
Porter, George (Endymion Porter's son), 100–101
Porter, Mrs (Endymion Porter's wife), 23
Portsmouth, England, 9, 49, 56, 185, 189, 208, 224
Portugal, King John IV of, *see* John IV
Portugal/Portuguese, 164–9, 172, 186–7, 245, 254
Powick Bridge, England, 60–1, 63, 89, 101, 111–2
Prague, 1–3, 6, 15, 45
Presbyterians, 151, 153–4, 156, 166
Pride, Colonel Thomas, 160–1
Prinsenhof, Holland, 7–10, 14, 17
Privy Council, 27, 187, 192, 212, 215
Protestants, 1, 5, 8–9, 11, 13–4, 17–8, 22–3, 29, 42, 48, 68, 119, 149, 205, 213–5, 217, 221
  see also Church of England
Puerto Rico, 174, 176, 188
Pym, John (MP), 48
Pyne, Valentine (Master Gunner of England), 181, 201

Raglan Castle, Wales, 139
Raglan, Lord Herbert of (Marquess of Worcester's son), 82–3, 95, 122
Ratisbon, 43–4
Reading, England, 75, 77, 79, 87–9, 107
Reeves, Sir William (Captain & Deputy Governor of Windsor Castle), 193–4, 209–11
Revenge of Whitehall (ship), *see* *Marmaduke*
Rheinburg, Germany, 18–9
Rhenen, Holland, 12, 44, 215, 221
Rich, Isabella, *see* Isabella Thynne
Richmond and Lennox, Duchess of, *see* Mary Villiers
River Thames, England, 1, 72, 169, 198, 207–208, 210
Rochdale, Baron Byron of, *see* John Byron

Rochester, England, 64
Roe, Sir Thomas, 10–1, 15, 21, 25–8, 32–3, 39, 43–6, 79
Roebuck (ship), 23, 162–3
Royal James (ship), 191, 197, 207
Royal Navy, 23, 28, 53, 154, 165, 198
   see also Navy Board
Royal Society, 41, 212
Royalists, 57–63, 66–70, 72–4, 77, 80–1, 84–6, 91–3, 95–7, 102, 104–106, 108–109, 111, 113–5, 117–8, 123, 125, 127, 129–32, 134–5, 137, 139–40, 142–3, 145, 148, 150, 152, 154–9, 161, 163–5, 172, 177, 180, 187, 224–5, 251
Ruthven, Patrick (Earl of Forth and Brentford), 68, 88, 94–6, 122–3, 155

Saint-Germain, 150, 152
Salisbury, Earl of, 81, 192
Sandwich, Earl of, 189, 191–2, 198, 207
Sandys, Colonel Edwin, 60–2, 64
Satisfaction (ship), 159
Schomberg, Count Frederick, 210
Scilly Isles, 162, 164
Scotland/Scottish, 1, 4–5, 8, 27, 38, 40, 44, 47, 51, 68, 98, 100–101, 105, 111, 115–7, 130, 135, 139–40, 142–5, 147, 149–51, 153–7, 159, 166, 170, 177–8, 183, 189, 215, 224, 250, 252, 254
   southern, 143
Scott, Edward (Lady Katherine Goring's husband & Thomas Scott's father), 223–7, 252
Scott, Katherine, *see* Lady Katherine Goring
Scott, Sir Thomas (Lady Katherine Goring's son), 227–8, 251
Scottish army, 101, 140, 144, 147, 150, 154, 157, 166, 170, 177
Scottish Parliament, 153
Seacroft Moor, England, 84, 114
Second Charles (ship), 164
Shaftesbury, Earl of *see* Anthony Ashley Cooper
Shrewsbury, England, 58–9, 61, 64–5, 68, 102–103, 105–106, 125–6, 222

Siegen, Colonel Louis von, *see* von Siegen
Skippon, Philip, 78
Somerset House, England, 204, 221
Sophia, Princess, (Prince Rupert's sister), 7–8, 162, 176–7, 186, 200, 203–205, 216–8, 221–2, 250
Southampton, Earl of, 55, 127
Sovereign of the Seas (ship), 23, 31
Spain, King of, 42, 46, 171
Spain/Spanish, 3–4, 6–13, 15, 18–9, 30, 42, 46, 75, 151, 164, 171, 174, 177–8, 180, 185–6, 192, 198, 206, 211
Spinola, Ambrogio, 8
Spragge, Sir Edward, 209–11
St Albans, Earl of, *see* Henry Jermyn
St Helens, 193, 197, 209
St John's College, 25
   see also Oxford University
St Michael the Archangel (ship), 169
Stafford, England, 58, 81–2, 130, 216–7, 251
Stapleton, Sir Philip, 97
Star Chamber, 29, 47
Strafford, Earl of (Thomas Wentworth), 22, 47
Stratford-upon-Avon, England, 84, 90–1
Stuart, Lord Bernard (Earl of Lichfield), 123, 142
Sudeley Castle, England, 79–80
Sunderland, Earl of, 97
Surrey, England, 149, 201, 212, 246, 252
Swallow (ship), 162, 171–6
Sweden, Christina of, 178–80
Sweden/Swedish, 12–5, 23, 32–4, 36–8, 41, 43, 51, 68, 78, 179–80, 184–5, 205–206
Swiftsure (ship), 193

t'Serclaes, Johann (Graf von Tilly), 14
Taafe, Viscount, 71, 229
Tadcaster, England, 113
Terceira, 168–9, 171
Tetworth, England, 89
Thame, England, 77, 89–90
Thirty Years War, 13, 23, 38, 150, 176, 254

Index

Thomas (ship), 162–3
Thynne, Isabella (née Rich), 228–9
Thynne, Sir James (Isabella's husband), 228
Tienen, Belgium *see* Tirlemont
Tillier, Major-General Henry, 103, 114, 130
Tirlemont, Belgium, 19, 40
Toulon, France, 167, 172, 176
Tromp, Admiral, 195, 209–10
Turnham Green, Battle of, 73

Upper Palatinate, *see* Palatinate
Urry, Sir John (often spelled Hurry), 89, 123

van Dyck, Sir Anthony (Charles I's court artist), 25
van Honthorst, Gerrit (artist), 7
Vane, Sir Henry, 11, 15, 21–2, 119
Venetian ambassador, 1, 40, 43, 47, 54, 57, 63, 72, 81, 112, 123, 193–4, 198, 206
Venlo (Spanish fortress), 18
Verney, Sir Edmund, 69, 86
Victory (ship), 18
Vienna, Austria, 40–2, 44–6, 176–7, 181, 183, 185, 221
Villiers, Barbara (King Charles II's mistress), 199, 220
Villiers, Mary (Duchess of Richmond and Lennox), 50, 229
Vlotho Bridge, Battle of, 34, 40, 90
Vlotho, Germany, 36–8, 114
von Degenfeld, Louise (Charles Louis's wife's maid), 178
von Hatzfeldt, Melchior, 34, 36, 38, 90
von Königsmarck, Count Hans Christoff, 34, 37–8
von Kuffstein, Count, 40, 42
von Kuffstein, Susanne Marie (Count von Kuffstein's daughter), 40
von Plessen, Count Volrad, 7
von Plessen, Sybille, 7
von Tilly, Graf, *see* Johann t'Serclaes
von Wallenstein, Albrecht Wenzel Eusebius, 15, 17, 39

Wales/Welsh, 2–3, 8, 13, 27, 58, 69, 75, 81, 83, 87–8, 90, 97, 100–102, 123–4, 126–7, 130–3, 135–41, 144, 150–2, 154–8, 164, 184, 222–3, 225–6, 252
North, 101, 124
South, 83, 135, 154
Walker, Sir Edward (Secretary-at-War), 107, 118, 143, 255
Wallenstein, Albrecht Wenzel Eusebius von, *see* von Wallenstein
Waller, Sir William, 4, 82–3, 87–8, 91, 97, 106, 109, 111, 117, 122–3
Walsingham, Edward (Digby's agent), 141, 176
Warwick Castle, England, 70, 81
Warwick, England, 66, 70, 81–2, 157–8
south-east, 66
Warwickshire, England, 58, 66–8, 81–2
Wentworth, Lord (the Earl of Cleveland's son), 224, 240
West Country, England, 77, 80, 87, 127, 153
West Indies, 159, 167–8, 171–3
Westminster Abbey, England, 204, 208, 220
Westminster Hall, England, 48, 162
Westminster, England, 1, 28, 48–9, 51, 55, 58, 93, 98, 125, 141, 145, 160, 162–3, 195, 224
Westphalia, Germany, 6, 32, 222
Whalley, Colonel Edward (Oliver Cromwell's cousin), 132, 153
Wharton, Lord, 74, 237, 253
Wharton, Nemiah, 59–64, 66
White Mountain, Battle of, 15
Whitehall Palace, England, 1, 19, 25, 28, 47, 73, 141, 162, 183–4, 186, 197, 206, 217
Widdrington, Sir Edward, 114
William, Prince of Orange, 16, 18–20, 27, 30, 32, 46, 53, 68, 75, 160, 214
Willis, Sir Richard, 124, 143–4
Willoughby of Parnham, Lord, 155, 158–9
Wilmot, Lord Henry, 30–1, 60, 63–4, 68–9, 77, 79, 90–1, 94, 96, 107, 109, 120, 122, 152–3, 170, 241, 253
Wiltshire, England, 77, 228, 253

265

Windsor Castle, England, 72, 186, 199, 210, 214
Windsor, England, 188, 199–200, 206, 217–8, 247, 254
Wolverhampton, England, 103
Woolwich, England, 23, 198
Worcester, England, 59–61, 64–6, 77, 82, 90, 95–6, 127, 145, 170, 250
Worcester, Marquess of, 82, 95
Worcestershire, England, 101, 124, 250, 253
Würtzburg, Germany, 39

York, Duchess of, 206, 213–4
York, Duke of (later King James VII/II), 52, 69, 129, 141, 154–5, 158, 178, 180, 184–5, 189–92, 199, 201, 206–208, 210, 212–5, 217–8, 220
York, England, 77, 86, 106, 108–14, 116–9
Yorkshire, England, 54, 74, 77–8, 83–4, 88, 105–106, 141–2, 145
   coast, 54
   West, 105

Zuider Zee, 190

Dear Reader,

We hope you have enjoyed this book, but why not share your views on social media? You can also follow our pages to see more about our other products: facebook.com/penandswordbooks or follow us on X @penswordbooks

You can also view our products at www.pen-and-sword.co.uk (UK and ROW) or www.penandswordbooks.com (North America).

To keep up to date with our latest releases and online catalogues, please sign up to our newsletter at: www.pen-and-sword.co.uk/newsletter

If you would like a printed catalogue with our latest books, then please email: enquiries@pen-and-sword.co.uk or telephone: 01226 734555 (UK and ROW) or email: uspen-and-sword@casematepublishers.com or telephone: (610) 853-9131 (North America).

We respect your privacy and we will only use personal information to send you information about our products.

Thank you!